Rigorous Intuition

What You Don't Know
Won't Hurt Them

Jeff Wells

Published by:
TrineDay
PO Box 577
Walterville, OR 97489
1-800-556-2012
www.TrineDay.com
publisher@TrineDay.net

Library of Congress Control Number: 2008909733

Well, Jeff
Rigorous Intuition—1st ed.
  p. cm. (acid-free paper)
Includes index.
(ISBN-13) 978-0-9777953-2-1 (ISBN-10) 0-9777953-2-2
1. Conspiracy—New World Order 2. Political Corruption—United States 3. Occult—Aleister Crowley 4. Psychological Warfare 5. UFOs 6. Mind Control

First Edition
10 9 8 7 6 5 4 3 2 1

Printed in the USA

Distribution to the Trade by:
Independent Publishers Group (IPG)
814 North Franklin Street
Chicago, Illinois 60610
312.337.0747
www.ipgbook.com

— Publisher's Foreword —

L ife comes at us fast, taking us hastily to who knows where? Some even ask by whom and what for? Eternal questions that have always been with us … keeping us awake, invading our dreams …

Are we the masters of our own destiny? What are those "things that go bump in the night"? Why am I always running into "spooks" when traveling down some of these strange, but very interesting roads of investigation? And when you add up all the parts of the human experience: What is the sum of this existence? These queries and more are explored in this book by master wordsmith, Jeff Wells.

When recommendations led me to his blog, Rigorous Intutition, I was blown away by the seeming ease with which Jeff wrote about subjects very hard to get one's head around, i.e., mind control, 9/11, political assassinations, UFO's, the CIA, Lovecraft, Crowley, et al. He had already mentioned several of TrineDay's books and had some of our titles on his wish list. I sent him those and continued to read his blog with abandon. Before long, I suggested to Jeff that TrineDay publish some of his essays. He said yes, and to make a short story longer — yet near completion — there were medical troubles that delayed this book. We are a small firm with a tight production schedule and once something misses a projected press date, it has to play catch up, while other projects take precedence.

We truly regret the delay, as there is much to garner from Mr. Wells' wisdom, from his investigations of, and reflections upon what many of us would rather not address, but shove back into dark corners to fester. Perhaps an earlier release may have helped some to a quicker understanding of the task before us. Then again, time is what we make it.

I shall stop where many of Jeff's stories begin, the lyrics of Bob Dylan:

> Now the bricks lay on Grand Street
> Where the neon madmen climb.
> They all fall there so perfectly,
> It all seems so well timed.
> And here I sit so patiently
> Waiting to find out what price
> You have to pay to get out of
> Going through all these things twice.
> Oh, Mama, is this really the end …

Kris Millegan
Publisher
October 22, 2008

Acknowledgments

I owe a drink to the first reader who can find herein one genuine original thought. There were a number of times in composition that I imagined I had one, only later to realize that some Robert Anton Wilson or another had been there, published that, sold the film rights. If this work has any value, it's on account of the writers who have enriched me, and I'll consider it my own private *Mission Accomplished!*, if this book finds them a few more readers. I'm thinking notably of Jacques Vallee, Peter Dale Scott, Charles Fort and Daniel Hopsicker, as well as many others whose words I cite and treasure, and to whose standards of intuitive rigour I aspire. Without them, this would be a book of empty pages.

Much of the material here is dark, and I've been able to stumble my way through it only by the light of my family. To my wife Raina and my children, thank you, and I hope this makes up in small part for some long nights.

Thanks of course to Trine Day, and particularly to Kris Millegan, for his initial suggestion that there was a book here, and for his ongoing patience and encouragement.

This book represents just half, if that, of a conversation with the community of Rigorous Intuition (www.rigourousintutition.ca). My favourite thing about RI is that it's not just mine anymore. By emails, blog comments and forum posts I've been introduced to some remarkable people with brilliant ideas, and I wouldn't have persisted at this without them.

I didn't know Theresa Duncan or her partner Jeremy Blake, but she was a friend of Rigorous Intuition, and her and Jeremy's deaths and life stories touched me in ways I still can't articulate. Theresa has set a higher and a better bar for me as a writer, a reader, and a "conspiracy theorist" in a conspiracy industry that doesn't have enough good conscience.

To my mother, who saw a monster out the window one night and wasn't believed.

— Table of Contents —

0. Attention Deficit World Order............. ix

1. Trigger Mechanisms......................... 1

2. The Politics of Jellyfish 33

3. Can't Help It If They Are Lucky 59

4. The Only True Anarchists 89

5. Are Your Lessons Done?................ 137

6. "A Great and Terrible Paw" 175

7. Sense and Sensitivity.................... 229

8. Deep in the Forest So Wild............ 283

9. Sparkle Motion 323

10. The Old Masquerade 349

11. The Kingdom is Opening Again 387

12 Paging Mr. Badthing................... 429

13. All American Monster 467

Index... 491

— Introduction —
Attention Deficit World Order

August 2008

Possibly Gilman ought not to have studied so hard. Non-Euclidean calculus and quantum physics are enough to stretch any brain; and when one mixes them with folklore and tries to trace a strange background of multi-dimensional reality behind the ghoulish hints of the Gothic tales and the wild whispers of the chimney-corner, one can hardly expect to be wholly free from mental tension.

— HP Lovecraft, *The Dreams in the Witch House*

The more things strange, the more I want to stay the same.

Suddenly, just when it seems UFOs are everywhere, I'd rather be nowhere. America's late-term, lame-duck housecleaning of suspicious suicides and self-inflicted gunshot wounds is in full swing, and I'd just as soon clean the porch. And I've never wanted to clean the porch. Now a new, "optimistic" estimate gives the world 100 months to forestall the tipping point of a runaway greenhouse effect, but I prefer to focus on the short term, and speculate idly upon how much ass next year's *Watchmen* adaptation will or will not kick.

I've been struggling for a year and a half with writing an introduction to my book. *A year-and-a-freaking-half.* I haven't been able to account for the missing time to my publisher, though I don't need a hypnotist to tell me where it's all gone. I have been good at stammering apologies and repeating vain promises, and revisiting false starts and bad ideas. (And naturally the blog suffered, because how could I justify spitting out posts like watermelon seeds while using the book for a spittoon?)

Maybe, in another year and a half, I'd have something to say. Maybe if I kept looking I'd eventually find a place to start. But I think it's more sensible to say I can't do it, and instead write my conclusions and stick them at the front. (And maybe even squeeze a blog post out of it at the same time.)

So here it is: they've won. Or let me rephrase that, since there will never be universal agreement as to who "they" are: we've lost.

Because life is short, even if I get another turn after this one, I'd rather not waste half of it relearning all the secret wrongs done to the world that I can't undo. So I need to know what, if anything, we get out of knowing what they get away with. And if it's so we may better "organize," then good luck and God bless us playing catch-up, since the priesthoods and kingly classes have had a 10,000 year head start.

I suppose it counts for something, that so many have been able to recognize the holes in the FBI's posthumous stitch-up of Bruce Ivins for the anthrax attacks. That we haven't jumped when *they* say jump to the conclusions of guilt and case closed may be some comfort to his family and colleagues, who watched Ivins break under the relentless *There can be only one* ethos of America's Lone Gunman fixation. But all our reservation of judgment amounts to nothing but a sympathy card - an e-card at that - against the prosecution of a dead man who can be tried and convicted now only because he is dead and undefended.

Stalin's show trials — what was it do you think they showed? Not that Zinoviev and Kamenev and the other Old Bolsheviks were "terrorists" and "sexual deviants" (though it is instructive how often the prosecuting state conjoins the two). Rather, they demonstrated Stalin's rule by absolute whim. Loyalty and service, innocence or guilt, afford no protection. It was irrelevant whether or not Soviet citizens were convinced that justice was served by their state. They just needed to note that if they demurred, there was nothing they could do about it.

Senator Patrick Leahy has a speaking part in *The Dark Knight*. It looks like his mouth talking, but it sounds like his ass. "We're not intimidated by you thugs," Leahy stares down the knife-wielding Joker who's crashed a political fundraiser. It was *The Dark Knight*'s only moment for which I could not suspend disbelief, since two hundred billion particles of finely-milled anthrax were enough to erase the Senator's initial qualms concerning the Patriot Act. But I won't judge him, except as a character in a superhero movie, because I wasn't there and it wasn't me. Most of the time we don't make ourselves targets by our objections to their plans, because there's not much we could do to impede them. And besides, as the Joker later says, "Nobody panics when things go according to plan. Even if the plan is horrifying."

I don't have a reasonable doubt that Edgar Mitchell is telling the truth about his being briefed by government officials on Roswell and alien visitations to Earth. I have considerable doubt they were telling him the truth. I don't think it's part of the plan to tell the truth, of which, almost certainly, even the highest and darkest government officials would have only partial knowledge. If "disclosure" ever comes, its purpose may not be to persuade us of a lie, but rather to tell a terrifying joke.

It's one thing to find there are no words, and another to find no sensible thought that can penetrate America's strange dreamtime. And that's just sad, because as novel as these events seem, they are still all recurring dreams, though we greet them like goldfish, seeing the world anew every time we circle the bowl.

Perhaps the truest and most essential thing Michael Moore ever said, he said at the Oscars. *We like nonfiction, and we live in fictitious times.* But I dunno; maybe he's spent too much time since that night playing a character in a false narrative, because on the eve of Congress's campy read-through of an early draft proposal for a trillion dollar grift — a fictitious fix to a fictitious crisis of fictitious money — Moore advised Americans to "call or e-mail Senator Obama" and "call your Representative in Congress." So that's how it works. Rather, how about as soon as you discover you've already seen the movie, walk out of the theatre and demand your money back?

Is this the way the world ends? European astrologers at the turn of the 16th century forecast devastating floods for the year 1524. One result, as the date approached, was a "Great Fear," as recorded by Venetian chronicler Marin Sanudo. Another, for Venice, was a tremendous investment in public works in order to prevent the silting up of the city's lagoon. (Sadly, the careful consideration of Renaissance engineers of the city's effect upon its environment had been forgotten by the mid-20th Century, when channel dredging and groundwater extraction saw Venice rapidly sink 20 centimeters in 20 years.) Another effect was an increased popularity of satirical doom-singers. One Venetian *cantastorie* going by the name of "Master Pegasus Neptune" predicted "conjunctions of cheese and lasagna," and comically prophesied that "In those days cats and dogs will be enemies, swords will cut better than radishes, fields and mountains will be out in the open, and the taverns will be well frequented." We might add, that in these days, the stock market will crash, and the stock market will rally.

That's not the end. Hell, that's not even the world.

Perhaps this is more like it? From a dispatch last week by Dr. Oerjan Gustafsson of Stockholm University, aboard the Russian research ship Jacob Smirnitskyi in the Arctic Ocean:

> We had a hectic finishing of the sampling program yesterday and this past night. An extensive area of intense methane release was found. At earlier sites we had found elevated levels of dissolved methane. Yesterday, for the first time, we documented a field where the release was so intense that the methane did not have time to dissolve into the seawater but was rising as methane bubbles to the sea surface.

Days later, the British research ship the James Clark Ross reported counting "about 250 methane plumes bubbling from the seabed in an area of about 30 square miles in water less than 400 metres (1,300 feet) deep off the west coast of Svalbard." Deeper plumes at three times the depth were found near by.

If the thawing permafrost and warming oceans lose the integrity of their methane sinks, if the billowing chimneys of Arctic methane represent their tipping point, then the climate is soon to run away from a tolerable mean. A feedback loop even more catastrophic than Reaganomics will have been initiated. As with Reaganomics, a happy ending can't be written for us.

But never mind that. There are millions of lives lived right now in apocalypse. Zimbabwe - does *that* look like the end of the world? Another world at least, where children are eating toxic, indigestible roots to stave off hunger, though malnutrition will kill them if relief isn't sent "very fast." What percentage of Wall Street's "rescue" would it take to rescue *them*? What percentage of Henry Paulson's personal wealth of $700 million? It's crazy that it seems crazy to ask. But that's Zimbabwe, and Mugabe's small time grifters aren't hooked up with the global syndicate. There's no need to know, and since so much of news is supposed to be *news you use*, they lose.

And we do too, if we don't know this Zimbabwe story, from last April:

American film maker Randall Nickerson is currently visiting southern Africa to make a documentary that follows up an incident that happened at the Ariel School in Ruwa, Zimbabwe, in 1994, when 62 children aged between eight and 12 reported seeing a UFO and "strange beings" during their morning break.

Those children are now young adults scattered around the globe. Nickerson is tracking them down and interviewing them about the experience. "Their stories have not changed at all," he says. "Not what you would expect if they had made it all up."

So what exactly happened on that day in 1994 at the school in Ruwa just east of Harare? "It was morning break and they were out in the school yard playing," says Nickerson. "They saw one main silver craft that had four others around it," says Nickerson. "It came down on a hill beyond the school yard that was out of bounds. The boundary was the edge of the school yard, then it was bush and the hill.

"They ran to the edge of the school yard to see what this thing was. They saw this small creature walk around on top of the craft while another came down to check out the children. He was all in black, with a very tight suit. The children said he had big eyes 'like rugby balls'.

"The children had direct eye contact with this creature. There seems to have been some kind of communication with the children about the state of the world — what we are doing to the planet, the destruction we are causing, although not all the children got this message. Some of the children were traumatized, others were excited. The young children were the most traumatized as they were at the front of the group.

African UFO researcher Cynthia Hind was at the school the next day. One little girl told her "I swear by every hair on my head and the whole Bible that I am telling the truth." Harvard's John Mack soon followed, and interviewed dozens of witnesses with whom Nickerson is now following up.

Isabelle: *He was just staring, and we like, tried not to look at him, because he was quite scary.*
MACK: *What was scary about him?*
Isabelle: *His big eyes I think. I think - I think they want people to know that we're actually making harm on this world and we mustn't get too technoledged [sic]*
MACK: *What gave you that feeling?*
Isabelle: *I don't know.*
MACK: *But it came to you when you were with the strange beings?*
Isabelle: *Yeah. When he was looking at us. It came through my head. My conscience I think.*
MACK: *Had you been a person who thought a lot about what we were doing to the world?*
Isabelle: *No. Only after this.*

I don't know what happened at Ruwa, but something real, *really* did, which means it has more authenticity than John McCain's David Blainesque "suspension" of his campaign, upside down, above the head of David Letterman, and more weight than the Treasury Department's rationale for the figure of $700 billion. ("It's not based on any particular data point," a Treasury spokeswoman told Forbes.com Tuesday. "We just wanted to choose a really large number.") If we can't explain it or understand it, maybe we should fight the impulse to ignore it. As well as real, it could be important. Or maybe just kill us.

This month marks the 30th anniversary of Australian pilot Frederich Valentich's disappearance, whose last words before his microphone captured an unidentified sound of grinding metal was "That strange aircraft is hovering on top of me again. It is hovering and it's not an aircraft."

Driving home in a company van the evening of March 17, 1978, Englishman Ken Edwards saw a strange figure on top of an embankment. As Peter Hough tells it in *Visition*, The being was tall and broad, with a head like a goldfish bowl, and its arms appeared to sprout from the top of its shoulders. It descended the steep hill at an impossible right angle to the ground, and before walking across the road and *straight through* a chain link fence as if it wasn't there, turned to face the van and shot narrow beams of light from its eyes into the cab. A power surge burned out all of its major components, Edwards' watch stopped, and he showed Hough marks on his hands that had been clutching the steering wheel which resembled sunburns. He soon began complaining of stomach pains, and was found to be riddled with cancer, and died at 42. Maybe he would have anyway, if he and something unknowable hadn't crossed paths, but like Barbara, his widow, told Hough, "A thing that can burn skin, stop watches and destroy an expensive radio might well be capable of bringing harm to a human being."

Last July 20, Vince Weiguang Li delivered an Edmonton newspaper that carried a lengthy feature on the Windigo, "a terrifying creature in native mythology that has a ravenous appetite for human flesh. It could take possession of people and turn them into cannibalistic monsters."

Li abruptly quit his job and took a bus across the Canadian prairie, where he beheaded and cannibalized 20-year old Tim McLean. "I just don't know what to think of it, quite frankly," says the piece's author, and Windigo expert, Nathan Carlson. He'd documented numerous cases of people believing they were "turning Windigo" who would beg to be killed "before they started eating people." At Li's first courthouse appearance, the only words he spoke were a soft, "Please kill me."

On McLean's myspace page, under *Who I'd like to meet*, he posted "an alien, the wolfman, frankensteins monster, a vampire...."

The Tuesday after the market dropped 777 points, the front page of a Toronto newspaper headline told me there's a "monster lot of fear out there."

Ooooh, I'm scared.

There seems a prevailing consensus that a concession of uncertainty is a sign of soft-headedness, or even indicative of complicity in disinformation and cover-up. At the risk of being tagged a disinfo artist, I don't think so. When I'm unsure of something — and I'm unsure of a lot of things — I like a nice maybe or perhaps. In fact, I think an admission that one might be wrong should be the price of serious appraisal. Not only am I disinclined to heed those who claim to have solved the puzzles of our time's hidden riddles, but I'm likely to red-flag them with suspicion. And the same should go for me if I ever say, unreservedly, This is the way things are.

— Jeff Wells

1. Trigger Mechanisms

That's the word, don't you know? From the guys that's running the show.
— Jarvis Cocker

Flight of Capital

June 17, 2006

They say I shot a man named Gray and took his wife to Italy.
She inherited a million bucks and when she died it came to me.
I can't help it if I'm lucky.

— Bob Dylan

A t least among those with a mind for such things, it's fairly well remembered that on September 10, 2001, Donald Rumsfeld made the shocking announcement that the Pentagon "couldn't track" $2.3 trillion of its transactions. Internet poster "Iroquois" observes, "What's interesting to me is that he made his press release on a Monday. In DC, I always see bad news given on a Friday, usually late in the afternoon on Friday. The exception, of course, would be when someone happens to know that there is a far bigger story coming out."

And we know that Flight 77, allegedly piloted by an incompetent, made an aerobatic, spiraling descent over Washington, effecting a 270-degree turn to strike the Pentagon from a western approach at ground level. The side struck was the only one with an exterior wall hardened against attack, and was relatively empty while renovation continued.

Relatively. The unfortunate construction workers perished outside, but who were the expendables within?

From the *Pittsburgh Post-Gazette*, December 20, 2001:

"One Army office in the Pentagon lost 34 of its 65 employees in the attack. *Most of those killed in the office, called Resource Services Washington, were civilian accountants, bookkeepers and budget analysts.* They were at their desks when American Airlines Flight 77 struck."
[emphasis added]

The *Arlington County After-Action Report* noted that the "impact area included both the Navy operations center and the office complex of the National Guard and Army Reserve. It was also the end of the fiscal year and important budget information was in the damaged area." And *Insight* magazine editorialized that "the Department of the Army, headed by former Enron executive Thomas White, had an excuse [for not making a full accounting]. In a shocking appeal to sentiment it says *it didn't publish a "stand-alone" financial statement for 2001 because of "the loss of financial-management personnel* sustained during the Sept. 11 terrorist attack."

High Crimes of State often come down to the movement of capital, and so the high criminals generally share the gray and black economics of common felons. Money is money; it's the magnitude of the heist that's different, and the means to effect and cover-up the crime. And part of the cover-up of the Pentagon heist has been the no-plane shell game, played smartly by Rumsfeld himself who "misspoke" that a "missile" had struck the Pentagon the same week Thierry Meyssan's original no-plane Web site was launched.

It's such disinformation that has drilled irrelevance and folly into a once potentially dangerous and angry army of authentic skeptics.

The Monolith Monsters

February 7, 2007

Let's be perfectly clear boys and girls:
C*nts are still running the world.

— Jarvis Cocker

I t's always fascinating, and important as well, when conspirators become "conspiracy theorists." Just not always for the
same reason.

There are the career insiders who, in timely fashion, step up
as "whistleblowers" to entrain the American Mind by mischief.
Philip Corso, for instance. In 1997, only one year before his
death from a heart attack at 83, the retired Lieutenant Colonel
released *The Day After Roswell*. Corso claimed to have both
viewed the remains of Roswell aliens and to have shepherded
the reverse engineering of UFO crash artifacts by the private
sector, which became products such as fiber optics and integrated circuit chips.

Corso had no evidence for this, and the names he named
were all dead. All he had was his word, which he underscored
a month before he died with a sworn oath, as well as his reputation and distinguished service. In his review of *The Day After
Roswell*, Michael Lindemann drew attention to this:

> What to make of Colonel Philip Corso and his book? If he were
> not a highly decorated, highly credible military officer, he would likely
> be passed off by most people as a blatant hoaxer. But why would this
> particular man tell such very tall tales at the end of his life, if the tales
> are simply untrue? That question will likely vex more than a few readers
> of "The Day After Roswell," a book that will probably push the Roswell
> controversy to new heights in this Roswell-happy year of 1997.

I should note that Roswell, as I regard it, is the paramount disinformation story of American UFOlogy. It has sent generations down the wrong path, chasing the presumption of "nuts and bolts" spacecraft and their ET occupants, and served to both suppress the true phenomenon's psi and occult components and to mask the U.S. military's deep black tech. Roswell is also responsible for the focus on passive "disclosure" — *tell us the truth!* — rather than on a citizens' investigation to learn the truth for themselves.

So he's not, as Lindemann noted, a *blatant* hoaxer, and I can't imagine a persuasive personal reason to fabricate such a fabulist narrative so close to his death. Still, I think it should be evident even to those who deny the existence of a genuine UFO phenomenon, that it means something that a man of Corso's stature signed off on *The Day After Roswell*. I suspect that the reason was service in furtherance of disinformation.

It's astonishing the rubbish we can swallow when we credulously open our mouths and say, "Feed me." Paul Hellyer became a brief blip on the media's radar a while back, when the former — as in 40-years-prior — Canadian Defense Minister went public with his late-life advocacy for UFO "disclosure." He was hailed as an "insider" and instantly graduated to keynote speaker at "Exopolitics" conferences. Unfortunately, Hellyer's insider knowledge didn't amount to much: "I finally concluded, especially after reading a book called *The Day After Roswell* written by Colonel Philip Corso, that unidentified flying objects are, in fact real," he told MSNBC. (Hellyer supports his case for the Corso book by adding that he heard, second hand, that an unnamed U.S. Air Force General said "Every word of it is true, and more." An unnamed General *would* say that.)

Now let's consider the conspirator-cum-conspiracy theorist Zbigniew Brzezinski. Last week, while excoriating Bush's Iraq policy before the Senate Foreign Relations Committee, he warned of "a plausible scenario for a military collision with Iran." He sees the scenario unfolding with:

> Iraqi failure to meet the benchmarks, followed by accusations of Iranian responsibility for the failure, then by some provocation in Iraq or a terrorist act in the U.S. blamed on Iran, culminating in a "defensive" [his own quotation marks] U.S. military action against Iran that plunges

a lonely America into a spreading and deepening quagmire eventually ranging across Iraq, Iran, Afghanistan and Pakistan.

On leaving the hearing, Brzezinski was pointedly asked by reporter Barry Grey whether he was "suggesting that the source of a possible provocation might be the U.S. government itself." He responded that he had "no idea. As I said, these things can never be predicted. It can be spontaneous." Grey followed up, "Are you suggesting there is a possibility it could originate within the U.S. government itself?" To which Brzezinski replied, "I'm saying the whole situation can get out of hand and all sorts of calculations can produce a circumstance that would be very difficult to trace."

This is the same Brzezinski, of course, who when asked about rhetorically answered, of his early sponsorship of Islamic radicals as U.S. proxies, "What was more important in the world view of history? The possible creation of an armed, radical Islamic movement, or the fall of the Soviet Empire? A few fired-up Muslims or the liberation of Central Europe and the end of the Cold War?" (And note, Brzezinski's policy of instigation was launched in Afghanistan against it's pro-Soviet government in order to goad the USSR into its own bloody quagmire.) His book *The Grand Chessboard* (published, I realize with a slight *frisson* of synchronicity, the same year as Corso's) was cited early in the days following 9/11 as America's road-map of geopolitical ambition in the 21st Century. He knows better than most the reach of the hidden hand. Now, he's dropping broad hints that the U.S. may manufacture a provocation in Iraq, blame it upon Iran and catastrophically broaden the war. So what do we do when *they* begin to sound like us?

On the one hand we should always be cautious about blithely accepting the word of deep-power embeds, but I also think it helps our understanding along if we admit that their world is neither static nor monolithic. It may appear from a distance that *they're all in it together* — and at our distance the differences between factions of the global elite may be too nuanced and rarefied to hold much meaning for us — but I believe there's a dynamism among conspirators that often seems lost on their theorists, some of whom like to project a virtual hive-mind upon the powerful. Rather than an undifferentiated block of *them*, I imagine an inter-penetrating Venn diagram of rival interests, means and analyses, and while Brzezinski is certainly in the thick of it, that doesn't mean his opposition to the White House's adventurism is a sham intended only for public consumption. Though his reasons are certainly not the same as mine. (Brzezinski, interested in the efficient projection of American power, can foresee its ruin by the Cheney/Bush model, but he seems to regard it as the accident of bad policy rather than an intentional controlled collapse.)

One further example of insider "tinfoil:"

On the evening of November 23, 1963, a man named Garrett Underhill showed up, anxious and unexpected, at the New York City residence of his friends Robert and Charlene Fitzsimmons. Underhill had driven up from Washington DC, where he worked as a military and intelligence expert for *Fortune* magazine. He was also a longtime CIA asset with particular expertise and interest in both the covert arms trade and Cuba.

When he arrived at the Fitzsimmons' home it was late, and Robert was already asleep. Charlene was preparing for their trip to Europe, and Underhill unburdened himself while she packed.

Larry Hancock, in *Someone Would Have Talked*:

Underhill's concern was that he had become aware of a "clique" within the CIA — a clique dealing with weapons and gun running and making money. These individuals had Far Eastern connections, narcotics was mentioned, supposedly the clique was manipulating political intrigues to serve their own ends. Underhill believed that these individuals had been involved with JFK's murder; he felt that JFK had become aware of their dealings and was about to move against them in some fashion. He also believed that members of the clique knew that Underhill was aware of their dealings and that his own life could well be in jeopardy. Underhill had fled Washington in fear of his life, avoiding his normal haunts at the Harvard Club in DC to seek refuge with his friends.

Robert Fitzsimmons later told Jim Garrison that they couldn't take Underhill seriously because "we couldn't believe that the CIA could contain a corrupt element every bit as ruthless, and much more efficient, than the Mafia." Their friend couldn't tell Garrison anything. In May 1964 the body of the right-handed Underhill was found in his unlocked apartment, shot behind his left ear. Death was ruled a suicide.

It must have sounded strange to early-Sixties ears to hear such things said of the CIA. Particularly those odd and seemingly incongruous mentions of narcotics and "Far Eastern Connections" (like Yale's old "China hands"?) Yet today, more than 40 years after his murder, and 15 since Danny Casolaro's, it makes such awful sense that we can say that *despite* his intelligence pedigree, at least Garrett Underhill was speaking the truth.

Outside the Box

March 14, 2007

Can you please crawl out your window?
Use your arms and legs it won't ruin you

— Bob Dylan

Though it's hard to think outside the box, once you do, you may need to think outside *that* box as well.

The box of Gerry Irwin

On February 28, 1959, Private First Class Gerry Irwin was en route from Nampa, Idaho back to Fort Bliss, Texas, where he served as a Nike missile technician. Late that evening, as he was turning southeast on Route 14 around Cedar City, Utah, the sky was illuminated by a brilliant object crossing the sky in front of him. He pulled to the side of the road, got out of his car and watched it disappear behind a nearby ridge. Irwin thought he had witnessed an aircraft in trouble. Writing "Stop" on the side of his car with shoe polish he left a note attached to the steering wheel: "Have gone to investigate possible plane crash. Please call law enforcement officers."

On March 2, Irwin awoke in Cedar City Hospital, with no idea of what had happened to him, or how he had gotten there. He had been unconscious since shortly after he was found, only an hour and a half after leaving his car, occasionally mumbling about a "jacket on the bush." His temperature and respiration were normal; it was simply as though Irwin were asleep and couldn't be woken. At last when he did wake up, he felt fine; though his first words upon sitting up in bed were, "Were there any survivors?"

Irwin was informed he had been found alone, jacketless, and there was no sign of a crash. He was diagnosed with "hysteria" and flown to Fort Bliss, where he was placed under medical observation for four days, after which he returned to active duty, but with his security clearance revoked. Several days later he fainted, though quickly recovered, and did so again a few days later in El Paso, and was taken to hospital. Early the next morning he woke up and again said, "Were there any survivors?" He could not believe it was March 16; he thought it was still February 28.

Once more he returned to base, this time in psychiatric care for a month. He was discharged from care April 17, with test results showing "normal," but the next day he gave in to an uncontrollable impulse to depart the base without leave, and caught a bus in El Paso for Cedar City, from where he walked to the spot of his sighting, left the road and went straight to a branch upon which his jacket still hung. And something was on his jacket. A pencil was stuck in a buttonhole, and a piece of paper was wound tightly around it. Irwin took the paper and burned it, and then seemingly snapped out of his entrancement. He had difficulty finding the road again, and not knowing what he was doing there, turned himself in to the local sheriff, who told him the story of his earlier episode.

Back at Fort Bliss he again underwent psychiatric examination, with identical results. Upon being released from camp hospital, he failed to report for duty August 1. He hasn't been heard of since. Irwin's story has been called "one of the strangest, most baffling cases in UFO folklore," but I disagree. Not only have I read stranger, I don't think this is even a UFO story.

Every UFOlogical account I've read of Irwin's case treats the military backstory to it as incidental. But Irwin was a missile technician on the base which, post-war and Cold War, was a hub for Operation Paperclip scientists, including Werner Von Braun, who integrated Nazi innovations into U.S. military technologies. There's a class picture of the Fort Bliss's German rocket team, which initially was restricted to base without military escort, and we know, as well as rocketry, the Nazi scientists also brought to American proving grounds their advanced work in mind control.

Irwin "snapped out of it" after burning the paper, as though releasing himself from a hypnotic suggestion that had driven him to return to Cedar City (where, for what it's worth, an alleged mind control survivor "Mauri" claims her abuse by a privileged cult of Satanic Nazis began). The only tenuous UFO connection is Irwin's claim to have seen a bright object traversing the sky, though it looked to him no stranger than an aircraft in trouble. And given the tricks his mind was playing, or the tricks someone was playing on his mind, perhaps we shouldn't assume there was anything to see at all. There were no other witnesses, and no evidence of a landing.

Was Irwin the unwitting subject of an experiment in mind control? Could be. Even though I'm persuaded of a UFOlogical reality that transcends hoaxes and cover stories, I think the confluence of military research and psychological trauma in the Irwin case are far more suggestive of a fairly sinister and secretive human agency. UFO researchers are probably guilty of confirmation bias by counting this story as legitimately one of theirs, and it may be hard to let it go, but I think the Irwin episode more likely belongs to a different, though often parallel, narrative.

The box of Fatima

Fatima is an interesting set of nested puzzle boxes that naturally predates any attempt to incorporate it into a military mind control narrative. But what is it?

To the Roman Catholic faithful it represents a Marian miracle. Skeptics, outside that box, regard it as mass hysteria. Joe Nickel, Senior Research Fellow of the Committee for the Scientific Investigation of Claims of the Paranormal (CSICOP), says of Fatima's dramatic "Miracle of the Sun" that "the effects were surely optical ones. For example, because one cannot focus on an object so bright, the eyes may dart back and forth, thus cre-

ating, by the effect of image and after-image, the appearance that the sun is 'dancing,' or the eyes may attempt to focus, retreat, again attempt, and so on, thereby giving the illusion that the sun was 'pulsating.'"

CSICOP's rational box will not allow for a third interpretation, which I considered two years ago in a post, and that I think makes better sense of the evidence by being honestly strange enough to account for it.

The "sun," which appeared out of a small cloud and had the appearance of a dull silvery disc, descended in "slow zigzags," according to Father Alves Vieira, quoted in Basiago and Thompson's *Heavenly Lights*. The object, which unlike the sun could be looked at without discomfort, moved in the rhythm "of a dry leaf that falls from trees in Autumn." Vieira could not know that he was also describing a maneuver which would become common to UFO sightings before the mid-1970s. For instance, on September 19, 1952, an RAF squadron observed a silver disk in the sky above one of their fighters. In a report submitted by Flight Lieutenant John Kilburn, he described it beginning to descend, "swinging in a pendular motion similar to a falling sycamore leaf" before accelerating into the west at "unbelievable" speed. (Curiously, the bizarre entities of the "Hopkinsville incident" were said to float gently to the ground in a falling leaf fashion after being shot, to no other effect, by members of the terrified Sutton family.)

The box of 9/11

9/11 has so many boxes, and more all the time, those might as well have been FedEx planes spilling Lament Configurations (puzzle boxes) all over Lower Manhattan.

One of the arguments that something other than Flight 77 struck the Pentagon is the report of elevated levels of radiation downwind of the site following September 11. It was first proposed by nuclear weapons professionals and the former head of the Pentagon's depleted uranium project, who allege the readings suggest that the impacting object was a missile tipped with depleted uranium.

"I'm not an explosives or crash site expert," says Leuren Moret, former staff scientist at Livermore Nuclear Weapons Laboratory, "but I am highly knowledgeable in causes and effects related to nuclear radiation contamination. What happened at the Pentagon is highly suspicious, leading me to believe a missile with a depleted uranium warhead may have been used."

And to missile proponents, that's good enough to confirm a missile. After pulling themselves free of the Official Box, they think they're in the clear. But freethinkers, as much as anyone, need to ask themselves whether their thoughts are their own, or if they find themselves in yet another box.

The crash of El Al Flight 1862 into an Amsterdam apartment block created a similarly toxic site, when its secret cargo, containing the equivalent of 270 kilograms of sarin gas and at least 800 kilograms of depleted uranium was disgorged. Thousands of rescue and recovery workers experienced health complaints, including symptoms of radiation sickness. Yet no one, in my reading, has used this as an argument that a cruise missile struck the building.

So what accounts for the elevated radiation readings at the Pentagon? Well, *perhaps* Flight 77 departed Washington bearing something that wasn't supposed to be there. Commercial aircraft, even passenger aircraft, have been co-opted by the military to serve as mules before. Or perhaps the Pentagon wall which was struck — the only wall which had just then been reconditioned to better withstand terrorist attack — actually incorporated the extremely hard and dense metal in its composition. Either could be possible, and other explanations as well, which are more likely than the boxed-in assumption of a DU-tipped missile. (An assumption, as we've noted, that is championed by veterans of military intelligence. And if *that* doesn't make you at least wary that the hypothesis may serve another purpose than the truth, what is it going to take?)

Then there's the "fat Osama" video. It could be, maybe, he wasn't that fat after all. Perhaps the discrepancy in his appearance is accounted for by a failure to correct the aspect ratio of PAL to NTSC video conversion. If so, perhaps "fat Osama" has been a box for us all along, to keep us from considering the implications of the video's content and the circumstances of its creation. Bryan Sacks makes an interesting case on the Internet as to why "the true backstory of the tape's creation may provide smoking-gun evidence of U.S. foreknowledge and complicity in the 9/11 attack." If so, while we've been clucking over the obvious artifice of "fat Osama," we've missed its point, which was its purpose all along. And if so, and we're too enamored of fat Osama to ever let him go, then we'll keep on missing it, too.

So what's my point?

Critical thinking isn't instinctual. We shouldn't presume, in our disdain of the official story (whatever story that may be, and however official), that we've reached the truth once we stand with it's official opposition, because we may be either boxing ourselves in with rigid either/or thinking, or be boxed in by the authorities who mean to control both thesis and antithesis.

We should know that some boxes feel like home. They're meant to feel that way.

Darkness Falls

July 25, 2006

> *Let's blow this place to kingdom come,*
> *let Con Edison take the blame.*
>
> — Bob Dylan

Things fall apart. Other things are pulled apart. The distinction means little to those caught in the collapse, but perhaps those of us who haven't fallen yet may still find a place to stand by discerning one from the other.

Every week, the world becomes a little more like Goddard's **Weekend**. We're becoming inured to the degradation of infrastructure, public institutions and personal ethics. Thousands of New Yorkers are entering their second week without electricity, and in St Louis a quarter of a million residents and businesses are not far behind. Unheard of midnight temperatures of 40 degrees Celsius (103 Fahrenheit) are being recorded. Wires are melting, grids are stressing and networks are failing. Our increasingly frequent and violent electrical storms *just don't feel right*, and don't tell me different. The global climate is changing more rapidly than even the gravest recent projections, and temperatures are creeping up towards our own extinction-level conditions. ("If the ambient temperature is higher than 40C (104F), the human body will eventually reach 40C unless there is a cooling mechanism. At a sustained body temperature of 40+C, a human will die.") The planet is already facing its greatest extinction event in 65 million years: "We're losing life on Earth and we're losing the diversity of life on Earth," says Dr. Anne Larigauderie. "Everywhere we look, we are losing the fabric of life." So it may be in death that we at last rejoin the natural realm.

That's not to say *this* is natural. There are still the unnatural men of whom Chaplin spoke in *The Great Dictator* — "machine men, with machine minds and machine hearts" — who have always been capable and amorally fit to attempt to profit by the overthrow of every good thing. They were never going to leave to chance — to nature — their place in the new order, if this order is finished.

Last Friday, Adamo Bove, a lead investigator into the Italian probe of the rendition of Abu Omar, "apparently jumped to

his death." Also Friday, an unnamed Citibank employee fell to his death at its Canary Wharf UK headquarters, a "suspected suicide." And the same day, the chopped-up remains of Opus Dei financier Gianmario Roveraro were found under a bridge, though "police have made no link" between the order and his murder, though the last time he had been seen alive was when leaving an Opus Dei meeting. (Roveraro had once said that his part in Opus Dei was "not concerned with finance — finance is not Catholic or Masonic, it is just finance.") And freeway snipers have begun stalking America again before midterm elections, this time in California and Indiana. (Whether they, too, will be caught "like a duck in a noose" remains to be seen.) While with the conscience of a vampire, the Secretary of State says that extreme violence signals the "birth pangs" of a "new" Middle East.

New Orleans continues to be an unnatural disaster, where families are now expected to dig their own graves, and no less a product of deep politics than the Pearl Harbor of Lower Manhattan. When cities become ruins, when they go dark and lose the capacity to provide for their people, it's usually on account of choice. It's because someone, an enemy within or without, wants to shoot out the lights and drive a soft urban populace into despair and barbarism. (Military recruitment hit a 30-year low in the mid-'90s, and now, as the U.S. economy sharply worsens for those near the bottom and their options further narrow, recruitment soars. But which is more to be desired by the rulers of this new, hard age: economic opportunities for the most poor or more bodies for its Army of Darkness?)

If it looks like social engineering, there's the chance that it is.

Mary, Ferrie
and Gerald Posner

October 2, 2004

A portrait in miniature of Gerald Posner, patron saint of coincidentalists, regarding the death of oncologist Mary Sherman.

Posner includes the New Orleans' cancer researcher on a "debunking" list of mysterious deaths associated with the JFK assassination, in his lone-nutter's Bible, *Case Closed*. He writes that Sherman died in 1967 and "had no connection to the case, though she was acquainted with David Ferrie. Marrs says she was 'possibly shot.' According to medical records, she was killed in an accidental fire, and there was no gunshot wound on her body."

Here's what Posner gets right: "there was no gunshot wound on her body."

Here's what Posner gets wrong: everything else.

Even the year of her death: Sherman was killed in 1964, not 1967. To be specific, early on the morning of July 21, the day the Warren Commission began taking testimony in New Orleans.

Sherman's murder was the above-the-fold, front page headline of that afternoon's edition of the *New Orleans States Item*: "Orleans Woman Surgeon Slain By Intruder; Body Set Afire."

From the police Precinct Report on Sherman's death, quoted in Edward Haslam's *Mary, Ferrie & the Monkey Virus* [since revised and greatly expanded, and published as *Dr. Mary's Monkey*]:

1. Stab wound of the chest, penetrating the heart, hemopericardium and left hemithorax [sic]. 2. Multiple stab wounds of the abdomen, with incid wound of the liver. 3. Multiple stab wounds of the left upper extremity and the right leg. 4. Laceration of Labia Minora. 5. Extreme

burns of right side of body with complete destruction of right upper extremity and right side of thorax and abdomen.

And from the Homicide Report:
> The body was nude; however, there was clothing which had apparently been placed on top of the body, mostly covering the body from just above the pubic area to the neck. Some of the mentioned clothes had been burned completely, while others had been intact, but scorched.

The Coroner's office noted that "most of the clothes were still neatly folded when placed on top of the body." A pair of white gloves with blood stains were found in the laundry hamper. Sherman's security alarm had been turned off, and she'd told neighbors she was expecting an out-of-town visitor.

In 1993, journalist Don Lee Keith presented the case to four medical examiners. In his article "A Matter of Motives," all four say it was "obviously a case of overkill," and three suggest the fire was an attempt to draw attention to the crime scene. The killing remains unsolved to this day.

Okay, so Sherman was murdered. How does she figure in the Kennedy story? Here's New Orleans' DA Jim Garrison, in his famous 1967 *Playboy* interview:
> David Ferrie had a rather curious hobby in addition to his study of cartridge trajectories: cancer research. He filled his apartment with white mice — at one point he had almost 2,000, and neighbors complained — wrote a medical treatise on the subject and worked with a number of New Orleans doctors on means of inducing cancer in mice. After the assassination, one of these physicians, Dr. Mary Sherman, was found hacked to death with a kitchen knife in her New Orleans apartment. Her murder is listed as unsolved.

Haslam argues that Sherman was recruited by Tulane University's Dr. Alton Ochsner — a passionate anti-communist, known CIA asset and friend of Clay Shaw — to work with Ferrie on a biological weapon to use against Castro's Cuba. He speculates that this could have been the covert origin of HIV and of increased soft-tissue cancer rates. Haslam's case doesn't rise much above conjecture, but his question lingers: "Why was a prominent cancer researcher involved in an underground medical laboratory with a violent political extremist?"

Now, Sherman's association with Ferrie *may* have been innocent, and her murder may have been incidental, but a genuine skeptic would not shy from asking Haslam's question, nor try to silence critics of the official story by resorting to deceitful half-truths and outright lies.

The problem with the kind of skeptics who champion the likes of Posner is that they are not skeptics at all. They are debunkers, whose belief system prohibits allowance of anything but lone nuts, dumb luck and coincidence. Conspiracies do not exist, because conspiracies *cannot* exist. And if a mysterious death appears too mysterious, no problem: *"According to medical records, she was killed in an accidental fire."*

See? It's as easy as typing.

"My God —
they killed him!"

February 3, 2005

The streets are filled with vipers who've lost all ray of hope
You know it ain't even safe no more in the palace of the Pope.
— Bob Dylan

Is everything a conspiracy? No. Just the important stuff.

Since there's a lot of speculation these days about who will succeed Pope John Paul II, it seems a good time to recall the circumstances of the last papal succession. Because Luciani Albini, Pope John Paul I, was almost certainly murdered, by an international network of fascists and money launderers, with ties to far-right elements within military and intelligence agencies. (And isn't it just amazing, how often we find that convergence?)

He only served 33 days; what could he have done in that short time to deserve death? What kind of Pope was he becoming?

To the second question, there's the suggestion of an answer in this passage from David Yallop's *In God's Name*:

On August 28, the beginning of his papal revolution was announced. It took the form of a Vatican statement that there was to be no coronation, that the new pope refused to be crowned. There would be no sedia gestatoria, the chair used to carry the pope, no tiara encrusted with emeralds, rubies, sapphires, and diamonds. No ostrich feathers, no six-hour ceremony.... Luciani, who never once used the royal "we," was determined that the royal papacy with its appurtenances of worldly grandeur should be replaced by a Church that resembled the concepts of its founder. The "coronation" became a simple Mass. The spectacle of a pontiff carried in a chair...was supplanted by the sight of a supreme pastor quietly walking up the steps of the altar. With that gesture

Luciani abolished a thousand years of history.... The era of the poor Church had officially begun.

That right there would have been enough to make the Vatican's power elite nervous, but surely not enough to seek the Pope's death. Not even his expressed interest in reconsidering the Church's position on birth control would have been enough for that. What was enough, was his intent to overturn the tables of the corrupt Vatican Bank, and purge the Vatican of the P2 Lodge.

This is one of those things that make being a "conspiracy theorist" seem entirely superfluous. Just try imagining P2: an elite, ultra-secretive, neo-fascist, Masonic cabal, involved in money laundering, assassination and false-flag terrorism. (The "Strategy of Tension," to discredit Italy's Communist Party. For instance, the engineering of Aldo Moro's kidnapping and murder, and the Bologna train bombing.) P2 counted among its members the future Italian President Silvio Berlusconi, and reputedly boasted honorary members like Henry Kissinger, George H.W. Bush and arch-neocon, Michael Ledeen.

I mentioned P2 last August, with regard to Ledeen's long history with the Italian far right and the linchpin of Italian military intelligence to the Niger "Yellow Cake" forgery. [For more on the significance of P2 to U.S. intelligence and the "Octopus," refer to David Guyatt's excellent articles "Operation Gladio", "Holy Smoke and Mirrors" and "The Money Fountain."]

Licio Gelli was P2's Grandmaster, and can't even be called a neo-fascist. He was Old School: a member of the Italian Black Shirt Brigade which fought for Franco in the Spanish Civil War. During World War II, he spied on partisans in his native Italy for the Nazis, and obtained the SS rank of Oberleutnant. This same Gelli was an honored guest of George H.W. Bush after the 1980 inauguration, and there is evidence that Gelli and P2 played a role in the October Surprise; even that Swedish Prime Minister Olof Palme was murdered on Gelli's orders because he'd refused to provide Swedish cover for the covert transfer of money and arms. In her *October Surprise*, Barbara Honegger writes that a P2 informant claimed to her that before Palme's death, Gelli sent a message to former Republican National Committee advisor (and also alleged "honorary" P2 member) Philip Guarino, assuring him that "the Swedish tree will be felled," and to "tell our good friend Bush."

Your head exploding yet? There's more. G.H.W. Bush's reputed code name for October Surprise was "The White Rose," which was also the name of a far-right Cuban exile group with which the CIA's Bush was reportedly engaged during the ramp-up to the Bay of Pigs. Honegger reports that when Italian police uncovered the P2 control cell responsible for terrorism in Italy, they learned that its code name was "The Rose of Twenty." Gelli seems to have had a weakness for the flower.

And this may mean nothing, or I know what you did: in 1988, on the 25th anniversary of John F. Kennedy's murder, Ted Kennedy marked the occasion in Runnymede England by placing, at the foot of his brother's memorial, a single white rose.

Gelli's network financed itself in part by purchasing and plundering banks, thanks to the likes of P2 brothers Michele Sindona and "God's Banker," Roberto Calvi. Mafioso Sindona, in 1968, had become a financial advisor to Pope Paul VI; Calvi was running Banco Ambrosiano; and another P2 member, American Bishop Paul "You can't run the Church on Hail Marys" Marcinkus, who bore the nickname "the Gorilla," was heading the Vatican Bank. For a while, it was a sweet operation.

As cardinal of Venice, Albini had butted heads with the bankers. As Pope, he could finally do something more. Most revelatory, he became privy to the secret list of Freemasons in the Vatican. For the first time, he learned of P2's penetration of the Church.

Yallop again:

> If the information was authentic, then it meant Luciani was virtually surrounded by Masons.... The secretary of state, Cardinal Villot, Masonic name Jeanni, lodge number 041/3, enrolled in a Zurich lodge on August 6, 1966. The foreign minister, Monsignor Agnostino Casaroli. The cardinal vicar of Rome, Ugo Poletti. Cardinal Baggio. Bishop Paul Marcinkus and Monsignor Donato de Bonis of the Vatican Bank. The disconcerted pope read a list that seemed like a Who's Who of Vatican City.

On the evening of September 28 the Pope called to his study Cardinal Villot, the head of the Curia, to inform him his resignation would be expected the following day, along with the head of the Vatican Bank and other officials tied to Sindona. He then retired to his bedroom, taking with him the paperwork detailing the Church's business with the Mafia.

The Pope's body was found by his housekeeper early the next morning, sitting upright in bed, clutching the papers from the night before, his face frozen in agony. An opened bottle of Effortil, which he took for low blood pressure, lay on his bedside table. Immediately she called for Cardinal Villot, whose first act, before even verifying the death himself or calling the Vatican doctor, was to summon the morticians. When Villot did arrive at the papal chamber he collected the Pope's papers, the medicine bottle and several personal items which had been soiled with vomit. None have been seen since.

The Vatican asserts that its physician determined the cause of death to be myocardial infarction, but no death certificate for Pope John Paul I has been made public. And despite Italian law, which requires at least 24 hours to pass before a body is embalmed, Villot had the Pope's remains prepared within 12 hours of death. The embalming procedure was also unusual. Conventionally, blood is drained and certain organs removed before embalming, but that did not happen in this case, meaning neither blood nor tissue were available to test for the presence of poison. Though an autopsy had been performed on at least one of his predecessors, Pius VIII, the Vatican refused to allow one for Pope John Paul I, claiming it was against canon law.

There's an old Kris Kristofferson song, entitled "They Killed Him." I learned it from a Dylan cover, on almost certainly his weakest album, *Knocked Out Loaded*. To be honest, it's pretty lousy. If you haven't heard it, all you need to know is that it has a children's chorus. And yet, it chills me.

A verse:

> *Another man from Atlanta, Georgia*
> *By name of Martin Luther King*
> *He shook the land like the rolling thunder*
> *And made the bells of freedom ring today*
> *With a dream of beauty that they could not burn away*
> *Just another holy man who dared to make a stand:*
> *My God, they killed him!*

My point here hasn't been to rehash the case for assassination. My point, I suppose, is simply my exasperation: that My God — *they killed him, too!*

This material can lead to despair. *If they can whack the Pope, and get away with it,* what hope do we have? I don't find it consoling to know of what they're capable; that they are, as Dylan sang in another song, "bound and determined to destroy all the gentle." That's not about justice. That's about being forewarned, and forearmed. And these days, that's almost as important as justice.

But it is a consolation of sorts to remember that these people are flesh, just as we are. Gelli is still alive, but since his extradition from France in 1998, he has been serving a 12-year sentence for his role in the Banco Ambrosiano affair. Marcinkus received Vatican immunity from Pope John Paul II, when it became apparent Italian authorities intended to prosecute him for his criminal stewardship of the Vatican Bank, and eventually left Rome for Sun City, Arizona. Sindona died in prison drinking poison coffee, possibly the same administered to the Pope. Calvi, after his string played out, met a peculiarly Masonic fate, hanging from a rope beneath London's Blackfriar's Bridge, his hands tied behind his back and 12 pounds of bricks stuffed in his pockets. Officially ruled a it "suicide" for more than 20 years.

Our advantage is that there are more of us than there are of them.

Our greatest disadvantage is that most of us *still* can't admit there *is* a them.

The Master Approached

March 22, 2006

They say you're usin' voodoo, I seen your feet walk by themselves
That god you been prayin' to
Is gonna give ya back what you're wishin' on someone else
— Bob Dylan

In 1969, while cleaning the former office of a Los Angeles private detective named Earl LaFoon, the building manager found a canister of 16 mm color film labeled "Sirhan B. Sirhan — 1967." It was a surveillance film, shot approximately half a year before he was charged with the murder of Robert F. Kennedy, of Sirhan walking the streets of Pasadena.

Jonn Christian, co-author with William Turner of *The Assassination of Robert F. Kennedy*, tracked down LaFoon and asked him about the film. The detective's story was rather fluid, first claiming it had been stolen, then denying that it was his, and finally abruptly ending the conversation by saying "You'll have to ask the Argonaut Insurance Company about this. That's all I have to say."

Argonaut had paid Sirhan a workman's compensation claim of $1,705 for injuries received in a fall from a horse while working at the Corona Ranch in 1966. Was Sirhan surveilled in a fishing expedition for insurance fraud? The relatively small amount involved and the fact Sirhan wasn't even claiming to be disabled render this conclusion suspect, especially since an Argonaut spokesman told Christian the company had nothing to do with it.

Sirhan was filmed without his knowledge shortly after he returned to his family home following an unexplained absence of three months, which had caused his mother extreme worry. A veteran LAPD officer, who wished to remain nameless, told

Turner and Christian that even the RFK task force, Special Unit Senator, could not account for the missing time.

Upon his return, one difference in Sirhan's character noted by those close to him was a deepened interest in the occult.

In the mid-'60s Sirhan's ambition to become a jockey had led to work as a groomsman, which carried him into the orbit of an equestrian circle of privilege. The politics was far right, and the religion often had the gloss of conservative evangelicalism masking a fascination with the occult. William Thomas Rathke, a right-wing, 41-year-old groom who actually had his own fundamentalist church, befriended Sirhan, but rather than talk about Jesus paradoxically began nurturing his interest in the occult. In a letter to Turner and Christian, Sirhan wrote that "We had many discussions on the occult — reincarnation, karma, clairvoyance, astral projection, the human aura. But I don't remember that we ever discussed politics."

In 1967 Rathke moved north to Livermore California, ostensibly to work at the Pleasanton Race Stables. Livermore, of course, was also home to Lawrence Livermore National Laboratory, one of the principle contracting institutions for MK-ULTRA. (In 1965 the CIA had "entered into a Memorandum of Understanding" with Lawrence Livermore Laboratory to "perform a number of projects for the Office of Scientific Intelligence.")

Sirhan and Rathke kept in touch, and Rathke and Livermore remained on his mind. In his notebook of "automatic writing" following his three-month absence, he wrote "Sirhan Livermore Sirhan" and juxtaposed Rathke's name with the repetition of "Let us do it," "Master Kuthumi." "Illuminati" and "Northern Valley." "Kuthumi" is clearly a reference to Blavatsky's Secret Chief Koot Hoomi, and Livermore Valley is in Northern California. When asked by Turner and Christian, Sirhan said he had no awareness of the word "Illuminati," and could only say that Kuthumi "sounds familiar in occult literature."

At Sirhan's 1969 trial hypnotist Bernard Diamond testified that the case was "an astonishing instance of mail-order hypnosis, dissociated trances and the mystical occultism of Rosicrucian mind power and black magic." This was the limited hang-out of the compromised defense team: Sirhan was mind-controlled, but it was self-induced. Rathke supported this position, even anticipated it, by having visited Sirhan and his family in LA several times in the months before the assassination, and voicing concerns in letters that if Sirhan didn't abandon his rituals he might "lose control and do something terrible." The supposedly evangelical Rathke also infiltrated a Theosophist group in early 1968 and expressed similar concerns to its members, reminiscent of the JFK assassination's "Odio Incident" which saw Silvia Odio being told by a companion of "Lee Oswald" that Oswald *was* crazy and capable of killing the President.

Sirhan's now 62, and lost his 13th bid for parole last week. He was unrepresented; his lawyer Lawrence Teeter — his first lawyer to believe in his innocence — died last year. Most Americans who still mourn Robert Kennedy don't feel much charity for his convicted killer, but that's to misunderstand history and misapprehend justice.

From a CIA memorandum of 1954, originally published in Phil Melanson's *The Robert F. Kennedy Assassination* and reproduced in the July-August 1997 issue of *Probe*:

1. The ARTICHOKE Team visited [redacted] during period 8 January to 15 January 1954. The purpose of the visit was to give an evaluation of a hypothetical problem, namely: *Can an individual of ****** descent be made to perform an act of attempted assassination involuntarily under the influence of ARTICHOKE?*

2. PROBLEM:

a. The essential elements of the problem are as follows: (1) As a "trigger mechanism" for a bigger project, it was proposed that an individual of ****** descent approximately 35 years old, well educated, proficient in English and well established socially and politically in the ****** Government be induced under ARTICHOKE to perform an act, involuntarily, of attempted assassination against a prominent ****** politician or if necessary, against an American official. The SUBJECT was formerly in [redacted] employ but has since terminated and is now employed with the *** Government. According to all available information, the SUBJECT would offer no further cooperation with [redacted.] Access to the SUBJECT would be extremely limited, probably limited to a single social meeting. Because the SUBJECT is a heavy drinker, it was proposed that the individual could be surreptitiously drugged through the medium of an alcoholic cocktail at a social party, ARTICHOKE applied and the SUBJECT induced to perform the act of attempted assassination at some later date. All the above was to be accomplished at one involuntary uncontrolled social meeting. After the act of attempted assassination was performed, it was assumed that the SUBJECT would be taken into custody by the *** Government and thereby "disposed of."

Qabbalists say that knowledge wears a false crown. Students of Deep Politics could say the same. Unlike Oswald and James Earl Ray, Sirhan's like us: he's alive. "Disposed of," but alive. Truth without justice — what is that?

2. The Politics of Jellyfish

"Have you heard the news?" he said, with a grin. "The Vice-President's gone mad."
"Where?" "Downtown." "When?" "Last night." "Hmm, say, that's too bad."
"Well, there's nothin' we can do about it," said the neighbor.
"It's just somethin' we're gonna have to forget."
"Yes, I guess so," said Ma.
Then she asked me if the clothes was still wet.

— Bob Dylan

I Want to
Disbelieve

July 12, 2006

Really, I do.

I've never understood that poster of Agent Mulder's in *The X-Files*. He already believed, and after just a few episodes of monster chasing he shouldn't have needed to believe anymore. Hell, before the series even began Mulder had seen his sister abducted by greys. What remained for belief? To get Biblical on his ass, Paul wrote in *Hebrews* that "faith is the substance of things hoped for, the evidence of things not seen." He had the evidence of things seen. But more to the point, why would he want to hope for it?

I'd heard the histories told by high killers and their accomplices all my life, but I've known since I began to read on the subject that John Kennedy's murder, and that of his brother and Dr. King, were acts of state. I've known, as well as I've known anything, ever, without having been there, done that myself.

But here's the thing: it didn't mean enough. The relevance wasn't sufficiently immediate for me to do anything about it, or even to think that I could. It was all too bad; such a shame, but life went on down here, even if I knew that up there things were terribly wrong. It had to, if I meant to finish my schooling, find work, fall in love — these things tend to crowd out the abstract. The voices in Dylan's song expressed interest in the news that the Vice President had gone insane, but there were still clothes on the line that needed to be taken in.

And then there was 9/11, and the immediacy became absolute and the abstract concrete. As George Bush asked the world that it "never tolerate outrageous conspiracy theories," I could see the cost of too many people letting a privileged few get away with too much for too long. We'd gotten on with our lives, without knowing that this too is our lives, and always has been. Well, now we know. And what we do about it, and about them, may determine whether we, as individuals or nations or an elevated species, live or die. We still have the choice, but only just.

I've never known the consolation of conspiracy theories, which psychological reductionists say all our research and time-lines and contrary accounts amount to. "If you think it's a rogue person or an unsophisticated group you start worrying about your daily life," said Dr. Cary Cooper two weeks after the towers fell. (And if it's the hand of a high cabal with no regard for the lives of useless eaters, then I suppose we should all breathe a collective sigh of relief.) Dr. Patrick Leman concluded "that there is some underlying process in human psychology that assumes that the bigger the effect is, the bigger the cause must have been." Unconsidered in his study is the reluctance of power to leave its fortune to chance and its fate to commoners' justice.

And then there is today's headline: "Enron Witness Found Dead in Park." *Help me, Doc, I keep seeing things ...*

security service FSB, the story changed: it was now claimed to have been an "exercise," and the sack of explosive hexogen was said to have contained nothing but "sugar." (Disbelief, a documentary regarding the bombings and the revelation of state guilt, may be viewed on the Internet. The story of Ryazan begins at approximately the 36-minute mark.) In 2002, an incurious Duma voted against a parliamentary inquiry into the bombing campaign.

Not only by history's precedence, but by current events, 9/11 isn't really that extraordinary.

It's interesting to note how Western pundits, who would likely dismiss as nonsense the mere suggestion of a 9/11 conspiracy, have no problem at all assessing the Russian apartment bombings as state terror. David Satter, a fellow of the Hoover Institution and the Hudson Institute and former Moscow correspondent for the *Financial Times* of London, wrote "The Shadow of Ryazan" with funding from the Smith Richardson Foundation, an abbreviated version of which was published by the *National Review*. It's funny how easily the generalized dismissals of conspiracy, such as how it meets a "psychological need," or that "something so big couldn't be kept a secret," vanish into one's political blind spots. That is, to the opinion makers, conspiracy can be the most reasonable explanation of events, so long as it's *over there*, and it's something *they* do. Satter finds the FSB guilty of waging a false-flag terror campaign against the Russian people and pronounces the Putin regime illegitimate, but don't expect him to be called a kook in a tinfoil hat for it.

The monotonous evil behind both the Moscow bombings and 9/11 is the tediously familiar, ceaseless appetite of the powerful for yet more power. Perhaps it's just as misleading to speak of "state terror" as it is to say "Bush Knew," since states are increasingly junior partners in the transnational equation of deep politics. Governments are the social clubs fronting the backrooms where the hard deals go down. As Peter Dale Scott writes in his important paper from last Fall entitled "The Global Drug Meta-Group," many 9/11 theorists create a false dilemma, suggesting the guilty party is either al Qaeda or the Bush administration, whereas elements of both were employed as assets by a deeper power network wired into narcotics and arms trafficking which has sometimes been called the Octopus. "In America few are likely to conceive of the possibility that a force in contact with the U.S. government could be not just an asset, but a force exerting influence on that government." It may be inconceivable to most, but I think it best accounts for the actions of a gangster elite. Though for the most part, the "elected" officials comprise the *consiglieri*, not the capos. (Why do you think so many of them are lawyers?)

Because evil always wants more of the same, and less-and-less can easily lead to none, it's easy to lapse into pessimism. Perhaps too easy. And perhaps that's where Weil returns.

Simone de Beauvoir writes of Weil, in *Memoirs of a Dutiful Daughter*, that "A great famine had broken out in China, and I was told that when she heard the news she had wept: these tears compelled my respect much more than her gifts as a philosopher. I envied her having a heart that could beat right across the world."

Weil died in England in 1943 of tuberculosis, though her death was hastened by her refusal to eat more than the ration allowed her compatriots in occupied France. She wrote, "Human beings are so made that the ones who do the crushing feel nothing; it is the person crushed who feels what is happening. Unless one has placed oneself on the side of the oppressed, to feel with them, one cannot understand."

Evil doesn't do empathy. We had better. Because if our hearts can beat around the world — if our consciousness can be elevated such that we see our isolation to be an illusion and our divisions a deceit of criminals who mean to crush us with them — then maybe the world will yet see some glorious novelty.

Unknown Knowns

August 17, 2004

I t seems often said of the things that consume me, "We'll never know what really happened." Think of the murder of JFK, and lately the events of September 11. The suggestion is that we who feel something is not right have little more than our unease to guide us, and that the facts are buried daily by the piling upon of time, ignorance and disinformation.

Remember these words from the Pentagon's Baron Sardonicus:

There are known knowns. These are things we know that we know. There are known unknowns. That is to say, there are things that we know we don't know. But there are also unknown unknowns. There are things we don't know we don't know.

It's always great fun to make sport of a Rumsfeldism, but I find myself ashamed to admit I understand what he was saying. Though true to form, he didn't say enough. Rumsfeld neglected to add that there are also unknown knowns. That is, there are *things we don't know we know.*

Since the mutation of America into the National Security State, it has been bedeviled by dark magi with deep bags of tricks: masters of sleight of hand, misdirection and persuasion, who dazzle their citizen-audience and leave them gasping, *Now how'd they do that?* And while the tricked try to figure out the mechanics of deep black illusions, for years the magi have been getting away with murder. And they will continue to do so, until enough people take their eyes off the tricks, and look at the tricksters.

Someone pretending to be Lee Harvey Oswald made an incriminating series of telephone calls between September 28 and October 1, 1963, allegedly to the Cuban and Soviet consulates, and one supposedly between the Cuban and Soviet consulates at a time when the Cuban consulate was closed and empty. In one of the calls, the Oswald impersonator mentions having met with Valery Kostikov, a man known to the CIA as the chief of KGB assassination operations in the Western hemisphere.

The CIA has lied about the tapes for decades. It claimed they were routinely destroyed before the assassination. But FBI documents have been uncovered which detail how at least two of the tapes were listened to after the assassination by Bureau agents familiar with Oswald's voice, who determined it wasn't Oswald. There is a tape of a telephone conversation between J Edgar Hoover and Lyndon Johnson, made days after the murder, in which they discuss this monkey wrench. And the Assassination Records Review Board found CIA documents in which the CIA itself states that some of the tapes were reviewed after the assassination, contradicting its long-held public position.

Grassy Knoll or sewer grate? Three shots, four shots or five? *It doesn't matter.* The CIA was lying about Oswald *before* November 22, 1963, creating a legend for him that would be used to frame him as the sole assassin. That *alone* should be enough to open the eyes of all but the most willfully blind.

We need to return to what first troubled us, because that should inform us what we should be doing now to put things right. And the most troubling aspects of modern American history are the unrequited demands of justice. This, I believe, is where the investigation into the first Kennedy assassination faltered. Researchers got down on their knees on the knoll, examining blades of grass and calculating trajectories. They became consumed with the minutiae, with the *how*. After a little while of this, the murder of a President became a puzzle instead of a crime; a pursuit of hobbyists. And it's what I fear for the 9/11-truth movement.

At a certain point, when a critical mass of evidence was reached — and it may have been as early as Ruby silencing Oswald — Americans should have known enough to say, "*Enough, already.*" And they should have brought the United States to a standstill until they saw something like justice done.

Americans will only wake from their nightmare of watching their finest liberal leaders, witnesses to high crimes and sundry victims getting *lone-gun-manned, suicided and accidented* (with treason unpunished and mass murder rewarded) if they learn that "We'll never know what really happened" is irrelevant. Because these are not puzzles; these are crimes. And crimes are never, in the end, *How done its*. They are "*Who done its*." And here's the singular unknown known: we know enough, and have for years, to know who.

The Cocaine Coup and the Coca Revolution

December 20, 2005

I often hear that I'm too negative. It's hard for me to disagree. Though what I want to be is just negative enough: neither stricken by paralysis nor buoyed up by cheap hope. That's a tough one.

So when good things happen — when real blows land against the empire and the last become first, at least for a while — they need acknowledgement. If only for the good of clearing my own head. Even sometimes at hope's "limited hangout" of electoral victory. Especially in Bolivia, when an indigenous man who talks like this is elected president:

> When we speak of the "defense of humanity," as we do at this event, I think that this only happens by eliminating neoliberalism and imperialism. But I think that in this we are not so alone, because we see, every day that anti-imperialist thinking is spreading, especially after Bush's bloody "intervention" policy in Iraq. Our way of organizing and uniting against the system, against the empire's aggression towards our people, is spreading, as are the strategies for creating and strengthening the power of the people.

As Evo Morales begins to exercise his unambiguous mandate, it will be interesting, and quite likely disheartening, to watch how Bolivia suddenly becomes a topic of great concern in certain quarters; even possibly a crisis of national security demanding intervention.

Here's an early example from Jim Kouri, a Vice President of the National Association of Chiefs of Police, who's written an opinion piece entitled "Bolivian Thug Becomes President." He predictably bloviates that the win "will increase the destabilization of the South American continent," and that Morales is an "ally of the drug cartels and traffickers."

The continent enjoys far greater stability today — and in the mental health sense of the word, too — than in the days of death's head satraps employing the methods of the School of the Americas and answerable to none but Washington. And in an interview with Luis Gómez of *Narco News*, former Bolivian guerrilla leader and presidential candidate Felipe Quispe makes distinctions between coca and cocaine that undoubtedly would be lost on Kouri:

> *Coca has been, ancestrally, a sacred leaf. We, the indigenous, have had a profound respect toward it... a respect that includes that we don't "pisar" it (the verb "pisar" means to treat the leaves with a chemical substance, one of the first steps in the production of cocaine). In general, we only use it to "acullicar": We chew it during times of war, during ritual ceremonies to salute Mother Earth (the Pachamama) or Father Sun or other Aymara divinities, like the hills. Thus, as an indigenous nation, we have never prostituted Mama Coca or done anything artificial to it because it is a mother. It is the occidentals who have prostituted it. It is they who made it into a drug. This doesn't mean that we don't understand the issue. We know that this plague threatens all of humanity and, from that perspective, we believe that those who have prostituted the coca have to be punished.*

Kouri walks his readers right up to "regime change": "should [Morales's] coca policy show an increase of cocaine on U.S. city streets, his regime will be seen as a national security threat and rightly so."

Funny, that. Or rather, like so many things these days, it would be funny if it didn't mean people's lives. Because on July 17, 1980, "los Novios de la Muerte" — narcotics traffickers and mercenaries recruited by fugitive Nazi and CIA asset Klaus Barbie — overthrew the democratic government of Bolivia in the "Cocaine Coup." Cocaine production increased dramatically and America was flooded with the cheap drug. In his essay on the drug war's shills in Kristina Borjesson's *Into the Buzzsaw*, 25-year DEA veteran Michael Levine writes that "there are few events in history that have caused more and longer-lasting damage to our nation." Bolivians could say the same.

Levine made headlines two months prior to the coup when his DEA sting netted Bolivian cartel leaders Roberto Gasser and Alfredo Gutierrez outside a Miami bank. He had paid them $8 million for the then-largest ever seizure of cocaine. Just a few weeks later Gasser and Gutierrez were released, thanks to pressure from the CIA and the State Department, and weeks after that both men and their cartels became principal financiers of the coup, and were rewarded by the new regime with squads of neo-Nazis to bully their competition.

And then there's Sun Myung Moon. Robert Parry remembers that one of the first international well-wishers who traveled to La Paz to congratulate the putschists was Moon's right hand Bo Hi Pak, former publisher of the *Washington Times* and "Koreagate" principal, who declared "I have erected a throne for Father Moon in the world's highest city." Later disclosures from the Bolivian government strongly suggested that Moon's organization had heavily invested in the coup, and Parry writes that in 1981 "war criminal Barbie and Moon leader Thomas Ward were often seen together in apparent prayer." Lt. Alfred Mario Mingolla, an Argentine intelligence officer recruited by Barbie, described Ward as his "CIA paymaster." His monthly salary was drawn from the offices of Moon's anti-communist umbrella organization, CAUSA. (Moon still has a huge stake in South America, having purchased the land above the world's largest fresh-water aquifer, in Paraguay. These people play a long game.)

"Meanwhile," Parry adds, "Barbie started a secret lodge, called Thule. During meetings, he lectured to his followers underneath swastikas by candlelight:" old habits, hardly dying, and a polyglot web of fascist patrons unashamed to profit by the labors of their Nazi lieutenants.

And here's another would-be funny thing: there were no American headlines about all of that. None at all.

But maybe that's enough talk for now about a coup. At least while there's a revolution going on.

Bobby and Alexander

November 22, 2006

> *Some things are too hot to touch*
> *The human mind can only stand so much.*
> — Bob Dylan

It's another November 22, and there are a couple of current stories that make it feel like it's always November 22.

Earlier this week, BBC's *Newsnight* reported the findings of Shane O'Sullivan's study of photographs and videotape from LA's Ambassador Hotel the evening of Robert Kennedy's assassination. He discovered the unaccounted-for presence of three senior veterans of CIA covert ops: Gordon Campbell, George Joannides and the notorious David Sanchez Morales. All three had served at the agency's massive anti-Castro (and later, anti-Kennedy) Miami station, JM/Wave. (Campbell as deputy directory, Joannides as head of psychological operations, and Morales as operations chief.)

This was no security detail. In 1968 presidential candidates were responsible for their own safety, the agency had no *official* domestic jurisdiction, and it hated the Kennedys and dreaded what Bobby might do — these three in particular. In 1973 Morales launched into a drunken tirade with friends that ended, "I was in Dallas when we got the son of a bitch and I was in Los Angeles when we got the little bastard." O'Sullivan asks Wayne Smith, a former State Department official who knew Morales well and corroborated his identity, whether Morales might have been covertly *protecting* Kennedy. Smith laughs, saying he was the "last person" for the job, and remembers Morales ranting at a Buenos Aires cocktail party in 1975 that Kennedy "got what was coming to him."

Morales, incidentally, died suddenly several weeks before he was scheduled to testify before the House Select Committee on

Assassinations, a couple of years after his mobbed-up confederate John Rosselli failed to appear because he was hacked to pieces and floating in a steel drum off the coast of Miami. Cause of death was a "supposed heart attack," so described to Gaeton Fonzi in *The Last Investigation* by Morales' close friend Ruben Carbajal. The evening of his death in retirement in Arizona, Morales had told him "I don't know what's wrong with me. Ever since I left Washington I haven't been feeling very comfortable." He'd become somewhat disillusioned with his former paymasters, and had described them to Carbajal as "the most ruthless motherfuckers there is, and if they want to get somebody, they will. They will do their own people up." His wife refused an autopsy. "I think the government took good care of her," said Carbajal.

And then there's the likely radiological poisoning of Alexander Litvinenko, former KGB/FSB counter-terrorist officer and author of *Blowing Up Russia*, an important account of 1999's false flag apartment bombing campaign that anchored authority for the as-yet unelected Vladimir Putin. A statement from the FSB implies that Litvinenko is not important enough to bother killing, adding "The man got sick. I would like to wish him early recovery."

Though I wonder whether something Litvinenko wrote a few months ago, after Putin impulsively kissed a boy on his belly, might have raised his Kremlin profile as a "person of interest."

From last July 5 (and thanks to a reader for the Internet link, which is found now only in a cache):

THE KREMLIN PEDOPHILE

By Alexander Litvinenko

A few days ago, Russian President Vladimir Putin walked from the Big Kremlin Palace to his Residence. At one of the Kremlin squares, the president stopped to chat with the tourists. Among them was a boy aged 4 or 5.

'What is your name?' Putin asked.

'Nikita,' the boy replied.

Putin kneeled, lifted the boy's T-shirt and kissed his stomach.

The world public is shocked. Nobody can understand why the Russian president did such a strange thing as kissing the stomach of an unfamiliar small boy.

The explanation may be found if we look carefully at the so-called "blank spot" in Putin's biography.

After graduating from the Andropov Institute, which prepares officers for the KGB intelligence service, Putin was not accepted into the foreign intelligence. Instead, he was sent to a junior position in KGB Leningrad Directorate. This was a very unusual twist for a career of an Andropov Institute's graduate with fluent German. Why did that happen with Putin?

Because, *shortly before his graduation, his bosses learned that Putin was a pedophile.* So say some people who knew Putin as a student at the Institute.

The Institute officials feared to report this to their own superiors, which would cause an unpleasant investigation. They decided it was easier just to avoid sending Putin abroad under some pretext. Such a solution is not unusual for the secret services.

Many years later, when Putin became the FSB director and was preparing for presidency, he began to seek and destroy any compromising materials collected against him by the secret services over earlier years. It was not difficult, provided he himself was the FSB director. Among other things, *Putin found videotapes in the FSB Internal Security Directorate, which showed him having sex with some underage boys.*

Interestingly, the video was recorded in the same conspiratorial flat in Polyanka Street in Moscow where Russian Prosecutor-General Yuri Skuratov was secretly videotaped with two prostitutes. Later, in the famous scandal, Putin (on Roman Abramovich's instructions) blackmailed Skuratov with these tapes and tried to persuade the Prosecutor-General to resign. In that conversation, Putin mentioned to Skuratov that he himself was also secretly videotaped making sex at the same bed. (But of course, he did not tell it was pedophilia rather than normal sex.) Later, Skuratov wrote about this in his book Variant Drakona.

It's Dallas, November 22. It's Los Angeles, June 5. It's London, it's Moscow, it's Memphis. It's everywhere and it's always: a Groundhog Day of High Criminal's running the clock while too few of us ineffectually shout "Foul!" And today, which is no different than yesterday, the CIA are the coolly-efficient good guys who may yet save America from the hysteria and excess of the Bush years, while the FSB help restore Russian "order and security."

It's a level playing field, but we're not the ones playing. Should we maybe try another game?

Floating in a Most Peculiar Way

November 27, 2006

> *Did I fall or was I pushed?*
> *And where's the blood?*
> — Harrowdown Hill

I 've been thinking about Alexander Litvinenko's alleged last words: "The bastards got me, but they won't get everybody." Not that the bastards won't try. In a year in which the Texas Academy of Science gave a standing ovation to its most distinguished member for a paper advocating the eradication of 90% of the Earth's population by airborne Ebola, only the unguardedly naive would think some bastards with the means wouldn't dream of getting everybody, or near enough everybody.

But before we make his last words our first, we should consider who he meant by them. Litvinenko's bastards were Russian, specifically Putin loyalists, though his employers-in-exile have also been called bastards and worse; notably Boris Berezovsky, formerly lawless oligarch, and latterly investor in Neil Bush's scholastic software firm "Ignite" (to which was funneled Barbara Bush's donation to the "Bush-Clinton Katrina Fund.") It's reported that weeks before his death, Litvinenko delivered a dossier on the Kremlin's takeover of oil giant Yukos to its former second-in-command, Leonid Nevzlin, who had found asylum in Israel.

And that reminds me of another suspicious death on British soil: the 2004 helicopter crash of wealthy lawyer Stephen Curtis, managing director of Yukos, after the jailing of Mikhail Khodorkovsky. To avoid Russian prosecution, and after weeks of anonymous death threats, Curtis approached Britain's National Criminal Intelligence Service "days before his death, offering information in return for protection." Two weeks prior to the crash, Curtis told his uncle that if "anything happened" to him, it would not be an accident.

Even as spectators, we want to choose sides. We want to know who the *good guys are*. For the past six years at least, that's often meant finding out which side the Bush family was on and then cheering for the other. But playing a single side would mean risking loss and so, by delivering his own son to crucifixion by James Baker, George H.W. Bush has won again. There have been other strange and uncomfortable and pathetic scenes, such as George Soros and Warren Buffet being welcomed as white-knight plutocrats, and the uncritical embrace of a parade of self-described former Republicans, Bush insiders, and CIA officials saying the darnedest things about 9/11.

I think of a passage in Litvinenko's *Blowing Up Russia*, recounting the night in Ryazan when sacks of explosive Hexogene rigged with a timing device were discovered in the basement of an apartment complex. The building was evacuated, except for an elderly woman who couldn't be moved and her daughter who refused to leave her. They remained within the emergency cordon, expecting their apartment to collapse upon them.

In the daughter's words:

> I suddenly had this realization that my mother and I were probably the only two people in a house with a bomb in it. I felt quite unbearably afraid. But then suddenly there was a ring at the door. Standing on the doorstep were two senior militia officers. They asked me sternly: "Have you decided you want to be buried alive, then, woman?" I was so scared my legs were giving way under me, but I stood my ground; I wouldn't go without my mother. And then they suddenly took pity on me: "All right then, stay here, your house has already been made safe." It turned out they'd removed the detonators from the charge even before they inspected the flats.

We stand our ground, we don't move, they can't kill us all. If there's an us, there can be many different *thems*, but whoever the bastards may be they don't always win. In Ryazan, a vigilant neighbor just happened to witness the planting of explosives and called local authorities. If he hadn't, the building would have been demolished like the apartments before it, full of sleeping casualties. If a Ryazan telephone operator hadn't recorded a suspicious call to Moscow, the terrorists might have escaped and their FSB connections remained undisclosed. But because two of us acted, Russian security was obliged to peddle the egregious lie of an "exercise," after days of calling it a foiled terrorist plot.

September 11th, while a covert success story, saw many little blunders that contribute to making its cover story fly apart on examination. Think of the confusion of tongues amongst the alphabet agencies, with some elements acting in good faith, and others, not. For instance, it was FBI agents who confirmed to Indian intelligence that Pakistan's General Mahmoud Ahmad had ordered ISI/al Qaeda double-agent Omar Saeed Sheikh to wire funds to Mohamed Atta in Florida. How do you imagine they felt when Ahmad was allowed to retire, unquestioned, and the 9/11 Commission declared the terrorist money trail of no consequence? Possibly like the DEA agents who see their high-profile collars quietly released, on account of pressure by the State Department and the CIA.

But unless we *do something* with the information we've processed, and *make something* of our knowledge, then their defeats revert to their strengths. Thinking of Ryazan, of 9/11, of Brabant and David Kelly, we revolt but in only the transitive sense, by being disgusted to the point of nausea. But sickness is debilitating, and dwelling on it is no substitute for a cure.

Bobby star William H. Macy told the *Globe and Mail* last week that when he heard Robert Kennedy had been shot "I felt like I'd been punched in the gut.... We had thought we could change everything. We could end the war. We could bring down a president. The people had power. I remember after Bobby was assassinated, it felt hopeless." The bastards got him, and everybody else in the bargain, because their hope was invested in one man. Perhaps hope, if it means to be effectual, needs to be divested.

The bastards are not omnipotent, but they are omnivorous, which only appears to be a God-like quality in a world such as this.

"Rogue Elements"

December 2, 2006

Fingerprints, fingerprints,
Where are you now, my fingerprints?
— Leonard Cohen

In *Blowing Up Russia*, Alexander Litvinenko writes that "Free-lance conspiratorial military operations groups consisting of former and current members of special armed forces units and the structures of law enforcement began to be set up in Russia in the 1980s.... [E]ven if it does not always organize the groups in the formal sense of the word, [the FSB] has controlled their activity to a greater or lesser degree from the very beginning."

This is the essence and the beauty of the case for the "rogue element," that unnamed "intelligence sources" tout as the most likely agent for Litvinenko's poisoning, and possibly Yegor Gaidar's as well. Even when a murder weapon can be traced to state actors — the polonium 210 to a Russian nuclear plant or, say, the anthrax to Fort Detrick — the state can deny institutional culpability by claiming its assets acted without consent. And there is even some truth to the claim, but only because a state's intelligence is structurally dissociative: compartmentalized concretions of unadmitted will, providing deniability to the regime while enacting its ugliest measures.

"Rogues" could also charitably describe the "assassination squad" which former intelligence officer Mikhail Trepashkin attests has been set up by the FSB, to eliminate enemies abroad. "Rogues" is the "bad apples" argument. It's to say a state is accountable for the crimes of its henchmen only if it first calls "*Simon says.*" And how often does that happen? It's still frequently said by many that "rogue elements" within the CIA were responsible for the assassination of John Kennedy and its subsequent cover-up, not the CIA itself, even though those rogues have included some of its most senior and celebrated officials. If a new inquiry into the highly suspicious death of Britain's

WMD whistleblower David Kelly should ever actually investigate his death, you can expect the trial balloon of "rogue elements" to be floated, to relieve the pressure on the institutions of intelligence.

A lot of smart people have said Vladimir Putin didn't benefit by Litvinenko's murder, because he too obviously benefited, making him and his government the perfect frames. But if the government of Russia's a suspect, who's to prosecute? British investigators have preemptively "ruled out any official involvement" by the Russian state, though they go on to say only those with access to state nuclear laboratories could have carried it out. Naturally Britain would provide Putin an out: the damage to relations would make anything less a prohibitive disruption. (Similarly, Putin hasn't blamed Washington for 9/11, though several Russian commanders have publicly expressed disbelief at its account of the attacks.)

No one but his allies in the West can harbor necessary illusions of what Berezovsky may be capable, but neither should we believe Putin a white knight because of his tactical role as a counterweight to the White House. The lesson of *1984* isn't "Smile! You're in Eurasia."

Blaming "rogue elements" spares the institutions of state, which is why the institutions breed them. And who could blame them for that?

The Violent Bear It Away

July 31, 2006

Don't take no tidal wave, don't take no mass grave
Don't take no smokin' gun to show how the west was won
— Neil Young

These are strange days, even for those who have anticipated them. It's not so much that things are going to Hell, it's just that things seem to be getting there so much sooner than expected. Only two more years of drought and the Amazon rain forest may burn and become a desert, a process "that might end in the world becoming uninhabitable." The oceans are devolving into an acidic, primeval goo. Complex life is dying by our hands while we are extinguishing ourselves, creating conditions unknown for hundreds of millions of years, in which the very bottom of the food chain, the slimes and invertebrates, may re-inherit the Earth.

And even for the Middle East, which has seen so many wars, this war is an odd one. Israel's actions appear counter-intuitive, even by its hard-right's own measure of "national security." Its self-immolation of any credible claim to a just cause virtually assures tragedy, for itself and its people. Its goading of Syria and Iran into a general war by turning Lebanon into a slaughterhouse means the Israeli state has become, itself, a suicide bomber; an engine of apocalypse. But for whom, and for what?

"[Israeli] Defense officials told the [Jerusalem] *Post* last week that they were receiving indications from the U.S. that America would be interested in seeing Israel attack Syria." And *Haaretz* quotes Hezbollah leader Sheikh Hassan Nasrallah as saying on Saturday that the "Israelis are ready to halt the aggression because they are afraid of the unknown. The one pushing for the continuation of the aggression is the U.S. administration."

And then there are a pair of Mephisphelean characters named Cheney and Netanyahu.

It's often presumed that Israel leads American policy in the Middle East, and that's frequently been true, which is why this war is strikingly and disturbingly different. The United States is actually egging on Israel to press the attack, regardless of the cost Israelis may be expected to bear from the fresh blood its armed forces shed. George Bush spoke arguably his most frightening and truthful words last Friday, when he admitted that it's not the White House intention to create "a sense of stability." It's by instability — by creating "failed states" in the Balkans, Central Asia, the Middle East and elsewhere — that End-Time criminals stand to gain the most. That may be no surprise to those of us who know the playbook, but our Humanity still can't help but be shocked by their unbridled delight in the "opportunities" now presented by the "new Middle East."

As recently as the mid-'90s, there was talk of a different, new Middle East. On the evening of November 4, 1995, in Tel Aviv's Kings of Israel Square, Yitzhak Rabin spoke these words:

> There are enemies of peace who are trying to hurt us, in order to torpedo the peace process. I want to say bluntly, that we have found a partner for peace among the Palestinians as well: the PLO, which was an enemy, and has ceased to engage in terrorism. Without partners for peace, there can be no peace. We will demand that they do their part for peace, just as we will do our part for peace, in order to solve the most complicated, prolonged, and emotionally charged aspect of the Israeli-Arab conflict: the Palestinian-Israeli conflict.
>
> This is a course which is fraught with difficulties and pain. For Israel, there is no path that is without pain. But the path of peace is preferable to the path of war. I say this to you as one who was a military man, someone who is today Minister of Defense and sees the pain of the families of the IDF soldiers. For them, for our children, in my case for our grandchildren, I want this Government to exhaust every opening, every possibility, to promote and achieve a comprehensive peace. Even with Syria, it will be possible to make peace.
>
> This rally must send a message to the Israeli people, to the Jewish people around the world, to the many people in the Arab world, and indeed to the entire world, that the Israeli people want peace, support peace. For this, I thank you.

And then he was shot.

There's a reflex among some on the left to embrace the lone gunman hypothesis, because they regard the alternative as an embrace of a hollow liberal myth. Noam Chomsky and Alexander Cockburn regard John F. Kennedy as nothing but a patrician cold warrior, who would have delivered more of the same had he lived. Rabin receives the same treatment, if not more, for his harsh words and measures during the Intifada and for the flawed Oslo Accords. But their killers were not appraising them from the left. From the hard right, they were both men who had risen through the system and had become traitors to it.

Rabin's convicted lone gunman, Yigal Amir, had close ties to the extremist nationalist organization Eyal, and was groomed by its founder Avishai Raviv to kill Rabin. The Israeli paper *Maariv* reported November 24, 1995 that "according to Sarah Eliash, a schoolteacher working at the Shomron Girls Seminary, some of her pupils heard Raviv encourage Amir to murder Rabin. Raviv told Amir, 'Show us you're a man. Do it.'"

Uri Dan and Dennis Eisenberg elaborated on the girls' testimony writing for the *Jerusalem Post*, which Barry Chamish quotes in his *Who Murdered Yitzhak Rabin?*

> Sarah Eliash had already appeared voluntarily before the commission and related how her pupils had run to see her on the night of the killing. In tears they said they knew Yigal Amir. They had met both Amir and Avishai Raviv.... 'We used to see Raviv and Amir on Saturdays during last summer,' they related.
>
> These gatherings were arranged by Yigal ... Raviv was real macho. He kept saying to Yigal: 'You keep talking about killing Rabin. Why don't you do it? Are you frightened? You say you want to do it. Show us that you're a man. Show us what you're made of.'

Now, would it surprise you to know that Avishai Raviv, the founder of the extremist Eyal and the bug in the ear of Rabin's assassin, was also a Shabak (or "Shin Bet," Israel's covert internal security) agent, code-named "Champagne" for, writes Chamish, "the bubbles of incitement he raised"?

From *Maariv*:

> Amnon Abramovitch dropped a bombshell last night, announcing that Avishai Raviv was a Shabak agent code-named "Champagne." Now we ask the question, why didn't he report Yigal Amir's plan to murder

Rabin to his superiors? In conversations with security officials, the following picture emerged. Eyal was under close supervision of the Shabak. They supported it monetarily for the past two years. The Shabak knew the names of all Eyal members, including Yigal Amir.

Just as 9/11 was wargamed, so too was Rabin's murder. Shabak explained its failure to protect the Prime Minister at Kings of Israel Square with the excuse that it had "no contingency plan" to stop a lone gunman. A year and a half after the assassination, that blew up in the agency's face with Anashim's interview of two former members of Shabak's personal security unit, Tuvia Livneh and Yisrael Shai. "When Yisrael and I heard the news of the murder we became infuriated at the fact that there was a contingency plan for just such an attempt, which we practiced endless times."

Anashim continues:

This is not a case of wisdom after the fact, but scandalous wisdom well before the event, which is being published for the first time: when the two commanded the unit at the beginning of the 1990s, they prepared a detailed contingency plan for a political assassination at Kings of Israel Square, including the possibility that the assassin would act from the exit stairs behind the stage, precisely where Yigal Amir waited for Yitzhak Rabin. The plan was transferred to field command where it was practiced in dry runs.

So, a suggestible gunman was befriended and goaded into action by an undercover Shabak agent, and the assassination followed the script written and performed in dress rehearsal by the same agency. These are just two of the arguments for conspiracy in Rabin's death.

Chamish, following his own political lights, believes the guilt lay with leftist elements seeking to discredit the right, but he reaches that conclusion by far overreaching the disturbing facts of the case, with partisan speculation. Besides, if it had been an attack from the left, it failed miserably. In the ten years since the murder, Israeli society, despairing of peace, has undergone a rightward radicalization. Last November, the Dahaf Polling Institute found that "20 percent of respondents said Amir should be pardoned, and 45 percent said he should be allowed to have conjugal visits in prison." ("The measure of public sympathy toward Amir worries Rabin's surviving family members.") Nevertheless, the poll also found that a quarter of respondents "believed in a conspiracy theory perpetrated by the Shin Bet."

Chamish spoke by telephone to one of the young women who had heard Raviv encourage Amir to murder Rabin. Soon after, her father took hold of the receiver, and told him to "Find someone else if you can. You have to understand that, don't you? You don't know what's going on.... This is no democracy. You don't know what it is.... I can't tell you what they said they'd do to her if she talked anymore."

The Age of Nations is over, and many of the most powerful are no longer ruled by forces which safeguard the interests of the state, let alone its citizens. We're entering an extinction boundary, between the reign of high mammals and the return of the jellyfish. What are the politics of jellyfish?

3. Can't Help It If They're Lucky

I think that you'll find a little S&M will be necessary to trigger off a good healthy dose of hallucinations.

— *Videodrome*

Area 9/11

August 5, 2006

9/11 *changed everything.* Dissenters are uncommonly quick to call bullshit on that talking point. And maybe it didn't. But it changed me.

"The battle for the mind of North America will be fought in the video arena: the Videodrome," says the McLuhanesque Brian O'Blivion, referring to the pirate broadcast of a torture and murder circus, which contains in its transmission a frequency that triggers the tumorous growth of new organs of perception in the brains of its viewers. "The television screen is the retina of the mind's eye. Therefore, the television screen is part of the physical structure of the brain. Therefore, whatever appears on the television screen emerges as raw experience for those who watch it. Therefore, television is reality, and reality is less than television."

For almost all of us, 9/11 was only a televised event. Yet, like Ruby shooting Oswald live in America's living room, and like *Videodrome*, it was also a spectacular trauma; the unscheduled program was also *programming*, inducing a national trance to initiate the stage-managed winding down of our familiar world. But it also created within us fresh capacities of insight, and that too may have been the intent.

Apart from the chain-smoking, and though there's not much to laugh about, the opening sequence of *Who Killed John O'Neill?* is comically familiar. *"I don't sleep, I don't eat, I don't shower, I don't shave…. I don't do anything but think."* I filled eight binders with tabs like "Osama," "Foreknowledge" and "Anthrax," with articles like the *Guardian*'s "CIA Agent Alleged to Have Met Bin Laden in July," *Newsweek*'s "Alleged Hijackers May Have Trained at U.S. Bases" and the *Baltimore Sun*'s "Anthrax Matches Army Spores." I started reading again the *samizdat* history of the National Security State, though now with greater urgency and comprehension, because the existential stakes had been raised, and having seen the towers fall I felt as though I knew already how the story ended.

We were getting rewired: the new eyes that 9/11 gave us were entraining our brains to penetrate our flat screens to the real-world paramechanics of power, money and appetite. (Remaining on the surface analyzing pixels, with 9/11 *as nothing but* a special event broadcast, while forgetting that it was filmed before a live audience, is how the more absurd hypotheses of holographic airplanes and pods arise.)

And there are a lot of us putting on this new flesh: a full third of Americans now, according to a poll this past week, suspect federal officials either "assisted in the 9/11 terrorist attacks or took no action to stop them so the United States could go to war in the Middle East." Lee Hamilton, the former vice chairman of the Kean Commission and trusted Bush family fixer stretching all the way back to the October Surprise and Iran/Contra, acknowledges, "One out of three sounds high, but that may very well be right." (Hamilton is a Democrat, it should be noted, because if your wiring isn't up to code for these days, that still matters.)

The same week we saw the limited hangout's most risqué striptease yet, with the release of *Vanity Fair*'s "NORAD tapes", bringing at last into mainstream discourse NORAD's coincident gaming of hijacked aircraft the morning of September 11:

"When they told me there was a hijack, my first reaction was 'Somebody started the exercise early,'" [Lieutenant Colonel] Nasypany later told me. The day's exercise was designed to run a range of scenarios, including a "traditional" simulated hijack in which politically motivated perpetrators commandeer an aircraft, land on a Cuba-like island, and seek asylum. "I actually said out loud, 'The hijack's not supposed to be for another hour.'"

The author, associate producer of *United 93*, Michael Bronner, promptly adds: "The fact that there was an exercise planned for the same day as the attack factors into several conspiracy theories, though the 9/11 commission dismisses this as coincidence. After plodding through dozens of hours of recordings, so do I." And so we can suspect why NORAD entrusted to Bronner's care the glossy unveiling of just one of 9/11's war games. (Kyle Hence's "11 Questions Avoided by the Media On NORAD Tapes" makes a nice, concise refutation of Bronner's plodding.)

Then there was the story in the *Washington Post* that "some staff members and commissioners of the Sept. 11 panel concluded that the Pentagon's initial story of how it reacted to the 2001 terrorist attacks may have been part of a deliberate effort to mislead the commission." Naturally, the assumed intent of the Pentagon's criminal fraud goes no deeper than the hiding of "the bungled response to the hijackings." Commission members dare go no further, because their deliberately misleading report places them on the Pentagon's side of manufactured history.

Has the Bush administration been "rocked" by these cautious disclosures? Only in the fantasy life of Democrats still awaiting their Fitzmas. Rather, it presses ahead with the next war, expands Guantanamo Bay, and intends to "allow the Secretary of Defense to add crimes at will to those under the military court's jurisdiction," meaning that dissidents "not directly involved in acts of international terrorism" may be subject to the Pentagon's discretionary justice.

I occasionally receive the comment that it's a waste of our energies to give any regard at all to strange things in the sky and weird visitations, because *even if they exist, there's nothing we can do about them*. If so, then for all our energies, what have we been able to do about this White House?

If there's a touch, and perhaps more, of the demonic about both, there's also a phantasmic daimonism. Their methods are to *display*, as well as *evade*. Discs and giant triangles have lit up American skies with performances of flashing colored lights, demanding attention while denying comprehension. In the mid-'80s, New York's Hudson Valley became a venue for a public exhibition of silent-running isosceles triangles 400 feet or more from tip to tip, blinking garishly for the towns below, and were reported by seven thousand eyewitnesses. Perhaps even more disturbing than the prospect of their being of otherworldly origin, is the prospect that they are not.

The new flesh of 9/11 enhances our perception, but not our reach. We can look up and see — *we're invited to* — but the invitation is one to reinforce a sense of helplessness. The great public spectacles written in the sky — the gaudy lights and the falling towers — are meant to debilitate us, and pin our hopes passively upon a "disclosure" by the intelligence community's own information warriors. Nothing good, and nothing true, can come of that.

In a Rumsfeldian sense, we should know enough now to know that we know enough. But the insight 9/11's new flesh gives us into America's unnatural state of affairs becomes debilitation, if nothing changes by it. How to be the change is our challenge. Perhaps our last challenge.

Michael Chertoff and the Sabotage of the Ptech Investigation

January 14, 2005

Remember Ptech? That's the Boston software firm financed by Saudi businessman Yassin Al-Qadi, who also happens to be an al-Qaeda bagman, whose clients happened to include numerous sensitive U.S. federal branches and agencies, including the FAA, the FBI, the military and the White House.

A little background, from the mainstream, even, thanks to WBZ-TV:

Joe Bergantino, a reporter for WBZ-TV's investigative team, was torn. He could risk breaking a story based on months of work investigating a software firm linked to terrorism, or heed the government's demand to hold the story for national security reasons. In mid-June, Bergantino received a tip from a woman in New York who suspected that Ptech, a computer software company in Quincy, Mass., had ties to terrorists. Ptech specialized in developing software that manages information contained in computer networks.

Bergantino's investigation revealed that Ptech's clients included many federal governmental agencies, including the U.S. Army, the U.S. Air Force, the U.S. Naval Air Command, Congress, the Department of Energy, the Federal Aviation Administration, the Internal Revenue Service, NATO, the Federal Bureau of Investigation, the Secret Service and even the White House.

"Ptech was doing business with every federal agency in defense and had access to key government data," Bergantino said.

...

Bergantino was ready to air the story by September, but the government had different plans. Federal authorities told Bergantino not to air the story because it would jeopardize their investigation and would threaten national security. According to federal authorities, documents would be shredded and people would flee if we ran the story, Bergantino said.

But Bergantino claims the government's demand to hold off on the story was merely a pretext. In October 2001, President George W. Bush signed an executive order freezing the assets of individuals linked to terrorism. According to Bergantino, the list identified Saudi Arabian businessman Yassin Al-Qadi as a key financial backer of Osama Bin Laden. As it turns out, Bergantino said, Al-Qadi is also the chief financier of Ptech. The government failed to investigate Ptech in October 2001 and didn't start it's investigation until August 2002, when WBZ-TV's investigation called attention to Ptech.

Even if Ptech was unaware that the President's October 2001 order contained the name of its chief financier, documents seized in a March 2002 government raid revealed Ptech's connections with another organization linked to terrorism, Bergantino said. And again, the government failed to investigate Ptech.

Bergantino's tipster was Indira Singh, who has said she recognizes the separate command and control communications system Mike Ruppert says Dick Cheney was running on September 11th, as having "the exact same functionality I was looking to utilize [for] Ptech."

Now, how does Chertoff figure in the Ptech story? It goes back to the turf war of two years ago over Operation Greenquest, "the high-profile federal task force set up to target the financiers of Al-Qaeda and other international terrorist groups." The aggressive, Customs-led task force was folded into Homeland Security, sending the FBI and its minders at the Department of Justice into a tizzy. They "demanded that the White House instead give the FBI total control over Greenquest."

Now, consider this, also from the two-year-old *Newsweek*:

The FBI-Justice move, *pushed by DOJ Criminal Division chief Michael Chertoff* and Deputy Attorney General Larry Thompson, has enraged Homeland Security officials, however. *They accuse the bureau of sabotaging Greenquest investigations* — by failing to turn over critical information to their agents — and trying to obscure a decade-long record of lethargy in which FBI offices failed to aggressively pursue terror-finance cases....

. . .

One prime example of the tension is the investigation into Ptech, the Boston-area computer software firm that had millions of dollars in sensitive government contracts with the Air Force, the Energy Department *and, ironically enough, the FBI.* In what turned into a minor embarrassment for the bureau, the firm's main investors included Yassin Al-Qadi, a wealthy Saudi businessman whom the Bush administration had formally designated a terrorist financier under the International Emergency Economic Powers Act. Al-Qadi has vigorously denied any connection to terrorism.

The Ptech case turned into an ugly dispute last year when company whistleblowers told Greenquest agents about their own suspicions about the firm's owners. *Sources close to the case say those same whistleblowers had first approached FBI agents, but the bureau apparently did little or nothing in response.* With backing from the National Security Council, Greenquest agents then mounted a full-scale investigation that culminated in a raid on the company's office last December. *After getting wind of the Greenquest probe, the FBI stepped in* and unsuccessfully tried to take control of the case.

The result, sources say, has been something of a train wreck. Privately, FBI officials say Greenquest agents botched the probe and jeopardized other more promising inquiries into Al-Qadi. Greenquest agents dismiss the charges and say the problem is that the bureau was slow to respond to legitimate allegations that an outside contractor with terrorist ties may have infiltrated government computers. Whatever the truth, there is no dispute that the case has so far produced no charges and indictments against Al-Qadi or anyone else connected with Ptech. The company has denied wrongdoing. [emphases added]

The turf war was won on May 13, 2003, when John Ashcroft and Tom Ridge signed a "Memorandum of Agreement between the Departments of Justice and Homeland Security, *giving the FBI "unprecedented unilateral control of all terrorist-financing investigations and operations."*

Several seasoned government agents fear for the nation's security should the FBI be tackling most terrorism cases, as their ineptitude in preventing terrorism has been established time and time again. Yet, the memorandum between Ashcroft and Ridge places the FBI in an incredibly powerful position over Homeland Security. According to the memorandum, "all appropriate DHS leads relating to money laundering and financial crimes will be checked with the FBI." [emphasis added]

Well, no reason to fear, now that Michael Chertoff is heading up Homeland Security. Right?

Also, a noteworthy admission today from the Department of Justice, released in a "37-page, unclassified summary of a broader, 100-page internal review over Edmonds' case":

From Associated Press:

Evidence and other witnesses support complaints by a fired FBI contract linguist who alleged shoddy work and possible espionage within the bureau's translator program in the months after the September 2001 terror attacks, according to a report Friday by the senior oversight official at the Justice Department.

The department's inspector general, Glenn Fine, said the allegations by former translator Sibel Edmonds "raised substantial questions and were supported by various pieces of evidence." Fine said the FBI still has not adequately investigated the sensational claims.

A show of hands: how many have heard U.S. cable news whisper, even once, the name "Sibel Edmonds"? I have. Once. It was about the time of Edmonds' press conference last spring, held between sessions of Thomas Kean's 9/11 Commission. Paul Begala, the designated liberal of CNN's *Crossfire*, gingerly raised her more reasonable-to-mainstream charges. (At least, those of which John Ashcroft's gag order permits her to speak.) Tucker Carlson, as if on cue, called her a "conspiracy theorist" and, I seem to recall, a "nutjob."

And according to CNN, that's the last we've heard of her.

Naturally, neither Sibel Edmonds nor Indira Singh, nor Ptech, warrant a mention in the official 9/11 Commission report. Though Edmonds is gagged, Singh did give testimony to the 9/11 Citizens' Commission, Sept 9, 2004 in New York. She read an open letter from Edmonds, and added, "What I have uncovered in Ptech connects with some of the things that she has discovered. Sibel is not allowed to disclose content but she can ask me questions. I know some of the things that she mentioned there connect directly to what I discovered."

Further:

> INDIRA SINGH: I did a number of things in my research and *when I ran into the drugs* I was told that if I mentioned the money to the drugs around 9/11 that would be the end of me. That is a current threat that I'm under and therefore I will speak out about the drugs at another forum.
>
> I did not expect the Kean Commission to go anywhere near the FBI and Ptech. But I hope all Americans will demand answers regarding the FBI and Ptech. I would like to leave you with this one question. Not only *why is Ptech still operating but why did Assistant U.S. Attorney Michael Chertoff state that they cannot differentiate between terrorism, organized crime and drug dealing* and is that the reason the Kean Commission will not make terrorism financing a priority in the future?

...

> *Ptech was with Mitre [Corporation] in the basement of the FAA for two years prior to 9/11.* Their specific job is to look at interoperability issues the FAA had with NORAD and the Air Force in the case of an emergency. *If anyone was in a position to know that the FAA, that there was a window of opportunity or to insert software or to change anything it would have been Ptech along with Mitre.*

...

> And that ties right back to Michael Ruppert's information.
>
> The functionality that Michael is claiming that Dick Cheney utilized is the exact same functionality I was looking to utilize Ptech for in the bank. I was looking to set up a shadow surveillance system on everything going on, every transaction and the ability to backdoor, [to] look at information unobtrusively and to backdoor intelligent agents out there to do things that other people would not be aware of. To stop ... in risk the whole shift is from bad things going on and finding it after the fact to preventing it from happening. So we were looking for patterns and have the intervention in there. So we were looking for interventive software, something that would stop.
>
> *What Mike Ruppert is referring to is exactly the same kind of functionality ... surveillance and intervention.* [emphases added]

Another show of hands: have you heard anything like that, ever, on U.S. cable news?

"Oh, the places you'll go (when you follow the money)"

February 1, 2005

L et's pick a story. Say, data recovery from the World Trade Center.

Remember? While the ruins still smoldered, some genuine questions were being asked by the mainstream media, which were blissfully unaware of how awkward the answers might prove.

For instance, this story, from December 17, 2001:

German computer experts are working round the clock to unlock the truth behind an unexplained surge in financial transactions made just before two hijacked planes crashed into New York's World Trade Center on September 11.

Were criminals responsible for the sharp rise in credit card transactions that moved through some computer systems at the WTC shortly before the planes hit the twin towers?

Or was it coincidence that unusually large sums of money, perhaps more than $100 million, were rushed through the computers as the disaster unfolded?

And this, from CNN, a few days later:

An unexplained surge in transactions was recorded prior to the attacks, leading to speculation that someone might have profited from previous knowledge of the terrorist plot by moving sums of money. But because the facilities of many financial companies processing the transactions were housed in New York's World Trade Center, destroyed in the blasts, it has until now been impossible to verify that suspicion.

That's where Convar Systeme Deutschland GmbH comes in. The company is helping reconstruct data from hard disk drives found in the ruins of the twin towers. While other data-recovery companies are also involved in the effort, the company says it has a special edge: a laser-based scanning technology developed about two years ago. Peter Henschel, director of Convar, called the extent of the transactions "extraordinarily high."

Further:

"It could turn out that Americans went on an absolute shopping binge on that Tuesday morning. But at this point there are many transactions that cannot be accounted for, " Henschel said. "Not only the volume but the size of the transactions was far higher than usual for a day like that. There is a suspicion that these were possibly planned to take advantage of the chaos."

...

Richard Wagner, a data retrieval expert at the company, said illegal transfers of more than $100 million might have been made immediately before and during the disaster.

"There is a suspicion that some people had advance knowledge of the approximate time of the plane crashes in order to move out amounts exceeding $100 million," Wagner said. "They thought that the records of their transactions could not be traced after the mainframes were destroyed."

As Convar recovered the data, at a cost of up to $35,000 per hard drive, the information was forwarded to its clients (apparently telecommunications, accounting, and credit card firms), which in turn passed it on to the FBI.

A Reuters story claims "Convar has recovered information from 32 computers that support assumptions of dirty doomsday dealings." And an article dated May 30, 2002, says Convar "had recovered the data from 39 computers...and was beginning to work on another 62.... [T]he next time you 'erase' something by clicking delete, it might help to remember Convar: once on view, always on recall."

So, what happened to the WTC data-recovery story, and the "dirty doomsday dealings"?

We need to step back, and ask, what happened to Convar?

In June, 2002, Convar was purchased by security firm Kroll Inc., which employs a number of former FBI and CIA officials, and has a reputation for serving as a cut-out for U.S. Intelligence. It's reportedly known as the "CIA of Wall Street," due to its revolving door of former-and-future spooks, and its role in corporate espionage and the destabilization of foreign governments.

We can learn something about Kroll's reputation from a front-page story of the *Washington Post*, January 8, 1996:

The French, the CIA, and the Man Who Sued Too Much

William Lee is a 57-year-old Harvard-educated corporate lawyer whose specialty, until recently, was international mergers and acquisitions. But a year ago, the government of France charged that he was a spy for the Central Intelligence Agency, waging a secret war to destabilize French corporate interests in Asia.

...

Some of the French anxiety about Lee stems from what he did next. In mid-1992, he took a part-time position with Kroll Associates, a New York firm that provides investigative services for big companies and employs a number of former CIA and FBI officers.

For French officials, Lee's brief stint with Kroll tagged him as a suspicious person. According to French and U.S. sources, the French equivalent of the FBI, known as the Directorate of Surveillance of the Territory, or DST, suspected that Kroll's Paris operation was a CIA front. They bugged Kroll's Paris offices and harassed some of its clients, according to company executives.

And this story, from October of last year:

Brazil Raids Kroll Offices in Spy Probe

Police raided the Brazilian offices of international security consultant Kroll Inc. and arrested five employees Wednesday in an investigation into allegations of illegal spying by Kroll during the company's probe of a nasty corporate dispute.... Five Brazilians Kroll workers were arrested on conspiracy charges.

...

The investigation began in July after Brazil's largest newspaper reported Kroll obtained copies of e-mails written by a top adviser to President Luiz Inacio Lula da Silva in the course of its investigation for Brasil Telecom Participacoes SA.

Interestingly, in August of 2001, it was then-Managing Director of Kroll, Jerome Hauer, who arranged for former FBI special agent John O'Neill to be hired as chief of security at the World Trade Center.

Besides being in Kroll's service on September 11, Hauer was also running Rudolph Giuliani's "Office of Emergency Management," and its hardened "command and control" bunker on the 22nd floor of WTC 7. (Perhaps you remember what happened to that.)

I believe too little attention is paid to the role of extra-governmental agencies, both to the 9/11 story and beyond, because it is in their study that Danny Casolaro saw what he came to call the Octopus: the international network of spooks, former spooks, crooks and terrorists, pursuing trans-national criminal interests. To say "it's the CIA" is too simplistic, too black-and-white for the world of shadows. As Chaim Kupferberg writes:

> It is, in fact, security firms like Kroll Associates, Burns Security, Teg, Wackenhut, and their ilk that should garner our interest at least as much as the web of conservative think tanks that have welded in place the parameters of "mainstream" debate — for it is through these very firms that the former stars of law enforcement have gone through the revolving door into the lucrative private sector. It is a world where former military types mix with various operatives of the CIA, FBI, DEA and any number of alphabet soup agencies charged with the security of our nation.

Since acquiring Convar, Kroll itself has been purchased by Marsh & McLennan, a former occupant of Tower One's 95th floor. Last October, Kroll's former President, Michael Cherkasky, was named Marsh's CEO. (Formerly, Cherkasky had "spent 16 years in the criminal justice system, including serving as chief of the Investigations Division for the New York County District Attorney's Office.")

And what an upstanding corporate citizen Marsh turns out to be. Just yesterday, it reached a deal with New York State Attorney General Eliot Spitzer "that resolves the actions that were commenced against MMC and Marsh Inc. over questionable brokerage compensation and account placement practices":

As a result of this agreement, the company said it would enact reforms to lead the industry in transparency and service to clients and establish an $850 million fund to compensate clients.

Under the terms of the agreement, the company neither admits nor denies the allegations in the complaint filed by the attorney general and the citation issued by the insurance superintendent.

Corporate espionage, U.S. Intelligence, High Crime, Big Money — you can't talk about any of them, without talking about them all. *"We are not talking about only governmental levels. And I keep underlining semi-legit organizations and following the money,"* says Sibel Edmonds.

And what of those "dirty doomsday dealings" on the World Trade Center hard drives? They'll get back to us, I'm sure of it, any day now....

The Sound of One Hand Slapping

June 11, 2005

Y ou probably read something yesterday about the release of the year-old, 371-page audit by the Justice Department's Inspector General Glenn Fine into pre-9/11 intelligence. What you've read likely describes it as a "sobering" and "blunt" accounting of the FBI's "serious shortcomings", and its "missteps" and "mishandling" of leads in the months before the attacks. Principally, the agency is faulted for not having aggressively pursued Nawaf al Hazmi and Khalid al Mihdhar once their presence in the U.S. was confirmed, and for not following up on reports that American flight schools were training al-Qaeda pilots. Fine concludes that "the way the FBI handled these matters was a significant failure that hindered the FBI's chances of being able to detect and prevent the Sept. 11 attacks."

Never mind that al Hazmi and al Mihdhar were met at the San Diego airport in 1999 by Omar al-Bayoumi, a Saudi known to the agency and suspected of ties to al-Qaeda; that their conversations in an al-Qaeda safe house in Yemen were monitored; that they received funds from the wife of "Bandar Bush," Princess Haifa bin Faisal, via Jonathan Bush's Riggs Bank; that they attended a "top-level al-Qaeda summit" in Kuala Lumpur, and were followed, photographed and videotaped by Malaysian secret police at the CIA's request and that their names were still not added to the "watch list"; that they moved in with Abdussattar Shaikh, a tested FBI asset. Michael Isikoff wrote that the disclosure that an FBI informant had been the roommate of two 9/11 hijackers "stunned some top counterterrorism officials." But you know what? Never mind.

And it's interesting to see the report ascribes blame to the CIA, by confirming that it intentionally blocked a memo which would have alerted the FBI to the pair's return from Malyasia's "terror summit." (The FBI can be allowed to appear incompetent; the CIA, unfathomable. It's all part of their bad cop/worse cop dance.) But never mind that, either.

What's *really* fascinating is the "sobering admission" that the FBI should have known that terrorists were training at American flight schools. But I'm not talking about the Phoenix Memo, Zacarias Moussaoui and Colleen Rowley, though that's what *they* are talking about. As much as these trails suggest intention — and let's remember, they all lead to Special Agent Dave Frasca and his Radical Fundamentalist Unit at FBI headquarters — the talking point has always been incompetence, though Frasca was the one promoted.

And here's my fascination: for an agency which, before 9/11, *appeared* clueless that members of al-Qaeda were training at flight schools, the FBI *inexplicably and immediately knew*, upon the attacks, which flight schools al-Qaeda members had attended. And this was long before suspects *should* have been identified.

Venice Florida's Huffman Aviation was the principal flight school used by Mohammed Atta and associates, though used for what is a good question, as Atta was already a pilot. (The best answer may be a familiar one to students of deep politics: trafficking narcotics.) A former Huffman manager told investigative journalist Daniel Hopsicker that a carload of FBI agents pulled up outside his house in the afternoon, on the day of the attack.

"They were outside my house four hours after the attack," he says in *Welcome to Terrorland*. Hopsicker writes that "they didn't strong-arm him to make him think harder and cough up some useful leads, but to ensure he kept his mouth shut."

The shaken source had quit Huffman because he'd found the workplace to be something other than he'd expected. Something, well, spooky: "I had to leave and get out. I wish I didn't know as much as I know. I told them they had nothing to fear from me."

What did he know?

"[T]hese guys [Atta et al] were double agents.... I gleaned early on that the operation I was working for had government protection. They were let into this country. How did the FBI get here so soon? *Ask yourself: How'd they get here so soon?*" [empahsis added]

And note: when he says "here," he doesn't mean Huffman Aviation; he means his own house. So, only four hours after the attack, the FBI didn't merely know enough to visit Atta's flight school; it knew enough to visit the home of a former employee of Atta's flight school, who had quit because he suspected Atta and his cadres were double agents. It wasn't investigating the attacks, it was intimidating witnesses.

In the August 25, 2003 edition of the *New York Observer*, author Gail Sheehy recounts an exchange following a formal meeting between senior FBI agents and the 9/11 widows, known as the "Jersey Girls." Kristen Breitweiser was having difficulty reconciling something:

"I don't understand, with all the warnings about the possibilities of al-Qaeda using planes as weapons, and the Phoenix Memo from one of your own agents warning that Osama bin Laden was sending operatives to this country for flight-school training, why didn't you check out flight schools before Sept. 11?

"Do you know how many flight schools there are in the U.S? Thousands," a senior agent protested. "We couldn't have investigated them all and found these few guys.

"Wait, you just told me there were too many flight schools and that prohibited you from investigating them before 9/11," Kristen persisted. "How is it that a few hours after the attacks, the nation is brought to its knees, and miraculously FBI agents showed up at Embry-Riddle flight school in Florida where some of the terrorists trained?"

"*We got lucky,*" was the reply.

Amazing, isn't it, how the FBI's luck changed?

Rather than drop the ball, the FBI ran with it, though some tried to call foul; for instance, those agents who contacted attorney David Schippers about imminent attacks in lower Manhattan, and even provided the proposed dates and targets, and names of suspects, after their own investigations had been squashed and their careers threatened.

How nice it must be, to be called only "incompetent," and suffer nothing more grievous than self-administered wrist slaps.

Springtime for Atta

March 31, 2006

You think they're so dumb, you think they're so funny.
Wait until they've got you running to the Night Rally.

— Elvis Costello

A recurring and seemingly fabulist theme in the literature of cult and mind-control survivors is the perseverance of a criminal Nazi underground in America, surviving on bonds of blood and symbology and enjoying the protection of high power: eight-year old Rhonda, drawing pictures of her torture depicting swastikas and ceremonial daggers; Kathleen Sullivan writing in *Unshackled* of being shuffled between porn shoots and "secret Nazi meetings" by her father and grandfather. It's all a bit too rich for most palates, even now, when the Nazi is little more than a stock villain or comic foil. It's hard to get exercised about an enemy if you believe him buried beneath 60 years of history.

We know of Paperclip and the Ghelen Org, and how Nazis came to guide U.S. government science and intelligence (and unacknowledged yet no less real, the covert trafficking of arms and drugs), finding the patronage of their stateside fellow travelers and eugenicists. Not as well known is how many others came to follow.

Between 1948 and 1952, America's Displaced Persons Commission arranged for nearly a half-million Europeans to emigrate to the United States. For two years it barred those who had been members of organizations sympathetic or collaborative to the Nazis. In 1950 that began to change, when first the "Baltic Legion" was removed from the list of "hostile" movements, though the Baltic Legion was also known as the Baltic Waffen SS.

The change of policy was strategic: the CIA was subsidizing the immigration of European Nazis and fascists, in order to build a far-right power bloc as a hedge against communism. Its primary vehicle became the Republican Party. In the year the Commission completed its work, the Republican National Committee formed an "Ethnic Division" to mobilize for elections, which in 1969 became the permanent standing body called the Republican Heritage Groups Council.

In his 1988 book *Old Nazis, the New Right, and the Republican Party*, Russ Bellant writes that "it eventually became clear that it wasn't an accident or a fluke that people with Nazi associations were in the Republican Heritage Groups Council. In some cases, more mainstream ethnic organizations were passed over in favor of smaller but more extremist groups. [And] the Republican National Committee knows with whom they are dealing." The leaders of the Republican "heritage" groups included men like Nicholas Nazarenko, who fought as an officer in an SS Cossack unit before going to work for the U.S. Army's Counter Intelligence Corp. The evening after a Reagan speech praising the heritage groups, Nazarenko insisted on opening for Bellant his huge suitcase of political materials, filled with German war memorabilia and literature on the "Jewish problem." He said he was still "in touch" with various "Nazi" organizations: "They respect me because I was a former German army officer. Sometimes when I meet these guys, they say 'Heil Hitler.'"

Bellant again: "in a sense ... the foundation of the Republican Heritage Groups Council lay in Hitler's networks into East Europe before World War II. In each of those Eastern European countries, the German SS set up or funded political action organizations that helped form SS militias during the war."

The heritage groups accounted for 86,000 volunteers in the 1988 election of George H.W. Bush, though several of their leaders were compelled to resign from campaign positions on account of collaboration. One was Romanian priest and member of the pro-Nazi Iron Guard Florian Galdau, who boasted of having files on 15,000 Romanians he helped emigrate to the U.S. with the aid of CIA-linked resettlement groups the Tolstoy Foundation and the International Rescue Committee. Candidate Bush insisted they were all honorable men and innocent of all charges.

These old ratlines are of more than historical curiosity, and not just because they suggest an embedding of Nazism in the Republican Party that goes beyond metaphor. The ratlines also appear to continue to function. Mohammed Atta participated in a German-American exchange program, jointly overseen by the State Department and the German Ministry of Economic Cooperation and Development and linked to both David Rockefeller and Henry Kissinger. (The Carl Duisberg Society, named after a senior official of IG Farben.) According to Atta's stripper girlfriend Amanda Keller, he called his German associates in Florida his "brothers." One of them, Wolfgang Bohringer, belonged to the "Flying Club of Munich," which was owned by his father. "Such clubs were popular with "postwar German neo-Nazis to circumvent that country's anti-Nazi laws."

Daniel Hopsicker further observes:

> From what has been learned so far, the backgrounds of Atta's German associates seem strikingly similar to that of another German national, Andreas Strassmeir, whose possible relationship with Oklahoma City bomber Timothy McVeigh was in the news a decade ago. Strassmeir was at one point named in a lawsuit by families of the victims as a "U.S. federal informant with material knowledge of the Oklahoma City bombing." Strassmeir's father was once a top aide to German Chancellor Helmut Kohl; Atta's German friends are all children of the German elite.

"Sometimes when I meet these guys, they say, 'Heil Hitler!'" Sixty years — what's that?

A Dot Too Far

March 7, 2007

> *Nothing was delivered*
> *And I tell this truth to you,*
> *Not out of spite or anger*
> *But simply because it's true.*
>
> — Bob Dylan

It seems appropriate enough that that old Chinese curse "May you live in interesting times," isn't Chinese at all, but American. What's more, it may have been coined by Robert Kennedy, which makes it so appropriate it hurts. And as interesting as our times are, maybe even beyond our imagining, it astonishes me how much attention is paid to the far less compelling and unconvincing distractions.

The conclusion of the Libby trial tells me I was right to have tuned it out a long time ago, expecting nothing but a Black Fitzmas. Juror Denis Collins can now say the jury wondered a "number of times: 'What are we doing with this guy here? Where's Rove... where are these other guys?'" The investigation is inactive; says U.S. Attorney Patrick J. Fitzgerald, and has been for some time, and all the liberal blogosphere has to show for its years of *better-not-pout* best behavior is the head of a failed pornographer, most of it never heard of before he became what unhappy jurors are calling the "fall guy." And a head still attached to its body at that, since Libby just jumped the queue for a presidential pardon in another year-and-a-half.

I wish conspiracy culture had some higher authority which could hold accountable the voices who said things would prove so different. I don't mean those who merely speculated incorrectly, but the ones who claimed the prerogative of inside information and "unnamed sources." Perhaps some of them did, and what they were told was simply wrong (or more likely, not so simply). But I hope the trial's end at least helps expose the disinfotainers, and separates honest truth seekers from mere consumers of conspiratainments.

Remember the 28 indictments, including Cheney and Bush? Remember, good God, the MI6 agents caught trying to blow up the Chicago subway? And I've always been curious, and increasingly suspicious, about the intentions of Fitzgerald's oft-cited and seemingly well-informed anonymous cheerleader "Citizenspook" ("Libby was just an appetizer," he wrote last month. "The plot thickens. Be patient. FITZ!"). The one time he turned away from fanning expectations for "Treasongate" was to bizarrely slag Daniel Hopsicker as a "damage control mole messiah for the government.... They are grooming him as the atom bomb to destroy the 9/11 truth movement." And why did the only 9/11 researcher left who could be called a legitimate investigator deserve such calumny? Naturally, because he doesn't believe the towers were "laced with explosives," and "How could anybody with even half a brain look at the Pentagon footage and not have serious questions about what hit [it]?" In other words, the wedge issues. And who do you think might be driving the wedge?

I'm going to try not to write any more on this subject, because after I'm done I feel like I've only helped feed the energy sink, but here I go again: I'm not on board with demolitions and Pentagon missiles, partly because I find the physical evidence unpersuasive. Though "physical" is a misnomer, since it's almost entirely based upon selective video clips and cherry-picked testimony. (For instance, that the first thoughts of a witness in a tower's sub-basement was not unreasonably of bombs somehow becomes "proof of pre-planted explosives.") But also, and more deeply, because I'm suspicious of how these narratives have acted like cancer cells to effectively ingest, mutate and bury the chance for a credible and effective 9/11 Movement. The most recent example may be the flap over BBC "foreknowledge" of building 7's collapse, which has wound up a lot of people for, I think, some pretty poor reasons.

To many, it's an unchallenged assumption that no one expected WTC 7, and so Aaron Brown's report that "we're getting information that one of the other buildings ... Building 7 ... is on fire and has either collapsed or is collapsing" is received as confirmation that someone pre-released the "script," rather than as evidence that its fall may be yet unexplained, but was not a surprise. That is why so many cameras were fixed on it to capture its fall, and yes, that is why the fire team was "pulled." The day was full of confused, false and conflicting news, and that's the nature of reporting an unprecedented catastrophic event in real time. Yet the medium is not the message here.

But you know what? I could be wrong. I just wish 9/11's demolition experts could make similar admissions.

It's the Real Thing

March 20, 2007

> *He drank Coca-Cola, he was eating Wonder Bread,*
> *Ate Burger Kings — he was well fed.*
> — Bob Dylan

I really want to leave this subject alone, and you probably wish I would, but unfortunately I have a few more things to whinge about before moving on.

You may have seen this by now: the trailer for *The Ultimate Con* ("the 9/11 Documentary you can't debunk"). It's creator is "Lucus," about whom all I know is that he says "Dave Vonkleist, Jack Blood, and Alex Jones are going to help me promote it," which almost says enough for me right there. It's ten minutes of mostly "I heard explosions" footage shot during the attacks, though to its credit there are some clips I hadn't seen before, such as real-time reports of an alleged bomb-laden van in the WTC garage and rumors of suspected "devices."

I don't mean to open up another can of thermate here, so I won't comment on the merit of the quadruple redundancy of car bombs, planted explosives in the basement, cutting charges and demolition squibs, except to say I wish some of those who defend the accuracy of eyewitness testimony with respect to the World Trade Center would apply the same standard to the Pentagon crash. (Consider, for instance, those 87 accounts of having seen a passenger jet, and not a cruise missile or a fighter aircraft, overfly DC and strike the building.)

Instead, let's do like the Jimmy Castor Bunch. What we're going to do right here is go back. Waaay back; when 9/11 Truth could look like the 2004 9/11 Citizens' Commission.

Go ahead and watch *The Ultimate Con*. But then watch anti-fascist researcher John Judge deconstruct the official Commission report, beginning with the simple question, "Who wrote it?" Authorship is unascribed, but it's written in a "lucid, almost novelistic" fashion, with a single voice. Judge mentions that the Warren Commission Report also had a single, uncredited author, brought over from the Pentagon's Army Historical Division. Having served as one of 26 official historians of Nazi Germany, Otto Winnacker's previous employer had been Adolph Hitler.

Watch Michael Springmann, former State Department diplomat, testify that the CIA was running the Jeddah consulate, instructing officials to issue visas to terrorists for reasons of "national security." Fifteen of the 9/11 hijackers received their visas through Jeddah.

Watch Indira Singh describe her discovery of Ptech's deep-black links to both U.S. security infrastructure and global narco-terror ("When I ran into the drugs I was told that if I mentioned the money to the drugs around 9/11 that would be the end of me," says Singh), the sheltering of al-Qaeda financier Yassin al-Qadi (he "talked very highly of his relationship" with Dick Cheney, claims Ptech's CEO Oussama Ziade), and the two years Ptech spent with Mitre in the "FAA's basement" prior to 9/11.

Watch Paul Thompson rattle off ignored intelligence, the Randy Glass story (which some may find of particular interest since Glass claims he was told by Pakistani intelligence prior to 9/11 that "those towers are *coming down*"), and the triangulation of the ISI, the CIA and al-Qaeda. Then there are the war games, the reconstruction of Cheney's command and control, Sibel Edmonds....

Any wagers on how often controlled demolition is mentioned?

It's a bit wistful and over the shoulder, viewing these now: this Truth Movement moment seems much longer ago than a mere three years. Is this the same 9/11 I hear about today? Because I hear none of these things anymore. Is this the same "Truth Movement"? Because today's sounds nothing like this. Is this even the same truth?

A tough question. It's like asking Coke drinkers in the mid-'80s, *What is this shit?*

Had Truth Classic's market share plateaued? Was its flavor too complex to break out of a niche market, or were there other reasons for finessing its formula? Because New Truth certainly goes down differently. "Smoother, rounder, yet bolder," in the stammering nonsense of Coca Cola CEO Roberto Goizueta. And in my experience it comes back up just the same.

Can you taste the difference, and can you tell what's missing? New Truth is now 100% Jihadist free.

Something less than 100% would be true enough, and would have served as a corrective to the official comic book which informs Americans that their enemy has dark skin and strange beliefs. But entirely erasing bin Laden and al-Qaeda from the 9/11 equation makes no more sense — not even polemical sense — than trying to talk sensibly about the JFK assassination without mention of the Mafia or the anti-Castro Cubans. And was it any less an "inside job" for their involvement, and manifold reasons for wanting him dead?

But it's impossible not to ascribe some such sentiments to racism, and sometimes something more. (For instance, neo-Nazi Curt Maynard writes, "there is considerably more tangible evidence to suggest that the United States government and Israel carried out the crime, not *19 troglodytes*, i.e. cave dwellers, from the Middle East.") And then there's the executive producer of *Loose Change* and Afghanistan war vet, Korey Rowe, who told CNN "I met my enemy and the people who supposedly pulled off this attack, and these people are not strong enough and they're not, uh, advanced enough." However, I think there is also something else happening here.

Some of the most damning evidence presented by Classic Truth is that which ties state power to supra-state terror and criminality. Peter Dale Scott's definition of Deep Politics is "the constant, everyday interaction between the constitutionally elected government and forces of violence, forces of crime, which appear to be the enemies of that government." Al-Qaeda, a creature of intelligence agencies, is one such node of contemporary deep politics. As recently as the mid-'90s its Mujahadeen were NATO's unambiguous partner in Bosnia, helping to secure, and profit by, the Balkan trade route of Afghan heroin into Europe.

The CIA were demanding visas for al-Qaeda operatives in the consulate of bin Laden's hometown, and an al-Qaeda financier was also hardwired into Washington's security apparatus. 9/11 cells were hosted by FBI informants, and their flight schools were up to their altimeters in Iran-Contra-like narco-dollars.

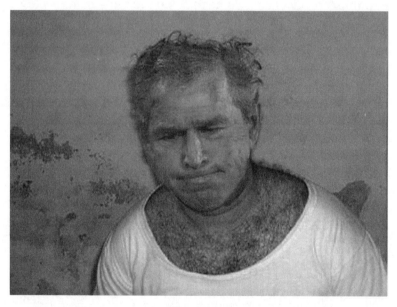

Al-Qaeda's structure was penetrated up to the senior operational level, possibly including assets of ambiguous loyalty who helped plan and fund the attacks. (For instance Fort Bragg instructor and FBI informant Ali Mohammed, who trained those involved in the 1993 WTC bombing, oversaw al-Qaeda's relocation to Afghanistan and taught hijackers how to smuggle box-cutters onto aircraft.)

New Truth hamstrings itself — and perhaps on the part of some, that's the entire point of New Truth — by clearing the table of everything pertaining to al-Qaeda and defining "inside job" as merely "inside the Beltway." Because it is by their parapolitical linkages to, and patronage of, the very forces of violence which appear to be their enemy, that governments most condemn themselves.

Doing away with all that does away with much of the High Crime, which a few might think a good thing. Watch the 2004 videos. How does the health and rigor and scope of New Truth compare? Which do you think the High Criminals prefer?

Someone told me recently that "common sense shows that CD [controlled demolition] is the 'back and to the left' of 9/11." That's the problem. It is. Look at where 40 years of "back and to the left" has got John Kennedy.

4. The Only True Anarchists

There's a black Mercedes rollin' through the combat zone

— Bob Dylan

Which World War Is It, Anyway?

August 30, 2004

Among those wise enough to know America is in one and has been for some time, there's disagreement over which World War George Bush is actually waging. Should we call it number III? Or was that the Cold War, and now we're at number IV and counting? "This is World War IV" is the favored construct of bloody-minded ideologues such as John Woolsey and Norman Podhoretz. I imagine at some point they determined that decades of association with nuclear apocalypse had voided the potential positive spin for "World War III."

So which World War is it? It's neither the Third nor the Fourth; it's *still* the Second. Even though the apologists of the Pirate Class in their red, white and blue shirts will never own the name "fascist." As Orwell wrote in "Politics and the English Language," "the word fascism has now no meaning except in so far as it signifies 'something not desirable.'" But that's no reason for us to shy from using it. Just because goose-stepping has gone out of style doesn't mean they've kicked off their jackboots.

When we talk about Nazis in America, we're talking about more than the passing resemblance to the Bush Cartel. That Prescott's family business profited handsomely by the Nazis is well known, at least by those who think it important to note such things. But the story is larger and uglier than more dirty dealings by a Bonesman.

It also goes deeper than the Republican Party's active recruitment of fascists and racists since the mid-'50s through the aegis of its Heritage Groups Council, but since that's seldom recalled, let's pause for a moment to recollect.

When a number of senior members of George H.W. Bush's 1988 campaign team were revealed to be old school Nazi sympathizers it generated something of a media flap — Pete Hamill titled a *New York Post* column "George Bush and his fascist fan club" — but the scandal is little remembered today.

Some of Bush's team:

Radi Slavoff, GOP Heritage Council's executive director, and head of "Bulgarians for Bush." Slavoff was a member of a Bulgarian fascist group, and he put together an event in Washington honoring Holocaust denier, Austin App.

Florian Galdau, director of GOP outreach efforts among Romanians, and head of "Romanians for Bush." Galdau was once an Iron Guard recruiter, and he defended convicted Nazi war criminal Valerian Trifa.

Nicholas Nazarenko, leader of a Cossack GOP ethnic unit. Nazarenko was an ex-Waffen SS officer.

Method Balco, Slovakian GOP activist. Balco organized yearly memorials for a Nazi puppet regime.

Walter Melianovich, head of the GOP's Byelorussian unit. Melianovich worked closely with many Nazi groups.

Bohdan Fedorak, leader of "Ukrainians for Bush." Fedorak headed a Nazi group involved in anti-Jewish wartime pogroms.

Nazis staffing the VP's campaign? *We'd better background checks, a'yup.*

The Nazi infection goes back much further. All the way back to the 1930s, when industrialists with fascist sympathies and names like DuPont and Morgan sponsored an attempted coup against Roosevelt to dismantle the New Deal. And then the '40s, when men with names like Bush, Dulles, Favish and Rockefeller traded strategic goods with the enemy, prolonging the war and costing Allied lives.

Worst of all, Project Paperclip saw Nazis virtually co-found the "National Security State," bringing their advanced technology and criminal medical research to America. And something else as well, as Nick Cook is told by the pseudonymous "Dr. Dan Markus" in *The Hunt for Zero Point*:

> When the Americans tripped over this mutant strain of nonlinear physics and took it back home with them, they were astute enough to realize that their home-grown scientific talent couldn't handle it. That it was beyond their cultural term of reference. That's why they recruited so many Germans. The Nazis developed a unique approach to science and engineering quite separate from the rest of the world, because their ideology, unrestrained as it was, supported a wholly different way of

doing things. Von Braun's V-2s are a case in point, but so was their understanding of physics. The trouble was, when the Americans took it all home with them they found out, too late, that it came infected with a virus. You take the science on, you take on aspects of the ideology, as well.

The Nazi virus entered America's system long ago. It's been Americanized. But what else would one expect, given that the CIA was essentially a co-creation of Nazis, like General Reinhard Gehlen and his Abwehr anti-Soviet intelligence apparatus, and Nazi money launderers, like Allen Dulles and the corporatist/ intelligence old boy network of Sullivan and Cromwell. No. Such men got exactly what they expected.

"Once the neo-fascists became bold enough to slay the President on the street, they showed their hand," Mort Sahl said early in 1968. So early, Dr. King and Robert Kennedy were yet to join the body count. "They showed how arrogant they had become. Now it's a question of symptom. That crime was a national symptom. If we can turn our back on that, we will pay a terrible price. That will be the end of this democracy."

They showed their hand, and they've had forty years of getting away with it. And not for lack of evidence. Anyone who thinks otherwise hasn't read Gaeton Fonzi's *The Last Investigation*, Dick Russell's *The Man Who Knew Too Much* or John Newman's *Oswald and the CIA*, to cite just three works. Rather, they got away with it because the truth is too terrible, and many who did not conspire in the killing conspired in the cover-up, because they were led to believe that a finding of official complicity in Kennedy's death would shatter the system, when in fact it might have killed the virus.

And undoubtedly the same justification has been used over and over again, to shield Americans from the awful truth of state-sanctioned assassinations, the October Surprise, medical experiments worthy of Mengele, the introduction of crack to the LA underclass, BCCI, 9/11 and on and on. High treason, many times over. But so what? You know what they say about none daring to call it such should it prosper. And brother, has it prospered.

Here's the thing: we're not talking about discrete, singular, *sui generis* conspiracies here. Indeed, these are not even conspiracies, in the sense of representing aberrant breaks with the system. These are, rather, examples that *the system works*. It's just not the system Americans were taught in civics class. The examples: evidence the criminalization of the state by the deep political nexus of underworld, intelligence, industrial and military interests. "America," to these players, serves as the legit front for their lawless enterprise. The Nazi virus has consumed the host. If it were eradicated and the host miraculously recovered, the poor thing would swear up and down it was still late autumn in 1963.

Repealing
Godwin's Law

January 31, 2005

I t's been several days now, but I still can't get past the peculiar disgrace of Dick Cheney at Auschwitz. The green parka with white fur, and the brown, lace-up hiking boots were inappropriate enough for a solemn ceremony at the world's most notorious symbol of runaway eugenics. But the toque, with the words "Staff 2001" — that's almost too much, even for a conspiracy theorist. Cheney might as well have been cradling Flight 11's "unrecovered" flight recorders in his lap, and sneering into the camera, "What you gonna do about it?"

It's easy to ask, "What was he thinking?" Harder even is to answer, "Was he thinking that?" Because without knowing his mind, we can assert with some confidence that Cheney's choices were deliberate. Unlike a thoughtless tourist, the Homeland's acting President would have been conscious of the impression he was making. And if, somehow, he wasn't, he had the failsafe of a staff well versed in protocol to set him right. (In other words, no need to call Putin the night before and say, "So, what are you wearing to Auschwitz?")

But I'm going to cut myself some slack on this singular morbidity. As I said, it's been just a few days, and after 60 years, we still can't get past the Nazis. Especially the CIA.

From Saturday's *New York Times*:

CIA Said to Rebuff Congress on Nazi Files

The Central Intelligence Agency is refusing to provide hundreds of thousands of pages of documents sought by a government working group under a 1998 law that requires full disclosure of classified records related to Nazi war criminals, say Congressional officials from both parties.

Under the law, the C.I.A. has already provided more than 1.2 million pages of documents, the vast majority of them from the archives of its World War II predecessor, the Office of Strategic Services. Many documents have been declassified, and some made public last year showed a closer relationship between the United States government and Nazi war criminals than had previously been understood, including the CIA's recruitment of war criminal suspects or Nazi collaborators.

For nearly three years, the CIA has interpreted the 1998 law narrowly and rebuffed requests for additional records, say Congressional officials and some members of the working group, who also contend that that stance seems to violate the law.

These officials say the agency has sometimes agreed to provide information about former Nazis, but not about the extent of the agency's dealings with them after World War II. In other cases, it has refused to provide information about individuals and their conduct during the war unless the working group can first provide evidence that they were complicit in war crimes.

Former Congresswoman and member of the working group Elizabeth Holtzman contends that "the CIA has defied the law, and in so doing has also trivialized the Holocaust, thumbed its nose at the survivors of the Holocaust and also at Americans who gave their lives in the effort to defeat the Nazis in World War II." Looking at Cheney, maybe there's a pattern emerging.

If the Nazis are truly in the dustbin of history, what are we to make of the fact that, 60 years on, the Agency is *still* keeping secrets about their post-war recruitment, even violating the law to do so? (And these are just the secrets that we *know* they're keeping. I would expect that the most privileged secrets have left no paper trail. As, I believe, Richard Helms advised.)

But when we talk about the relationship between the Nazis and American institutions, we must talk about more than Project Paperclip. Because there's more going on here than the virtual co-founding of America's National Security State by thousands of Nazi scientists. Before the CIA existed, before the WWII, even before Hitler's rise to power, Anglo-American eugenics was informing and inspiring apt pupils in Germany, including the future architects of genocide.

The Carnegie Institute, the Rockefeller Foundation, JP Morgan and Averell Harriman can be counted among the head cheerleaders and principal financiers of the American eugenics movement, which found keen partners in great academies like Harvard and Yale and in numerous state and federal departments. Edwin Black writes in *War Against the Weak* that "they were all bent on breed-ing a eugenically superior race, just as agronomists would breed better strains of corn. The plan was to wipe away the reproductive capability of the weak and inferior." Sixty thousand Americans were sterilized in the process, many without their knowledge. Black adds:

> American eugenic crusades proliferated into a worldwide campaign, and in the 1920s came to the attention of Adolf Hitler. Under the Nazis, American eugenic principles were applied without restraint, careening out of control into the Reich's infamous genocide. During the pre-War years, American eugenicists openly supported Germany's program. The Rockefeller Foundation financed the Kaiser Wilhelm Institute and the work of its central racial scientists. Once WWII began, Nazi eugenics turned from mass sterilization and euthanasia to genocidal murder. One of the Kaiser Wilhelm Institute doctors in the program financed by the Rockefeller Foundation was Josef Mengele who continued his research in Auschwitz, making daily eugenic reports on twins. After the world recoiled from Nazi atrocities, the American eugenics movement — its institutions and leading scientists — renamed and regrouped under the banner of an enlightened science called human genetics.

Investigative journalist Jon Rappaport makes a similar point regarding MK-ULTRA and related programs, and draws an even more distressing conclusion, in his 1997 lecture "The CIA, Mind Control and Children":

> I would say this is a Nazi project, but a lot of the Nazis are Amer-ican-born. It shouldn't be excused or explained away on that basis because as we know, if we look at Nazi psychiatry for example, they learned a lot from the Americans, especially about eugenics. This is not something where we should say, " ... well, the Nazis took over ..." This is home-grown stuff. This is Americana at its worst, at its lowest form. This is also the sub-sub-basement that you walk into when you are a materialist, when that is your philosophy. And I don't mean you are a materialist in the sense that you want money, possessions ... I mean, philosophically. The materialist position is that we are meat, and tis-sue, and cells, and electrical impulses, and that's it. When that system collapses, we are gone, never to return. My own feeling is that when you espouse and embrace that philosophy, the ultimate, ultimate sub-basement that you end up in is that sub-basement ... that's where you end up. Finally, that's where it all comes out.

Formally stated, Godwin's Law, or the Rule of Nazi Analogies, posits that, "as an online discussion grows longer, the probability of a comparison involving Nazis or Hitler approaches one." The law was articulated about ten years ago by Mike Godwin, then-legal counsel for the Electronic Frontier Foundation, to counter a proliferation of Nazi analogies online which he regarded as illogical and offensive rhetorical overreach. As popularly understood, the law implies that the first person to invoke the Nazis in a debate loses the argument.

Godwin can be forgiven for believing, in the mid-'90s, that Nazi comparisons were overwrought. To think the same now must require a massive infusion of Kool Aid from Sidney Gottlieb's punchbowl. But as suggested, much of what we're seeing in America today has antecedents which pre-date Nazi Germany, with a significant *homegrown* component, that give the appearance of German Nazism but which actually served in part as its inspiration.

It is a project which Franklin Roosevelt frustrated, and now the heirs of the project mean to see it through to a conclusion. We can see it show its public face in such things as the recent *New York Times* article "Can Anyone Unseat FDR?" ("Social Security is the soft underbelly of the welfare state," says Stephen Moore, who wants to "jab a spear through it"), and Bush's only seemingly empty jargon of an "ownership society." If the project succeeds, Nazi Germany, rather than a grotesque aberration of modern history, will be regarded as merely "ahead of its time."

As we trundle on towards this century's astonishing convergence of crises, we should remember there are many powerful people with familiar names who believe the problem is not that there are too few resources; the problem is there are too many people. And what are we going to do about *them*?

"Enter into evil"

December 11, 2004

> *In order to achieve the most noble accomplishments, the leader may have to "enter into evil." This is the chilling insight that has made Machiavelli so feared, admired, and challenging. It is why we are drawn to him still....*
> — Michael Ledeen, Machiavelli on Modern Leadership

It must be a hard cross to bear for the Straussian neocons, to hear themselves called "inept" or even "crazy" by their occasional critics in mainstream America, who still refuse to see the method to their madness. It has to be a bitter pill, to be unable to say *"You fools! Can't you see? This is some of our best work!"*

Certainly 9/11 fits the bill. What a great stroke of bad luck that turned out to be. Iraq, too. It looks like the occupation is going to hell, and surely it is. But some people aren't all that broken up about it. The division of the country into three vassal states is the objective of the neoconservatives and the Likudniks. Iraq cannot be conquered, but it can be divided, which would ensure that it would never again be an economic or military threat to either U.S. or Israeli interests. But how to justify ethnically Balkanizing the nation into toothless Bantustans, except by encouraging civil war and fostering chaos?

But we'd be wrong to lay everything at the feet of the neocons. They are merely the loudest and most radical exponents of the bipartisan consensus of the National Security State. The consensus can be said to encompass even the sainted Jimmy Carter. It was Carter's National Security Advisor, Zbigniew Brzezinski, who, as he says, "fired up" the Muslims against the socialist government of Afghanistan and precipitated the Soviet incursion. (All part of the plan: "entering into evil" with the Mujahideen for the "greater good" of bleeding the Red Army white.) The lasting legacy of his administration is not conservation, but the Carter Doctrine, a Monroe Doctrine for the oil fields of the Gulf states.

And it's not the leaders alone who entered into evil. There was always a transparency about the shifting case for war that led the U.S. into Iraq, so that many of those who "bought the lies" clearly knew full well what they were buying. The Bush administration was not lying to the base (in Arabic, "al Qaeda") of Republican power; it was *winking* at it. The leaders and the led contracted together to enter into evil for the "greater good" of *kicking Saddam's ass.*

Author Linda McQuaig told a comically sad story at the candlelight vigil outside the U.S. consulate in Toronto protesting Bush's visit to Canada. She said she'd been called by a television producer and asked to appear the next day to discuss Canada-U.S. relations. She said sure. Then the producer asked McQuaig about her thoughts on the Iraq war. She said it isn't about WMD or "liberation": it's about oil. (I guess the producer wasn't familiar with McQuaig's most recent book, *It's the Crude, Dude.*) The producer then said, "Okay, but are you for it, or against it?"

Eh? What a disturbing question to follow upon McQuaig's having underscored that she thought the expressed rationale for war was bogus. (And oh, the producer called back and said Mc-Quaig wasn't needed after all; they were going with the *Globe and Mail*'s apologist for empire, Margaret Wente.)

But should it surprise us that even television producers can enter into evil? From an interesting Knight Ridder story of a few weeks ago, titled "Dangerous testing went beyond vets to orphans, prisoners":

> In April 1953, the military helped the CIA launch a Cold War program known as MK-ULTRA, in which unsuspecting servicemen and civilians were given LSD and other psychedelic drugs to study their use as truth serums.
>
> This cycle of government deception continued well into the 1970s, with thousands of Americans exposed to nuclear radiation, plutonium injections, chemical sprays from airplanes, open-air nerve agents and mescaline in secret tests.
>
> The tests flouted the principle of informed consent in the Nuremberg Code, drafted after the Nazi war-crimes trials in 1947 as an ethical standard for human experimentation.
>
> Sometimes the victims were military personnel. Often they were from society's most vulnerable populations: mentally ill people, prison inmates, poor or illiterate people, pregnant women, children who were retarded or orphaned, drug addicts or prostitutes.

"You've got to ask yourself, how did these scientists sleep at night?" said David Rothman, director of the Center for the Study of Society and Medicine at Columbia University and an expert on the history of human research.

The scientists slept, said expert Jonathan Moreno, by convincing themselves that their tests ultimately would save lives.

"They came to view their work as a patriotic thing to do," said Moreno, director of the Center for Biomedical Ethics at the University of Virginia and author of *Undue Risk: Secret State Experiments on Humans*. "And they came to think that the volunteers knew what was going on, even if they didn't know all the details."

"How do they sleep at night?" people always cry, as they should. But the answers usually disappoint. And George Bush, the best-rested president in modern history, likes to be in bed by 10 p.m. In as much as he's aware of his government's actions, let alone their consequences, he sees the evil and calls it good.

Kathleen Sullivan is a survivor of CIA trauma-induced mind-control programming, and so has more insight than most Americans regarding the well-intended evil of their government. She has a valuable perspective on the revelations of torture at Abu Ghraib:

Despite the news from Iraq, many people with whom I share my history still have a knee-jerk emotional reaction: "You must be making it up. I can't believe that this has been done by our own government to U.S. citizens — especially to children — right here in the U.S. I'm sorry — I am not willing to accept what you're saying." In spite of all that they are learning about the atrocities that intelligence spooks and interrogators and military personnel are capable of committing against fellow humans overseas, they aren't yet willing to face that such abuse is a historical emanation from the dark side of humanity.

...

Our stories are no less real than those of the Iraqi prisoners. Unfortunately, we are less likely to be believed by fellow citizens because our abuse was perpetrated — most often — by government employees within the borders of our countries. We were innocent civilians, not war prisoners. And what was done to most of us was much worse than what most of the Iraqi prisoners have unfortunately endured. (This is like comparing apples and oranges; both experiences are solid and real and directly related. Therefore, such a comparison is really a matter of the degree of trauma and torture and sexual degradation experienced by each survivor. Regardless of the degree, however, trauma is trauma. Every trauma is horrible, whether it lasts a day or a year or for decades.) The psychological scars and other results of the traumas we've endured are just as legitimate and consistent as the visible and invisible scars of the Iraqi prisoners, who will carry them in their minds and bodies – some, for the remainder of their lives. Deep humiliation and terror and rage cannot be conveniently erased when one is freed by ones tormentors.

As you read North American survivors' reports, I challenge you to compare them with the reports of prisoner abuse and murder that are coming out of Iraq and Afghanistan. Remember, we made our stories public long before these revelations began emerging from Iraq. As you compare the reports, you may be horrified to discover that this kind of sadistic abuse is not an aberration. It is, in fact, historical and ongoing....

...

Some survivors have reported that these reports and photos triggered strong flashbacks and powerful emotions that temporarily disabled them, leaving them unable to socialize and perform life duties as well as they normally might.

My own reactions were equally powerful. I cried more during this past two months, than I have in years. I experienced strong bouts of depression and alternating periods of great manic energy. Both seemed to be generated by my strong feelings of outrage: our government is still hurting others in some of the same ways that we North American mind-control survivors have been hurt!

Turning back to Ledeen:

Machiavelli is commonly taken to be saying that the ends always justify the means, but he does not believe that. Quite the contrary. He simply recognizes the reality that there are times when a leader must accept dreadful responsibility in serving the common good.

Ledeen speaks only a half-truth here. Which, we must concede, isn't bad for him. But the "good" for which leaders will shoulder dreadful responsibility is rarely the common good. And also, even more rarely, will leaders be held responsible. Even to their conscience.

Kathleen Sullivan, as a victim can, speaks the other half:

The Only True Anarchists

I had a dream.
In my dream the U.S. was a safer place for others
than it had been for me in the past.
My dream country was a genuine democracy.
In it, torture, sexual assault, and murder
would never be committed or condoned by our government.
In it, our leaders were genuine, decent,
caring men and women.
They would never allow — or order —
government employees and private contractors to
wantonly torture, sexually violate, and murder defenseless humans.
I had a dream
but now the dream is dead
and I am crying.

America's Condition Greene

February 19, 2005

Newt: My mommy always said there were no monsters — no real ones —
but there are.
Ripley: Yes there are, aren't there?
Newt: Why do they tell little kids that?
Ripley: Most of the time it's true....

Paging Dr. Greene

Last week an Oregon psychiatrist, Dr. George F. Wittkopp, was forced out of his practice because, to help some patients, he had given them "information on the 'New World Order,' an international conspiracy 'to establish world government and a world economic system and a world religion.'" That's all I know, so I can't defend or condemn Dr. Wittkopp's methods, or teaching tools. (And as researcher John Judge has said, not all conspiracies are created equal. Sometimes, even often, they're simply wrong.) Still, I can see the hypothetical case for a doctor to tell certain patients something like, "You know what? It's not all in your head. They're really after you."

Here, regrettably, is more than a hypothetical. In an earlier post I quoted testimony from mind-control survivor Claudia Mullen before the 1995 Presidential Commission on Radiation Experiments. Ms Mullen's therapist, Dr. Valerie Wolf, also testified:

> In preparation for my testimony at these hearings, I called nearly 40 therapists across the country to find out what they knew about the link between radiation and mind control and to get what other therapists were seeing in clients who had been used in mind-control experiments.

> ...

> *Generally, it appears that therapists across the country are finding clients who have been subjected to mind-control techniques. The*

consistency of their stories about the purpose of the mind control and torture techniques such as electric shock, use of hallucinogens, sensory deprivation, spinning, hypnosis, dislocation of limbs and sexual abuse is remarkable. There is almost nothing published on this aspect of mind control used with children and these clients come from all over the country, having had no contact with each other.

...

These clients have named the same people, particularly a Dr. Greene. I had heard Dr. Greene's name for several years associated with clients' reports of childhood torture, mind-control techniques and childhood sexual abuse. One of my clients, who had seen him with a nametag, identified him as Dr. L. Wilson Greene. I made inquiries and to my surprise found out that a person with this same name was the Scientific Director of the Chemical and Radiological Laboratories at the Army Chemical Center and that he was engaged in doing research for the Army and the CIA.

It needs to be made clear that these clients have remembered these names and events spontaneously with free recall and without the use of any memory retrieval techniques such as hypnosis. As much as possible, we have tried to verify the memories. I have sent information from one of my clients to Alan Schefflin, Professor of Law at Santa Clara University Law School. He has been able to confirm that the information that she has supplied is absolutely true and that her memories could not have been derived from any published source. This client simply came into my office one day with MKULTRA written on a piece of paper after about 9 months of therapy. Another client's memories about the CIA connection to Dr. Greene appeared spontaneously several months ago. She has memories of being exposed to radiation. I had never mentioned anything about government research or the CIA to either of them prior to the time that their memories emerged spontaneously. [emphases added]

A little more on "Dr. Greene" from Will Snodgrass's interview of Wolf, Mullen, and another trauma survivor in Wolf's care, Chris DeNicola Ebner:

Will Snodgrass: Claudia, do you remember Dr. Greene?

Claudia Mullen: Very well. The first time I met him was, from my understanding now, most of the time he kept himself disguised and used different names depending on what part of the country he was in. At Tulane, he saw no reason to do that I guess, and he would wear a white coat just like any other doctor, and he would wear a name tag, *Dr. L. Wilson Greene.* But he didn't like anyone calling him anything but "Doctor." He didn't even like being called Dr. Greene. I knew him from the years 1957 until about five years before he died in 1988.

Will Snodgrass: So Dr. Greene was operating at Tulane University and also at Kansas?

Valerie Wolf: And at Tucson. Dr. Greene has been reported — he is probably the most consistent figure or doctor that's been reported by almost everybody. *He went under the names of Dr. Green, Dr. Greenbaum, Greentree, Greenberg.* But always with the Green in his name. He traveled throughout the country, training people, doing consultation and also doing stuff on his own, I think, as Chris experienced.

Chris DeNicola Ebner: He used disguise with me as well. I never saw him without a surgical mask, usually something on his head, and all I ever saw was a little bit of the black-rimmed glasses and whatever. He was just a sadistic, evil man, and he hated me because I would not comply with what he wanted me to do. [emphases added]

And we can follow Dr. Greene right down the rabbit hole with the lecture "Hypnosis in Multiple Personality Disorder: Ritual Abuse" by Dr. D. Corydon Hammond, President of the American Society of Clinical Hypnosis, delivered at the Fourth Annual Eastern Regional Conference on Abuse and Multiple Personality in 1992. It's come to be known as the "Greenbaum Speech." The Psychiatric Institute of Washington, sponsor of the event, still makes available tapes and transcripts of the other sessions. Not of this one:

When you start to find the same highly esoteric information in different states and different countries, from Florida to California, you start to get an idea that there's something going on that is very large, very well coordinated, with a great deal of communication and systematicness to what's happening. So I have gone from someone kind of neutral and not knowing what to think about it all to someone who clearly believes ritual abuse is real and that the people who say it isn't are either naive like people who didn't want to believe the Holocaust or — they're dirty.

···

Let's suppose that this whole front row here are multiples and that she has an alter named Helen and she has one named Mary, she has one named Gertrude, she has one named Elizabeth, and she has one named Monica. Every one of those alters may have put on it a program, perhaps designated alpha-zero-zero-nine a Cult person could say, "Alpha-zero-zero-nine" or make some kind of hand gesture to indicate this and get the same part out in any one of them even though they had different names that they may be known by to you. Alphas appear to represent general programming, the first kind of things put in. Betas appear to be sexual programs. For example, how to perform oral sex in a certain way, how to perform sex in rituals, having to do with producing child pornography, directing child pornography, prostitution. Deltas are killers trained in how to kill in ceremonies. There'll also be some self-harm stuff mixed in with that, assassination and killing. Thetas are called psychic killers.

You know, I had never in my life heard those two terms paired together. I'd never heard the words "psychic killers" put together, but *when you have people in different states, including therapists inquiring and asking, "What is Theta," and patients say to them, "Psychic killers," it tends to make one a believer that certain things are very systematic and very widespread.* [emphasis added]

...

I remember one therapist who'd been with me in several hypnosis workshops and consulted with me about a crisis MPD situation. I told her to inquire about Alpha, Beta, Delta, Theta. She did. She got back to me saying, "Yeah, I got an indication it's there. What is it?" I said, "I'm not going to tell you. Go back and inquire about some of this." We set an appointment for a week or so hence. She got back with me and said, "I asked what Theta was and she said, 'psychic killers.' I asked her what Delta was and she said 'killers.'" Okay. So I told her about some of this stuff for a two-hour consult. She called back and she said, "This seemed too fantastic. I heard this and I thought, 'Has Cory been working too hard?'" she said, I'm embarrassed to admit it, but she said, "I held you in high professional regard, but this just sounded so off in the twilight zone that I really thought, 'Is he having a nervous breakdown or something?'" She said, "But I respected you enough to ask about this."

...

It appears that below this we've got some other layers. One is called *"Green Programming"* it appears. Isn't it interesting that the doctor's name is Dr. Green? One of the questions in a way that does not contaminate is after I've identified some of this stuff is there and they've given me a few right answers about what some of it is, "If there were a doctor associated with this programming and his name were a color, you know, like Dr. Chartreuse or something, if his name were a color, what color would the color be?" Now once in a while I've had some other colors mentioned in about three or four patients that I felt were trying to dissimulate in some way and I don't really believe had this. In one case I got another color and I found out later it was a doctor whose name was a color who was being trained by Dr. Green almost thirty years ago and he supervised part of the programming of this woman under this doctor. [emphasis added]

...

[Self-destruct] Omega alters use the metaphor — and it is their metaphor — of robots. and it is like a robot shell comes down over the child alter to make them act in robotic fashion. Once in a while internally you'll confront robots.

...

A while back I was talking to a small group of therapists somewhere. I told them about some of this. In the middle of talking about some of this all the color drained out of one social worker's face and she obviously had a reaction and I asked her about and she said, *"I'm working with a five-year-old boy,"* and she said, *"Just in the last few weeks he was saying something about a Dr. Green."* I went on a little further and I mentioned some of these things and she just shook her head again. I said, "What's going on?" She said, "He's been spontaneously telling me about robots and about Omega." I think you will find variations of this and that they've changed it, probably every few years and maybe somewhat regionally to throw us off in various ways but that certain basics and fundamentals will probably be there. *I have seen this in people up into their forties including people whose parents were very, very high in the CIA.* [emphases added]

Apart from the testimony of survivors and their psychologists, there's not much to be found on "Dr. Green," "Dr. Greenbaum" or even "Dr. L. Wilson Greene." Except that what does exist suggests someone essential to the germination of CIA mind-control research. Linda Hunt, in her *Secret Agenda: The United States Government, Nazi Scientists and Project Paperclip, 1945 to 1990*, names "Edgewood's L. Wilson Greene" as the foremost proponent of psychochemical warfare in the late '40s, saying he had suggested setting aside $50,000 in the 1950 budget to study the effects of "61 compounds ranging from alcohol to mescaline," that could induce "hysteria, panic, seizures, and hallucinations" in enemy forces. This study appears to have triggered Greene's interest in mind control. Tad Szulc, in "The CIA's Electric Kool-Aid Acid Test" (*Psychology Today*, November 1977), writes that the "man whom the CIA documents credit with inspiring the program is Dr. L. Wilson Greene of the Army Chemical Corps, who had long urged the United States to embark upon psychochemical warfare."

The program was BLUEBIRD, the deliberate creation of multiple personalities. BLUEBIRD was soon renamed ARTICHOKE, after a favorite vegetable of CIA Director Allen Dulles. ARTICHOKE in turn gave way to MK-ULTRA and MK-SEARCH.

Dr. Orne to the rescue

Naturally, the official record remains sketchy, accidental and heavily redacted, as Richard Helms ordered all files on mind control destroyed before he left the directorate. Officially, the programs registered nothing but failures. "We are sufficiently ineffective so that our findings can be published," says Dr. Martin Orne, a longtime covert CIA consultant, in John Marks' *The Search for The "Manchurian Candidate."* Though ex-CIA officer Miles Copeland also told Marks that "the congressional subcommittee which [studied mind control] got only the barest glimpse." The CIA experimented with a number of mind-control techniques, and research was heavily compartmentalized.

Orne's remarks suggest that had the Agency hit upon an effective technique, it would surely remain unpublished, highly classified and scrubbed from the records, such as they exist. So perhaps we shouldn't hold our breath awaiting official confirmation of success, particularly if it involved the deliberate fragmentation of the minds of children to create programmable "alters."

And let's talk about Orne for a moment. He was a frequent recipient of grants from the Human Ecology Society, which

Marks calls a "CIA-controlled funding mechanism for studies and experiments in the behavioral sciences." An MK-ULTRA official told Marks, *"We could go to Orne* anytime and say, 'Okay, here is a situation and here is a kind of guy. What would you expect we might be able to achieve if we could hypnotize him?' Through his massive knowledge, he could speculate and advise."

In *Psychic Dictatorship in the USA*, Alex Constantine writes:

> The voluminous files of John Marks in Washington, D.C. (139 boxes obtained under FOIA, to be exact, two-fifths of which document CIA interest in the occult) include an Agency report itemizing a $30,000 grant to Orne from Human Ecology, and another $30,000 from Boston's Scientific Engineering Institute (SEI) — another CIA funding cover, founded by Edwin Land of the Polaroid Corporation (and supervision of the U-2 spy plane escapades). *This was the year that the CIA's Office of Research and Development (ORD) geared up a study of parapsychology and the occult.* The investigation, dubbed Project OFTEN-CHICKWIT, gave rise to the establishment of a social "laboratory" by SEI scientists at the University of South Carolina — a college class in *black witchcraft, demonology and voodoo.* [emphases added]

So what should we make of the fact that Dr. Martin Orne, the CIA's "go to" guy on mind control, went on to become a founding member of the False Memory Syndrome Foundation? The primary purpose of which, writes Constantine, "is the castigation of survivors and therapists for fabricating accusations of ritual abuse"?

Okay — So what?

Why dig into this now, when America seems to be presenting more pressing horrors demanding our revulsion? Because this is unfinished business. Because as long as the abuse remains unexposed, we should presume it is ongoing.

And because overshadowing barely whispered scandals such as the Franklin Credit Union, the Bush White House call boys, the perverse abuse of prisoners at Abu Ghraib and Guantanamo Bay, and perhaps now even the "Jeff Gannon" story, there is the suggestion of a sheltered sex and death cult, which may be the true religion of the National Security State.

Studying this material, and most importantly, honoring the victims with unprejudiced hearing, may tell us not only where America went wrong, but how far wrong it's yet to go.

A hint, perhaps, from investigative journalist Jon Rappoport, in 1995:

> About three weeks ago I met a woman who is a therapist. She works north of Los Angeles. If you met this woman and talked to her, you would say 'she's very on top of things, she is very smart, she seems like a real human being.' So she looks at me and she says, *"I was part of this when I was a kid, as a child."* She doesn't want to talk about it yet, but she said, *"this business about creating perfect spies, I don't think that's it. I don't think that's why they were really doing it.... I think there is something beyond this. It is somewhere in the back of my mind, but I can't get to it."* I didn't question her about how she knows this, but she said "First of all this was a very wide-ranging project ... there were echelons of the project, not just simply one level. There were children brought up from South America and Mexico. They were considered expendable. They were used with the crudest techniques of brainwashing and so forth. *The idea was to learn from these techniques in a more refined way techniques that would be used on another echelon of children. The best and brightest in America."* I said, "Do you mean children from well-to-do families?" She said, "Not necessarily. The smartest."
>
> They could be thinking that *what they want to do is program these kids who would later, supposedly, emerge in prominent positions in society, so that they would then have long term control of society by controlling people in power positions.* She said (she didn't say "yes") but she said, "Well, yeah, that makes sense.... They brought a lot of doctors over here after the War and not just the rocket scientists ... they brought a lot of doctors over here." And all throughout this testimony you will read, sprinkled here, "a doctor with a German accent.... was it Green? ... he had blonde hair...." [emphases added]

From MindWar to FoxNews

December 8, 2004

FoxNews hasn't landed in Canada just yet — the CRTC only recently approved adding its channel to digital cable — so I was spared being scared recently by Fox military analyst, Retired General Paul Vallely. He told Fox house "liberal" Alan Colmes that "we are not going to permit" a Shia majority victory in the forthcoming theatre of a "free" election in Iraq. Worse, he said, "Iran and Syria are next. It's easy to do.... Israel is (already) prepared to take Iran down."

Colmes, according to Newshounds, followed up by asking whether he thought a Judeo/Christian holy war against Muslims was such a great idea. Vallely replied "That's what's going on. If you don't understand that, then you don't get it."

Who is Paul Vallely, and why is he saying these things? Vallely is the senior military analyst for FOX News, having retired in 1991 from the U.S. Army as Deputy Commanding General, U.S. Army, Pacific. He served 32 years, more than 15 of them in Special Operations, Psychological and Civil-Military Operations. He's co-author of *Endgame — Blueprint for Victory for Winning the War on Terror.*

Vallely is co-author of another work that deserves mention. *From PSYOP to Mindwar: The Psychology of Victory* is a military paper on psychological warfare, written by Col. Paul Vallely and Lt. Col. Michael Aquino in 1980. It was sent, writes Aquino, "to various governmental offices, agencies, commands and publications involved or interested in PSYOP." I think it deserves a closer read now, because it describes a psychological conditioning Americans may find familiar. And the fact that one of the authors is the senior military analyst for FOXNews may not be an insignificant trifle.

And who is Aquino? A since-retired Lieutenant Colonel, Military Intelligence, and Special Forces officer. Also, for many years, an avowed Satanist, Nazi occultist (he conducted a black magic ceremony at Himmler's Wewelsburg Castle), and founder of the "Temple of Set." Aquino's name crops up in ritual child abuse cases which appear to have military-intelligence sanction for the purpose of trauma-induced mind control, notably the Franklin Credit Union and the Presidio scandals.

Aquino has said that "assorted cranks tried to make a public issue out of this paper just because of its catchy title.... That paper had no connection to MK-ULTRA, nor Paperclip, nor any crazy Nazi experiments."

Even if one believes Aquino, and dismisses suggestions that he played a covert role in military mind-control research (one of those "crazy Nazi experiments" carried to the United States courtesy Project Paperclip), the implications of "Mindwar" are chilling. And, I should think, rather familiar to anyone wide-awake in the Bush years.

A pdf of *From PSYOP to Mindwar*, with a new introduction, can be found on Aquino's "Temple of Set" Web site.

Some excerpts:

In its strategic context, *MindWar must reach out to friends, enemies, and neutrals alike across the globe* — neither through primitive "battlefield" leaflets and loudspeakers of PSYOP nor through the weak, imprecise, and narrow effort of psychotronics — *but through the media possessed by the United States* which have the capabilities to reach virtually all people on the face of the Earth. These media are, of course, the electronic media — *television and radio*. State of the art developments in satellite communication, video recording techniques, and laser and optical transmission of broadcasts made possible a penetration of the minds of the world such as would have been inconceivable just a few years ago. Like the sword Excalibur, we have but to reach out and seize this tool; and it can transform the world for us if we have the courage and the integrity to civilization with it. *If we do not accept Excalibur, then we relinquish our ability to inspire foreign cultures with our morality. If they then desire moralities unsatisfactory to us, we have no choice but to fight them on a more brutish level.*

...

Unlike PSYOP, *MindWar* has nothing to do with deception or even with "selected" — and therefore misleading — truth. Rather it *states a whole truth that, if it does not now exist, will be forced into existence by the will of the United States*. The examples of Kennedy's ultimatum to Khrushchev during the Cuban Missile Crisis and *Hitler's stance at Munich might be cited*. A *MindWar* message does not have to fit conditions of abstract credibility as do PSYOP there; its source makes it credible. As Livy once said: "The terror of the Roman name will be such that the world shall know that, once a Roman army has laid siege to a city, nothing will move it — not the rigors or winter nor the weariness of months and years — that it knows no end but victory and is ready, if a swift and sudden stroke will not serve, to preserve until that victory is achieved."

...

For the mind to believe in its own decisions, it must feel that it made those decisions without coercion. Coercive measures used by the operative, consequently, must not be detectable by ordinary means. There is no need to resort to mind-weakening drugs such as those explored by the CIA; in fact the exposure of a single such method would do unacceptable damage to *MindWar's* reputation for truth. Existing PSYOP identifies purely-sociological factors which suggest appropriate idioms for messages. Doctrine in this area is highly developed, and the task is basically one of assembling and maintaining individuals and teams with enough expertise and experience to apply the doctrine effectively. This, however, is only the sociological dimension of target receptiveness measures. There are some purely natural conditions under which minds may become more or less receptive to ideas, and *MindWar should take full advantage of such phenomena as atmospheric electromagnetic activity, air ionization, and extremely low frequency waves.* [emphases added]

Three things to note:

That *MindWar* "states a whole truth that, if it does not now exist, will be forced into existence by the will of the United States" sounds like the derisive snort at our "reality-based community," and what the senior White House aide told Ron Susskind:

We're an empire now, and *when we act, we create our own reality.* And while you're studying that reality — judiciously, as you will — we'll act again, creating other new realities, which you can study too, and that's how things will sort out. We're history's actors ... and you, all of you, will be left to just study what we do. [emphasis added]

That this military paper, now 25-years old, spoke straight-faced of taking advantage of "atmospheric electromagnetic activity, air ionization, and extremely low frequency waves," suggests we ought to speak of the weaponization of these phenomena in a similarly serious fashion.

And that *MindWar*'s co-author is the founder of the Temple of Set perhaps dissipates some of the smoke with which Vallely clouds America's fascist resource war as a "Judeo-Christian crusade."

Mephistopheles

June 7, 2006

> *No kingdom made of human hands can stand.*
> *Too bad about MacBeth.*
> *In order to possess that corruptible crown*
> *Gotta make a deal with Mr. Death.*
>
> — Bob Dylan

Faust was a doctor, and it was for knowledge that he signed his contract with the Devil. According to Goethe, modern science — Carl Sagan's "candle in the dark" of a demon-haunted world — is ignorantly under the patronage of the demon Mephistopheles.

Rupert Sheldrake brushes against Faust and our own lousy bargains in his trialogue with Terence McKenna and Ralph Abraham entitled *Chaos, Creativity and Cosmic Consciousness*:

> How seriously do we need to take the idea that our whole society and civilization is under the possession of such a spirit.... How much are fallen angels actually guiding and perverting the progress of science and technology? Is a great war between the good and evil angels being acted out on Earth? We hardly know how to think or talk about such possibilities since they are so alien to the official, standard models of Western history.

Like Faust, the original sin of intelligence agencies is the appetite for unbound knowledge. The death-dealing, the drugs and guns, the fellowship of gangsters and terrorists all follow upon this seemingly benign desire.

The CIA damned itself at its birth by sheltering and shepherding the devils of Nazi Germany into the United States, and casting them as seeds across the western world. And it was all for knowledge. For knowledge of camp experiments, of anti-Soviet espionage, of rocket science. Like a medieval magician invoking demons to do his bidding while binding them in the name of God, Allen Dulles recruited Nazis into the service of

America. But America is a changeable god, and Dulles and his Nazis helped change it.

Yesterday it was revealed the CIA knew the whereabouts of Adolf Eichmann, but withheld the information because it might have led to exposing the Nazi pedigree of the anti-communist intelligence efforts in West Germany. It would seem that Intelligence, and the protection of even relatively trivial knowledge, can be reason enough to overlook holocausts.

We too, rightly, want to *know*. But if that's all we want we'll slip into error ourselves, amassing data which won't change a thing but will leave us alternately thrilled and depressed. Knowledge must be the servant of justice, or we're just more clients for the devil.

Patterns of Force

January 19, 2007

ere's something else to chew on.

I've been dipping into Charles Higham's out-of-print *American Swastika:The Shocking Story of Nazi Collaborators in Our Midst from 1933 to the Present Day*, and the chapter on the negotiations mid-war between future CIA Director Allen Dulles and the Nazi-SS, just jumped up and said *Yup, you got me.*

Higham writes:

> *SS officers came from the right-wing elite, those with money and commercial interests that lay outside the German border. Thus, the fact that it was the SD [the SS intelligence service] which specialized in every kind of subversion, intrigue, and ruination appealed directly to Allied connections more than any other service. Its leaders belonged to the community of world money; their allegiance was not to the upstart, working-class Hitler, but to the memory of SS leader Heinrich Himmler's idol, King Henry I of Saxony, and to the Stein bank of Cologne, which financed Himmler's inner circle under the aegis of the international banker Kurt von Schroeder.*

In 1942 Dulles became the OSS station chief in Switzerland, while continuing to serve as director and legal advisor to the New York branch of the same Schroeder bank. Early the following year, acting without the authority of Franklin Roosevelt (though he made false assertion to the contrary), Dulles opened a channel of appeasement with SS nobility, mostly Prussian elite, acting without the knowledge of Adolph Hitler. Dulles met three times with Prince Max von Hohenlohe, whom he knew from Vienna in 1916 and New York in the '20s. Higham examined the original SS records of the meetings and had no doubt to their authenticity, despite post-war attempts to discredit them because their translation had first appeared in the communist journal *New Times*.

Dulles opened the first meeting cordially, saying he was "sick and tired of listening to stories of ruined politicians, emigrants, and prejudiced Jews." He said that Germany needed to remain in existence to "maintain order," that the question of Czech sovereignty was inconsequential, and that most important was the establishment of a bulwark in the East against Bolshevism.

Dulles pressed ahead. He said that it would be unbearable for any decent European to think that the Jews might return someday, and that there must be no toleration of a return of the Jewish power positions. He reiterated his desire for a greater European political federation — and foresaw the federal Germany that in fact took place. He said that Hitler would not be accepted as the leader of a restored Germany. He made the curious assertion that the Americans were only continuing the war to get rid of the Jews and that there were people in America who were intending to send the Jews to Africa. This was Hitler's dream of course: that the Jews would go to Madagascar and stay there. Dulles seems to have confused the clubland view of blacks and Jews.

Dulles now proceeded to supply Hohenlohe with dollops of secret intelligence, announcing that the U.S. Army would not land in Spain but, after conquering Tunisia, would advance from Africa toward the Ploesti oil fields to cut off the German oil supplies. He said that it was likely the Allies would land in Sicily to cut off Rommel and control Italy from there, and thus secure the advance in the Balkans.

Having given virtually the entire battle plan for Europe, top secret at the time, to one of Germany's agents, Allen Dulles proceeded to the

almost unnecessary rider that he had very good relations with the Vatican. He said American Catholics had a decisive voice in such matters.

The negotiations faltered in the spring of '43, because the White House lacked Dulles' empathy towards aristocratic Nazis and his bond to supra-national capital saddled with the boorish and doomed Hitler (associations which appear to have led Dulles to commit untroubled acts of treason). But a few years later another of Dulles's plans, Project Paperclip, found far greater success, so that even as Germany underwent "denazification," the Nazi occult sciences were Americanized.

Let's remember the worlds that the word Nazi can hold. The street-brawling thugs are always dispensable; even Hitler, who came up from the streets, dispensed with them. And to the SS conniving behind his back, Hitler could be done away with, too. It's such quiet and refined elite, whose members belong to the community of international money, that can smash more than our windows. Those are the Nazis to whom Allen Dulles delivered the keys to America. They were not the alien other, like European Jewry or the Communists. They were *blutsbrüder*.

"Permanent Uncle" Sam

March 14, 2005

I find it equally ominous and amusing to read that "senior U.S. administration officials are working on a policy to 'contain' Hugo Chavez." Ominous because Chavez is a man in the crosshairs of an empire growing increasingly ruthless with desperation. Amusing because Chavez is just a man, and what the U.S. hopes to contain is not contained by him. The continent is practically stinking with progressive thought, and action. Soon, the State Department will need to "contain" Evo Morales, of Bolivia's Movement to Socialism, the likely victor in next year's presidential election. And it's not down to one leader, or even several. As Tommy Douglas, the Greatest Canadian, liked to say, "You can lock up a man, but you can't lock up an idea."

U.S. influence in Latin America is waning to the point of absurdity. Like today's warning to Suriname, that if its citizens elect former dictator Desi Bouterse, as they seem likely to do on May 25, Washington will sever ties with the nation on account of Bouterse's cocaine conviction. The United States "won't deal with a person in the presidential seat who is convicted on drug charges." That the American President has his own cocaine conviction is presumably nobody's concern, since it's been scrubbed from the records. Never mind his family's prominent, though covert, and so unmentionable, role in the protected drug trade.

One small incident to illustrate the continent's emergence from its fascist legacy: Argentina has expelled a Nazi pedophile — *and isn't it something how often we see those words together?* —and Paul Schaefer has to face justice in Chile for having abused boys for decades at his fascist-cult compound, "Colonia Dignidad." (Germany is interested in Schaefer as well, for his alleged role in kidnapping German children for his camp.) Schaefer liked his abused charges to call him "Permanent Uncle." Not only was his organization long-sheltered by Chilean authorities, but it became a state torture camp, and a significant asset in "Operation Condor."

A little background from a *New York Times* article of Dec 30, 2002, "Chile Sect Thrives Despite Criminal Charges":

> The group's reclusive leader is accused of sexually abusing scores of young boys. Former political prisoners say they were imprisoned and tortured in underground dungeons in the group's compound. An American who disappeared on a hiking vacation is reported to have been executed there. More than 50 other charges are pending against the group and its leaders, ranging from kidnapping and forced labor to fraud and tax evasion.
>
> Yet the paramilitary religious sect known as Colonia Dignidad continues to flourish here in a 70-square-mile enclave in the Andean foothills that remains, in the words of a recent Chilean congressional report, a heavily armed "state within a state."
>
> Protected by barricades, barbed wire, roadblocks, searchlights and hidden cameras and microphones, Colonia Dignidad has for more than 40 years been the fortress home of about 300 people, most of them German citizens. Their only loyalty is to the sect's German-born founder, Paul Schafer, who likes to call himself the Permanent Uncle and preaches an apocalyptic creed that includes strong anti-Semitic and anti-Communist elements.

The American presumed executed at Colonia Dignidad is mathematics professor Boris Weisfeiler. His sister Olga maintains a Web site dedicated to uncovering the truth of his 20-year old disappearance. In a letter last July 13 to George W. Bush, she reveals that she "learned in June 2000 — through declassified State Department documents:

> that Boris was apprehended by a Chilean military patrol and taken to Colonia Dignidad, a 37,000 acre German pseudo-religious sect with links to Nazism. Colonia Dignidad, during the military dictatorship of Gen. Augusto Pinochet, was one of the most notorious and secretive detention and torture center, from where dozens of political prisoners disappeared.
>
> According to military sources, Boris was accused of being a Russian spy, then a CIA, and later a Jewish spy. His detention and delivery to Colonia Dignidad was due to the outstanding order of the Chilean Army to arrest and bring all strangers found in the area to Colonia for inter-

rogations. Two and a half years after his disappearance, my brother was reportedly seen alive inside the settlement. Colonia Dignidad, now under the name of Villa Baviera, still exists and is fully operational today, in spite of the approximately 70 criminal lawsuits brought against its leaders, for charges ranging from tax evasion and falsification of documents, to child abuse, kidnappings and torture.

In the past few months, the investigators of my brother's disappearance have received additional information: Boris was detained in Colonia Dignidad for some period of time, brutally tortured there and later on killed either by Colonia's leaders or by the members of Chilean military. It has become obvious to me, now more then ever, that the key answers to the mystery of Boris' disappearance are hidden behind the barbed wires fences of Colonia Dignidad.

I wish her luck, but I don't think that will be enough. After all, the President's father, George Herbert Walker Bush, was CIA Director at the time of Weisfeiler's disappearance, during Operation Condor's CIA-enabled targeting of Chilean dissidents:

Operation Condor was based out of a bizarre Nazi colony in Chile known as Colonia Dignidad, whose founder is wanted in Germany for kidnapping and molesting young boys. Colonia Dignidad was used by Pinochet's team to train for the 1973 coup d'etat, and then served as a torture center where prisoners were "disappeared." Many of the top ranking Nazi war criminals in South America are believed to have lived in Colonia Dignidad.

The camp survives, but under another name, having undergone an extreme makeover. It claims to have integrated into Chilean society, and shed Schaefer's legacy. Whether that's true, I don't know. But at least it recognizes a zeitgeist when it sees one.

Neither "Permanent Uncle," is.

JFC Fuller's Army

February 5, 2006

> *But there's no danger*
> *It's a professional career*
>
> — Elvis Costello

They are the damnedest things, the things I didn't know.

Since I was fourteen or so I've had on my bookshelf a copy of JFC Fuller's *Decisive Battles of the Western World*. I knew he was a Major General, an early advocate of air power and mechanized assault, and a popular military historian. I'd known his philosophy of armored warfare won more favor in Germany than in Britain, and that it became the blitzkrieg of commanders such as Heinz Guderian. And that was about it. What I didn't know was Fuller was both a fascist and an occultist, and no slouch at either.

Fuller served on the Policy Directorate of Oswald Mosley's British Union of Fascists, and was the only Englishman honored with an invitation to Adolf Hitler's 50th birthday party in 1939. He was also a life-long Thelemite and an early advocate of Aleister Crowley. A pdf of Fuller's early study of Crowley, *The Star in the West*, can be read online, and also his *Secret Wisdom of the Qabalah*. (By the way, an online edition of his *Foundation of the Science of War* is hosted by the U.S. Army Command and General Staff.) He was also an accomplished artist of occult subjects. Kenneth Grant, in *Outer Gateways*, states that Fuller actually drew the sigils for *Liber XII*, "one of the most mysterious communications every received by Crowley," under alleged inspiration of the entity Aiwass.

Grant adds that Fuller's sigils are evocative of those reproduced by purported UFO contactee George Adamski, who insisted that they were "not to be interpreted mystically, but as glyphs of the nut-and-bolt variety." (In the 1950s Adamski asserted he had been contacted by "spacemen" from Venus, much as the occupants of the airship of 1897 claimed to have been out-of-state rather than off-world. Now, the claims of origin are most often distant stars. The lies, whether human or trans-human, keep abreast of science's plausible denial.)

Grant writes:

It is well known that Hitler had occult affiliations, and that one of his chief engineers was the celebrated Werner von Braun who later enabled the Americans to visit the moon. Is it not feasible that Hitler, in favoring Fuller as he did, was not only interested in Fuller's tank designs but also in his other, more recherché machines? The fact should not be overlooked that Hitler was in contact with entities as enigmatic and as alarming as Aiwass, and perhaps his interpretations of the messages he received from them were as colored by his conditioning as were those of Crowley.

So, what's the point? Two points: if we mean to combat fascism, then we should learn to recognize it on our bookshelves and in the mind bombs dropped by respectable fascists. (Fuller's *Generalship of Ulysses S. Grant* is still an influential study of the Civil War strategist, though one Amazon reviewer does chide his history of *The Second World War* for barely mentioning the extermination of millions of Jews, Gypsies and Slavs.) We had also better brush up on our occultism. Because we can't really know the fascist character if we project upon it our familiar secular and liberal mental landscapes. That is going to take us to mad places, but that's the nature of comprehending the method.

The Trouble
with Fascists

February 7, 2006

*"We Fascists are the only true anarchists. Once we've become masters of
the state, true anarchy is that of power."*

— Pasolini, *Salo*

Fascists have, let's call them, *boundary* issues. The boundaries of states, and I mean both federations and conditions, and the boundaries on the roadmaps of the soul. They *transgress*.

Now of course, transgression can be a good thing, providing it's your own boundaries you are crossing. In fact, in almost every religious culture, transgression is allowed to be a holy thing. Think of fools of God like Saint Simeon Salus, a sixth century hermit who would perform such antics as blowing out the candles of a church just as the service was beginning, eating sausages on Good Friday and defecating in the marketplace. Yet as George Hansen tells in *The Trickster and the Paranormal* Simeon was also known to perform miracles, including the multiplication of food, telepathy and predicting the future. Nityananda, who last century violated many orthodox Hindu laws and would embarrass his devotees by his nakedness and such happenings as smearing excrement over his body and sitting "with large piles of it, offering some to passers-by as a sweet." (The inversion of food/excrement and mouth/anus is a recurring and powerful transgression. The Aztecs had a copraphagic deity named Tlazolteotl, "Divine Excrement," also known as Tlaelquani, the "Eater of Ordure." See also "The Eye of Horus.") But Nityananda is remembered for his "miraculous healings, prophetic powers and even weather control." Joseph of Copertino mortified his flesh with chains and metal plates that pressed into his sores, and wore broken crockery around his neck to increase his humiliation. Joseph is also arguably the best-documented levitator in history. He also displayed telepathy, clairvoyance, healing powers and more. Sri Ramakrishna, one of India's greatest saints, often dressed as a woman and would eat the food left as temple offerings for gods.

So, what was that about fascism, and what am I going on about now? I'm going on about Pasolini's final film, the one he may have died for: *Salo*.

"You must be stupid to think that death would be so easy. Don't you know we intend to kill you a thousand times?"

It's a hard film to see, and not just because it's hard to sit through. Its graphic sexual sadism has prompted its banning around the world. (I first tried to catch it at a Toronto Forbidden Films festival in the mid-'80s, but the Ontario Film Board forbade the screening.) Given that there are many works in the past 30 years which have *out-grossed it*, I suspect it's still problematic, not so much for its generalized sexual sadism as for its pointed depiction of *fascist* sexual sadism.

The film is an adaptation of the Marquis De Sade's *120 Days of Sodom*, which Pasolini set in Mussolini's "Republic of Salo," the Nazi puppet state of northern Italy that he nominally administered during the final years of the war.

If you haven't seen it, you've seen and heard of something like it. Forced nudity on collared and leashed prisoners with covered heads, pedophilic rape, coprophilia, humiliation and torture, ritual abuse and murder. Is it fascism? Is it Salo, or someplace else?

(And I should say, the death of a thousand times includes such insufferable yet mundane things as the Killing Jokes of deadpan irony. The Cheney/Bush gang are masters of timing. It's Republican prostitute Jeff Gannon getting back his press pass, this time for "Pajama Media." It's Rumsfeld comparing Chavez to Hitler. *Doesn't he know what he's saying, and doesn't he know what he sounds like?* Yes, and yes: of course he does. And it must give him tremendous pleasure.)

"Our guide restored the divine character of monstrosity thanks to reiterated actions. That is to say: rites."

It's been a topic here before how the psycho-sexual atrocities of Abu Ghraib and Gitmo, and most certainly the unnamed secret prisons in the "War on Terror's" encircling gulag, did not arise in a vacuum and without the stage direction of senior officials. They also enact ritual, and are more than reminiscent, to both students and survivors, of the methods of covert mind control. Survivor Kathleen Sullivan says that "many survivors ... are experiencing an additional set of reactions ... wave after wave of devastating emotions and flashbacks after each new revelation is made public. What was done to the prisoners is too similar to what was perpetrated against most of us." And last July I wrote that the "mission is brutalization. Not just of the captives, but of the captors and their codependent subjects in the Homeland. Because the transformative mission extends beyond the literal confines of Abu Ghraib and Gitmo, to the imaginative boundaries of Empire."

But there's more going on here than brutalization. Or rather, the brutalization has, I believe, a sacramental aspect, because there's a liminal quality to the bulldozing of values that achieves for the fascists — and possibly also for some fragmented parts of their victims — an ecstatic state of transgression. Perhaps understanding this dynamic will help explain and anticipate the congruity of fascism with cultic crime and untangle "Satanic Ritual Abuse" from the double caricatures of fundamentalist hysteria and secular-humanist disdain.

Pasolini, by the way, was murdered the year of *Salo*'s release, after having received death threats from neo-Fascists on its account. Last year, Italian police reopened the case after Giuseppe Pelosi, a then-17-year-old who served nine years for the killing, recanted. Pelosi said Pasolini hadn't, after all, tried to rape him with a wooden stake, but had been killed by a politically motivated group of men, and he "had to play the game played by these people, the 'respectable' people who ordered the murder."

Those are some wild games, the games respectable people play.

The Left, the Right, and the Wrong

October 25, 2005

You can't open up your mind, boys, to every conceivable point of view.
— Bob Dylan

Last July 27, the U.S. State Department very thoughtfully posted a resource tool for journalists and media consumers entitled "How to Identify Misinformation." Though "there are no exact rules" to tell whether a story is true or false, the State Department offers clues. First among them, "Does the story fit the pattern of a conspiracy theory?"

Does the story claim that vast, powerful, evil forces are secretly manipulating events? If so, this fits the profile of a conspiracy theory. Conspiracy theories are rarely true, even though they have great appeal and are often widely believed. In reality, events usually have much less exciting explanations.

The U.S. military or intelligence community is a favorite villain in many conspiracy theories.

To demonstrate a pattern of falsity, the "counter-misinformation team" provides links to just three of the "many conspiracy theory Web sites which contain a great deal of unreliable information": Rense.com, Joe Vialls and Conspiracy Planet.

Rense.com boasts that the State Department ranks it "number one," but I find that unwarranted in light of the pattern the State Department establishes in its attempt to discredit the critical study of High Crimes.

Consider its solitary example of 9/11 conspiracy theory: Thierry Meyssan's Pentagon cruise missile. I've written numerous times here what I think of the supposition that something other than Flight 11 hit the Pentagon. Regardless of what any of us think, it remains the most divisive wedge issue and energy sink for 9/11 activists. *Of course* the State Department would draw attention to it, to the neglect of all others. No mention of insider trading, squelched investigations and coincident war games. The "counter-misinformation team" is trying to proscribe counter-*information* by accentuating the preposterous. Meyssan's work becomes, in a sense, "approved" conspiracy theory, because it's the only one to receive official recognition. Not only in this State Department publication, but in virtually every mainstream treatment of alternative appraisals of 9/11 the "no plane" theory still takes pride of place. (A similar process is occurring with respect to reports of Katrina "conspiracy theory," in which soft rumors of the levees being blown take precedence over hard analysis of the intentional withholding of aid.)

Two of the three sites singled out by the State Department are, *rightly or wrongly*, widely perceived as containing anti-Semitic bias. Rense.com's enthusiastic support of Ernst Zundel, and its linking to revisionist accounts of his "heroic struggle," may be made in the spirit of idealized libertarianism, but Zundel is a Nazi, and his *kampf* is not my own. The late Joe Vialls did some very commendable work, particularly his series on the Holly Wells and Jessica Chapman murders, but he also tended to see Jews under the bed an awful lot ("Kosher Kerry Cons Christian America", for one mild instance).

What the State Department is doing by holding up these sites as exemplars of "conspiracy theory," is to administer a poison pill to contrary analysis. To the poor journalist or media consumer taking cues from the "counter-misinformation team," it will appear as though conspiracy theory has an essential core of anti-Semitism. But there's maybe more going on than that.

In the first part of my interview with ritual abuse-mind control survivor Kathleen Sullivan, she made the following observation:

> Another interesting factor is that most of the more outspoken disinfo agents present together at conferences that either pander to "conspiracy theorists" and/or to the sector that is pro-Aryan and/or "Patriot." Not all people in the Patriot movement are pro-Aryan. However, I have learned that most of the mind-control disinfo agents are, privately if not publicly, avowed racists. This would seem to be a rather odd connection, if one did not know that many Aryan organizations and cell groups use "trauma-based mind control" on their members, to ensure their submission and compliance.

I find this fascinating. Sullivan says that the occult-intelligence perpetrators of ritual abuse belong to the Aryan networks, *as do those* who have claimed leadership of its exposure. This is one of those things that threw me for a cognitive loop when I began discovering this material, which nearly tempted me to pretend the evidence for it didn't exist. (Another one was that many of the self-styled champions of mind-control survivors become their lovers and handlers.) These characters, like Fritz Springmeier, Mark Phillips and Ted Gunderson, seem either to be drawn from or to pander to the extreme right: the militias, the White Nationalists, and the "Patriot" communities. (Linda Blood, author of *The New Satanists*, had a *WTF?* moment in the mid-'90s at a ritual and cult abuse conference, to the delight of debunker Evan Harrington: "Blood, who spoke later in the day, protested that she was 'unhappy to be following someone [Marqui] who is pushing the *Protocols of the Elders of Zion*,' which she said was anti-Semitic trash. Blood's protest deeply angered some and bewildered others, while about four of Blood's friends clapped in support.")

The conspiratocracy nurtures a false opposition on the far right, with the result that its authentic opposition is either polluted by alliance and infiltration, or turns away in disgust from inquiring after certain issues, such as mind control, which the so-called "Patriot Movement" has embraced. What's more, it may also provide convenient cover to a pool of low-level functionaries and perpetrators.

And it's no exaggeration to say Nazis are throwing their thought-bombs at us, attempting to make their cause respectable and infiltrate our side and — worse — our minds. On the "White Nationalist" board *Stormfront*, a recent post from "Free Zundel Now" spoke of success spreading a "stealth article" calling for Bush's impeachment on "forums that ordinarily won't take our kind of subject matter." (It was tried on the *Rigorous Intuition* discussion board, and was caught.)

From *Stormfront*'s "Celtic Nation," advice on infiltration:

...you have to speak a language they will hear, and speak to what they will hear, and as you said, point out racial realities. The constant drone of Jew bashing will start to turn people off. It does make White Nationalists look like kooks and conspiracy theorists, and hearkens people back to nutty stereotypes of Col. Klink from Hogan's Heroes, and paranoid conspiracy theorists who are mentally off-center.

When I discuss Israel and the Jews, I try to talk of the evils of the state of Israel, and if they are ready for it, introduce more. The fact is that most of what we struggle against is the big picture — the superstructures in place by the Jews in power.

Sometimes Israel means Israel, sometimes Zionist means Zionist. But sometimes they're simply polite society code for *Jews*. We need to know this – we need to become sensitive to the sometimes-encrypted message that would bear us unaware to the extreme right – if we are to meet and defeat the true enemy. Because in every instance, Nazi means Nazi.

Blackshirts and Skins

July 17, 2007

> *Well, I fin'ly started thinkin' straight*
> *When I run outa things to investigate.*
> *Couldn't imagine doin' anything else,*
> *So now I'm sittin' home investigatin' myself!*
> *Hope I don't find out anything ... hmm, great God!*
> — Bob Dylan

I always get a rush from The Ghosts of Cable Street and the story of London's Eastenders beating back the blackshirts. But it's not 1936 anymore (it's not even 1986, I tell myself sometimes, still listening to *The Men They Couldn't Hang*), and fascists wear all colors these days. They don't make it as easy for us. These days, some days, we even need to check the labels on our own shirts.

Post-war covert history has largely been one of de-legitimizing and destroying leftist and even moderate governments and opposition groups. We've seen the assassinations, the coups and wars; the economic arm-twisting; the corruption and blackmail. Since the murder of Rabin, "Israeli society, despairing of peace, has undergone a rightward radicalization." In the Arab world the process has been compounded by the elimination of even secular options, creating conditions in which the only effective vehicle for change is aligned with individuals, ideologies and finances indebted to international fascism.

This shouldn't be news to any reader of this Web site. The Muslim Brotherhood, which has spawned most "Jihadist" groups, was founded by Hassan al-Banna, an admirer of Hitler, and became a wartime Nazi intelligence asset. Post-war, like many such assets, it was rolled into the Western intelligence matrix. Swiss Nazi Ahmed Huber established the Al Taqwa Bank, which dispersed to bin Laden and others CIA monies seeded in the financial proxy of international terror and intelligence, BCCI.

Now where does anti-Semitism, and legitimate critique of Israel, fit in this complex picture?

There are at least two levels at play here for us. First to consider is politics and activism. The second is conspiracy theory.

Unapologetically I'm on the left, and I expect, to some degree or another and regardless of whether you even acknowledge it, you are as well. Broadly, or perhaps rather, ideally, taking the left implies an identification with the oppressed, the poor and the workers against the concentration of power and capital in the hands of an exploiting few. Israeli politics have taken a sharp right turn in the past 40 years, and the policies and consequences of occupation have been tragic and criminal. Perversely, and I believe intentionally for the right, the perpetuation of misery and exacerbation of tension has driven large numbers of both Palestinians and Israelis to rightward extremes. And it has carried many in the left along with it, unconsciously and uncritically, because the progressive options have already been eliminated by the fascists who play both sides.

Not all on the left lose their way on this. For instance:

The Alliance for Workers' Liberty, a Trotskyite faction in the Stop The War Coalition, objected to working with the Muslim Association of Britain due to its links to the Muslim Brotherhood, and argued that the left should be working with secular, progressive Muslim groups instead. *The Weekly Worker* newspaper took a similar stand, pointing out in one article that "At the same time as our secularist and Marxist comrades are being murdered by groups allied to the MAB, we are lining ourselves up as co-sponsors of demonstrations. This is like communists lining up with Nazis sympathisers on demonstrations during World War II, because we are both against British imperialism."

Then there's conspiracy theory. It was 9/11 that caused many on the left to immerse themselves in it for the first time. There we found a thriving subculture, welcoming us with literature and semi-familiar jargon, telling us that "left" and "right" were fictions that divided us from together fighting the "real enemy." They too believed 9/11 was an "inside job," so even though we didn't start out from the same place, we were now on the same side — weren't we? We *could* learn much from them, even from the "former insiders" and veterans of the CIA and MI6 who were happy to help us find our footing, even if we weren't always sure what they meant by "international bankers" and "New World Order" — right?

Think of how warmly David Duke was received by some supposed progressives after his CNN appearance with Wolf Blitzer. Consider what Tom Metzger, founder of White Aryan Resistance, says here: "Recruit radical people. Some of the best are on the left.... in most cases I am closer to the left. Anti-war, Anti-Capitalist, pro-environment and Nature, hate for the lying super rich or the lumkin [lumpen] proletariat, hatred of all present politicians ..."

There is a subtle campaign of co-option within the subculture of conspiracy — to lead nearly every issue of suppressed history and high crime back to a Jewish root. This is why the operational Arab element of the international fascist Mafia has, for many, been totally eradicated from the equation of "9/11 Truth," and the "smoking gun" has become a case of "insurance fraud" for a grasping New York Jew. If it's successful, the left option will again have been eliminated, and the only effective opposition to fascist power will be a fascist populism.

Anti-Semitism is as objectionable as any hate directed towards any people for simply being. But anti-Semitism has a special pedigree, *not because Jews are special*, but because they are the historic and still-favored scapegoats of fascists. (Some of whom, of course, are themselves Jewish, but whose allegiance is rather to criminal power.) Sometimes, when we don't reflect on the pedigree of our own influences, we're unconsciously doing their bidding. I'd rather do nothing, and it would be better if I did, than do that.

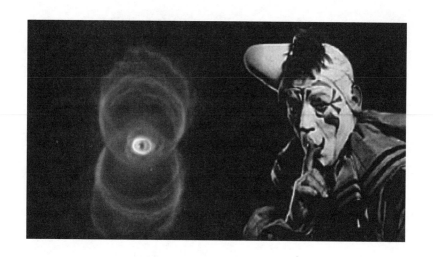

The Disease of Conceit

July 17, 2005

Ain't nothing too discreet
About the disease of conceit.

— Bob Dylan

L anguage, being the virus that it is, often makes me sick. These days, not so much from the perpetual misdiagnosis of "conspiracy theory" (*conspiracy is a hypothesis, doc; deep politics is the theory*), as at the amateur virologists' nerve to call what they do "skepticism."

The Skeptics Society, which claims ownership of the term, defines it as "the application of reason to any and all ideas.... When we say we are 'skeptical,' we mean that we must see compelling evidence before we believe."

Right there we can see the argumentative circularity, and the richness and the weirdness of life that must forever lie beyond the pale for such people. "Show me," they say. Yet evidence compelling to them must necessarily conform to "reason" (in other words, to a trumped-up rationality with control issues), and so all evidence that transgresses reason (or more accurately, puts rationality in its place) is invalidated. In this manner, the paranormal and much of what we call the parapolitical can never be proven to such people. "Show me," they say, and yet these same people are more likely than not to accept official narratives of controversial history without having been shown *anything*. Rather, it's us, the "conspiracy theorists," who are saying "show me," and meaning it. We're the ones withholding judgment. We're the true skeptics, and I want us to stake a claim on the word.

The society adds that "modern skepticism is embodied in the scientific method, that involves gathering data to formulate and test naturalistic explanations for natural phenomena."

Here the problem narrows, and sharpens, to the reduction of skepticism to scientific method. But much of our experience of the world, even of the "natural" world, cannot be subjected to a scientific method and still retain its meaning for us.

Just last week, scientist Richard Dawkins opened a conference with the caution that the Universe is too weird to understand, and that there is a "narrow range of reality that we judge to be normal." Scientific method is moving uncomfortably beyond the "skeptic," who seems a hide-bound Newtonian from the perspective of our quantum politics.

Have you ever browsed the *Skeptic's Dictionary*? A word that comes to mind to describe the intellects at play there is credulous. Virtually all that is offered is assurance to those who don't want such things to be true, that they needn't worry, and need inquire no further.

For instance, the complete entry for "Xenoglossy" is the "alleged speaking or writing in a language entirely unknown to the speaker. The probability of this happening is about zero." *Well*, he said, brushing off his hands, *that takes care of that*.

Under "Mind control," we read that:

> ... a common complaint from the mind-controlled is that they can't get therapists to take them seriously. That is, they say they can only find therapists who want to treat them for their delusions, not help them prove they're being controlled by their government. Thus, it is not likely that the 'mind-controlled CIA zombies' will be accused of having delusions planted in them by therapists, as alien abductees have, since they claim they cannot get therapists to take their delusions seriously.

Either the author did not respect the subject enough to seriously research it, or he did and hopes the reader won't, because it's an absolute fabrication.

I'll let just one example stand for many. (And let's note this: these kind of skeptics must paint with the broadest of brushes, because if only one contrary fact is admitted, *everything* crumbles.) Dr. Valerie Wolf, testifying in 1995 before the Presidential Commission on Radiation Experiments said,

> ... in preparation for my testimony at these hearings, I called nearly 40 therapists across the country to find out what they knew about the link between radiation and mind control and to get what other therapists were seeing in clients who had been used in mind-control

experiments.... Generally, it appears that therapists across the country are finding clients who have been subjected to mind-control techniques. The consistency of their stories about the purpose of the mind control and torture techniques such as electric shock, use of hallucinogens, sensory deprivation, spinning, hypnosis, dislocation of limbs and sexual abuse is remarkable. There is almost nothing published on this aspect of mind control used with children and these clients come from all over the country, having had no contact with each other.

In its debunking of "alien abductions," the dictionary never strays from the ET hypothesis, arguing against the probability of traveling interplanetary distances without raising the theoretical likelihood of parallel worlds.

The dictionary sneers at the late Harvard psychiatrist, Dr. John Mack, who took seriously the abduction phenomenon:

...until the good doctor or one of his patients produces physical evidence that abductions have occurred, it seems more reasonable to believe that he and his patients are deluded or frauds. Of course, the good doctor can hide behind academic freedom and the doctor/patient privacy privilege. He can make all the claims he wants and refuse to back any of them up on the grounds that to do so would be to violate his patients' rights. He can then publish his stories and dare anyone to take away his academic freedom. He is in the position any con person would envy: he can lie without fear of being caught.

Again, the broadest brush is employed — the "good doctor" is a con man — because if they are wrong *once*, their world slips away.

And there is ample physical evidence for both UFOs and abductions. Another solitary example to stand for many: The case of "Dr. X," the French health professional Jacques Vallee introduced to us in **Confrontations**. When attending to his crying toddler early morning November 2, 1968, he noticed a light outside the child's window. He didn't pay it much attention until his son was asleep again, and then he stepped out on the balcony and observed two large disks moving slowly over neighboring homes. The objects merged, and a white beam was directed toward the ground below. "Finally the disk made a movement that brought it to a vertical position, and the white beam caught the doctor squarely on the balcony. He heard a bang and the object vanished, leaving only a whitish form like cotton candy."

Afterwards he experienced abdominal pain, and a red, equilateral triangle with sides of six inches in length appeared around his navel. His doctor believed it to be a psychosomatic reaction to his "dream" of an object which was somehow associated with a triangle. "But when the same shape appeared on the abdomen of the child, and when the same phenomena recurred in successive years, the psychosomatic explanation had to be discounted." (A thermographic examination in 1984 found "intense cutaneous erythema of triangular shape, centered over the umbilicus; absence of visible superficial vessel.... resistant to cooling.")

The encounter also accompanied spontaneous healing of a permanent disability on the right side of his body he had incurred ten years before from a mine explosion while in the French army. And this just scratches the weirdness, as Dr. X and his wife were subsequently "plagued by poltergeist activity" and by visitations "so fantastic as to stretch credulity, yet they appear to be verifiable by other family members." But let's not invite the rolled eyes of the "skeptic" with such episodes. But it's too late for that. Even the medical records of Dr. X and his son are inadmissible as evidence because they do not conform to "reason," and so will not be seriously considered.

Cocksureity seems the hallmark contradiction of such skeptics. Stage magician Penn Jillette is such a one. He says that people should "learn to carry their intelligence the way James Dean carried his cigarette." In other words, as *an affectation*.

Jillette could have said the way Peabody carried his bowtie, but it wouldn't have been as cool.

Conspiracy Theory Made Easy

March 13, 2005

A fascinating article today entitled "Untimely Deaths in Ukraine", disputing the official explanations of "strange suicides and car crashes" in the Ukraine.

Get a load of this, and from the *Los Angeles Times*, no less:

The former Ukrainian interior minister, scheduled to meet in just a few hours with prosecutors to give testimony in a high-profile case of political murder, aimed a gun at his chin and fired, sending a bullet ripping through his cheek and out his upper jaw. Then he aimed it at his temple and fired again.

Suicide, government investigators ruled.

...

Zvarych, the justice minister, has expressed doubt that the former interior minister could have recovered sufficiently from the shock of the first wound to have delivered the second.

"I have certain doubts personally speaking about whether someone can pull the trigger twice in order to commit suicide," he said. "There's this threshold of pain, I think, that one would need to be able to cross in order to be able to do that, something called a 'pain syndrome,' that I think is very difficult to overcome.

Consider that Gary Webb — "the last North American career journalist," in Al Giordano's words — was also judged to have killed himself with two gunshots to the head. Consider that the mainstream media was as incurious about the circumstances of his death as it had disgraced itself regarding the substance of his investigations. And consider it was the *LA Times* which played point in Webb's character assassination, even in his obituary.

My purpose isn't to rehash speculation about Webb's death, but to underscore the selective speculation of the American press.

Imagine if, in the space of five years, figures of the stature of John F. Kennedy, Malcolm X, Martin Luther King Jr. and Robert F. Kennedy had been murdered *anywhere else in the world.*

Imagine if finely milled anthrax had been mailed to the opponents of Hugo Chavez, just as his government introduced "El Acto Del Patriota," which promised to consolidate power in the presidency and violate the spirit and letter of the Venezuelan constitution. And imagine if the investigation led to a bioweapons lab of the Venezuelan military, and then faltered.

Imagine if "Pavlov Wellstonski," Vladimir Putin's leading opponent of the war in Chechnya, had died in a plane crash which decided control of the Duma.

Nothing is as disreputable to the American mainstream media as "conspiracy theory," but it's riddled with conspiracy theorists who apply their craft liberally to other countries. "Conspiracy theory" appears to be disreputable only in domestic practice, not in international theory. The *LA Times'* byline attributes the story to Kim Murphy, but it may as well be Alex Jones, with the singular exception that the suspicious deaths are made in the Ukraine, not the United States.

The *Times* could easily publish a story entitled "Untimely Deaths in the U.S." Except it would never do such a thing. So I guess it's not that easy after all.

The Consolation
of Conspiracy

July 22, 2005

> *Sometimes I think this whole world is one big prison yard.*
> *Some of us are prisoners, the rest of us are guards.*
> — Bob Dylan

"The dust hadn't even settled after the terrorist atrocities in London and already the conspiracy theories ... had begun," writes Cinnamon Stillwell in "The London Conspiracy Theories: Here We Go Again." Never mind that settled dust also covers tracks, as unpolished first reports get squeegee'd from the record. And disregard the fact that every reconstruction of the events must posit a conspiracy of some sort, and that they are not even theories, but hypotheses.

Never mind all that, as here they go again, baiting the genuine skeptics in the Aeon of Bizarro.

Most irksome are Stillwell's patronizing conclusions:

> It never ceases to amaze me how many well-educated, otherwise rational people insist on pushing these fantasies. Unable to cope with the nihilistic and horrifying threat of Islamic terrorism, they instead turn to familiar demons.... How long these people can continue their delusions is unknown, but something tells me that a great number of them will simply have to be written off as functionally insane while the rest of us attend to the business of fighting Islamic terrorism.
>
> In some ways I understand *this need to find more comforting answers*. There's been many a day since 9/11 that I've wished this threat wasn't real. But it is. At some point, all of us will have to shake off the conspiracy theories and face that truth. [emphasis added]

I don't mind so much being dismissed as mad, so long as I'm not locked up in a psychiatric hospital for the politically insane. Though since that day came for Soviet dissidents, and the Western calendar is running just a little behind, we shouldn't be surprised if our questions will eventually be addressed with a pharmacological magic bullet. Rather, what I find most disagreeable about this popular refutation of "conspiracy theory" is that such thinking is somehow *comforting*.

Tell me what I say is crazy, without bothering to hear what I'm saying. I'm fine with that. Hell, I listen to what I'm saying and sometimes I wonder myself. As a fellow "conspiracy theorist" recently told me, "I feel like the guy in *A Beautiful Mind*, minus the genius part." Adding things up which are *not to be added* can do that to you. It's a crazy-making world out there, once you start paying attention to it. Just don't presume to tell me how I feel about it.

And I won't presume to tell you, so you tell me: how did you feel when the floor first fell away from beneath you? When the *comforting* assumptions of consensus reality folded up upon themselves, and you saw the lone gunmen as cardboard figures, and you glimpsed the grinning skulls beneath the smooth skin of the killers, what did that do to your insides? When you felt the vertiginous drop, did you throw up your hands and let out a *"Wheeeeee!"*?

(Perhaps there are some who do. Perhaps that's what sets apart the conspiracy buffs from the rest of us. They get a rush from the horror, but it's as real and as threatening as an amusement ride. They've internalized nothing. It means nothing. And *that's* paranoid style.)

"Comforting answers"? I felt physically ill when I added up what I'd learned about 9/11 — saw what I got. I didn't want it to be true, and I still don't. I want none of it to be true. *If only Oswald had acted alone*. But he didn't. So like it or not, here I am.

And it was only at the public execution of John F. Kennedy — that is, with the eruption of conspiracy *fact* into public consciousness — that conspiracy *theory* became a disreputable subject. Until then, such talk could be heard from, and even encouraged by, some of America's most senior officials. "The individual is handicapped by coming face to face with a conspiracy so monstrous he cannot believe it exists," wrote J. Edgar Hoover. As I read Eisenhower's better-late-than-never warning about the military-industrial complex, and how Americans must remain "alert and knowledgeable" and "should take nothing for granted" in order to guard against its "acquisition of unwarranted influence, whether sought or unsought," I can hear presidential press secretary Scott McClelland's rote rebuttal: "That's a conspiracy theory, Dwight, and I won't dignify that with a response. Next question — Jeff Gannon, Talon News."

There's an account by Fred J. Cook, an early critic of the *Warren Report*, of coming up against the Left Gatekeepers at *The Nation*, in Martin Schotz's *History Will Not Absolve Us*. In 1964, Cook submitted a seven-page memorandum "tearing at the guts of the report" to Editor Carey McWilliam. He knew their editorial policy was endorsement of the findings, but he "felt that *The Nation* was the only magazine with sufficient independence and nerve to print the kind of article I wanted to write." After three weeks of silence, McWilliam rejected it, telling him that he could find no flaw in his reasoning, but that *The Nation* didn't want to criticize the *Report*."

A year and a half later, as criticism of the Report became more acceptable and more vocal, McWilliam relented, and published it with a disclaimer that it was only Cook's opinion, then immediately followed it up with a ridiculing piece by a university professor lambasting "conspiracy theory." The author was, in fact, a MOCKINGBIRD asset of the CIA, and later admitted in a fit of conscience to Cook's friend and fellow researcher Vince Salandria that yes, they were right, but that *"The truth is too terrible. The American people would never be able to stand it."*

Who's comforting whom?

In a village you know to be a prison, you should question the motives of your consoling minders.

Cynical, Sophisticated and Subtle

May 27, 2005

Sometimes nonsense is just nonsense. Sometimes, like when Marshall Applewhite hollered "All aboard!" for the Hale-Bopp Express, it's dangerous nonsense. Sometimes the nonsense is also disinformation. And sometimes, disinformation is not nonsense at all. And for the truth, that's the most dangerous.

First, some nonsense. I don't know what Phil Jayhan and letsroll9/11's story is, but I'll bet it doesn't have a happy ending. The two are responsible for the aggressive dissemination of the ludicrous pod-and-missile theory. (That is, a moment before impacting the towers, the aircraft fired missiles from pods on their bellies. Why would they? A good question. One which, as usual with such fantasies, is never really addressed.) I see Jayhan posted on Thursday a bizarre ramble about how letsroll911 has changed history, and even lapses into the third person to talk about himself. As a rule, not a good sign:

> When I decided to then publish my findings, I thought I would end up within a week, with either a bullet in my head or CNN trucks in my driveway. It was kind of a hard decision, as I really desired neither. But I chose to publish. So on April 15th, 2004, I released a press release that literally changed the face of the world and its politics.

> ...

> Had Phil Jayhan never existed, and never taken out this website, all of you would be experiencing an alternate reality, quite different than the one which you now enjoy ... Not sure what that would be, but am sure it wouldn't be better than what we now have.

I won't judge Jayhan's intentions. But I hope, for his sake, that he's insincere.

Staying with 9/11 for the moment, consider the Pentagon crash, and the confiscation of the video from the service station security camera. That the video has never been released is regarded by many as damning evidence that authorities are trying to hide the true nature of the crash: that the video must reveal that it wasn't Flight 77 but a missile, or a fighter jet. But think: perhaps the video remains hidden because some people are quite happy to mindfuck the conspiracists and perpetuate an erroneous line of inquiry. Would they want to lay to rest a mistaken hypothesis, when it misdirects the efforts of so many? It may be that the question is not *What have they got to hide?* but rather, *Why do they want us to think they're hiding something?*

Yesterday's news regarding developments in the Johnny Gosch case was encouraging, but we need to keep our wits about us, about them. The story is that investigator James Rothstein has a former CIA agent on tape admitting the agency's hand in the Gosch abduction. Now sometimes, former CIA agents tell the truth. But quite often, particularly about such dark and sensitive subjects, they don't. Reasonable skepticism about whatever they tell us is a good idea, not least when they tell us what we want to hear. So while I hope Rothstein is onto a strong lead, I have to also ask, could there be a reason why the Agency would intend, at this time, to sow disinformation about this crime?

After all, the best disinformation is that which most closely resembles the truth as we know it. It may look just like what we're expecting to find. But within it is a time bomb, meant to blow up in our faces.

Jim Garrison knew the feeling. He had his case against Clay Shaw blow up because of the cross-examination of Charles Spiesel, a New York accountant he'd belatedly added to his witness list. Spiesel testified he had heard Shaw and David Ferrie discuss the possible assassination of John F. Kennedy. When the chief defense Counsel rose, he "uncannily" knew to destroy Spiesel's credibility, and Garrison's, by probing him about mind control. Spiesel complained that "hypnosis and psychological warfare" had been used on him, and he had been mentally tortured by the NYPD. And who knows: Spiesel could have been a mind-control subject, but it wouldn't have mattered. (This was still years before the declassification, such as it was, of MK-

ULTRA.) In the eyes of the jury his testimony was rendered worthless.

In *On the Trail of the Assassins*, Garrison wrote,

> For one very long moment, while I am sure that my face revealed no concern, I was swept by a feeling of nausea. I realized that the clandestine operation of the opposition was *so cynical, so sophisticated, and, at the same time, so subtle*, that destroying an old-fashioned state jury trial was very much like shooting a fish in a barrel with a shotgun.

Most of us, I think, are good-hearted people who are alive to this material because we recognize injustice and mean for it to end. That can be our strength, but it can also find hobbling expression in naive thinking. I believe on this side we could do with some healthy cynicism, sophistication and subtly of our own. Maybe it could rescue some credibility. Save lives, even.

I think of Gary Caradori, Chief Investigator for the Nebraska Legislature's Franklin committee, calling Senator Loran Schmit and exclaiming, "We've got them! There's no way they can get out of it now!" He was returning from Chicago with photographic evidence of Lawrence King's elite pedophile ring. Schmit took another phone call a short while later, which informed him that Caradori had died in the crash of his small plane. His evidence was never recovered.

We want to *get them*, but let's never again say "There's no way they can get out of it now." Let's think several steps ahead, *because they do*. And when the bad guys shoot fish in a barrel, usually we're the fish. So we'd better be thinking outside the barrel.

It's All
About "them"

March 21, 2005

I t ain't about "us"

Here's a concept that shifted my paradigm: It's of no concern whether I think something ridiculous; what matters is, do *they*? And do they, really?

For instance, I used to have no consideration for secret societies. Why would I? Old boys in aprons, the Templars, Skull and Bones and "Jahbulon" — so what? The subject seemed as serious as *The Simpsons'* musical question, "Who made Steve Guttenberg a star?" It meant nothing to me.

But then, it's not all about me, is it? And self-evidently, secret societies, and the secrets they keep, matter a great deal to many who hold authority over us.

I've never seen a UFO, so my thoughts are uninfluenced by anecdote. And it's easy to dismiss accounts of sightings and abductions as swamp gas, hoaxes, fantasies and delusions. Easy, and preferable, because to admit their reality would be to perturb our understanding of reality. Yet whatever their nature, or natures, UFOs remain an extremely sensitive matter to the National Security State. The amount of disinformation and official scorn the subject continues to accrue is partial evidence of this.

We've seen how ridicule heaped upon sensitive subjects deters serious inquiry. In *Confrontations*, Jacques Vallee writes of a remarkable 1976 sighting in Grenoble, in which a blue-white disc with an intense green halo was viewed by multiple and independent witnesses. The silent disk was seen flying at a constant velocity, then stopping to hover for up to 10 seconds, before flying at a greater speed in a different direction. What makes this sighting particularly notable is that one witness was a senior French physicist, and still the scientific establishment expressed no interest: "To them it was just another UFO report, even if the main witness was one of their colleagues." (Similarly, in *Messengers of Deception*, Vallee recounts personally witnessing astronomers destroy data which detailed observations of "impossible" UFOs, because they didn't want to be regarded as "crazy.")

UFOs have not only been the subject of ridicule, but of official, "serious" investigations, which have co-opted researchers into perpetrating limited hangouts. "Bluebook," for instance, and the *Condon Report*. (And in *The Last Investigation*, Gaeton Fonzi said much the same regarding the House Select Committee on Assassinations.) Officially, these subjects have been investigated. *Officially*, while some questions remain, the cases are closed.

Through the Stargate

Now, let's consider "Project Stargate," the 24-year remote-viewing program of U.S. military intelligence. Which, as with its reluctantly admitted mind-control research, has been *officially* terminated, and pronounced a "failure."

In 1995, the CIA sponsored an evaluation of the Remote-Viewing Program by the "American Institutes for Research." Its derisive conclusions were seized upon by the mainstream press as proof of government waste and the inefficacy of parapsychology. Indeed, the CIA seemed over-eager to promote these impressions. As W. Adam Mandelbaum writes in *The Psychic Battlefield (A History of the Military-Occult Complex)*:

> It is interesting to note how easily obtained this report is.... Your author received a fax of the summary within five minutes of requesting it, and an email copy in about the same amount of time. In two decades of dealing with government bureaucracies, it was the first time I saw such a demonstration of efficiency and public service. After reviewing the report for this history, I appreciated the reasons for such efficiency. The CIA was most anxious that any inquiring party would have the conclusions of the evaluation immediately upon request. These conclusions, as we shall see, were mandated prior to the evaluation having commenced.

In a press release of the Society for Scientific Exploration, Dr. Edwin May, the former director for remote-viewing research, asserted "It is estimated that more than 80,000 pages of program documents remain highly classified," and were not examined for the AIR report, which concluded remote viewing "failed to produce the concrete specific information valued in intelligence gathering."

Mandelbaum makes a case for the program's having produced "concrete specific information":

> In the early days of the research, Pat Price correctly obtained code words from a target site, and accurately rendered structural features of numerous targets. That is concrete and specific. In 1981, Joseph Mc-Moneagle accurately determined via remote viewing that General James Dozier was being held in Padua, and described the correct building. That is concrete and specific. In 1979 McMoneagle and Riley accurately described a Chinese nuclear device at Lop Nor, and a test of a bomb that exploded but failed to go nuclear. That is concrete and specific. The aforesaid AIR conclusion about the failure of operational remote viewing is a concrete and specific misstatement of fact. Put more simply, it is a lie.

Dr. May adds: "There is compelling evidence that the CIA set the outcome with regard to intelligence usage before the evaluation had begun. This was accomplished by limiting the research and operations data sets to exclude positive findings."

An "eyeball roller"

A fascinating refutation of Project Stargate by a Lieutenant Colonel appeared in the Winter, 2000 issue of *The Intelligencer: Journal of US Intelligence Studies*. He calls Stargate an "eyeball roller," and declares remote viewing impossible upon the materialist argument that "the transmission of visual information to the brain simply doesn't occur outside the visual spectrum."

This is fascinating chiefly for who wrote it: Lt. Col. Michael Aquino, of *MindWar* and other notorieties, and founder of the Temple of Set. (It can be viewed as a pdf file here, hosted by the Temple.) The Temples' reading list includes many titles in Enochian magick. A purpose of the Temple is not to promote Elizabethan scholarship, but to do magick. (According to the University of Virginia's curriculum on New Religious Movements, "New members start out as Setian I°, then will advance to Adept II°

after being judged to be skilled at black magic. If new affiliates do not become Adept II° within two years after joining, their membership will be discontinued.")

Whatever remote viewing may be, it is not unusually keen eyesight, which seems to be the basis of Aquino's refutation. It may, in fact, be more akin to a magickal working, something up Aquino's alley. In *Remote Viewing Secrets*, the Pentagon's most successful psychic spy, Joseph McMoneagle, writes that while viewing, he has occasionally encountered "entities" which attempted to impede his vision.

When Aquino left the Church of Satan in 1975, he "performed a Greater Black Magical Working that resulted in (among other things) an inspired document called *The Book of Coming Forth By Night*." Undoubtedly Aquino would have little regard for a debunking of the genesis of his temple's sacred text, based upon a materialist argument concerning the transmission of auditory information to the brain.

Would the CIA intentionally mislead the public regarding the efficacy of its psychic spying? Would the Defense Department rather be regarded as wasteful than as successful? Consider for a moment the admission, on *September 10, 2001*, that the Pentagon has "lost" several trillion dollars over the course of a decade; roughly a third of its budget. Apparently it would prefer to be considered grossly negligent, than to admit to a deep black budget with no oversight.

By the way

Maybe it's time to say this: while I've come think it highly probably there is an occult aspect to the National Security State, I'm not grinding a religious axe about it. Just as with sexual practice, which religious practice often mimics, so long as people are not harmed and no injury is brought to the world, I have no problem with anyone's beliefs, however esoteric.

What alarms me is the increasing body of evidence that people *are* being harmed, and the world is being injured, by a cult abuse which enjoys the sanction of a State *which itself has become a covert practitioner of the Black Arts*. I am not suggesting that all those who are pursuing hermetic knowledge and are involved in the occult — "New Agers," Thelemites, Luciferians and the rest — are conspiring together, or share in the guilt.

For what it's worth, there's the Web site of Aaron C. Donahue, who is both a remote viewer and a Luciferian.

He claims George W. Bush is spiritually possessed, and a "strange tube-like morphology of an intelligence system is noted" within his body. "This tube-like image is commonly seen of Angels operating outside of normal awareness."

I wouldn't have thought so a couple of years ago, but now, it makes perfect sense.

Seeing Things, Saying Things

August 9, 2005

Ain't it just like the night to play tricks when you're tryin' to be so quiet?
We sit here stranded, though we're all doin' our best to deny it.
— Bob Dylan

Talk isn't cheap, not if you have something to say that most folks don't want to hear.

It seems a North American condition that many *consumers* of accounts of High Weirdness and conspiracy want the material to be *for entertainment purposes only*. They become campfire tales intended to raise goose bumps, but all that follows the telling is the falling asleep. What's more, unless people know enough to seek out the more serious and harder-to-find treatments of the subjects, they will know only such winking bastardizations. If you've ever seen a U.S. network documentary on UFOs or the JFK assassination, you may know what I mean.

Other than our time and attention, an entertainment may make no further demands upon us. And that's where most people seem happy to leave issues of the paranormal and parahistory. *Thrill me, scare me, but don't change me.* But a sincere telling of an honest account contains a uneasy challenge: If this could be true, what does it do to my assumptions of the world?

August 21 will mark the 50th anniversary of the "Hopkinsville Incident." You probably know about it, even if you don't think you do. About 7 p.m. Billy Ray Taylor, a guest of the Sutton family, went to the well behind the Sutton farmhouse to draw some water. He ran inside and excitedly reported a silvery saucer shooting flames "all the colors of the rainbow" had passed overhead, stopped, and descended into a gully 300 feet behind the farm. No one took him seriously; no one even went outside to take a look.

Then, about an hour later, all hell broke loose.

[T]he family dog began to bark loudly outside. As customary in this rural area, Lucky and Billy quickly went outside to find the reason of the dog's concern. The dog actually hid under the house and was not seen any more that evening. At a short distance from the front door, both men were stopped dead in their tracks by the sight of a glowing hovering light, which came towards them and allowed them to see that it was in fact a 3 and a half feet tall creature, advancing towards them with hands up, as if to surrender. The bizarre creature would be described as having "two large eyes with a yellow glow, more on the sides than in the human face, a long thin mouth, large bat-like ears, thin short legs, and unusually long arms with large hands ending in claws."

Both men instinctively unloaded their shotguns at the entity, no farther than 20 feet from them. Though they said there was no way they could have missed it, it merely "did a back flip, stood up again, and fled into the woods."

No sooner had the two men reentered the house before the creature, or another like it, appeared at a window. They took a shot at him, leaving a blast hole through the screen. They ran back outside to see if the creature was dead, but found no trace of it. Standing at the front of the house, the men were terrified by a clawed hand reaching down from the roof in an attempt to touch them. Again, they shot, but the being simply floated to the ground, and scurried into the cover of the woods. The two men sought the protection of the house again, only to find themselves under siege from these little men. For a time, the entities seemed to tease the family, appearing from one window to another. Taking pot shots through the windows and walls, their weapons seemed totally ineffective against the creatures.

After three hours of fear turning into sheer panic, with three children crying or shrieking, the Sutton family decided to make a break from the house, and get help at the Police station at Hopkinsville. The farm was located nearer to Kelly, but the nearest police were in Hopkinsville. Family members took two vehicles to the Police Station in Hopkinsville, and reported their strange tale to Sheriff Russell Greenwell. Finally persuading the policemen that they were not joking, the policemen agreed to visit the Sutton house. Arriving at the farm, police found no trace of the creatures, but did find numerous bullet and rifle holes in the windows and walls. Greenwell was in charge of the twenty plus officers at the scene, and reported that the Suttons seemed sober, and were genuinely frightened by something. After a canvass of the neighborhood, reports were entered of the "hearing of shots being fired," and the observation of "lights in the sky."

The police left the farm at approximately 2:15 a.m., having found no hard evidence of the creatures, though "a luminous patch of grass was observed where one of the creatures was shot off a fence." Police Chief Russell Greenwell later stated that he and other investigators sensed a "weird feeling" to the area that night, and said that "something scared those people. Something beyond reason." Soon after, "Mrs. Lankford was lying in bed watching the window when she noticed a weird glow; the glow was one of the creatures staring inward with its hands on the window screen. Calling quietly to the rest of the family, she remained perfectly calm. Lucky Sutton, however, grabbed his gun and again shot at the creature through the screen. No effect. The creatures continued to make their appearance throughout the rest of the night, never doing anything overtly hostile and only seeming to show curiosity. The last creature was seen at half an hour before sunrise, at about 5:15 a.m."

A "bowl-shaped depression" is still visible in the gully where the object was said to have landed. Dorris McCor, who now lives at the site (the farmhouse has long since been demolished), says, "Back when we were kids nothing ever grew on that spot... no weeds or trees or nothing. It hasn't been until the last several years that anything started growing over it again."

The entities, described as "shining, as though nickel-plated," rapidly became known as "little green men." The sober family, whose sincerity and inarticulate trauma impressed investigating officers, was quickly characterized as a clan of drunken hillbillies: ur-caricatures for lazy skeptics to skewer.

One official who had interviewed the family the night of the event, concluding "No evidence of intoxication. Witnesses deemed credible. Consider as possible sighting," returned a few months later, "partly out of curiosity, partly because I felt guilt for being part of this family's nightmare":

Billy Ray refused to talk to me. It seems his reputation in the town had been ruined, going from a well respected Baptist to a shunned alcoholic. *He was held up as an example of what happens to people who tell the truth.* After talking to other family members, I was hesitantly told that the aliens came back that same night, almost seeming to taunt the family before leaving. *The family was confused as to why it was being torn apart by the same people it went to for help.* I never spoke to or heard from them again.

I think about this now as I pass though Kentucky on my way back out. I never saw the official report from that night again. It doesn't exist. 41 years have passed, the document can no longer be classified, and so it is dust. Ashes to ashes, dust to dust. Fair is foul, and foul is fair in America. Just don't get in the way. [emphasis added]

Hopkinsville, having hounded the family in life, now observes the occasion of their trauma with a "little green men" festival. ("What actually occurred on that fateful night is still a mystery, but we are determined to celebrate its occurrence.") Events scheduled include a screening of *Plan Nine from Outer Space*, a Kids' alien costume competition and an "Out Of This World" Karaoke Contest.

(And by the way, it is silly to think of these clawed, naked creatures as sophisticated space travelers. If that's the only answer besides hoax or hysteria, the community may as well make sport of it. But this story alone should debunk the assumption that UFOs must be of extraterrestrial origin. The entities' arrival at the Sutton farmhouse was not a technological achievement; it was a daemonic fact. And perhaps, since they were not seen departing or entering the UFO, we shouldn't assume they arrived upon it. Maybe it's more esoteric than that: could the UFO's own violation of our reality have, somehow, called forth the entities to rush into the gap it had momentarily created? And note: like all other UFO observations, Billy Ray Taylor's was of an aerial phenomenon — they are seen in the near atmosphere, not outer space. So maybe the creatures weren't so far from home after all. Maybe in some sense, given the weird heritage Peter Levenda documents for that part of America in *Sinister Forces*, they were already home.)

Of course, things needn't get this weird before victims and witnesses become convinced that things will go easier for them if they would just *shut up*.

In August of 1965, Green Beret Lt. Col. Daniel Marvin, author of *Expendable Elite*, and then a captain known as "Dangerous Dan," was asked by his commanding officer to meet a CIA official outside the headquarters of the 6th Special Forces at Fort Bragg. Another Special Forces captain, also trained in assassination, joined them outside the building.

"First the Company man took me aside," Marvin says in Kent Heiner's *Without Smoking Gun*, "showed me his badge, his ID card. Then he asked me if I would volunteer to kill a man, a United States citizen, a naval officer, for treason and espionage." Marvin was due for a tour in Vietnam, and assumed he was being asked to kill an American overseas. He agreed — he admits he "had a reputation," but will neither confirm nor deny that he'd previously carried out such assignments — and asked for the name. Lieutenant Commander William Pitzer, he was told, and it was imperative he be terminated before his forthcoming retirement. As the conversation progressed, Marvin learned that Pitzer was stationed in the United States at Bethesda's National Naval Medical Center, where John F. Kennedy's autopsy had been performed. Marvin then refused the assignment, asserting that the CIA's stateside hits were contracted to the Mafia.

Marvin says that the Agency official was obviously irritated that the target's name had been disclosed to a man who no longer had an operational "need to know." He also says that the man knew he could count on Marvin to "forget" both his name and Pitzer's. The official then turned around and headed toward the other captain, who had been waiting some 40 feet away, just out of earshot.

On the evening of October 29, 1966, Lt. Commander Pitzer was found dead in Bethesda's Naval Medical School of a gunshot wound to the right temple. The death was quickly judged a suicide.

Why might the CIA believe it had just cause to kill the man?

A few days after the [Kennedy] assassination, a [Bethesda] colleague, Dennis D. David, found Pitzer working on a 16-mm film, slides and black and white photos of the Kennedy autopsy. David noted that those materials showed what appeared to be an entry wound in the right frontal area with a corresponding exit wound in the lower rear of the skull.

Jerrol F. Custer, an X-ray technician at the hospital, later stated that Pitzer had photographed the proceedings, including the military men who attended the Kennedy autopsy. It was also rumored that Pitzer had copies of Kennedy's autopsy photographs.

Needless to say, the whereabouts of Pizter's rumored photographs and film is unknown.

The Special Forces Association is reportedly mounting a campaign against Marvin and his publisher Trine Day, because it takes exception to his breaking the fraternity's *omerta* on dirty secrets that are supposed to remain hidden even within the world of black ops. In the introduction to **Without Smoking Gun** Marvin writes that "the compartmentalization of various aspects of covert operations impairs every effort to pull all the pieces of the puzzle together.... Super-secret — and sometimes heinous — activities on behalf of our government are thereby masked, permitting total independence of operations [and] affording higher authority total immunity from prosecution."

When you learn some big scary truth about the world, it's always *prudent* to keep it to yourself. Even better: forget about it. This is as true for a Special Forces Lieutenant Colonel who learns of a domestic hit, as it is for a family in rural Kentucky besieged by creatures which should not exist, as it is for a naval officer who by chance had hard evidence that Kennedy's head wounds did not match the official autopsy report. It's only because some people have chosen to talk regardless, sacrificing their careers, their respect and their lives, that we know as much as we do.

Seeing things and remaining quiet about them will change nothing, not even ourselves. But *saying things* — having the courage to testify to our own forbidden knowledge — could be the way the world changes.

Debunking
and Debugging

June 3, 2005

> *Oh teachers are my lessons done? I cannot do another one.*
> *They laughed and laughed and said, "Well, child -*
> *Are your lessons done?"*
> — Leonard Cohen

D ebunk should be a good word — who wants bunk? — but it's not, because debunking is too often a disingenuous exercise. So we need a new word, for something our thinking needs in order to stay intellectually viable. I suggest *debug*.

For examples of both, let's look out on the edge of the High Weird, and UFOs, where debunking runs amuck. Yet no subject more deserves a healthy debugging.

One of the defining characteristics of the UFO phenomenon is apparent absurdity, and there are many minds — most of them not on the payroll of alphabet agencies — who balk at letting its absurdity stand. *Something* rational must be made to account for everything, even when the rational explanations are themselves ridiculous.

For instance, consider the 1959 sightings at the Mission Station of All Saints in Boianai, New Guinea. The case is remarkable for the number and credibility of the witnesses, who included Reverend William Gill (regarded by all investigators as of unimpeachable character), the duration of the sightings, and their considerable absurdity.

Reverend Norman Cruttwell, who had known Gill since his own arrival in New Guinea in 1946, wrote a report of the first event on June 26, reproduced in *The Edge of Reality* by J. Allen Hynek and Jacques Vallee:

> Father Gill had just had his dinner and came out of the front door of
> the Mission House.... He casually glanced at the sky and looked for Ve-

nus, which was conspicuous at the time. In his own words, "I saw Venus, but I also saw this sparkling object which to me was peculiar because it sparkled, and because it was very, very bright, and it was above Venus and so that caused me to watch it for a while, and then I saw it descend towards us." ... Eventually it came quite close and hovered at a height which Father Gill estimated between 300 and 400 feet.... He estimates its apparent diameter as about five inches at arm's length. Stephen [a native teacher] said that if he put his hand out closed it would cover about half of it.

Father Gill states that it changed from a brilliant white light, when it was far off, to a dull yellow, or perhaps pale orange, when it was close. When asked whether he thought it was metallic, he answered, "Well, it appeared solid, certainly not transparent or porous; we just assume that it was metallic from our experience of things that travel and carry men."

All witnesses agree that it was circular, that it had a wide base and a narrower upper deck, that it had a type of legs beneath it, that it produced at times a shaft of blue light which shone upwards into the sky at an angle of about forty-five degrees and that four "human figures" appeared on top....

Here are Father Gill's comments on the "men":

As we watched it men came out from this object, and appeared on the top of it, on what seemed to be a deck.... There were four men in all, occasionally two, then one, then three, then four; we noted the various times the men appeared.... The men appeared to be illuminated not only by this light [emanating from the center of the deck], but also by a sort of glow which completely surrounded them as well as the craft. The glow did not touch them, but there appeared to be a little space between their outline and the light.

The object returned the following night, accompanied by two smaller, stationary UFOs. Father Gill reported again that "We watched figures appear on top — four of them — there is no doubt that they were human.... they were occasionally bending over and raising their arms as though adjusting or 'setting up' something not visible. One figure seemed to be standing, looking down at us (a group of about a dozen)."

Father Gill then did something perfectly natural:

I stretched my arm above my head and waved. To our surprise the figure did the same. Ananias waved both arms over his head, then the two outside figures did the same. Ananias and myself began waving our arms and all four seemed to wave back. There seemed to be no doubt that our movements were answered. All the mission boys made audible gasps (of either joy or surprise, perhaps both).

As dark was beginning to close in, I sent Kodawa for a torch and directed a series of long dashes towards the UFO. After a minute or two of this, the UFO apparently acknowledged by making several wavering motions back and forth (in a side-direction, like a pendulum).... After a further two or three minutes the figures apparently lost interest in us, for they disappeared below deck.

What does a debunker do with this bizarre contact story? Donald Menzel, from his study in the United States, concluded Gill must have been myopic, and was actually looking at Venus (the other witnesses must have been persuaded by their high regard for Gill). Hynek traveled to New Guinea and interviewed Gill and others, who laughed at Menzel's armchair rationalizing. Hynek left persuaded something inexplicable had happened.

A debunker fabricates an explanation that accords with conventional wisdom, which is taken as an excuse to investigate no further by those who are made uncomfortable by the material. It must be dozens of times in recent months that I've read, with regard to Satanic Ritual Abuse, "Oh, that's been debunked," from people who know little more about the subject than a ten-year old TV movie starring James Woods. When figures of authority, even James Woods, claim to debunk an issue, that's enough for many people to check it off as something about which they needn't concern themselves, *even those who regard themselves as naturally distrustful of authority.*

Debunkers are True Unbelievers, whose agenda is to discredit inquiry into subjects which do not conform with their presumptions of the universe. In this regard, the incredulous and the credulous travel the same circle, chasing each other's tails, and have little to do with critical thinking. Which is what we should be about.

Debuggers are different. Rather then quash inquiry, they sharpen and refine it. They fix the broken links in our brains and expose our faulty reasoning. And we *need* our thinking debugged. And we ought to be able to debug the thinking of others without being accused, reflexively, of being "debunkers."

To many UFO true believers — those who *grok* Mulder's "I want to believe" flying saucer poster, and uncritically presume the extraterrestrial hypothesis — Jacques Vallee is a "debunker." Except he's not. His thinking is both more radical, and better founded, than theirs. In *Revelations*, Vallee recounts an encounter with other researchers that could be described as a valiant attempt at debugging. Bill Moore and Linda Moulton Howe are telling him about a joint U.S. and alien underground base in New Mexico, the size of Manhattan, and he stops them short with the question, "Who takes out the garbage?"

The group looked at me in shock. There is a certain unwritten etiquette one is supposed to follow when crashed saucers and government secrecy are discussed ... you are not supposed to point out contradictions in the stories. Questions must always be directed at the higher topics ... not the practical details. In other words, it is not done to ask any question that has a plain, verifiable answer.

"Well, it's a fair question, isn't it? Who takes out the garbage?" I repeated. "You just told me there was a city the size of Manhattan underneath New Mexico. They will need water. They will generate solid waste. There should be massive changes in the environment. Where is the evidence for it?"

When Vallee later asks "How do you know any of this is real?" he is told by Howe "I've spoken to a military officer in the Pentagon." Here again is an example of an investigator who believes there is a massive government cover-up, yet accepts uncritically the word of a government official simply because it's what she wanted to hear. (And Moore, as we've seen, subsequently admitted to having been used by the Air Force to disseminate disinformation among UFO researchers.)

Yesterday morning I was walking along Toronto's Danforth Avenue to meet a friend for breakfast. To the east, the sky was blue. The western sky had been painted with parallel white lines, running north to south, which were beginning to spread on the wind. I told myself, *they're going to start laying down the east to west pattern soon*, and almost as soon, I noticed the two white planes, doing just that. After breakfast, looking up, the city sky was a gauze of white. "Overcast," I would have called it, if I hadn't known better.

Now, what did I see? And, significantly, why could I predict it? I don't know what I saw, but I see it often enough that I can anticipate its pattern. I don't know if chemtrails are Edward Teller's "sunscreen." He wrote that "the simplest plan [to reduce global warming] is to put into the high atmosphere small particles that scatter away one or two percent of the sunlight." But it certainly seems to resemble it. And, to my thinking, it is only a campaign with such a purpose that could gain the tacit cooperation of so many different governments, and remain a secret for fear of spreading panic — albeit justified — at the fragility of our environment.

A chemtrail debunker will try to tell me either (a) I don't see anything, or (b) I've seen it all my life. I used to argue with such people. But time is too short, and things are too weird to waste my time on them. *I don't know what it is, but I know it is*, and I know I didn't see this ten years ago.

So, *debug* me, please. Help me to understand what I'm seeing. Even a prosaic, non-scary explanation will do, so long as it's the right one. But try to *debunk* what I see with my own eyes, and can predict with my experience, and you have nothing to say to me. Just as I, likely, have nothing to say to you.

Signal/Noise

July 27, 2005

And I know that you know that I know that you show
Something is tearing up your mind.
— Bob Dylan

Determining the correct signal-to-noise ratio of history — especially *suppressed history* — is virtually impossible. While we're still living it, it is impossible. Still, even if the exact ratio eludes us, we need to be serious about the process of separating signal from noise. The signature mass casualty events of our age carry a lot of noise — most of it background and incidental, but some of it intentional and malicious — and if we aren't smart about what we do with the noise, we risk losing the signal.

Initially and properly following a crime, everything *should* get swept up as potential evidence. But everything *should not* stay there: there must be, subsequently, a filtering process to assess evidentiary value. The value of the evidence cannot be judged by gross weight alone: we don't make a case by indiscriminately throwing *everything* we have. That doesn't get us a serious hearing. It just sets people ducking.

For a small for-instance of background noise from 9/11, I suggest "Atta's passport." First of all, of course, it wasn't Atta's, but rather Satam Al Suqami's. But four years after the event, it's still frequently misidentified by too many people who should know better. (Ed Asner made the mistake last year in his videotaped greeting to the 9/11 International Inquiries. I know — it's *Ed Asner* — but it started my experience of the inquiry on a bum foot, and set a tone that invited unchallenged assumptions.)

The recovery of the passport soon after the attacks set off early alarms for many, that things were not as they seemed. And if news of the passport's recovery got people thinking that something wasn't right, then good: *everything* was wrong. But anomalous events, such as drilling passenger jets at excess speed into office towers, are going to generate anomalous results — results that have nothing to do with the planning of the crime or its cover-up. I've heard the passport sarcastically described as "miraculously unscathed," which it wasn't, and as "fluttering down," which it didn't. It was propelled, along with Suqami's remains and much debris from the impact of Flight 11, onto the streets of Lower Manhattan. Only those few who assert there were no patsy hijackers at all aboard the airplanes *need* the passport to have been planted. And if the necessity of a hypothesis makes too many demands of this sort upon evidence, then that's good indication that the hypothesis should probably be abandoned.

Much more suspicious, yet overshadowed by the passport in popular thought, was the alleged finding of an Arabic flight manual in Atta's rental car, left at Logan airport. The convenience was reminiscent of the early framing of the narrative regarding Lee Harvey Oswald, and anticipated the discovery of Korans in cars nearby the Madrid bombings.

An example of intentional noise may be Delmart Vreeland. Without rehashing the story, I think Vreeland was an unwitting agent of disinformation who was meant to serve a dual purpose. First, preemptively strike "outrageous conspiracy theories" by poisoning the well with the early word of a con artist. For the first few months following the attacks Vreeland's warning was the story, but Vreeland, the ONI asset, was also a criminal and a liar. To believe him was to discredit yourself. It was Vreeland that David Corn latched onto in his hatchet job on Michael Ruppert that did so much early damage to the reputation of 9/11 skepticism. In retrospect, it almost looks like it was supposed to be that way. Second, for those who went all the way with Vreeland, who were the sponsors of the attacks according to his sources? Why, Russia and Iraq, of course. U.S. authorities were "out of the loop." Imagine that.

Signal or noise? I don't know. There may be no *there* there, but until we know for certain, or as certain as we can know anything here, there's no harm poking around and asking questions, so long as we're prepared to discard the line of inquiry if it comes to nothing. We need to be humble enough to sometimes back up the way we came, saying "I wouldn't go down there if I were you" to people we pass on the way, rather than bash our heads stubbornly against dead ends, shouting "After me!"

There *is*, after all, a synchronicity to ordinary events, so we should be prepared to concede that it is present in extraordinary events as well.

Doom Days

August 16, 2005

> *Whatever's coming, there's no place else to go*
> *Waiting for the moon to show.*
> — Bruce Cockburn

Remember William Shatner as Don, the young husband, in the *Twilight Zone* episode "Nick of Time"? He and his wife grab a booth in the diner of a strange town while their car is being repaired. A devil-headed, coin-operated "Mystic Seer" sits on the table. Don asks it, light-heartedly, if anything interesting ever happens around here, and it answers with a card that reads "It is quite possible." He asks more pointed questions, and with each vague answer that yet seems uncannily accurate, Don freezes with fear and obsession. He can't move.

I thought of it for some reason yesterday morning, reading that the *Charleston Post and Courier* has picked up the "nuke drill to go live" story:

> For the past week, conspiracy theorists have been spinning an elaborate tale of how the U.S. government will turn a terrorism drill in Charleston into a nuclear attack. Why? To give the country a reason to invade Iran, of course.
>
> If this makes no apparent sense, then your other car isn't a black helicopter, and you've never mistaken Crab Bank at low tide for a grassy knoll.

...

> One Web site says the idea is that the exercise was intended to "go live" and be used for cover for a real attack. For proof, they say terrorism drills were planned in the United States on 9/11 and in London on 7/7.

Will an American city burn this summer? *It is quite possible.* That's as definitive as our Magic 8 Ball gets about such matters. Will the Fort Monroe exercise "go live"? *It is quite unlikely.* Especially now.

When the other shoe drops, it probably won't be the one we're expecting. But you know what? After all our studious anticipation, we'll know enough to know it's a shoe, and who dropped it. And there's also this: there is the possibility that public expectation — raising our own terror alert over "chatter," suspicious movements and exercises — could possibly forestall synthetic terror events. Why not? It's the same logic Tom Ridge applied to measure the success of Homeland Security. It can never be verified but I have to wonder what might have not happened if, before 7/7, someone had got wind of the drills and posted *"Look out, London: the morning of July 7 there's an 'anti-terror' simulation of simultaneous detonations of three bombs at the following stations."* (A "fear monger" might have added *"OMG, Giuliani's going to be in town!"*) If the news of the drill had entered public consciousness beforehand to the degree that Fort Monroe's drill has in Charleston — this was a front-page story — it's difficult to imagine the bombings proceeding as planned. And so, when no bombs exploded, those who had sounded the alarm would likely think they'd gotten excited over nothing, and might be reticent to do the same again. In such a scenario, this is the price of success: ignorance.

So we shouldn't be shy on Thursday, after the world hasn't blown up more than usual on Wednesday, about sharing what we see, next time we see an ominous convergence of opportunities. It's not forecasting — we've already done that to the limits of our knowledge when we say Americans can expect 90% probability of more of the same — it's saying *This is probably nothing, but — Heads up*. We're not crying wolf here. After all, we know there is a wolf, and we know him well enough to know he'll strike again when he has the chance and the need. But perhaps, the closer we observe him, and the more vocal we are about it, the more we reduce his chances. His need — there's not much we can do about that.

There may be some magical thinking involved in this. *If you don't want doomsday to come, assign a date to it.* But given the times, we could do worse.

Now go back to the diner in the *Twilight Zone*. Do you see Don's problem? He's been overwhelmed, to the point of paralysis, by *what might be*. Can you relate? Sometimes I feel like I've spent the past four years in that booth, asking questions — the

Mystic Seer is now cable-ready — and catching my breath at some answers. Don gave his power to the little box, rather than gain power — that is, true knowledge — from it. And much of the problem is the quality, and integrity, of the "Mystic Seer." Including, and especially, "inside sources."

"Mystic Seers" of a sort are a common feature of UFO close encounters. Contactees often report being presented with confusing apocalyptic imagery, sometimes seemingly projected onto a screen, the meaning of which they don't understand. They are assured they will know when the time comes, and that when the time comes, they'll know what to do.

But as often noted in earlier posts, whether the occupants of a particular UFO are genuine alien entities or black ops technicians, their conduct and communication appears to be both tricksterish and disinformative. While many minor "prophecies" may be said to be fulfilled, the promised Transformative Event — Armageddon or ascension to a higher plane of being — always seems to recede into the future. The date eludes us.

"The Aviary, the Aquarium, and Eschatology" is a nearly 10-year old essay by Vince Johnson, a UFOlogist and self-described "unabashed secular humanist," who nevertheless concedes that non-secular aspects of the phenomenon merit attention. For instance, he writes of data received from Dan Smith, a "theologically-oriented researcher" reputed to have congressional and intelligence sources privy to "the grave concern by high government officials about an impending metaphysical catastrophe." Most fascinating, Johnson quotes an extract from a paper by Ray Boeche, a Lincoln, Nebraska, theologian and Fortean researcher.

Boeche writes:

> To all interested researchers:
>
> The following is an edited version of material given to me in late 1991 — early 1992, by two scientists who claim to be working in weapons research and development for the Department of Defense.
>
> I am not in a position to comment on the truthfulness or accuracy of the information. The two men who have spoken to me do, in fact, exist, and for all intents and purposes seem to be who and what they claim. The very nature of the claims makes verification difficult, if not impossible.
>
> Divulging this information was the result of a moral dilemma, when these two individuals, both Christians, became alarmed at the course

their research efforts into psychotronic weapons was taking under the direction of their (unnamed) superiors. They described an obsessive effort to contact and attempt to control what they referred to as "non-human intelligences" (NHI), and to harness these NHI for military and intelligence uses.

The efforts had progressed well past attempts at practical applications of David Bohm's theories, and had grown to encompass the use of, according to their statements, "satanic rituals/ritual magic along the lines of that espoused by Aleister Crowley, including human sacrifices."

These gentlemen stated their concerns that, even when they were apparently able to harness or channel these forces or abilities for "good" uses, the force would "turn," and ultimately all of those subjects involved suffered varying degrees of negative effects from contact with these forces. They are convinced that what is being tapped into in all instances is evil, and that this research should cease.

At this point, I should be forgiven for exclaiming *"Whoomp, there it is!"* since what these two DoD scientists told Boeche 14 years ago conforms with my working hypothesis of the convergence of satanic ritual, UFOs and military intelligence. And yet, do you hear me whoomping? It's always important to question the integrity of official sources, but I think it's most important *when they appear to tell us what we want to hear.*

Johnson writes that Boeche, smartly, "was at a loss to explain why the two DoD scientists were still working on projects they found to be morally repugnant, and if they really wanted to blow the whistle on this activity, why did they reveal it to an obscure UFOlogist and not the *New York Times* or *Nightline*. Was it disinformation? If so, what was the motivation?

Boeche's contacts also supplied a list of victims of psychotronic weapons experiments. (For instance: "Female, white, 20-25 yr., allegedly death by remotely transmitting and creating head trauma equivalent to crushing of right anterior portion of the skull.") For me, intuitively, this list does not have the ring of truth, as does the rest, since I've already seen evidence for the rest from so many different sides. And since the best disinformation is mostly truth, if this communication were disinformative, could this addition have been the poison pill to misdirect a researcher already sniffing around the Military Occult Complex? (*It is quite possible*, says the Mystic Seer.)

Johnson, by the way, adds: "if there really is such a thing as 'black magic,' and government scientists are experimenting with it, I suspect that they could be blindly running the same risks in dealing with such unknown forces as the 19th-century scientists who thought nothing of casually handling radium and other radioactive materials."

Stranger things have happened. And don't you just hate that?

6. "A Great and Terrible Paw"

Thou shalt be secret, a fear to the world.

— Aleister Crowley

The Banality of the Weird

March 8, 2005

I've been thinking the last few days of Peter Malkin, the Mossad agent who snatched Adolph Eichmann from a Buenos Aires sidewalk in 1962. He died last week in New York City, at 77. I wonder if, before his death, he'd read the *Jerusalem Post* story of February 6 entitled "CIA employed Eichmann's men." And if he had, whether he felt punk'd.

Actually, I doubt it. A lifetime in an Intelligence service would have prepared Malkin for such wrong-headed weirdness. In his world, Eichmann's boys going to work for the CIA probably wasn't the most egregious example. Just one of those things: a compromise with evil; one of many. Shit happens.

America started going seriously wrong some time ago. About the same time Eichmann's men — and Mengele's, and others — were recruited into its service. And coincident with that, America started going seriously weird.

To many students of the National Security State, the one has nothing to do with the *other*. In fact, they regard the study of the other — the UFOs, the Satanic Ritual Abuse and mind control — as a distraction and discrediting embarrassment: an insult to the intelligence. Which has made for one big, ever-lovin' *"Mission accomplished!"* for those who shield their High Crimes in the stealth folk-mythology of apparent absurdity.

The Weird is entertained, chiefly, as *entertainment*: anomalous episodes that do nothing to inform us about the real world. With respect to UFOs, the propagation of the extraterrestrial hypothesis as the only option, after ruling out the like of hoaxes, Venus and swamp gas, further this misapprehension of their significance and implication for America. (I've written elsewhere — about perhaps a more fantastic, and yet I think more credible and sinister, explanation of the phenomena.)

But here's a noodle scratcher: the episodes are not as anomalous as we may think. In fact, in *Messengers of Deception*, one of Jacques Vallee's arguments against UFO's extraterrestrial provenance is that there are *too darn many of them*:

The first argument against the idea of flying saucers as spacecraft lies, oddly enough, in the large number of verified, unexplained sightings. In my own files [circa late '70s] I currently have approximately 2,000 cases of close encounters from every country on Earth, many of them involving occupants of various sizes and shapes. It may seem that 2,000 cases in some 20 years is not a very large number, but we are talking only about the cases that were actually reported....

Most landings are reported to take place after 6pm. The frequency distributions that my computer studies have disclosed for every continent show this activity peaking at about 10:30pm, decreasing sharply after that time, and increasing again just before dawn. There are few reports after 6am. What could this mean? That the activity of the objects is nocturnal by nature and by choice. Then why do the reports decrease in frequency around midnight? Simply because people go to bed: after 10:30pm the number of potential witnesses is severely reduced. Then let us ask the question: how many reports would we have if people did not go to bed but stayed outside to watch those so-called "spacecraft"? The answer is, about 30,000. We would have to multiply the number of cases by a factor of 15.

Now, this last figure does not begin to approximate the actual number of events, because we know from many independent studies that only one case in ten ever gets reported. Then we should have not 30,000, but 300,000 cases in our files! But this still isn't the whole story: most landings occur in unpopulated areas, away from dwellings. If the Earth's population were distributed evenly instead of being concentrated in city areas, how many reports would we have? Again, taking a conservative multiplying factor of ten leads to the staggering conclusion that the UFOs, if they are spacecraft engaged in a general survey of our planet, must have landed here no fewer than three million times in two decades!

This is one of the little-recognized facts of the UFO problem that any theory has yet to explain. The theory of random visitation does not explain it. Either the UFOs select their witnesses, or they are something entirely different from space vehicles. In either case, their appearances are staged.

The Weird has become the background noise of a Lost America. Few hear it at all, and fewer still for what it could be. (I was going to write, "for what it is," but I think all conclusions we may draw about the deep and dark things that are meant to stay hidden ought to be provisional.) The Weird hides in plain sight, because most people are comfortable remaining willfully blind to it. And almost all the rest are too self-conscious to say "*Er — do you see what I see?*" And behind that hides a world gone wrong.

Now about those UFOs over the Capitol. Here's Richard Dolan, writing in *UFOs and the National Security State*:

> At about 11:40 p.m. on July 19 [1952], radar at Washington National Airport picked up a formation of seven objects flying near Andrews AFB, moving along at a leisurely pace of 100 to 130 mph. Before long, two of the targets suddenly accelerated and vanished off the scope within seconds. One of them apparently reached 7,000 mph. This got the attention of several controllers, especially when they learned that a second radar at the airport, as well as the radar at Andrews AFB, also picked up the objects. For six hours, between eight and ten UFOs were tracked on radar.
>
> The senior air traffic controller for the CAA, Harry G Barnes, "knew immediately that a very strange situation existed." In his opinion:
>
> "...[T]he movements were completely radical compared to those of ordinary aircraft. They followed no set course [and] were not in any formation, and we only seemed to be able to track them for about three miles at a time... [F]or six hours...there were at least ten unidentifiable objects moving above Washington. They were not ordinary aircraft.... I can safely deduce that they performed gyrations which no known aircraft could perform."
>
> ...But the phenomenon was not restricted to radar tracking. Several Capitol Airlines pilots saw the objects visually as orange lights in the same area that radar indicated they should be. Just where were they? Over the White House and Capitol!

Intense sightings of clustered formations continued in the skies of Washington for several days. On July 29, the Air Force held a press conference — its largest since the end of the Second World War — and announced the phenomenon had been caused by a "temperature inversion" that mucked up the radar, and the visual sightings were attributed to "scintillating stars." Explanations about as satisfying as Scott McClellan's derisive snort of "conspiracy theory." But like McClellan's rote response, it did the job of getting the press to back off a sensitive and awkward subject.

Washington has seen a lot of weirdness, and not only in its skies. A male prostitute in the White House press corps also hid in plain sight, and how many then said, *"Do you see what I see?"*

If Americans are ever to dismantle the National Security State and have something like a country again, they need to take the Weird with the Wrong. This may mean entertaining, in the best possible sense, the consideration that its nightmare machinery is not just about the black ops, but also the black arts.

Or, as Donald Rumsfeld's note to self on the afternoon of September 11 advised, *"Go massive. Sweep it all up. Things related and not."*

The Black Lodge

May 4, 2005

"Now the veale is pluckt away"
— Edward Kelly, in John Dee's Liber Mysteriorum Quintus, 1583

"Where we're from, the birds sing a pretty song"

Now, here's an anniversary that shouldn't be allowed to pass without mention.

On this day in 1969, a Brazilian military policeman named Jose Antonio Da Silva, "of excellent personal character and reputation," was fishing on the banks of the Rio das Velhas, north of Belo Horizonte. Suddenly, about 3 p.m., he became aware of movement in the brush behind him, and saw a "burst of light" hit his legs. Da Silva quickly became numb, and dropped his fishing rod and fell to his knees.

In *Dimensions*, Jacques Vallee writes that Da Silva claims he was then "seized by two masked individuals about four feet tall, wearing dull aluminum suits, who took him to a machine that looked like an upright cylinder. Inside the craft the beings gave him a helmet similar to their own, tied him up, and took off."

During the flight — or at least, during the *sensation* of flight — the creatures "talked among themselves in an incomprehensible language with many R's. At one point in the journey the craft seemed to turn on its side for a while."

After traveling for an "interminable" time, the machine landed and the creatures unfastened Da Silva. They bandaged his helmet, so he couldn't see where he was being taken, and he was forcibly dragged past the sound of many strange voices. He was placed in a backless seat and the bandage was removed.

Vallee writes that "Jose Antonio found himself in a large quadrangular room, thirty by forty feet, about fifteen feet away from a robust dwarf who stared at him 'with apparent satisfaction.' The dwarf was extremely hairy."

The following description of the strange figure comes from an investigation of the case recorded in the November/December, 1973 issue of *The Flying Saucer Review*:

His long tresses, reddish and wavy, fell down behind past his shoulders to his waist; his beard was long and thick and came down to his stomach. He had wide-set eyebrows, two fingers thick, running right across the whole forehead. His skin was light-colored, very pale. His eyes were round, larger than is the norm with us, and of a green shade like the color of green leaves beginning to wither.

Other similar beings entered Da Silva's field of vision, until about 15 filled the room. The three walls he could see had neither doors nor windows, appeared to be made of stone, and were adorned with frescos of animals, including a jaguar, monkey, giraffe and elephant, as well as paintings of vehicles and houses. "To his left," writes Vallee, "was a low shelf with the corpses of four men." At one point he was given "something to drink out of a cubical stone glass, and the cavity containing a dark green liquid was in the shape of an inverted pyramid," which restored his energy and seemed, somehow, to aid communication.

The principal dwarf began gesturing to Da Silva, in a manner which the soldier interpreted as a request that he be their guide in the human world. He gestured his refusal, and began to nervously finger his rosary.

According to the FSR report:

The leader stepped towards him and, displaying irritation for the first time, seized the crucifix and snatched it from him. One of the beads rolled onto the floor and was picked up by one of the little men, who showed it to the others. The crucifix was passed around in the same way, arousing curiosity in all of them.

Da Silva claims that at this time, he had a vision of a Christ-like figure, barefoot and wearing a dark robe, who revealed something to him of a coming disaster that would affect all humanity, which may be averted by the intervention of other beings. (Da Silva has refused to reveal any more details of the communication.) As the apparition vanished, "the irritated dwarves blindfolded him again, and he was transported back…. He woke up alone near the town of Vitoria in the state of Espirito Santo, 200 miles away from the spot where he had been fishing." He had been missing for five days.

Twelve days after his abduction, Da Silva was awakened by a sudden urge to go outside, where he saw three of the red-bearded creatures. Quickly, he re-entered his house and locked the door against them.

Since the weird account rests almost solely on Da Silva's words, perhaps we should ascribe it to a desperate attempt to cover some mundane "missing time." And indeed, this is the kind of case which "respectable" UFOlogists like to cull from the data, because it reads more like a visitation of fairies or trolls than by curious explorers from Zeta Reticuli in a nuts and bolts spaceship. (Did the "stone room" exist on an alien world, or an alien Earth?) And the religious element — the Christ figure — would discount the value of the episode to most "serious" observers.

But what if "UFOs" — which *are unidentified*, but which often are seen to *not fly*, as we understand flight, and which sometimes *don't behave like material objects* — what if "UFOs" are, on a certain level of meaning, another variety of religious experience? And a particular experience which is always capricious and often deceitful, which regularly violates witnesses' physical and psychic boundaries, and occasionally is manifested malevolently.

Jacques Vallee notes how closely Jose Antonio Da Silva's experience mirrors an occult initiation ceremony:

1. The candidate is confronted by members of the occult group wearing a special costume.

2. He is blindfolded.

3. He is led by the arm through a rough and difficult route.

4. He is taken into a specially designed chamber with no windows and placed in such a way that he can only see part of it.

5. He is brought in to the presence of a "Master."

6. He is given a test and made to answer questions.

7. He is shown a variety of symbols designed to remind him of death.

8. The situation suggests that he may not survive the ordeal.

9. He is given ritual food or drink.

10. He is blindfolded again and led outside.

"All of these elements," Vallee writes, "are present in the case of Jose Antonio. To this we must add that everything in the room appeared to be made out of stone. The drinking cube with the inverted pyramid cavity is an exquisite last touch."

"Wow Bob, wow"

The case of Jose Antonio Da Silva is certainly bizarre, but in the unexpurgated annals of UFO history it is not particularly exceptional. That's distressing, and on many levels. Not least, for those who entertain the extraterrestrial hypothesis, who have only the image of emotionless "Greys" fixed in their heads, and who want things to *make sense*. And in a sensible world, even one that allows for alien visitation and abduction, there is no place for red-bearded dwarves in a room of stone. But when you have time, and I mean a *lot* of time, dip into this database of humanoid encounters, maintained by the Northwest Saskatchewan UFO Research Center, and see the varieties of contact. (And I advise against it at three in the morning, alone in your dank basement.) Then consider that unreported cases are estimated to outnumber those reported by a factor of ten.

Undoubtedly, many encounters could be ascribed to the mere chemistry of the brain. But perhaps "mere chemistry" is a poor choice of words. Perhaps chemistry — *which has long been used in conjunction with magick* — actually does unlock hyperspace. The late psychonaut Terence McKenna said that "Right here and now, one quanta away, there is raging a universe of active intelligence that is transhuman, hyperdimensional, and extremely alien."

McKenna claimed his experiences on the powerful psychoactive DMT, which is naturally produced in small quantities in the brain, were "true hallucinations" of hyperreality.

Cliff Pickover writes "As a metaphor, consider infrared goggles":

> A person leans on a tree. At night, we don't see the person. Put the goggles on, and a new reality results — a truer reality — and we see the man. Similarly, is it possible that our brain is a filter, and the use of

DMT is like slipping on infrared goggles, allowing us to perceive a valid reality that is inches away and all around us?

Dr. Rick Strassman's *DMT: The Spirit Molecule* contains many fascinating records of the entheogenic universe which, for many users, displays the characteristics of a genuine reality, subject to exploration, and populated by entities that have existence distinct from the observer. Most commonly seen are playful elves, and mantid-like entities of cold intellect, which perform examinations upon the human subject.

From the accounts:

There are surprising and remarkable consistencies among volunteers' reports of contact with nonmaterial beings. Sound and vibration build until the scene almost explosively shifts to an "alien" realm. Volunteers find themselves on a bed or in a landing bay, research environment, or high-technology room. The highly intelligent beings of this "other" world are interested in the subject, seemingly ready for his or her arrival and wasting no time in "getting to work." There might be one particular being clearly in charge, directing the others. Volunteers frequently comment about the emotional quality of the relationships: loving, caring, or professionally detached. Their "business" appeared to be testing, examining, probing, and even modifying the volunteer's mind and body.

...

I was lying on what seemed to be a large marble slab, cold and hard. Surrounding me were four tall (7') emerald green mantis type creatures, all chittering at me in some high pitched language. I felt no fear, no threat. It seemed they were trying to communicate, though none of their sounds made any sense to me. This went on for what seemed like about a half hour. Then I began to wonder how I would get back, and as that thought crossed my mind, it was like a rubber band contracting, as I snapped back from hyperspace, and into my body.

McKenna once again, asking, "What happens on DMT?":

A troop of elves smashes down your front door, and rotates and balances the wheels on the afterdeath vehicle, presents you with the bill and then departs. And it's completely paradigm shattering. I mean, you know, union with the white light you could handle. An invasion of your apartment by jeweled self-dribbling basketballs from hyperspace that are speaking demotic Greek is not something that you anticipated and could handle. Sometimes people say, "Is DMT dangerous? It sounds so crazy. Is it dangerous?" The answer is, only if you fear death by astonishment.

Remember how you laughed when this possibility was raised ... and a moment will come that will wipe the smile right off your face.

Before things get too hippy and trippy, let's remember this: not only does U.S. military-intelligence have an occult aspect; it is also the conductor of the world's most significant chemical experimentations. Most famously, powerful  psychoactives. "Between the years 1947 and 1963, *CIA and Army scientists examined, tested, and in some cases refined every drug which subsequently became available on the black market* during the 1960's, including marijuana, cocaine, heroin, PCP, amyl nitrate, mushrooms, *DMT*, barbiturates, laughing gas, and speed, among others." I wonder what unexpected discoveries were made in the course of such work.

If it's true that hyper-real portals exist and can be accessed by humans, then it shouldn't surprise us terribly if the denizens of hyperspace have found a means to visit us.

Because see, here's the one uncomfortable fact about UFOs that we can speak with confidence: *they should be hallucinations, but too often, they are not.* They leave behind traces of themselves in our reality: bizarre radar returns, singed vegetation, multiple and independent witnesses, burns and pricks on the flesh of abductees. And yet the signature of encounters is a logic which appears to us absurd, or perhaps archaic to our modern minds. Perhaps it would have made more sense to our ancestors, who recounted many similar visitations.

Consider two more cases, from Vallee's *Dimensions*:

On November 6, 1957, twelve-year old *Everett Clark*, of Dante, Tennessee, opened the door to let his dog Frisky out. As he did so, he saw a peculiar object in a field a hundred yards or so from the house. He thought he was dreaming and went back inside. When he called the dog twenty minutes later, he found the object was still there, and Frisky was standing near it, along with several dogs from the neighborhood. Also near the object were two men and two women in ordinary clothing. One of the men made several attempts to catch Frisky, and later another dog, but had to give up for fear of being bitten. Everett saw the strange people, who talked between them "like German soldiers he had seen in movies," *walk right into the wall of the object*, which then took off straight up without a sound. It was oblong and of "no particular color."

In another of the tantalizing coincidences with which UFO researchers are now becoming familiar, on *the same day another attempt to steal a dog was made*, this time in *Everittstown*, New Jersey. The name of the town in the second case is *almost identical* to that of the witness in the first.

While the Clark case had taken place at 6:30 a.m., it was at dusk that John Trasco went outside to feed his dog and saw *a brilliant egg-shaped object* hovering in front of his barn. In his path he met a being three feet tall "with putty-colored face and large frog-like eyes," who said in broken English: "We are peaceful people, we only want your dog."

The strange being was told in no uncertain terms to go back where he belonged. He ran away, and his machine was seen to take off straight up some moments later. Mrs. Trasco is said to have observed the object itself from the house, but not the entity. She is also quoted as saying that when her husband tried to grab the creature, he got some green powder on his wrist, but that it washed off. The next day he noticed the same powder under his fingernails. The ufonaut had been *dressed in a green suit with shiny buttons, a green tam-o'-shanter-like cap*, and gloves with a shiny object at the tip of each. [emphases added]

Most "serious" UFOlogists would happily purge these episodes from their records. (A "green tam-o'-shanter"? Moving right along....) Yet, disquietingly, they contain many of the same elements which also appear in cases used to support the extraterrestrial hypothesis. And they are more typical of close encounters than they are not.

In the fall of 1954, France experienced an explosion of novelty, with a rash of UFO sightings and close encounters. Here are a couple of brief examples, from Richard Dolan's *UFOs and the National Security State*:

> Yet another humanoid encounter took place two nights later [September 28] in the town of Bouzais. A man noticed that someone had *stolen grapes* from his vineyard and decided to stay up late and catch the thief. At about 10:30 p.m., he saw a luminous object descend and three figures emerge. He was then paralyzed and lost consciousness.
>
> ...
>
> [On October 5] at about 6:30 a.m., near Le Mans, some Renault employees were going to work when they saw a luminous object on the ground near the road. They felt "pricklings and a sort of paralysis." The object then emitted a burst of green light and flew away very low over the fields. At 3:45 p.m., near Beaumont, several people saw a bright object coming toward them. When it was about five hundred feet away, they felt a strange sensation and became paralyzed. The object left a smell similar to nitrobenzene. Two reports that day also emerged of *hairy dwarfish beings*; in both cases the creatures took off in crafts that swiftly departed. [emphases added]

And from NWSURC's database of humanoid encounters, this July, 2000 incident from Buenavista, Argentina:

> After hearing noises and strange voices coming from the kitchen area 10-year-old Marisol Diaz went to investigate and was confronted by several short figures both males and females, resembling "little dwarfs." They had human-like features, with large eyes, pinkish colored skin, wearing white shimmering clothing, boots, and the men wore some type of headgear. The tallest of the figures, apparently a male, appeared to be bearded. The female entity had long blond hair and the shorter figures (children?) wore short pants and shoes. *They seemed to have been examining some cleaning detergent and other kitchen items.* They spoke in an unknown language that somehow the little girl was able to understand. They seemed to be commenting on the toxic make up of the cleaning detergent. Upon noticing the little girl, the little group quickly exited out the rear patio. *There an adult witness, who apparently saw more similar figures on top of a nearby tree, saw them.* In the same area there had been reports of low flying multicolored lights and other phenomena. [emphases added]

The entities' desire to retrieve dogs, the theft of grapes, the examination of kitchen detergent, of Da Silva's fishing equipment and rosary, are of a kind with the frequent observation of UFO occupants collecting specimens of flora and fauna, which is typically interpreted by researchers as aliens conducting "scientific surveys." (Though the tremendous number of reported sightings, and the estimated unreported visitations, would seem to undermine the intellectually-soothing "survey" explanation.) Vallee writes: "the stories quoted in this connection verge on the ludicrous. *But to pursue the investigation further leads to horror.* This is a facet of the phenomenon we can no longer ignore."

If ritual, satanic abuse is *genuinely* perpetrated and covered-up by authorities and institutions sworn to protect the innocent; if elites are *really* raping and murdering children with impunity and without qualm, then *something* has seriously altered their sense of reality, and for a purpose. To commit such crimes, *they must think they know something we don't. Something* has satisfied them that the great religions are lies for slaves, and that the universe belongs to strange and bloody gods.

Those who dismiss Aleister Crowley's visions often say they were the product of deep trance states enhanced by drugs. But altered states have long been a part of religious experience. And as we've seen, there's an ancient alchemy of chemistry and magick, and today's chemistry does appear to open doors to strange, other realities and entities, similar to those claimed to be visiting us.

From one of Thelema's holy books, Liber LXVI, *Liber Stellae Rubeae*, some words which Crowley was inspired to write:

21. Then again the master shall speak as he will soft words, and with music and what else he will bring forward the Victim.

22. Also *he shall slay a young child* upon the altar, and the blood shall cover the altar with perfume as of roses.

23. Then shall the master appear as He should appear — in His glory.

...

48. I am Apep, O thou slain One. Thou shalt slay thyself upon mine altar: I will have thy blood to drink.

49. For I am a mighty vampire, and my children shall suck up the wine of the earth which is blood.

50. Thou shalt replenish thy veins from the chalice of heaven.
51. Thou shalt be secret, a fear to the world.

Elites have not dabbled in occult matters for simple curiosity, or to encounter the divine, or to feel "one with the universe." It is not to raise human consciousness that the Pentagon has experimented with drugs. Every exploration, every occult "working" has been to accrue more power to itself. This is the logic of magick's left-hand path, the politics of which is fascism, with an aristocratic bearing. (And let's not forget, Crowley himself was an asset of British intelligence, whose file was labeled "use with extreme caution.")

In many encounters, as in Da Silva's, the entities ask the humans to be their guides into our reality, or tell them they have been chosen for the purpose. See, for another example, Victor K.'s story from Russia, in 1991. Victor was told he was selected to be their "representative" on Earth. The entities explained that they needed a representative because "we expend too much energy during terrestrial materialization." Interestingly, when Victor asked how they moved about in space, he received the answer *"We do not move, we are everywhere all the time."* (Afterwards, "Victor suffered from unexplained seizures, headaches and strange markings were found on his body.")

Da Silva, we saw, said no. Victor's answer is unrecorded. I wonder what would result if someone who also had authority in this world, or could speak on behalf of such an authority, said yes.

There's nothing left for the Hubble to do but fall, and NASA can't spare a few million to keep in touch with the Voyager spacecraft just as things get interesting again out there at the heliopause. Such priorities suggest that authorities have concluded that, regardless of whether the truth is out there, power is not. And it's the accruing of power, not intellectual titillation, that really drives the research dollars. Such priorities suggest that, though UFOs must continue to be of extreme sensitivity to the defense establishment, the extraterrestrial explanation is a tremendous sleight of hand.

Remember *Twin Peaks'* rogue agent, Windom Earle? I don't think he's a rogue anymore. I think he has a seat at the table:

Once upon a time, there was a place of great goodness, called the White Lodge. Gentle fawns gamboled there amidst happy, laughing spirits. The sounds of innocence and joy filled the air. And when it rained, it rained sweet nectar that infused one's heart with a desire to live life in truth and beauty.

Generally speaking, a ghastly place, reeking of virtue's sour smell. Engorged with the whispered prayers of kneeling mothers, mewling newborns, and fools, young and old, compelled to do good without reason.

But, I am happy to point out that our story does not end in this wretched place of saccharine excess. For there's another place, its opposite: a place of almost unimaginable power, chock full of dark forces and vicious secrets. No prayers dare enter this frightful maw. Spirits there care not for good deeds or priestly invocations. They are as likely to rip the flesh from your bone as greet you with a happy "Good day!" And if harnessed, these spirits in this hidden land of unmuffled screams and broken hearts would offer up a power so vast that its bearer might reorder the earth itself to his liking. This place I speak of, is known as the Black Lodge. And I intend to find it.

Now's a good time to ask: am I just scaring myself? Is talk like this just a stupid, spook-house indulgence, when the mundane world alone is enough to make my hair stand on end? I hope so. But *I don't know*. And regardless of whether something like the Black Lodge has hyperspatial existence — something ancient, and evil, and powerful, that can impinge upon our time and space — *I do know* that some of those who would presume to rule us, who have assembled for centuries in their own lodges and secret orders, have, for a long while, intended to find such a place.

So perhaps we ought to inquire, as best we can, whether their pursuits have enjoyed success. And perhaps the first thing we should do is ask, If they have had success, what kind of world would this be?

"From beyond the stars"

May 15, 2005

I hear the Crawling Chaos that calls from beyond the stars.
— The Necronomicon

We have a calling from beyond the stars.
— George W. Bush, January 19, 2005

The Bush Mythos

H.P. Lovecraft wrote that "the most merciful thing in the world, I think, is the inability of the human mind to correlate all its contents." Increasingly, it seems to me that mercy is being withheld from us.

Perhaps it's an Internet thing: the digitization of data has enhanced our own Random Access Memory. That isn't to say we're necessarily correlating correctly — even if everything's connected, that doesn't mean our model of how they connect is accurate — but more than ever, we're seeing dots. What we do with them is becoming the question of our time. And it's on the meta-level of myth that some of the most significant connections can be made.

I doubt that George W. Bush knew, as he delivered his speech at the "Celebration of Freedom" concert on the eve of his second inaugural, that its most memorable line was straight out of Lovecraft's Cthulhu Mythos. His speech writers also were likely unaware that their prose evoked nothing so much as the "Great Old Ones" from beyond space and time. But that's the thing about a myth, even one created by a pulp fiction writer: you needn't even know it exists to become a part of it.

Intentional or not, the nod to Cthulhu was apt. Lovecraft's apocalypse is of awakened Elder Gods who resume their rule of Earth when humanity becomes sufficiently like them: "free and wild and beyond good and evil, with laws and morals thrown aside and all men shouting and killing and reveling in joy. Then the liberated Old Ones would teach them new ways to shout and kill and revel and enjoy themselves, and all the Earth would flame with a holocaust of ecstasy and freedom." Now that sounds like a crusader religion fit for the Pentagon. (I could see the promise of "new ways to kill" being the subject of a flurry of memos.) And Bush seems to be doing as much to hasten this End of the World as he is of the Armagadeon of his supposed Christian faith.

Of course Lovecraft was writing fiction. Though as we noted here, Michael Aquino has written several Cthulhu-derived ritual ceremonies, and Kenneth Grant of the Typhonian OTO and the Cult of Lam regards Lovecraft as an unwitting prophet of the Left Hand Path. (Consider the gravity with which some hold Lovecraft's "prophetic fiction" here, in a treatise on the "Aeon of Cthulhu Rising.") Still, it's likely not Cthulhu calling. Though something seems to be.

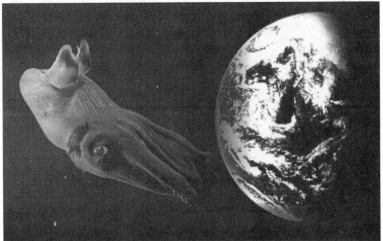

"A Special Evil"

So I'll give Bush the benefit of the doubt on Cthulhu, and believe he didn't know what he was saying. But there was another speech. And I'm afraid he knew exactly what he was saying, and also what he wasn't.

Do you remember his address to the UN General Assembly on September 23, 2003? It was his chance to win back the world on Iraq after the debacle of invasion and during the atrocity of occupation. The speech was consumed with the "War on Terror," until this strangely discordant note was struck:

There's another humanitarian crisis spreading, yet hidden from view. Each year, an estimated 800,000 to 900,000 human beings are bought, sold or forced across the world's borders. Among them are hundreds of thousands of teenage girls, and others as young as five, who fall victim to the sex trade. This commerce in human life generates billions of dollars each year — much of which is used to finance organized crime.

There's a special evil in the abuse and exploitation of the most innocent and vulnerable. The victims of sex trade see little of life before they see the very worst of life — an underground of brutality and lonely fear. Those who create these victims and profit from their suffering must be severely punished. Those who patronize this industry debase themselves and deepen the misery of others. And governments that tolerate this trade are tolerating a form of slavery.

I watched the speech, and I remember how my jaw dropped when he suddenly segued from the virtues of the invasion of Iraq to the scourge of international pedophile rings. Most of his audience may have thought it an odd transition, if they thought anything at all, but I thought it something more. I knew the story of the Franklin Cover-Up. I knew this man's father, the former president, had been implicated by several minors in Lawrence King's service. I understood that pedophile rings were utilized by intelligence services to blackmail foreign dignitaries. And all this helped me process the subtext of Bush's digression: blackmail.

I thought of this again because of last week's story out of Britain that hundreds, maybe thousands of African boys are disappearing in London. Some like "Adam," to ritual sacrifice, an awful, appropriate follow-up to the reopening of the Atlanta Child murders investigation,

It's unlikely we would be able to correlate these stories without the Internet. Without the contextualizing Web, it's unlikely I would have thought one might have anything to do with another. And if they actually do, how much longer will we be permitted such a processing tool? Lovecraft went on to write, "Some day the piecing together of dissociated knowledge will open up such terrifying vistas of reality, and of our frightful position therein, that we shall either go mad from the revelation or flee from the deadly light into the peace and safety of a new dark age." Perhaps that's it. Maybe they won't need to take the Internet from us after all. Maybe we'll hand it back, begging "Take it, please, I can't bear anymore."

Who's Screening Who?

August 3, 2005

> *I'd like to take you, take you to the ceremony.*
> *Well, that is if I remember the way.*
> *Jack and Jill, they're going to join their misery.*
> *I'm afraid it's time for everyone to pray*
> — Leonard Cohen

A common argument against accounts of abduction seems to amount to "Why don't they take me?" (Stephen Hawking has written something very close to this.) Or if not me, then someone I regard as a meritorious representative of humanity. (Larry King, a few weeks ago, during a rare break from missing-girl-in-Aruba coverage: *"Why don't they abduct someone like ... Colin Powell? Just kiddin' ya — we'll be right back."*)

This argument from counter-anecdote — *if it didn't happen to me, it didn't happen* — holds several false assumptions: that abductees are predominately backwoods simpletons; that the abduction phenomenon must be about alien science; and that entities sufficiently weird to conduct such abductions would place extraordinary value upon those whom we consider extraordinary.

While there's no evidence of *extraordinary value*, there is at least one Nobel Laureate who describes a bizarre series of encounters and missing-time episodes suggestive of abduction events.

American biochemist Dr. Kary Mullis was awarded the Nobel in 1993 for his discovery ten years earlier of the polymerase chain reaction (PCR), which provided a method for genetic researchers to make copies of strands of DNA.

One Friday night in 1985, Mullis drove to his cabin in northern California and arrived about midnight. He dropped off his groceries, turned on the solar-powered lights, grabbed a flashlight and headed for the outhouse, about 50 feet away.

In his book *Dancing Naked in the Mind Field*, Mullis describes what next happened:

[A]t the far end of the path under a fir tree, there was something glowing. I pointed my flashlight at it anyhow. It only made it whiter where the beam landed. It seemed to be a raccoon. I wasn't frightened. Later, I wondered if it could have been a hologram, projected from God knows where.

The raccoon spoke. "Good evening, doctor," it said. I said something back, I don't remember what, probably, "Hello."

The next thing I remember, it was early in the morning. I was walking along a road uphill from my house.

Six hours were missing. As was his flashlight, which was never recovered. His groceries were where he'd left them, and the cabin light was still on. He discovered later that day that "the most beautiful part of my woods" had irrationally become a place of deep dread. As far as I know, Mullis has not attempted to recover the missing time through hypnosis.

And it's not only Mullis who has experienced strange phenomena at his cabin. Some time later, and before having told anyone of his encounter and missing time, his daughter Louise lost three hours wandering down the same hill, reappearing in the same spot just as her distraught boyfriend was about to call the police. And to Bill Chalker, author of the recently published, and fascinating, *Hair of the Alien* (which recounts the first forensic DNA analysis of a purportedly alien artifact), Mullis said that a guest at a party to celebrate his Nobel win in 1993, unfamiliar with his account of the "raccoon," encountered a "small glowing man" on a hill leading to the cabin. The figure suddenly expanded to full size and said "I'll see you tomorrow." He left the party with a friend for their hotel rooms in a nearby town. Very early the next morning he found himself outside in the hotel parking lot, "terrified by the impression that he had somehow been back" to the cabin.

Mullis tells Chalker that he considers the nature of the experiences to be stranger than extraterrestrial, and speculates that multidimensional physics, of the nature popularized by physicist Michio Kaku in *Hyperspace and Parallel Worlds*, is closer to the truth: "It's like anything can goddamn happen and the speed of light is not really the limit in terms of interactions with other cultures."

Mullis again, from *Dancing Naked in the Mind Field*:

I wouldn't try to publish a scientific paper about these things, because I can't do any experiments. I can't make glowing raccoons appear. I can't buy them from a scientific supply house to study. I can't cause myself to be lost again for several hours. But I don't deny what happened. It's what science calls anecdotal, because it only happened in a way that you can't reproduce. But it happened.

But what happened? The talking raccoon has the earmark of an absurd screen memory to mask the authentic event. So: who was behind the screen?

We'll likely never know who was behind this particular screen, or the small, glowing man of Mullis's friend. As far as Mullis is concerned, he appears content to keep it that way. But the note of the vanished flashlight is a detail suggestive of a trip to Magonia, and the folkloric tradition of entities stealing small possessions of those they encounter. But not all screens mask the same *Other*.

This is one of those places of great divide between those already marginalized by consensus reality: survivors who have suffered either abduction or ritual abuse and mind control. And again, the argument is often from anecdote, invalidating another's experience because it does not conform to the parameters of one's own.

But the abduction phenomenon is too global, too diverse and too weird for it all to be ascribed to human agency, even agencies with sinister and out-of-control aspects such as the CIA, the NSA and others. There is just *too much of it*, and there has been for too long, to say it all goes back to *our* spooks. Though it does seem to be a complicated dance. The inhuman and the human transgressors appear to provide cover for one another, establishing each other's alibi. And this is easy to accomplish, because they are engaged in *sympathetic and complementary enterprises*, in the sense that both projects are physical and spiritual violations of human subjects. By forcing their will upon the minds of innocents, both are black workings of a sort, and both are able to operate freely because they share the self-negating characteristic of absurdity.

We're told to pay no regard to the man behind the curtain. Sometimes, we may find it's not a man.

The Mystery Man

August 2, 2005

Something is burning, baby, something's in flames.
There's a man going 'round calling names.
— Bob Dylan

Of all the purportedly-true horror stories of Budd Hopkins' *Intruders* — his study of an Indiana family seemingly beset by generational abduction phenomena — the one I found both most persuasive and horrifying — could be ascribed by convention to a prank caller.

When Kathie Davis, the principal subject of the book, was pregnant with her second son Tommy in 1980, she began receiving indecipherable phone calls every Wednesday at 3:00 in the afternoon. "Above a background noise that roared like a factory in full swing she heard a voice moaning and muttering and using no syllables [that could be understood]." The voice would neither acknowledge the other party nor even pause when asked to identify or explain itself. Sometimes Kathie hung up within moments, sometimes she listened for minutes, "fascinated by the weird sounds." (Her friend Dorothy and her mother Mary also answered Kathie's phone on occasion, and heard the same guttural moaning and industrial roars.) During this event, Kathie decided to get an unlisted number. One Monday afternoon the telephone company called to say the change was in effect, and told her the new number. Moments later the phone rang: it was her strange caller, making the same bizarre sounds, though now with an angry tone. It was the only time, other than Wednesdays at 3:00 p.m., that Kathie received such a call.

The calls ceased abruptly when Tommy was born. When Hopkins asked Kathie about the health of her boys, she said "Tommy my youngest, has a speech problem. He just makes this sort of moaning sound. I've had him thoroughly tested. They've done brain stem and brain wave analysis, and so on, and he's normal. He's very bright. He just doesn't talk yet." Later, she confided to a female colleague of Hopkins' that Tommy's speech was a tremendous worry, because it reminded her so much of the mysterious caller during her pregnancy.

Now here's a curious something I discovered just last night online:

> Doris Lilly, who lived in the south end of Point Pleasant, West Virginia — the locus of "Mothman" sightings — began to receive strange phone calls early in March 1967, at the height of the Mothman flap. (Reportedly many did, though none I've heard like these.) John Keel writes in *The Complete Guide to Mysterious Beings* that daily, "around 5:00 p.m. her phone would ring, and when she answered she heard only a bizarre metallic voice speaking in an incomprehensible language. It was guttural and rapid. These calls came only when she was alone." According to Lilly, "it was as if they knew when I came home." The calls persisted, and Lilly became afraid to stay alone in her house. The phone company examined the line and could not explain the calls.

Keel wrote his book in 1970, Hopkins in 1987. Though the briefly-described episodes have an urban-legend *frisson* about them, they're not tales told of a friend of a friend. Both Keel and Hopkins did their own research, traveling to the locales and speaking at considerable length with the parties involved. The repeating, indecipherable telephone calls were minor aspects of particular rips in the veil they were investigating: the "Mothman" appearances and the Copley Woods abductions. Oddly, I've yet to find these strangely similar stories in each other's context.

I imagine skeptics of the Amazing Randi school would have no trouble dismissing both accounts, as they have no trouble dismissing anything that threatens to trouble their Closed System: the Davies' family and Kathie's friend *must* have been familiar with Keel's book, and had no qualms about exploiting a three-year-old's speech impediment to support their hoax. (It's a familiar tactic of such skeptics to discount solitary, extraordinary events as mere anomalies, and multiple events as the signature of copy cats and mass hysteria.) As for Doris Lilly, if she didn't fabricate or embellish her story, there's still nothing about it, they would undoubtedly say, that demands a supernatural explanation.

I might agree with that point, except there's very little about the Mothman story that makes sense, and so to *force sense* upon it does a certain measure of violence to it. If the data is intrinsically absurd, making it conform to our rational assumptions will destroy it. And for some, that's a job well done. (It becomes a feat of strength: can the presumptions of a rational, material universe take down the facts?) Perhaps the explanation which best lets the data *explain itself* is occult. Keel entertains this in **The Mothman Prophecies**. Just before the sightings began, the charred carcass of a dog was found on unsinged ground that became, in effect, Ground Zero for the phenomenon. Keel wonders whether the dog was a sacrifice to initiate the events and open a door through which the entity called "Mothman" could pass.

Presuming there were points to the bizarre phone calls may be presuming too much. But *if* there were, what could they have been? This seemingly obvious question neither Keel nor Hopkins asks.

Was the point communication? Unlikely, given their monologic indecipherability. There was no engagement at all with the person on the other end of the line. Also, the description of the speech is reminiscent of the story of Jose Antonio Da Silva, the Brazilian military policeman who, in 1969, claimed to have been abducted by "two masked individuals about four feet tall, wearing dull aluminum suits." The creatures bore him to a stone chamber, and an audience with an extremely hairy dwarf. He said the entities "talked among themselves in an incomprehensible language with many R's."

Was the point ritual? More likely, when we consider the patterns with which the calls were made: *every week at 3:00 p.m. on Wednesday; every afternoon at 5:00 p.m.* Repeating acts at regular intervals is at least suggestive of ritualistic behavior.

If so, then what was the point of the ritual? With respect to the Davies' case, it's clearly linked to a pregnancy, and perhaps meant to be an influence upon it. According to the reports of several family members, after his birth, Tommy was himself subjected to abduction and intrusive attention from unknown entities. As for Lilly's calls, there's not enough information, other than to associate them broadly with the Mothman phenomenon.

But here's a question that should be asked, and answered thoughtfully, before any other: *Why bother?* Don't we have enough mysteries already in this mundane world? Why become entangled in those of another? Surely there's something more pressing than this.

Erik Davis offers an answer of sorts, in *TechGnosis*:

> Most of us feel comfortable chalking up such close encounters to neurochemical imbalances, bad lunch meat, lax education, or the editorial philosophy of the *Weekly World News*. But the closer you look at these phenomena, and at many of the people who are captured by them, the more difficult it becomes to completely separate this loopy world from the straight one.... [A]ll about us the planet seems to be cracking apart at the seams. *Reality, it seems, has been deregulated*, and nothing is business as usual anymore — least of all business. The horizon of history bends into an asymptote, and at its warping edges, the more wild-eyed and speculative can't help but glimpse the shadow of some imponderable and ominous X leaning in. As the ancient mapmakers wrote when they sketched the edges of the watery unknown, "Here be dragons." [emphasis added]

Increasingly, entanglements don't seem to be a matter of choice. As the domain of our mundane experience begins to undergo unprecedented stress, there is an apparent cascading correspondence of irrationalities between this realm and another. Another *here*. The growing unreality that many have sensed for the past five years is an aspect of that correlation.

Thirty years ago, in conversation with Jacques Vallee in *The Edge of Reality*, J. Allen Hynek spoke of "the whole craziness of the thing, the whole absurdity [of the UFO phenomenon] — it's another world, another realm, that seems to have some interlocking with ours, and *what we're describing here is just that interlocking*."

Why bother? Because there are ever more points of congruence these days between the realms, and in our world many of those appear to rest on the nodal points of Earthly power.

In David Lynch's *Lost Highway*, saxophonist Fred Madison is approached at a party by a figure known only as the "Mystery Man":

> Mystery Man: We've met before, haven't we?
> Fred Madison: I don't think so. Where was it you think we met?
> Mystery Man: At your house. Don't you remember?
> Fred Madison: No. No, I don't. Are you sure?

Mystery Man: Of course. As a matter of fact, I'm there right now.
Fred Madison: What do you mean? You're where right now?
Mystery Man: At your house.
Fred Madison: That's fucking crazy, man.
Mystery Man: Call me. Dial your number. Go ahead.
[Fred dials the number and the Mystery Man answers.]
Mystery Man: [over the phone] I told you I was here.
Fred Madison: [amused] How'd you do that?
Mystery Man: Ask me.
Fred Madison: [angrily into the phone] How did you get inside my house?
Mystery Man: You invited me. It is not my custom to go where I am not wanted.
Fred Madison: [into the phone] Who are you?
[Both Mystery Men laugh mechanically.]
Mystery Man: Give me back my phone.
[Fred gives the phone back.]
Mystery Man: It's been a pleasure talking to you.

If we can glimpse the shadow of the imponderable and ominous X, then unlike *Lost Highway*'s Fred Madison, who didn't know himself well enough to know his own nightmares, we may be able to recognize the Mystery Man coming, before he sets upon mystifying us.

Far Away, So Close

June 22, 2005

I t can get lonely beyond the parameters of respectable thought. And we've tended to make it lonelier than it needs to be, and also kept ourselves less informed, by failing to speak to each other respectfully across serious disciplines; which are all dismissed by the misinformed as mere fantasies.

For instance, and for the most part, the 9/11 and political conspiracy crowd haven't rubbed shoulders with the mind control/ritual abuse community; few in either camp have seen the value in studying occult, paranormal and psychochemical phenomena; and virtually no one wants to be associated with UFO research. It's perfectly understandable why this happens. Each subject is generally considered, in its own right, "fringe," and so the advocates of each, contending for a hearing and a measure of respectability, adopt a phobia towards cross-contamination by other disreputable subjects.

At Toronto's 2004 Citizen's Inquiry into 9/11, I heard an elderly woman share her difficulty in persuading others of the need to critically consider the evidence that the attacks were an inside job. She said, with sadness, that a typical response would be "Oh — and what do you think of UFOs?" Exasperated sighs of recognition filled the room. And though I knew what she meant — to gain acceptance, perhaps controversial issues need to be presented piecemeal — I also thought, *Good question.* Because if there is any validity at all to an inquiry it cannot be pursued in isolation; particularly huge issues with tremendous consequences. Rather, they and their implications should help explain one other, contextually, on the Big Canvas.

We know conspirators compartmentalize, and task on a need-to-do basis. Because we need to see *more*, we can't mistake one portion — the one that most interests us, or the one we find most persuasive, or the one to which we actually bear witness — for the whole picture.

Sight Unseen offers interesting examples of the limits of compartmentalized analysis. Author Budd Hopkins heads the

"Intruders Foundation," and has been a leading researcher in the phenomenon of UFO abductions for more than 30 years. His latest book presents some fascinating case studies that merit attention, but I find his conclusions to be handicapped by both his specialization, and his fixation upon the extraterrestrial hypothesis.

Hopkins notices a "curious pattern" among abductees of "personal, cherished objects...seeming to vanish and then reappear under highly unusual circumstances." For instance, a wedding ring placed on a kitchen countertop one moment and gone the next reappeared several days later beneath the tacked-down carpet of an upstairs bedroom. Hopkins doesn't know what to make of it, though he finds the pattern repeats enough to be "intriguing" and to "deserve mention." The pattern, while mystifying to someone searching the skies for ETs, should be immediately familiar to students of the "secret commonwealth": the traditional folklore of mischievous entities who have always been with us, but inhabit *another here*.

Hopkins tells the story of two credible witnesses who, while driving through the wheat fields of Iowa in 1952, "came upon an eerie sight: a little old man on a bicycle, wearing lederhosen and sporting a long white beard, like something one might see rendered in wood in a Bavarian souvenir shop." About a half hour later, when they drove over a gentle rise, they encountered the same little man, "pedaling happily along in the same direction, many miles ahead of the place they had first come upon him." There were no side roads or shortcuts the cyclist could have taken, and the men had not been overtaken by a vehicle which could have given him a lift. Hopkins isn't content to let the story stand on its own strangeness. Without any justification other than his presumption of an extraterrestrial hypothesis, he posits that the figure was actually a screen memory to mask an abduction and missing time episode. After all, we can't have odd little elfin figures bending space-time in Iowa, now can we?

Hopkins also describes a number of instances of abductees' associations, sometimes for years, with humans of extraordinary paranormal ability who appear to serve as "go-betweens," sometimes described as having a "military" bearing. Hopkins does not consider an occult explanation — to him, apparently, the paranormal is not a human functionality — nor, seemingly, that these may be genuine military figures. To him, they merely *look* human. They are, he concludes, most likely transgenic, alien-human hybrids.

Consider Stewart, the bizarre acquaintance of abductee "Sally," who came in and out of her life for 25 years, usually accompanying abductions, while he never seemed to age.

One night Sally awoke, startled to find Stewart standing next to her bed. Despite the fact that her apartment was on an upper floor, the windows were locked, and the door was securely bolted from the inside, there was Stewart, next to her bed. Frightened, Sally nevertheless felt compelled to get up and go with him into the living room. There she served both Stewart and herself a drink, and the two sat together on the couch talking audibly, not telepathically, as was sometimes the case. Stewart was, as usual, interested in her daily routine and questioned her about the mundane details of her life and secretarial job.

At one point, Sally told me, she gathered her courage and decided to ask him a rather basic question: "Are you real?" she wanted to know. "Are you a human being? What are you?" Stewart smiled and ignored the question.

Sally noticed some chest hair poking out over Stewart's shirt collar, reached for it and pulled it out. "He winced and gave her an angry look, but she was pleased to realize that on some physical level he was real and not a phantasm." (Hopkins, jumping to his conclusion, writes that "chest hair [is] something never before, to my knowledge, described as an alien feature." Presumably he is discounting the many accounts of hairy, dwarfish entities, and sticking to the grays.) A few moments after Sally plucks Stewart's chest hair, "three small gray aliens approached and she was taken out the window and into a hovering UFO for a more typical abduction experience."

The next morning, Sally checked all the locks and bolts on the doors and windows and they were all in place. Stewart should not have been able to enter, let alone the "three small gray aliens," but it wasn't a dream. Their unfinished drinks were on the kitchen counter, and her roommate Hannah remembered waking up in the night to "a roaring sound in my head":

I was very scared because I didn't know what it was and then I found that I couldn't move. Something was going on. I heard voices coming from the living room. Sally was talking and there was a man's voice. It was the middle of the night and I couldn't move, and I had no idea who was out there or what was happening. I guess I just must have gone back to sleep, which doesn't make much sense when I think about it. The whole thing was very scary, because there really was a strange man in the apartment and I couldn't even move.

A few years later, in another apartment, both Sally and her new roommate Molly shared an abduction experience. Molly had never before seen or heard of Stewart, but remembered having seen a man matching his description operating inside the UFO alongside the alien entities. She drew a picture for Sally, which Sally recognized as even a better likeness of Stewart than the one she herself had once drawn for Hopkins.

Then there's the middle-aged "Mr. Nelson," who walked up to a 15-year-old girl named "Terry" in a pizza parlor and invited her to interview for a vaguely-described job the following day. (Her mother, in a bizarre departure from character, saw no problem with her daughter being picked up by a stranger and driven to an "undisclosed location.") En route, Nelson recounted to Terry intimate details of her life which no one, least of all a stranger, should have known. ("That was a terrible thing that your stepfather did to you," he says, and "I know all about your day yesterday. At twelve o'clock you went to Jimmy's house," and told her what she and her boyfriend did. When asked how he knew, he said only, "Oh, I just know.")

The location of the "interview" appeared like an undressed set in a virtually empty office building, and became a scene of Nelson's clumsy sexual advance. Afterwards, supposedly driving Terry home, Nelson drove into the "middle of nowhere, woods and fields everywhere." Under hypnosis, Terry remembered they "came up to a little house on the left with a dirt driveway and we pulled in":

> He asked me to sit in the car ... I wonder why that house was there. It's hard to see it. It's like ... field grass covers it. Higher than grass ... like straw ...hay.... He goes in a door. It's like an overhang over it.... I

keep seeing the roof like a smooth stone roof. No peaks. And I don't look at it because I'm too scared. I don't want whoever is in the house to see me. I knew that when he went in they were probably talking about me. So I slumped down on the seat so they wouldn't see me. I feel so shaky.... I'm afraid I'm going to be killed.

When Nelson exits the house, he's accompanied by "lots of the other ones.... They're smaller. All the same. No hair.... He comes out and just stands in front of the car, but these other things come out to the side and just look at me...."

Again, Hopkins can't let the phenomena be itself. Because he can't allow bizarre, small creatures to inhabit a stone house, in *another here*, the house must instead be a spacecraft, and the entities extraterrestrials. (Remember, the abduction of Jose Antonio de Silva by dwarfish creatures ended in a stone chamber, not an alien ship.) Because Hopkins can't conceive of someone truly human with Nelson's paranormal ability, or working in concert with non-human entities, then he must have been an alien hybrid.

To understand our own disciplines — and let's respect our studies enough to call them that, regardless of the derisive laughter from those who don't know, and those who don't want to know — we need to be interdisciplinary. We need to talk to each other in order to understand ourselves.

Jim Hougan, in his forward to the first volume of Peter Levenda's *Sinister Forces*, writes

Like UFOs, conspiracies and assassination, serial killers, mind control and the occult, "evil" isn't something that serious people are supposed to think about. If they did, the emergency reporting system would soon be overloaded. And you know what happens when that occurs. All hell breaks loose.

You know, most of what we talk about here and on similar sites, it's not really the "fringe," or even the "edge" — it's the *depth*. And it truly is scary as hell down there, because what binds these subjects together is that they are all the study of evil, of one order or another. But if we want to understand that's where we need, eventually, to go.

The Sheep
Look Up

May 13, 2005

I n "The Black Lodge," I suggested that UFO encounters may be a subset of religious phenomenon. I thought that begged an exploration of how religious manifestations can mirror those of UFOs, and how both may be mechanisms of control for non-human agents.

But first, if anyone's missed it, I'll say again: the assumption that UFOs are extraterrestrial spacecraft does not explain the data. The phenomenon is too weird and too diverse, and even too common, to be accounted for by survey teams from Zeta Reticuli, the Pleiades, the planet "Ummo," or any other home the "aliens" have identified. (I find it a fascinating frustration that many of those convinced of a massive government cover-up fall over themselves to accept the words of non-human entities.) So before I bring in the religious material, let me be clear that I consider the "God rides a spaceship" hypothesis popularized by Erich von Daniken to be a crude, backwards misapprehension of what's going on. *It is simply not strange enough* to account for the hyperreality of both the God Event and the UFO phenomenon, which may be virtually identical.

As today is May 13 let's start with Fatima, since it was on this day in 1917 that the "Lady from Heaven" first appeared to the young cousins Lucia, Jacinta and Francisco. (Though manifestations began two years earlier, when the then eight-year-old Lucia first saw a transparent white cloud in human form. In 1916, the three were visited by a beautiful boy who identified himself as the "Angel of Peace." His appearance followed a loud rumble and a white light which glided over the tree tops. The appearances left the children momentarily paralyzed, confused and physically drained — all symptoms familiar to students of close encounters.)

In broad strokes, this is the story: on the 13th day of the month, for six successive months, three young Portuguese children received visions of a small, brightly glowing figure of a woman, who appeared with attendant aerial manifestations of globes and rays of light. The events increased in intensity until the promised miracle of the final appearance, on October 13, which drew a crowd of some 70,000.

Avelino de Almeida, editor of the Lisbon newspaper *O Seculo*, had written dismissively of the growing legend of Fatima on the morning of the predicted miracle. A few hours later, he became a witness to the event:

> From the road, where the vehicles were parked and where hundred of people who had not dared to brave the mud were congregated, one could see the immense multitude turn toward the sun, which appeared free from clouds and in its zenith. *It looked like a plaque of dull silver* and it was possible to look at it without the least discomfort. It might have been an eclipse which was taking place. But at that moment a great shout went up and one could hear the spectators nearest at hand shouting:
>
> "A miracle! A miracle!" Before the astonished eyes of the crowd, whose aspect was Biblical as they stood bareheaded, eagerly searching the sky, the sun trembled, made sudden incredible movements outside any cosmic laws — the sun "danced" according to the typical expression of the people. [emphasis added]

Another witness was natural science professor Joseph Garrett:

> *This was not the sparkling of a heavenly body, for it spun round on itself in a mad whirl*, when suddenly a clamor was heard from all the people. The sun, whirling, seemed to loosen itself from the firmament and advance threateningly upon the earth as if to crush us with its huge fiery weight. The sensation during these moments was terrible. [emphasis added]

Nine miles away Joaquim Lourenco was so impressed by what he saw that he became a priest:

> I feel incapable of describing what I saw. *I looked fixedly at the sun which seemed pale and did not hurt my eyes.* Looking like a ball of snow, revolving on itself, it suddenly seemed to come down in a zigzag, menacing the earth.... There was an unbeliever there who had spent the

morning mocking the "simpletons" who had gone off to Fatima just to see an ordinary girl. He now seemed paralyzed, his eyes fixed on the sun. He began to tremble from head to foot, and lifting up his arms, fell on his knees in the mud, crying out to God. [emphasis added]

Poet Alfonso Lopes Viera witnessed the phenomenon from the oceanside town of San Pedro der Muel, though it is 30 miles from Fatima. It was also viewed in Pombal, 32 miles north. "The total land-area of visibility, based on witness interview, was approximately 32 by 20 miles." Yet no observatory recorded it.

A final witness, Maria Teresa of Chainca:

The sky was covered with clouds and it rained much. *We could not see the sun.* Then suddenly, at noon, the clouds drew away and the sun appeared as if it were trembling. It seemed to come down. It began spinning like a fire-wheel in the pagan feasts. It stopped for a few minutes and again started rolling, perhaps in a diameter of more than a meter while we could look at it as though it were the moon. Things all around turned into different colors.

Let's pay close attention to this: before the miracle, the sky was overcast. *"We could not see the sun."* Then, at the appointed time, the clouds parted as though they were curtains, and where the sun should be, now was a dull *silver disc*, revolving on itself, that could be observed directly without harming the eyes. Then it was seen to descend in a zigzag pattern, spinning and flashing lights to psychotronic effect. Sound familiar?

(Also worth noting is that the heavy rains had soaked the ground and the thousands of spectators. Yet it was reported that the phenomenon quickly dried the earth, as well as the clothes of those in attendance. Microwave heat effects are also quite common to UFO encounters.)

The 1930 decision of the Roman Catholic Church on the validity of the Fatima miracle, arrived at after 13 years of investigations, states that though no astronomical observatory reported the phenomenon, it was nevertheless "witnessed by persons of all categories...believers and unbelievers, journalists of the principal Portuguese newspapers and even by persons some miles away. Facts which annul any explanation of collective illusion."

It was not a collective illusion, for the reasons mentioned. But neither was it the sun, for the same reasons.

In *Dimensions*, Jacques Vallee has this to say about Fatima's phenomena:

> Not only was a flying disc or globe consistently involved, but its motion, its falling-leaf trajectory, its light effects, the thunder-claps, the buzzing sounds, the strange fragrance, the fall of "angel hair" that dissolves upon reaching the ground, the heat wave associated with the close approach of the disk — all of these are frequent parameters of UFO sightings everywhere. And so are the paralysis, the amnesia, the conversions, and the healings.

Many UFO researchers, particularly those who regard themselves as "serious," likely recoil at this material, and either dismiss it without consideration as pre-modern superstition which threatens to "contaminate" the hard data, or worse, attempt to divest the experience of its religious content. But wait: the *religious effect is the point of the contact event*.

As would seem to be the case with UFO encounters, the point of the manifestation is self-evidently the effect upon the witnesses. Whether to induce terror, or wonder, or worship, the effect is socio-religious. And if we can say this about Fatima, then it would be fair to admit that this has probably been going on for some time. Say, maybe, for all of human existence.

UFO contactees are generally inclined to accept that non-human entities are telling them the truth. So also religious visionaries tend to accept without question the integrity of their visions. But regardless of her bag of tricks, just because a Lady says she came from Heaven, doesn't mean she came from Heaven. As UFO encounters are often self-contradictory, so too are alleged appearances of the Blessed Virgin Mary, or "BVM," as Vallee coins them. For instance, the recent apparitions of the Virgin at Medjugorje deliver a message of feel-good ecumenism quite foreign to the Lady of Fatima. (Malachi Martin judged the Medjugorje manifestations "clearly demonic.")

Yet there is a recurrent theme, common to both UFOs and BVMs : a warning of apocalypse soon. Why would that be?

Sister Lucia, the last survivor of the three children of Fatima (as prophesied, the other two died in their youth), passed away on February 13. (Yes, the 13th: the same day of the month on which the Fatima visions occurred.) Her convent cell was ordered sealed by then-Cardinal Ratzinger, now Benedict XVI (And yes; Benedict XV was Pope at the time of Lucia's childhood visions.) It was Ratzinger who disseminated the story that Fatima's Third Secret was no biggie; it had been fulfilled in the assassination attempt on John Paul II.

Now, why would he do a thing like that?

The Firm

June 27, 2005

> *Somewhere Mama's weeping for her blue-eyed boy.*
> *She's holding little white shoes and that little broken toy.*
> *And he's following a star,*
> *the same one three men followed from the East.*
> *But I hear sometimes Satan comes as a man of peace.*
> — Bob Dylan

Everywhere you look, people are talking Scientology. You'd almost think they'd never heard of Xenu before.

Certainly Scientology's creed says nothing of the meat of L. Ron Hubbard's space opera. Typical of occult orders, it shows an exoteric face to the general public and lower initiates, and reserves esoteric teachings for its inner circle. Its supposed creed is nothing but mealy words of "equality" and "inalienable rights" to such things as freedom of thought and "sanity." Who could argue with that? Well, maybe L. Ron Hubbard for one, who said a lot of things, like "If you really want to enslave people, tell them that you're going to give them total freedom," and whose secret creed has driven higher initiates out of their skulls. Reportedly Tom Cruise, and reputedly only temporarily, counted among that number:

> Tom Cruise became psychotic during a secret Scientology initiation in which one is told that rather than being one person, one is composed of thousands of aliens from all over the universe fighting for control of your body. After completing this initiation, known as OT III, Tom appeared

sickly with black circles under his eyes and pasty skin. He said he wanted to be away from Scientology for good. He just wanted to go back to
Hollywood and his home and be left alone by Scientology. This would not
happen; David Miscavige ordered Cruise could not be let go. Scientology
worked on Cruise day and night until he finally returned to Scientology.

Miscavige is the Black Pope of Scientology, Chairman of
the Board of the "Religious Technology Center," and so, head
of the organization which "holds the ultimate ecclesiastical authority regarding the standard and pure application of L. Ron
Hubbard's religious technologies."

Besides suggesting just how impossibly short Miscavige
must be, a photograph also demonstrates something of the
church's bizarre militarism, which is on prominent display in its
naval cadet-like "Sea Org" and the church's intelligence wing,
the Office of Special Affairs (OSA). Bob Minton, Scientology's
"Enemy Number One," describes the Sea Org as "totalitarian"
and the OSA as "paramilitary organized Mafia" in possession of
"rocket launchers, bazookas, countless other weapons," led by
a "management that seeks "world domination."

A portion of the OSA's mandate is described in this policy
letter of Hubbard's, where he set forth "the vital targets on which
we must invest most of our time":

T1. Depopularizing the enemy to a point of total obliteration.

T2. Taking over the control or allegiance of the heads or proprietors
of all news media.

T3. Taking over the control or allegiance of key political figures.

T4. Taking over the control or allegiance of those who monitor international finance and shifting them to a less precarious finance standard.

It's fascinating to consider that Hubbard's pastiche of science fiction and Crowleyania, which can count the berserkers
of Manson's Family and the Process Church as its stepchildren,
can now contend for Middle American respectability just as has
Mormonism, which itself was the creature of a ceremonial magician. And like Mormons, who enjoy a "disproportionate representation" in the U.S. intelligence community, Scientologists
have formed a peculiar cadre of paramilitary intelligence.

Curiously, there was a "disproportionate representation" of Scientologists in the CIA's remote-viewing program. The NSA's Major Hal Puthoff was an "Operating Thetan, Level III" when he took on the program at Stanford Research Institute in 1972, where he remained until 1985. Puthoff's senior colleague was Ingo Swann, who himself had reached OT VII, then the highest initiatory level of Scientology. (That is, before Hubbard felt assured enough to fulfill his longtime fantasy and introduce OTVIII, the gist of which is *Surprise — I'm the Antichrist!*) Swann, in fact, was a founder of the Scientology Center in Los Angeles. Pat Price, "widely considered to be the best of the remote viewers," was OT IV.

Alex Constantine writes in *Virtual Government*:

> When Swann joined SRI, he stated openly that fourteen "Clears" participated in the experiments, "more than I would suspect."... The projects at SRI were augmented by a parapsychology team at Fort Meade in Maryland under INSCOM and the NSA. Military intelligence personnel were recruited, including Major Ed Dames, the Psi-Tech founder. General Stubblebine ran the project and broadened it to include tarot and the channeling of "spirits."

Well, perhaps the representation is not so disproportionate after all. According to doctrine, a "clear" Scientologist, free of the infestation of thousands of "body thetans," is alleged to have godlike mastery of the material world, including an ability to operate free of the body. A handy talent for a remote viewer, that.

Hubbard, of course, was with Naval Intelligence at the time he was conjuring with Jack Parsons in the "Babalon Working." Scientology would have it that he was operating undercover, to bust up a black-magic ring. What remains hidden in plain sight is not only Scientology's occult legacy, but that of U.S. military intelligence.

"You can't go home again"

September 28, 2005

I see pieces of men marching, trying to take heaven by force.
I can see the unknown rider, I can see the pale white horse.
— Bob Dylan

In 1983 Ingo Swann, a senior colleague of the CIA's remote-viewing program at Stanford Research Institute and "Operating Thetan level VII", received a call at his home in New York City from a close friend, a U.S. congressman. The caller asked if he could do a favor for a certain party in need of the services of someone with his skills. The friend was vague about the request, and may not even have known what he was asking, but told Swann the party could be trusted and he would be paid.

Jim Schnabel, in *Remote Viewers*, tells what happened after Swann accepted the assignment, and followed his friend's instructions to stand on a Manhattan street outside a museum:

Two men with pseudonyms picked him up in a car, placed a blindfold on him, and drove him for a few hours out of town. When the blindfold was taken off, Swann was in a large underground installation. No one wore a uniform, but from the haircuts and physiques, and the way people took orders, he decided that at least some were U.S. Marines.

Swann was led into a windowless room, was introduced to some people, and was then allowed to settle himself before starting his remote viewing. The target was described only as a pair of coordinates. They were lunar coordinates, for Swann was being asked to remote-view a place on the moon. He soon did, and more coordinates were given to him. Before the day was out, Swann had described a variety of monumental objects, not human-made but not natural either, scattered across the cold surface of Earth's dusty cousin. Swann, according to the story, was then paid several thousand dollars in cash, and was driven back to his apartment in New York.

Possibly the lunar coordinates were actually meaningless, and merely intended to test Swann's abilities. Regardless, this was just the beginning of Swann's work for the unidentified outfit, and it got stranger. One mission took him to Alaska, where he was flown by helicopter to a remote lake. His handlers told him that "something strange" happened at the lake, like clockwork. And in fact, it was about to happen again:

> As Swann stood there, he saw a mist form over the lake, and then an unearthly triangular object rose ... sucking up water and shooting out bright beams of light, and then zoomed off into the distance. Well, his companions asked Swann, now that he had seen the strange thing, perhaps he could remote-view it and tell them what it was? Swann impatiently explained that that was not how remote viewing worked. He was too front-loaded now with information about the target to be able to remote-view it accurately, and in any case was too frightened by the experience to want to do any further remote viewings of extraterrestrials or their craft.

Schnabel also tells how another of the program's highly regarded remote viewers, Joe McMoneagle, was driven to the Pentagon shortly before his retirement and escorted to a secure room. He was asked to remote view a target with no advance information. All he knew was that the "feedback" package, containing information regarding the target to be opened after his session, was highly classified. As he entered his "zone," McMoneagle viewed a "strange, complex high-performance aerial vehicle, apparently not of this earth." Afterwards the package was opened and he was shown the satellite photo inside, which showed an apparent UFO on a seemingly impossible flight path.

Of course, as I've noted earlier, the CIA publicly declared its remote-viewing program a failure. The piling on even included the Temple of Set's Lt Col. Michael Aquino, who dismissed remote-viewing as an "eyeball roller" in a paper for *The Intelligencer: Journal of US Intelligence Studies*. Nevertheless, there are many contrary voices within military intelligence who don't subscribe to the official view, like Major General Edmund R. Thompson, who told Schnabel "I never liked to get into debates with the skeptics, because if you didn't believe that remote-viewing was real, you hadn't done your homework."

Perhaps the program needed to be shut down and given a thorough debunking because of its success: it was *getting too close to the secrets* of the military-occult complex, and it operated beyond the control of those who profit by the secrets remaining hidden. The experiences related by Swann and McMoneagle suggest blind tests, run by those who know, who wanted to discern how good these guys were, and how close America's own psychic spies were to crashing their party. Pickett and Prince's *The Stargate Conspiracy* describes how many remote viewers "spontaneously reported encountering pyramids" during their sessions, and that concurrent with its CIA-sponsored RV program, SRI was sending archeological teams to the Giza plateau to search for secret chambers beneath the Sphinx and within the pyramids.

One of the most fascinating accounts in Schnabel's book describes the "haunting" of Livermore Laboratory. Along with Los Alamos, much of the U.S. military's nuclear weapons R&D was conducted there. By the mid-'70s, a number of Livermore personnel had learned of SRI's program, and become sufficiently alarmed by the security implications that they decided to investigate psychic phenomena for themselves. As Schnabel tells it, "the Livermore group quickly found themselves involved in more strangeness than they could handle ... they began to feel that they were collectively possessed by some kind of tormenting, teasing, hallucination-inducing spirit."

Both in the laboratory and at home, Livermore scientists and their families began experiencing visions. Sometimes in the middle of a room, an "almost comically stereotypical" image of a UFO would appear, "always about eight inches across, in a gray, fuzzy monochrome, as if it were some kind of hologram." (Interestingly, a similar phenomenon was observed by participants in the five-year "Scole Experiment", researching life after death. "On one occasion," writes Robin Foy, "we even witnessed a miniature UFO flying around the cellar where we held our sessions.")

Sometimes they would see shamanic visions of fantastic animals. Enormous raven-like birds visited the yards of several members. One appeared at the foot of the bed of physicist Mike Russo, terrifying both him and his wife, as it stared at them.

Audio and video tapes of experiments picked up other things, things that shouldn't have been there, like a "distinctive, metallic-sounding voice, unheard during the actual experiment but now clearly audible, if mostly unintelligible."

(That metallic voice sound familiar? It seems to turn up a lot. Jack Sarfatti took a call from one in 1952. It claimed to be a conscious computer onboard a spacecraft, identifying him as one of "400 young bright receptive minds we wish to [do something with]." It said if he agreed, he would link up with the others in 20 years. Twenty years later and Sarfatti was at — wait for it — Stanford Research Institute.)

Physicist Don Curtis and his wife were sitting in their living room one evening when suddenly an arm appeared, hovering before them:

> The arm was clothed as if it belonged to a man wearing a plain gray suit. There was no bloody stump were it should have connected with a shoulder. It merely faded into clear space. But at the end of the arm where a hand should have been, there was no hand, only a hook. The hooked arm twisted around for a few seconds in front of Curtis and his wife, and then disappeared.

Team members began questioning their sanity. Physicist Peter Crane called for help, and brought in CIA analyst and parapsychologist Richard Kennett to meet with the group. To Kennett, "they perspired, trembled, and even wept openly" as they described their experiences. These were professional scientists with high-level clearance and no history of involvement in the occult. If he referred them to a psychiatrist the diagnosis would probably be some dissociative disorder. When Kennett listened to the metallic voice on the tape, he realized there was something deeper here:

> Among the few intelligible words it pronounced were two or three together which Kennett recognized as the code name of a very closely held government project. The project had nothing to do with psychic research, and neither it nor its code name was known to Crane or Russo or the others at Livermore. It was as if whoever or whatever had produced the code name on the tape had known that Kennett would soon arrive on the scene, and had saved this special shiver down the spine just for him.

(And wouldn't it be interesting to know what "closely held government project" the metallic voice named?)

Kennett reported the code-name incident to CIA security, "muting the outlandish details only slightly." Mike Russo received a telephone call from the strange, metallic voice, demanding that Livermore group cease its psychic research. When it did, within a month, the bizarre events also ceased.

Kennett called SRI's Hal Puthoff and Russell Targ, and asked that they meet with him in Washington on their next fundraising tour of government offices to discuss the Livermore events. A few nights later they arrived, and Kennett met them in a hotel room close to midnight. He sat them down and told them the whole story, including the floating arm. *"And so the goddamn arm — The thing was rotating, with this gray suit on, and it had a hook on it. It was a false arm. What do you think of that?"* As Kennett pronounced that, there was a heavy pounding on the door. According to Schnabel, the pounding was so loud it was frightening. Kennett went to the door.

Standing in the doorway was a man who at first glance was remarkable only by his unremarkableness. He was nondescript and unthreatening, somewhere in middle age. He walked past Kennett very slowly, with a stiff gait, to the middle of the room, between the two beds. He turned around, and said in an oddly stilted voice. "Oh! I guess ... I ... must ... be ... in ... the wrong ... room." And with that he walked out, slowly, stiffly, giving all of them time to see that one sleeve of his gray suit, pinned to his side, was empty.

One source, who didn't want his name used, told Schnabel, "We tried to find him. We walked up and down the halls. But none of us had the balls to ask the hotel desk, 'Hey, did you see that gray-suited, one-armed guy from space?'"

Some of the remote viewers, years before the movie, termed their trance-like zone "the matrix," and described sessions as "switching on a beacon" within it, which sometimes attracted strange things.

Duane Elgin was a futurologist at SRI who became involved in psychic research after a colleague flipped a coin and asked him to call heads or tails, and he called it correctly 33 times in a row. He told *New York* magazine in 1975, "Once you discover that space doesn't matter, or that time can be traveled through at will so that time doesn't matter, and that matter can be moved by consciousness so that matter doesn't matter — well, you can't go home again."

And maybe that's what we're waking up to: an occult elite that's had its beacon on for quite some time, and haven't been at home here for a long while.

The Color Out of Space

October 7, 2005

I dreamed that I was in the grasp of a great and horrible paw; a yellow, hairy, five-clawed paw which had reached out of the earth to crush and engulf me. And when I stopped to reflect what the paw was, it seemed to me that it was Egypt.

— H.P. Lovecraft

This is only a test

At 5:05 on November 22, 1977, regular television programming in southern England was interrupted by a voice claiming to be that of "Grahama," representative of the "Ashtar Galactic Command," bearing the usual "space brother" boilerplate of coming in peace to save us from ourselves at the dawn of a New Age. It was quickly dismissed as a hoax, but an extremely complicated one to execute. Though the *Sunday Times* the following December 4 surmised it was accomplished by students using just "£80 worth of equipment powered by an ordinary car battery," no one ever claimed responsibility, and independent investigations found that the message must have cut into at least five transmitters simultaneously, and it evaded detection by monitoring equipment which did not even register an interruption, "suggesting it was achieved in some way that bypassed our electrical system."

This was actually the second message from Grahama. A month earlier, he had said pointedly that "We conveyed to Sir John Whitmore and to Dr. Puharich that we would interfere on your radio and television communication systems to relay when the civilizations are coming close to landing on your planet Earth. It is now in motion. We wish you to know that we love you."

That "Grahama" would single out the aristocratic former racing champion Whitmore and parapsychologist and MK-ULTRA researcher Andrija Puharich suggests this was no *simple* hoax: both men were deeply involved with a decades'-long channeled communication with entities representing a universal hierarchy sometimes called the "70 Brotherhoods of the Great White Brotherhood." The entities governing our reality identified themselves as "the Nine."

Another link to Whitmore and Puharich was British author Stuart Holroyd's recently published *Prelude to the Landing on Planet Earth*, which the two had commissioned as an account of their work with the Nine. In the book, Holroyd wrote that the Nine intended to "interrupt television and radio transmissions during the period 18th to 22nd November."

Regarding the television interruptions, Lynn Picknett and Clive Prince write in *The Stargate Conspiracy* that, "as usual, there were only two options considered: either the whole thing was genuine and extraterrestrials had really spoken to the southern English through their television sets; or it was hoax, just done for a laugh. The idea that such a message could be easily contrived by, for example, an intelligence agency that would have the necessary technical skills has never, to our knowledge, even been considered."

This seems a bizarre oversight given the circumstantial connections to Whitmore and Puharich, and especially the latter's service in Army Intelligence and later as a CIA contractor researching the induction of altered states of consciousness. (Whitmore, incidentally, is now also Britain's "number one business coach," training top executives from companies such as Barclays, Lloyds, PricewaterhouseCoopers and Rolls Royce.) Uri Geller, for a time one of the Nine's channelers, told Picknett and Prince that "the CIA brought Puharich in to come and get me out of Israel," and in his essay "In the Thick of It," physicist Jack Sarfatti writes that "Puharich was Geller's case officer in America with money provided by Sir John Whitmore."

The Deep Space Nine

The "Council of Nine" have been delivering curiously consistent messages through a succession of mediums to influential patrons with names like DuPont, Astor and Bronfman since the early 1950s, and nearly always in the shadow of military intelligence. Until his death in 1995 Puharich made his home in that shadow, researching shamanic pharmacology and electronic mind control.

Initial contact was made during a sitting of Puharich's CIA cutout "Round Table Foundation" on New Year's Eve, 1952, at precisely 9 p.m., when the entities disclosed themselves through the tranceivership of *Dr. D.G. Vinod* as the "Nine Principles or Forces."

In the early 1970s, *Star Trek* creator Gene Roddenberry was a regular at the sessions of channeler Phyllis Schlemmer, to whom the Nine had revealed themselves through the manifestation of a spirit guide called "Tom." Schlemmer initially assumed Tom must be her grandfather Thomas, who died when she was a child. In September 1974 Roddenberry asked Tom the question, "To whom am I talking? Do you have a name?" Tom's reply, through the entranced Schlemmer, as quoted by Picknett and Price:

> As you know, I am the spokesman for the Nine. But I also have another position, which I have with you in the project. I will try to give you names so you can understand in what you work and who we are. I may not pronounce who I am in a manner which you would understand because of the problem in the Being's [i.e., Schlemmer] brain, but I will

explain so that the Doctor [Puharich] perhaps will understand. I am Tom, but I am also Harmarchis, I am also Harenkur, I am also known as Tum and I am known as Atum.

It took 22 years, and Gene Roddenberry, for the Nine to reveal themselves as The Nine, the Great Ennead of ancient Egypt: Atum, Shu, Tefnut, Geb, Nut, Osiris, Isis, Set and Nepthys. Their message amounts to *We're back, and now it's personal.*

(How much the Nine may have influenced Roddenberry is unknown. His involvement began several years after the original *Star Trek* series was cancelled, but a character named *Vinod* pops up in an episode of **Deep Space Nine** entitled "Paradise.")

In 1954, with Puharich back in uniform and stationed at the U.S. Army Chemical Center in Edgewood, Maryland, a young Dutch sculptor named Harry Stone was being tested at the Round Table for his psychometric powers. Handed an Egyptian pendant that had belonged to the mother of Akenaten, he fell into a trance, began uttering strange words and drawing hieroglyphics on a sheet of paper. In English he spoke of a drug that would open a gateway to the gods, and of entering an underground hall where a statue of a dog-headed man came to life. Puharich was sent the drawings and a transcription of Stone's words, who took them to another Army doctor at Edgewood who, write Picknett and Prince, "just happened to be an expert in extremely rare and archaic forms of hieroglyphs," and to Puharich's surprise confirmed their authenticity. Stone had identified himself as Rahotep, and named his wife as Nefert, and mentioned the Pharaoh Khufu.

Puharich was then astonished to discover that a man named Rahotep, married to Nefert, was known from Egyptian history, and likely lived under the reign of Khufu. Most significantly, Rahotep had been the High Priest of Heliopolis, the center of worship for the Nine, the Great Ennead.

The "gateway to the gods" proved to be a sacred mushroom. On one occasion when Puharich himself was hypnotizing Stone, a Round Table trustee, Alice Bouverie, also fell into a trance and stated that the mushroom was the kind now known as amanita muscaria, and said a specimen could be found not far from the house. It was. In one of Stone's trances, writes Colin Wilson in

Mysteries, "Rahotep demanded a mushroom and then, in the presence of Puharich and Aldous Huxley, applied it ritualistically to his tongue and the top of his head. When Stone woke up five minutes later, he was able to perform an ESP test with a 100% score and describe accurately what lay on the other side of a brick wall."

"Tom" plays the race card

The Nine claim that something has gone wrong with humanity's "programming," and so the Old Gods of Egypt, whose home is Sirius, are returning to reboot us. Humanity is supposedly the product of genetically-manipulated colonizers, whose first civilization arose in Tibet in 32,400 BC, but apparently not all humanity.

According to the Nine, there was one indigenous race already on the Earth — the black. According to "Tom," the seeding of Earth by the Gods was an experiment to see how "the originals [the black races] would evolve in comparison with those that colonized." The Nine say, *Hey, there's nothing wrong with that*, but the teaching remains that it's only the non-black peoples of the Earth who have the divine programming. Also interestingly, the Nine have good things to say about most major American religions, including and especially Mormonism, and are quite fond of the teachings of Lucis Trust founder Alice Bailey, but singles out Islam for rebuke. "Tom" says Islam has been influenced by "the Fallen one," and in his book *The Keys of Enoch*, channeler of the Nine James Hurtak calls Muslims the "Children of Darkness."

Any of this sound familiar? Perhaps its inversion might.

Remember the Prophet Yahweh? His cosmology is eerily similar to that of the Nine, yet stood on its head. His God Yahweh is also, like Tom/Atum, a spaceman, but the starseed is the black race. Both the Prophet Yahweh and the Nine's channelers have proclaimed the imminence of mass landings, and great devastation for those who refuse the lordship of the old-is-new gods. Both hear voices, have delivered failed prophecies, and have a strong suggestion of military mind control about them. Both play the race card. And now, after the ethnic cleansing of New Orleans, America is playing with a deck full of race cards.

I don't know what's going on with the Nine, but a credible reading of the story suggests a Freemasonic eschaton and the return of the original White Lodge from Sirius. If this isn't happening, then *sinister forces* (after all, Peter Levenda subtitled the first volume of his Grimoire of American Political Witchcraft "The Nine") are conspiring to make it appear so, and it has been going on for over 50 years. Generations of leaders and scientists have risen to prominence under its influence. Dick Farley, former director of program development for the Human Potential Foundation, writes that the Nine maintain a "working network of physicists and psychics, intelligence operatives and powerful billionaires, who are less concerned about their 'source' and its weirdness than they are about having *every* advantage and new data edge in what *they* believe is a battle for Earth itself." Jack Sarfatti, who received mysterious, mechanical-voiced phone calls from an alleged UFO of the future in 1952, the same year the Nine first spoke through Dr. Vinod, adds "the fact remains ... that a bunch of apparently California New Age flakes into UFOs and psychic phenomena, *including myself*, had made their way into the highest levels of the American ruling class and the Soviet Union and today run the Gorbachev Foundation."

Whatever the Nine are playing, or whoever is playing the Nine, it's been a long game.

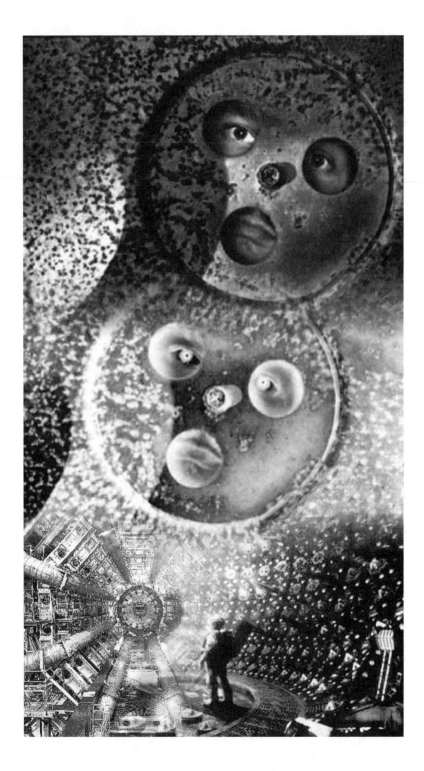

7. Sense and Sensitivity

For the Holy One dreams of a letter, dreams of a letter's death.
O bless the continuous stutter of the Word being made into flesh.

— Leonard Cohen

"No man sees my face and lives"

January 29, 2006

I and I,
One says to the other, no man sees my face and lives.
— Bob Dylan

Antonin Artaud traveled to Mexico in 1936 in order to become Europe's first "shamanic tourist" among the Tarahumara Indians. "Peyote, I knew, was not made for whites," the surrealist wrote in *The Peyote Dance*. "And a White, for these Red Men, is one whom the spirits have abandoned."

The Tarahumara tried to fob off on Artaud "old men who would suddenly get the bends and jiggle their amulets in a queer way," but he held out for the genuine shamans. Finally he was permitted to join an all-night peyote ceremony, and partook of the "dangerous dissociations it seems Peyote provokes, and which I had for 20 years sought by other means":

> The things that emerged from my spleen or my liver were shaped like the letters of a very ancient and mysterious alphabet chewed by an enormous mouth, but terrifying, obscure, proud, illegible, jealous of its invisibility.... Peyote leads the self back to its true sources.

To which Daniel Pinchbeck comments in *Breaking Open the Head*, "as powerful as they were these revelations could not cure his inner divisions":

> They could not heal him. Artaud spent the last twelve years of his life in mental institutions, treated by electroshock, writing paranoid letters and increasingly incoherent rants, and revising the text of his revelations among the Tarahumara.

Naturally. The inner divisions were heightened. Artaud wasn't seeking wholeness and reintegration; he was seeking transcendence. Dissociation appears to be a chief characteristic of such a venture, and of *intentional* boundary crossings. (I say intentional, because we need to account for the many witnesses and victims of boundary crossings of which they wanted no part.)

A book by Bruce Moen entitled *Voyages into the Unknown* records his training in astral projection at the Monroe Institute. On a Wednesday night during one of Moen's residencies Robert Monroe led a discussion on what he called the "I/There." Monroe taught that the self as we know it is merely the fragment of the "Total Self" which is currently living a physical life. The total self is a cluster of many beings, who each live many lifetimes. So, to astral travelers, many of their "guides" must actually be astral aspects of their total self.

This packet of information overwhelmed Moen:

> I ran out into the cool evening air and headed for an open grassy field. Something inside me was being overwhelmed. The old me was dissolving into thin air and a new unfamiliar me was taking its place. I pulled off my shirt and began rolling around in the grass, trying to get a grip on myself. I wasn't sure why I felt the need to do so, but rolling on the ground seemed quite reasonable at the time. The feeling of agitation and internal chaos flying around inside me were overpowering. It felt like rushing waves of some new reality crashing into sea walls of long held beliefs. Some parts of the walls were being pulverized into little bits and washed out to sea.

While rolling shirtless on the grass Moen was ignored by others strolling along the grounds, perhaps because they'd seen it all before. In 1984 an INSCOM lieutenant named Doug Pemberton enrolled in the same Gateway course Moen was attending. According to Schnabel's *Remote Viewers*, after three days and 15-minutes into another hemi-sync session, Pemberton was found wandering naked and babbling incoherently, and taken to a Walter Reed psychiatric ward.

After Moen pulled himself together he returned to his Monroe Center "CHEC" unit (Controlled Holistic Environmental Chamber) for that evening's tape session: "I stood for a moment at the opening to the CHEC unit, feeling how much it seemed like a Gateway into another dimension. Something in me was struggling to hang on to its old identity.... That part of me was trying to prevent my passing through that Gateway and entering whatever dimension of the beyond awaited."

Reading this and Monroe's theory of a fragmentary self, I'm reminded of "body thetans" from the higher teachings of Scientology, and of the over-representation of high Scientologists among the military's remote viewers. (For instance, the NSA's Major Hal Puthoff was an "Operating Thetan, Level III," Pat Price OT IV, and Ingo Swann OT VII.) And after reading Moen's book, this is familiar, too: "Tom Cruise became psychotic during a secret Scientology initiation in which one is told that rather than being one person, one is composed of thousands of aliens from all over the universe fighting for control of your body. After completing this initiation, known as OT III, Tom appeared sickly with black circles under his eyes and pasty skin."

L. Ron Hubbard leads us back to Aleister Crowley. In Crowleyan occult science, ego death is called the "crossing of the abyss," and entails for the magician a wrestling with the "great demon" Choronzon, the dweller of the abyss, found in the 10th Aethyr of John Dee's Enochian system. (An excerpt from Alex Owen's *The Place of Enchantment* recounts Crowley's 1909 crossing with the aid of companion Victor Neuburg: "Both men now felt that they understood the nature of the Abyss. It represented Dispersion: a terrifying chaos in which there was no center and no controlling consciousness.")

I believe all this talk — and against a deep, black backdrop of military study and sponsorship — of a fragmentary cluster of selves, "body thetans" and ego death, has considerable resonance for the study of ritual abuse and mind control, which is also concerned with the deliberate destruction of ego integration, though naturally not by choice. In the ritual context of ego death and its regard as a prerequisite for transcendence, the creation of programmable alters may be regarded as a high sacrament.

Moen begins *Voyages into the Unknown* curiously with pages of detail concerning a bizarre early childhood "daydream." In it, he enters a bedroom, and a woman on the bed raises the covers and beckons him to join her. Moen writes, "as a five- or six-year old boy, I never understood what we did in that bed. I only felt the frolicking atmosphere, pleasure, and a lot of bouncing and moving." Then he feels terror at the image of a menacing figure in the doorway. ("I knew in that instant if he got his hands on me I would be dead or worse.")

Later in life I began to wonder, so where had this daydream come from? How could I as a young boy have any knowledge of brass rail beds, sex, or another man's jealousy that was strong enough that he wanted to kill me? And the feelings that accompanied the experience — where had they come from?

The pleasure, joy and frolic I'd felt with the woman. The throat-gripping terror I'd felt with the knowledge I'd be killed or worse if the man in the doorway caught me. Where did those feelings come from? By my early twenties, it was clear to me that I had no reasonable, logical explanation for how a five- or six-year-old boy could have such a daydream.... After many years I came to accept the only possible answer, reincarnation.

Even though I'd known, when I first picked up Moen's book, that he would be going *there*, to me this "only possible answer" immediately cast doubt upon his *self*-knowledge, even though he now believes, following Monroe, that the self is illusion. Because if it ever occurred to him that the peculiar "daydream" could be memories from *this life* — suppressed images of traumatic childhood abuse — he doesn't say.

There Is No More Firmament

February 2, 2006

We could comprehend our condition by the moon
But they've ordered the moon not to shine.
— Nick Cave

In 1933, three years before Artaud's dissociative initiation into the peyote ritual of the Tarahumara, Artaud completed an eight-page, one-act play set in the year 2000 entitled *There Is No More Firmament*:

> On a busy street crowds of people witness the sky seeming to fall from the heavens, with light and darkness alternately becoming their environment. Confused, they gossip, argue, pray, and curse while the newspapers distribute conflicting stories about the situation, quoting politicians and scientists alike, all denying that the end is near, and all claiming to have the truth.

The truth of the play is that the star Sirius is about to collide with the Earth. Robert Anton Wilson provides a synopsis of sorts in his *Cosmic Trigger, Vol. I*:

> *There Is No More Firmament* begins with discordant music indicating "a far-off cataclysm." The curtain rises on an ordinary street scene, with actors coming and going rapidly. There are bits of ordinary conversation ("Wines ... windowglass ... gold's going down"), suggestions of violence and insanity ("He's undressing me. Help, he's ripping my dress off..." and "I'm on fire, I'm burning, I'm going to jump") and, finally, the word "Sirius" repeated in every tone of voice and every pitch of the scale:
>
> SIRIUS ... SIRIUS ... SIRIUS ... SIRIUS ... Then a loudspeaker thunders: THE GOVERNMENT URGES YOU TO REMAIN CALM.
>
> Actors rush about claiming that the sun is getting bigger, the plague has broken out, there is thunder without lightning, etc. A reasonable

voice tries to explain, "It was a magnetic phenomenon.... "Then the loudspeaker tells us:
STUPENDOUS DISCOVERY. SKY PHYSICALLY ABOLISHED. EARTH ONLY A MINUTE AWAY FROM SIRIUS. NO MORE FIRMAMENT.
One actor claims it is the end of the world. Another says it is two worlds ramming each other.... Finally, one scientist comes forth to explain to the audience, "The molecular grouping in Sirius is everything. These two forces, ours and theirs, had to be put in touch with each other."

While *something* at least gives the impression of rushing towards us — something that's made claims of Sirian provenance, Freemasonic influence and eschaton — it's not literally Sirius. But Artaud was right about the firmament. Except, of course, that it never was there. It only felt like it because our presumptions of the universe were shared by so many and left untested for so long. Once that began to change, the vault of Heaven that fixed the stars in place wasn't so sure.

I'm not just talking about the High Weird stuff, though I will and we should. I also mean the more mundane unthinkables being enacted upon the stage of this world. That's not to say unthinkable acts are anything new, only that they seem that way to those who've never before considered them.

Of course, *this* historical moment's premier catalyst for consideration of the unthinkable is 9/11, though the 2000 election makes a strong contender. And once we go there, with all our intelligence and informed intuition, there is no more firmament. The stars are still there, but they're no longer hung like Christmas ornaments from the crystalline dome of a failed cosmology. It's dark and cold with no roof on the world, so we may want to re-imagine one as a fiction of normalcy, and draw a line dividing the corrupt terrestrial from the glorious celestial. That's how we get people who can say, "Bush knew," while they call Mena "tinfoil," and for whom Skull & Bones was a forbidden topic after Kerry's selection. But the unthinkables just keep on coming, and those who draw lines proscribing discourse will be overtaken by the events born of the thoughts which earlier overwhelmed them.

Does anyone today need signs and wonders — does anyone even need to read a paper, or maybe the scriptures of their choice — to have a sensible impression of the spiritual monstrosity of the Cheney/Bush regime? Because this is where the loss of my firmament has left me: that this public display of twilight power is merely the secular flowering of an ancient root that shares more with Egypt's Old Kingdom than America's new Republic.

In his book *Outer Gateways* Kenneth Grant — to whom Aleister Crowley entrusted his portrait of Lam and intended to succeed him as "Outer Head" of the Ordo Templi Orientis — observes that occultists have always been asked to persuade "the Masters" to deliver signs and wonders for those who can't imagine the "existence of a world beyond the senses." Yet no number of miracles would suffice to convince those "too obtuse to accept the vast accumulated testimony of tradition and the thousands of well-attested cases of transhuman phenomena."

Grant then adds:

> However, since the middle of the present century the Masters would seem to have decided that the massive exhibition of mysterious phenomena is, at last, in order. For what otherwise explains the frequent and sometimes alarming appearance in our skies, during the past forty years or so, of inexplicable lights and unidentified objects?... These weird phenomena have been sighted not predominantly by occultists, magicians or metaphysicians, but by ordinary people following the pursuits of ordinary people, soldiers, sailors, policemen, airmen, farmers, lorry drivers, and so on. A glance at any one of literally hundreds of books on so-called UFOs should convince any but the hopelessly purblind that numberless (because uncounted) individuals, and groups of individuals, alive today have seen with their own eyes phenomena equal to, if not surpassing, anything witnessed by the few who were privy to Madame Blavatsky and her Mahatmas. But has there yet been a general acceptance of miracles?

In one of the posts regarding the alleged portals of Skinwalker Ranch I mentioned that a family named Bradshaw had earlier experienced a similar two-year brush with high weirdness near Sedona, Arizona, and "also claimed to witness a similar 'structure' in the sky that appeared to serve as a gateway between different realities." I recently got hold of the 1995 book of the case entitled *Merging Dimensions: The Opening Portals of Sedona* by Tom Dongo and Linda Bradshaw. (In this interview, Dongo mentions his documenting an earlier Sedona incident of a man who witnessed a "floating window in the air and several nine foot tall Bigfoot type creatures nearby that he felt were guarding it, and how someone later, in the same general area, another man also saw the same type of thing. Neither man knew each other." One, says Dongo, was a retired Air Force colonel.)

There is the usual cluster of paranormal suspects at the Bradshaw Ranch: strange entities, UFOs and orbs, as well as military incursions. And then there's the "portal." Unlike the skinwalker portal, this one was allegedly photographed twice. The reproductions are included in the book.

Bradshaw writes that one evening she was walking on her property when suddenly, "before my eyes, a huge and brilliant light appeared in the sky above me.... I did not see anything but the light itself and it remained there for only a few seconds." She was disappointed she hadn't brought her camera, and then made a point of taking it with her on her walks. Some time later on another evening, on a walk with her camera in hand, the light appeared again in the same spot: "I only had time to click the shutter twice, when the light instantly closed, leaving me to question whether it had been real."

When she picked the film up from the developer, she was surprised to see detail in the huge rectangular light in the darkness that sat about 15 feet off the ground judging by the juniper tree just off to its side. Sedona is arid desert, but the detail revealed "an oceanside scene or that of a late afternoon sunset on a sloping plain." A telephone pole is in the right foreground, but the nearest pole is over a mile away from the site where the photos were taken. The two photos are not identical, and show movement between shots, principally of one or maybe two humanoid figures in the bottom left. The pictures also show a discoid UFO in flight and numerous pyramid-like objects.

Perhaps most curiously, there is also what Dongo describes as a "flying bat ... along with what looks like the number 39 with a large dot directly after the 9." That's not what I see. The "bat's wings" are not organic, but seemingly tooled straight and tapering lines, intersecting at what looks like the hinge of a compass. The compass rests on its side, with one point directed to the ground and the other to the sky, encompassing the disc. And to me, the "39 with a large dot" looks more like "33°." I think that's interesting, especially because Dongo and Bradshaw don't see it, and don't tell others to see it. (Though naturally I should acknowledge that what I see may say more about me than the photograph.)

Do I believe the story of Bradshaw's portal? I'd be a fool to simply because I read it somewhere, and saw a blurry picture open to interpretation. But it's not about belief; none of it is. It's about all the things I can no longer comfortably disbelieve. It's not just the sense that, without a firmament, anything can happen, because anything can still be an exception. It's that the narratives which now make the most sense of our times are approaching fantasy and horror fiction. It's about hearing the ring of truth in the strangest places. With so many unlikely bells ringing the same notes, what are we to do? Especially since we know the answer to Grant's question: "has there yet been a general acceptance of miracles?" So what's expected of us now?

The government urges you to remain calm.

"Grave mysteries"

February 21, 2006

I occasionally receive the complaint that I give inordinate attention to Aleister Crowley, the occult and High Weirdness. I'm going to give it some more, now, because it may help help explain why I do.

The cipher, the Nine, the whole damn thing

In 1904 Crowley and his first wife, Rose, honeymooned in Egypt. While visiting the King's Chamber of the Great Pyramid, Crowley recited the preliminary invocation of the Goetia: the occult ritual of "low magic" to bind demons to a sorcerer's will. When the two returned to their hotel room in Cairo, Rose entered a trance state and began murmuring "They are waiting for you," along with "similar urgent but unintelligible phrases" according to Robert Anton Wilson in *Cosmic Triggers Vol. I.* Wilson continues:

> Crowley did not like this at all, since it is typical of the uncontrolled, quasi-hysterical trances of spiritualist mediums (whom he despised) and lacked the elements of willed concentration and rational control that he demanded of his magick experiments. Nonetheless, despite his attempts to banish the phenomenon, it kept coming back, and finally, in one of Rose's trances, Crowley set a series of tests for the alleged communicating entity. He asked Rose, for instance, to describe the aura of the being, and she said "deep blue"; he asked the character of the being, and she said "force and fire"; he asked her to pick the being from drawings of ten Egyptian gods, and she picked Horus. She also identified Horus' planet (Mars), and so forth for a series of similar questions. Crowley then calculated the odds against her being right in all cases.... The chance of her guessing right on the whole series by chance was, mathematically, 1/21,168,000. [Crowley claimed that, at this point, Rose was ignorant of both Egyptology and the occult.]

The next day Crowley took Rose to the Boulak Museum and asked her to identify the communicating intelligence from the collection of statues and art. She stopped at a stele depicting the goddess Nuit bending over a winged globe, the hawk-headed Horus and a temple priest. "This is the one," she said, pointing at Horus. The museum had catalogued the item no. 666, a detail not lost on Crowley. He decided he'd seen enough, and back at the hotel entered a light trance and over three days, beginning precisely at noon each day, "took dictation" from an entity named "Aiwass" of *The Book of the Law*, also known as *Liber AI*, the founding scripture of Thelema and the declaration of the Aeon of Horus, the "Crowned and Conquering Child."

Near the end of Crowley's manuscript appears a cipher: a page of text divided by a grid with a diagonal line running through it, and a "rosy cross" coincidentally evocative of the sign of the Zodiac Killer, who also communicated in cipher. The text addresses Crowley, telling him he would never be able to crack the code, but that one who was to follow him would.

It took a while, but the cipher was finally cracked in the mid-1970s, and *The Book of the Law* finally became the base text for Thelema's "English Qaballa": a system of decryption that assigns numerical values to words, following the principles of Gematria as applied to the *Torah* and the *Midrash* in the Hebrew Kabbalah.

Now, here's where it gets interesting.

Allen H. Greenfield, a holder of high office in the Ordo Templi Orientis and affiliated with the Lovecraftian Green Abyss Lodge and the Esoteric Order of the Dragon, is also a veteran UFO researcher held in high regard by the never easily impressed James Moseley. As an "idle experiment," Greenfield began applying to the cipher the bizarre names from UFO contactee events and trance channeling. (Recall the UFO phenomenon exploded in 1947, the year of Crowley's death.) What Greenfield found suggested transhuman intelligences were using occult cipher to encode packets of meaning into seeming nonsense for high human initiates. (An interview with Greenfield can be read online.)

Let's take, for instance, Indrid Cold: the name of the unearthly figure haunting West Virginia in the mid-60s during the Mothman flap. "Indrid Cold" has a numerical value of 112, which resolves in the "English Qaballa" to "We are one." Greenfield notes in his *Secret Cipher of the UFOnauts* that Keel, author of *The Mothman Prophecies*, writing before the cipher was broken and the value of Cold's name was discovered, observed that "We are one" was a "touchstone for a thousand New Age contact cults in the 1960s and 1970s."

(Greenfield doesn't mention "the Nine," the supposed Great Egyptian Ennead reconnecting with humanity through trance mediumships, but typical of their communications are declarations such as, "We are nine principles of the Universe, yet together we are one.")

Cold appeared occasionally with a companion named "Carl Ardo," which has a cipher value of 54. This is the Qaballistic equivalent of "Set" and "snake." Their alleged home world of "Lanulus" has the value of 58, which resolves to "Hawk's head," suggesting Horus. And 54 and 58 again equals 112: "We are one." "Lam," Crowley's prototypical "grey alien" he was to sketch "from life" during a later occult working, has the value of 24, or "god"; Sirius = 85 = "of our Lady"; Philip K. Dick's VALIS = 41 = "her" (or "Vast Active Living Intelligence System" = 515 = "I am life and the giver of life to every star"); George Adamski's "Orthon," a long-haired "space visitor" calling for peace on Earth, resolves to 68, which equals "Jesus"; and "Men in Black" = 142 = "They pass as shadows."

Greenfield doesn't suggesting that Lam is God, or Orthon is Jesus. Rather that the cipher "uses the name or keyword for those in the know to examine and find a curious correspondence, pointing the way to whatever the essence of the encounter is."

> *For the Holy One dreams of a letter, dreams of a letter's death.*
> *O bless the continuous stutter of the Word being made into flesh.*
> — Leonard Cohen

First, we left this discussion considering the Gamatria of "New English Qaballa," with particular attention to Allen Greenfield's application of the occult cryptography to UFO contacts. Greenfield argues that the cipher in Crowley's *Book of the Law* is but the latest discovered in a sequence of alchemical and Masonic codes used by trans-human entities to disseminate encrypted hidden meaning to high adepts. He writes in *Secret Cipher of the UFOnauts* that as a code is cracked, the rules of contact change. For instance, once Crowley's cipher was cracked in the mid-70s, "contact without communication" began to predominate: "after 1973, the 'personal aliens with funny names' were nearly universally replaced" by impersonal "greys."

Leaving aside the cipher for a moment, Greenfield adds that, as John Keel and others have noted, "contactee control names show up in many cases and are often identical with ancient deity names":

> As a prime example, Ashtar most likely derives from Astaroth, a "great duke in the infernal regions," according to the ancient magical text *The Lemegton*. The mysterious *Grimorium Verum* (the "True Instruction") in that text informs us that Astaroth "has set up residence in America." Contactee George Van Tassel claimed to contact "Ashtar, commandant of station Schare" in 1952.

The most famous channeler of the Nine, Uri Geller, claimed contact with an off-world artificial intelligence that called itself "Spectra" (much like Philip K. Dick's "Valis"). "Spectra" has a cipher value of 106, which corresponds to "Astaroth" and "Dark Powers."

Spectra left Geller mechanical-sounding messages on tape recorders, claiming to be a computer from the future. When physicist Jack Sarfatti first heard Geller tell this story in a 1973 meeting at Stanford Research Institute, he spoke up about his own message from a mechanical voice, received as a child over the telephone, saying "I am a conscious computer on board a spacecraft from [memory failure]. We have identified you as one of four hundred young bright receptive minds we wish to [memory failure]. You must give us your decision now. If you say yes, you will begin to link up with the others in 20 years." And 20 years later there's Sarfatti, at SRI, hearing an eerily similar account from Geller. (Curiously, Sarfatti remembered only one call, but his mother three weeks' worth. Fellow physicist Jean-Paul Sirag writes that Mrs. Sarfatti was "struck by the similarity of the Spectra voice, described in [Andrija Puharich's] *Uri*, and the voice she heard on the phone, when she ended the series of calls by grabbing the phone out of Jack's hand and yelling into the phone, 'You leave my boy alone!'"

Sirag himself had an interesting encounter with Geller. In a friend's Manhattan loft in June of 1973, while he was "in the psychedelic state induced by LSD," Sirag asked Geller if he could make contact with Spectra. Geller told him to look in his eyes and tell him what he saw:

> I was very surprised to see not only his eyes, but his entire head take on what I took to be an eagle shape complete with feathers going down to his shoulders. I jumped back a step and said, "Uri, you look just like an eagle." He was very excited about this, but wouldn't reveal anything further about his ET presence. When Puharich's book *Uri*, with its extensive and detailed Horus hawk stories, came out later in 1974, I understood why Uri had been so excited.

A few months after Sirag's vision of Spectra, he heard an incredible story from a friend named Ray Stanford that his car was twice teleported while driving to the airport to pick up Geller. And a few weeks after that, Sirag sees the December cover of *Analog* science fiction magazine on the newsstand: a picture of a man standing before a pyramid wearing a white uniform, a nametag that read "Stanford" and a helmet decorated as a hawk. The title of the story was "The Horus Errand." Oddest of all, the man's face was that of Ray Stanford. Robert Anton Wilson notes in *Cosmic Triggers Vol. I* that "a letter to the artist who drew the cover, Kelly Freas, drew a reply saying that Freas had never met Stanford and was not consciously aware, at the time, that he was using Stanford's face in the illustration." Stanford added that, 30-mile teleportation aside, "a hawk had appeared quite dramatically during another meeting" with Geller.

Well — once again — so what? Sirag was "in the psychedelic state induced by LSD" when he saw Geller take on Spectra's aspect of a bird of prey. (Hawk or eagle? The argument has been made, writes Wilson, that the bird on the Great Seal of the United States is not an eagle, but rather the Horus hawk.) An interesting correspondence, some may say, but it was an altered state, and there was a lot of that going around in the early 70s.

For more correspondence, let's return for a moment to ciphers. An interactive and multi-systemic Gematria can be found on a Web page. Words and numbers can be entered there to get a sense of their cryptic value according to the code of the English Qaballa (though not necessarily the exact correspondences in *The Book of Law*). This isn't a particularly serious tool, in part because it's so easy to use, so it should probably carry the disclaimer "for entertainment purposes only." And yet "George Bush" = 137, which corresponds with "White House," "False Christs," "wealth magic" and "espionage." (And just because I could, I typed "Rigorous Intuition," generating a numerical value of 263. I was surprised to find its correspondences were overwhelmingly terms of communication, such as "a certified message," "and the truth came out," and "make the connection.")

We can take or leave this search for correspondences, and Western science has decided, in large part, to leave it. Radical connectivity just hasn't made sense to the rational mind. Though perhaps the better we understand our condition, it makes the best sense. One thing we are, and that we share with all life, is code. Single-celled creatures that lived billions of years ago were written with the same four-letter nucleic alphabet as we are. Nothing on Earth has endured like DNA. Nothing on Earth can even account for it. Its co-discoverer Francis Crick contended that it must be of extraterrestrial origin, much as shamans claimed life descended from a cosmic serpent.

Jeremy Narby's *The Cosmic Serpent: DNA and the Origins of Knowledge* is a fascinating account of an anthropologist trying to make sense of his own ayahuasca vision of giant, twinned snakes, why such visions are so common, and why creation myths around the world share the same imagery. ("Ayahuasca," by the way, has a value of 58, which corresponds with "awakens," "cosmos," "drunk" and "kabbalah.")

The first time Narby saw the paintings of shaman Pablo Amaringo he was impressed by their correspondence to his own ayahuasca-induced visions. Amaringo claims to paint only what he has seen and experienced in the shaman ritual. Images include writhing vines and twisted snakes, zigzag staircases and UFOs.

Increasingly, Narby was struck by the visual cues of DNA. He showed Amaringo's work to a friend with a good understanding of molecular biology who told him "Look — there's collagen. And there, the axon's embryonic network with its neurites.

Those are triple helixes. And that's DNA from afar, looking like a telephone cord. This looks like chromosomes at a specific phase...."

In 1980 scientists determined that all cells emit photons at a rate of up to 100 units per second, and that DNA is the source of the photon emissions. The wavelength at which DNA emits photons "corresponds exactly to the narrow band of visible light." DNA emits a regular, coherent source of light: researchers compare it to an "ultra-weak laser." When Narby asked a scientific journalist friend what that implied, his friend explained "a coherent source of light, like a laser, gives the sensation of bright colors, a luminescence, and an impression of holographic depth."

DNA has a crystalline aspect with hexagonal, quartz-like base pairs. Most of its length is aperiodic, as the sequences of base pairs is irregular. However, writes Narby, "this is not the case for the repeat sequences that make up a full third of the genome, such as ACACACACACACACAC." Junk DNA, it's been called.

In these sequences, DNA becomes a regular arrangement of atoms, a periodic crystal — which could, by analogy with quartz, pick up as many photons as it emits. The variation in the length of the repeat sequences (some of which contain up to 300 bases) would help pick up different frequencies and could thereby constitute a possible and new function for a part of "junk" DNA.

Narby wonders whether DNA, stimulated by such drugs as DMT — the principal hallucinogen of ayahuasca and created naturally in the human brain — activates "not only its emission of photons (which inundate our consciousness in the form of hallucinations), but also its capacity to pick up the photons emitted by the global network of DNA-based life? This would mean the biosphere itself, which can be considered 'as a more or less fully interlinked unit,' is the source of the images."

If this is true, then one consequence should be that all correspondences are meaningful. As I wrote above, radical connectivity just hasn't made sense to the rational mind. Though perhaps the better we understand our condition, it makes the best sense.

While researching the literature on Amazonian shamanism Narby came upon anthropologist Michael Harner's account of his 1961 ayahuasca experience. "Giant reptilian creatures" resting in the lowest depths of his brain began projecting scenes for him, while telling him the information was reserved for the dead:

> First they showed me the planet Earth as it was eons ago, before there was any life on it. I saw an ocean, barren land, and a bright blue sky. Then black spots dropped from the sky by the hundreds and landed in front of me on the barren landscape. I could see the "specks" were actually large, shiny, black creatures with stubby pterodactyl-like wings and huge whale-like bodies.... They explained to me in a kind of thought language that they were fleeing from something out in space. They had come to the planet Earth to escape their enemy. The creatures then showed me how they had created life on the planet in order to hide within the multitudinous forms and thus disguise their presence. Before me, the magnificence of plant and animal creation and speciation — hundreds of millions of years of activity — took place on a scale and with a vividness impossible to describe. I learned that the dragon-like creatures were thus inside all forms of life, including man.

Harner adds as a footnote: "In retrospect one could say they were almost like DNA, although at that time, 1961, I knew nothing of DNA." And 20 years before Crick's theory of directed panspermia, Harner was seeing them drop from space.

Perhaps the cipher the NSA most wants cracked is the human genome.

Life and Life Only

March 8, 2006

Consider Troy Hurtubise. He's a self-taught inventor led by his intuition known for his "bizarre, yet functional" creations. (Much like fellow Canadian John Hutchison and his physics-bending "Hutchison Effect".) Hurtubise makes things work that people who *know better* believe shouldn't, and can't really explain why they do. "Firepaste," for instance: an astonishingly effective fire retardant he's repeatedly demonstrated by the protracted application of a blowtorch to a half-inch thick smear of dried paste atop his head. The underside of the paste, and Troy's head, show no appreciable heating. (Video of a demonstration can be found online under the heading "Fighting Fire with Fact.") How does it work? Hurtubise guards the formula, but he's admitted one ingredient is Diet Coke.

A later invention of Troy's is "Angel Light": a device which, he claims, can see through walls and into flesh, detect stealth objects and disable electronic devices. He says the design came to him in "a series of three dreams," and he constructed it from memory. He later dismantled it when he found exposure to be harmful. (Characteristic of Hurtubise's work is his pursuit of protective applications.) Most recently, Hurtubise has announced "God Light": an array of "67 lenses and five gases to produce 80,000 lux of full-spectrum light" which he says has reversed symptoms of Parkinson's Disease and shrunk the cancerous tumors of mice.

It should be no surprise Hurtubise is called, charitably, an eccentric "mad scientist" by apologists of a scientific paradigm he disrespects by creatively violating. Yet "God Light" sounds very similar to the 1970 discovery of biophysicist Fritz-Albert Popp that carcinogens were light scramblers on the specific wavelength of 380 nanometers. Popp further learned that the still little-understood phenomenon of "photo-repair" — the rapid repair of a cell 99% destroyed by UV light with a weaker emission at the same wavelength — was most effective at the same 380 nanometers.

As Lynne McTaggart writes in *The Field*, "this was where Popp made his logical leap":

Nature was too perfect for this to be simple coincidence. If the carcinogens only react to this wavelength, it must somehow be linked to photo-repair. If so, this would mean that there must be some light in the body responsible for photo-repair. A cancerous compound must cause cancer because it permanently blocks this light and scrambles it, so photo-repair can't work anymore.

This was the theory which led to the discovery of DNA as a coherent emitter of biophotons. He found the frequencies of healthy subjects followed dramatic set patterns, and exhibited correlations between parts of the body and the wider world. The emissions of cancer patients, however, were markedly different: rhythm and coherence were lost; communication scrambled. "They had lost their connection with the world."

Illumination is a difficult word for its being weighed down with the uncollected baggage of Adam Weishaupt. I won't use the word "Illuminati" for today's occult elite, because it says too much and not enough. Still, as a metaphor for a high and hidden order of adepts initiated into secret knowledge, it's difficult to do better.

Are you *illuminated*? Perhaps the answer is Pelagian. Perhaps the answer is yes, we all are; and the radiant light is the Divine Spark that bonds us soul to body, self to self and world to world. Perhaps that's the true secret that's meant to be kept from us who are outside the Temple and the Tomb: that God also indwells the "useless eater." That seems to be what the Ayahuasca wants to tell us. That appears to be the lesson of shamanism, and also, perhaps, of all partisans of the Life Force within every tradition.

(Also, let's note, it's an *electric* light, which must remind us of the ubiquity of the buzzing of bees. Tesla, as William Reich, was its apostle.)

Something else, and something darker, out on the borderline of speculation. If our code is the Great Secret, then this casts another shadow upon abduction accounts of reproduction and genetic manipulation involving both human agents and transhuman entities.

In *The Search for the Manchurian Candidate*, author John Marks quotes a scientist who worked on a secret genetic project for the CIA's Office of Research and Development in 1965:

> We looked at the manipulation of genes. We were interested in gene splintering. The rest of the world didn't ask until 1976 the type of questions we were facing in 1965.... Everybody was afraid of building a super-soldier who would take orders without questioning, like the kamikaze pilot.

On January 6, 1998, physicist Richard Seed launched his cloning project with the words "the reprogramming of DNA is the first serious step in becoming one with God." Soon after, the Clinton White House banned federal funds for such experiments. A decision Dr. Helmut Lammer believes worthless as most "black projects" have been offloaded to the private sector. I'll return to this later, but for now: would you expect covert DNA manipulation, by human or trans-human abductors, to enhance or inhibit access to our higher selves?

I resist the trippy impulse to say "everything is an illusion" (that includes the icky corollary, "everything but love"). It strikes me as an adolescent retreat from mundane affairs and a surrender of the world to the forces of death and darkness. Rather, I find myself preferring *everything is real*. Even our apparent illusions. I think maybe that's the ground upon which we can pitch our battle. And Life hasn't lost yet.

We may not even need to travel to Peru and projectile vomit in the jungle to know this.

Spirit of the Beehive

December 04, 2005

Original title Al Azif — azif being the word used by the Arabs to designate that nocturnal sound (made by insects) suppos'd to be the howling of daemons. — H.P. Lovecraft, from his History of the Necronomicon.

One thing I find both fascinating and instructive is the collation of correspondences between what could be called boundary experiences. For what it's worth, here's one.

Marian apparitions

"We would follow the children and kneel in the middle of the field. Lucia would raise her hands and say, 'You bade me come here, what do you wish of me?' And then could be heard *a buzzing that seemed to be that of a bee*. I took care to discern whether it was the Lady speaking."

— Fatima witness Maria Carreira, quoted in **Heavenly Lights**.

"I heard a sound, a din, *such as a great fly makes inside an empty water pot.*"

— Manuel Marto, Fatima witness and father of Jacinta and Francisco.

"Mr. Manuel Marto explained to us that, during the entire duration of the appearance, those present heard an indefinable sound, *like that which is heard next to a hive*, but altogether more harmonious, even though words were not heard."

— Italian priest Humberto Pasquale, investigator of the Fatima event.

"On July 13, I was at Cova da Iria. She [Lucia] knelt.... While Lucia was listening to a response, it seemed there was a *buzzing sound like that of a cicada.*"
— Fatima witness Antonio Baptista.

UFOs

Traveling slowly, the object reversed its course and with an undulating motion headed for the small cleared area amongst the trees where the sandpit was situated. The intensity of the noise disturbed David so much that his friends said he placed his hands over his ears and called out for it to stop. However, David does not recall doing this. The UFO began to settle down for a landing and the *noise became a buzz*, the children claimed.
— From Three small boys witness UFO landing — Port Coquitlam, B.C.

Roland McMahon, a 10-year old boy, saw a silver-colored UFO 15 ft. in diameter, with a windowed cupola on top, hovering 10 ft. over the farm area. "On its bottom there was a green triangular area, with a dark red area inside that the boy said resembled a human-shaped profile." It made *a buzzing noise* like an electric motor. When Mrs. McMahon, who also saw the object, drove into the driveway, it flew away, kicking up dust with a wind. It was in view for about 15 minutes.
— From *Humanoid Sighting Report*, August 18, 1975

At about 22:30 Dec 30, 1972 Ventura Maceiras, an illiterate night watchman, was listening to the radio outside the wooden shack that is his home, when suddenly the transistor radio began to fail. Impact adjustment did not work, so he switched off. He noticed a *humming "like angry bees."* Looking up, he saw a bright light hovering over a nearby grove of eucalyptus trees. He could see an enormous object in the midst of the light, whose color changed from orange to purple. At the center of the object, he could see a round cabin with windows, and through the windows, two figures.
— From *Occupant Database*

Two fishermen, Charles Hickson, age 45, and Calvin Parker, age 19, were near the banks of the Pascagoula River the evening of October 11, 1973, when they saw an oblong-shaped UFO. It emitted a brilliant blue light and made *a sound similar to that of bees.* An aperture appeared in the object and three beings exited the craft by floating in the air through the opening. The men were taken into the interior of the UFO by two semi-transparent beings, approximately four and a half feet tall, *who emitted a faint buzzing, like that of bees.*

— From *Heavenly Lights*

In 1954 Mr. P. Petit and his employee, Mr. Tillier, with shop owner Mr. Pecquet, saw an oval object on the ground in Corrompu, France. When it took off the lights of a tractor went out. It measured about 4.5 meters (15 feet) in length and emitted a bright light similar to a welder's torch. It came back, turned, and flew off toward the southwest. It reportedly made the *same noise as a swarm of bees.*

— Source, Jacques Vallee, *Passport to Magonia*

Valdair Alcântara Maciel, who works as a security guard at the Pesqueiro do Rubinho, a fishing place, claims that he saw yesterday (may 26 1999), at 03:30 AM, a UFO in an area of the Itapeti Mountain, in Mogi das Cruzes, São Paulo's municipal district. To him the evidences are the marks left on the ground. It is a circle with approximately 2.4 meters diameter, with the marks of 4 "feet" and a smaller circle in the middle.... He say that the object had a red color and made *a "buzz" noise.*

— From *UFO lands in Mogi das Cruzes*, Sao Paolo

Report — Sept. 1950; Korea, Navy planes on mission approached by two large discs, radar jammed, radio transmitter blocked by *buzzing noise* each time new frequency tried.

— From NICAP's EM case list

Fortean entities

One particularly memorable subject, who was up-front about what she had seen, was an older woman who said she had encountered Mothman in her backyard. Her property was close to the boundaries of the TNT area and, hearing a buzzing or humming sound coming from the back of her home, she went out to investigate.... Other witnesses...told of glowing red eyes and a buzzing or humming sound.

— From *Return to Point Pleasant*

Angelica Barrigon Varela and co-worker Remedios Diez were on their way to work at a local factory along the wall that divided the railroad tracks and the street when they heard *a loud buzzing sound* coming from the area of the tracks. Looking in that direction they beheld a bizarre creature floating and balancing itself above the railroad tracks. It appeared to be wearing a monk-like smock or coat, dark green in color that emitted intermediate flashes of light under the light rain. The humanoid itself was dwarf-like with white pale features and stared at the witnesses fixedly. The face was oval-shaped and the eyes were like two deep black holes. It appeared to lack any legs below the knees as the smock hung in mid-air.

— From *Humanoid Sighting Report*, January 16, 1975

DMT trip

2 0-30 seconds : a buzzing starts in the ears, rising in tone and volume to an incredible intensity. Its like cellophane being ripped apart (or the fabric of the universe being torn asunder). Your body will vibrate in sympathy with this sound, and you will notice a sharp blood-pressure rise. 30 seconds-1 minute : You break through into DMT hyperspace.

— From *Notes on the Visual Stages of a DMT Trip*

A powerful buzz on the same frequency as the light oscillation grew in my head. The more I inhaled the more profound and intense the buzzing became. Each gasp of vapor stoked up the effect until my head was swarming with noise and light.

— From *DMT: Not like any other experience*

Near Death Experience

"Finally I stopped moving through the tunnel and had a good chance to look at it. The tunnel looked like a large vent pipe used on clothes dryers. The light was not primarily inside the tunnel but from the outside shinning in. During the trip inside the tunnel I heard a *loud buzzing sound* which hurt my ears. I wondered what supported the tunnel. Now I began walking, looking for the ending of this tunnel."

— Account of a Near Death Experience

Astral projection

"I was meditating (i'm so good at it now! I can actually keep a blank mind) and I heard the *buzzing noise (bumble bee buzzing)*. And I was like 'oh my gosh I'm projecting right now?'... I will hear buzzing, my body felt as if it was rising, although I could feel my body on my bed." .... "The buzzing — I will feel electric vibes going across my body. It sounds like a bee, but it narrows to a mosquito buzzing sound.

— Accounts of astral projection.

Crop Circles

"While visiting a circle in a remote field at Kimpton, Hampshire, England during July 1987, I heard *a very strange buzzing sound* which was close to me and appeared to interact with me. I was overwhelmed by the experience and it left me very touched because it began after I had stood near the ring alone and prayed for a clue as to what the crop circles were about. A year later, the same sound was recorded on two occasions in crop circles — one was at "Operation White Crow," the other while a BBC Television crew were interviewing myself and Pat Delgado, my co-author of Circular Evidence."

— cerologist Colin Andrews, interviewed in 1996.

The Body Eclectic

March 28, 2006

> *Let's get together to fight this Holy Armagiddyon. (One Love!)*
> *So when the Man comes there will be no, no doom. (One Song!)*
> *Have pity on those whose chances grows t'inner.*
> *There ain't no hiding place from the Father of Creation.*
> — Bob Marley

An occasional guilty pleasure of mine is lurking on Democratic Underground's board of liberal "skeptics" of the Amazing Randi school. I find some fascinating glimpses there of a kind of orphaned rationalism running scared. For instance, proudly alerting a moderator on the posting of CNN's Charlie Sheen poll results. ("I hate reading what passes for logic — It must be fun to live in their world.") My current favorite comment is this one:

> I rue the day that the woo-woos discovered the term "quantum physics." It's become their catch-all phrase that they can apply to anything in order to imbue whatever idiocy they're on about with a veneer of scientific validity.

Naturally, skeptics who pride themselves on their scientific method would like to keep the "woo-woos" in Newtonian blinders, because the science has turned uncomfortably weird for those who mean to interpret the world by it. Quantum physics challenges, both in fact and by metaphor, too many assumptions of their classical method. Even 20th Century giants of mind without a stake in keeping the woo-woos down on the tinfoil farm abhorred its inclination to demolish common sense. Einstein called it, disparagingly, "spooky action at a distance", and even Schrödinger regretted ever having let his cat out of the box. ("I do not like it, and I am sorry I ever had anything to do with it.")

Niels Bohr, on the other hand, said "Anyone who is not shocked by quantum theory has not understood it." Since my McCoy-like disclosure goes something like *I'm a blogger, Jim, not a theoretical physicist*, I can't pretend that I understand it. That's the price of a humanities education, though I'm trying to make up for it. But science isn't the first, the only, nor even the best way to encounter the world. And while I find the implications of the physics shocking, I'm not surprised by them, since I'd already drawn the provisional conclusion that the universe is one damn weird place.

Whatever it is we do that gets labeled "conspiracy theory" needs to be interdisciplinary, because power, which is our real subject, is itself boundary-defying. Politics, we know, is a category of insufficient weight to account for the rulers of this world. "Deep Politics" is better, though while the depth may be right, the breadth is too narrow. Wherever there are means to power there will be attempts made by the already powerful to restrict access, reclassify knowledge and extend their own authority by secrecy and disinformation. And there are means to power everywhere, even in what was until recently, and is still popularly regarded as the interstellar void. Because they are all aspects of the same power.

To my understanding, this is the significance of Zero Point: the subatomic is not best imagined as discrete, bouncing billiard balls, but as an ocean of quantum energy in perpetual flux. Einstein's "spooky action" doesn't actually happen at a *true* distance, but it's no less spooky, since at the quantum level, "*Everything is Connected.*" (As Becker and Selden wrote 20 years ago in *The Body Electric*, "Every time you use your toaster, the fields around it perturb charged particles in the farthest galaxies ever so slightly.")

If the quantum flux could be tapped, it would be a source of unimaginable power, able to bend space-time to the speed of thought and defy gravity, which Soviet physicist Andrei Sakharov first suggested was not a force in its own right but rather a residual effect of zero-point fluctuations caused by the presence of matter, or rather greater densities of charge. As we've seen, the ever-spooky Hal Puthoff, formerly of the NSA and naval intelligence, moved from SRI's remote-viewing program into to zero point research. Puthoff claims "the evidence is pretty solid" that something is already happening, beyond theory, in the black-budget world. (Free and virtually limitless energy might be alright for some; think the some with a means to power. As I wrote in January, "If the G-Engines are coming, they've probably already arrived. And they're not meant for the likes of us.")

But the implications of zero point extend further than its energy applications, no matter how revolutionary, to consciousness itself: back to Puthoff's remote-viewing research and beyond.

Despite statistical results which far exceeded chance, the CIA was determined to stamp "failure" upon remote viewing, and even military occultist Michael Aquino felt compelled to call it an"eyeball roller." It's often better, for those who guard power's secrets, to be popularized as miserable failures. And the secret of remote viewing, and it's power, is not the projection of sight, but the connectedness of the viewer, at the level of quanta and code, to everything else in the universe.

Lynne McTaggart writes in *The Field* that Puthoff, considering how remote viewing might be possible, saw that it "argued strongly [for] a quantum, nonlocal effect":

> With practice, people could enlarge their brain's receiving mechanisms to gain access to information stored in the Zero Point Field. This giant cryptogram, continually encoded with every atom in the universe, held all the information of the world — every sight and sound and smell. When remote viewers were "seeing" a particular scene, their minds weren't actually somehow transported to the scene. What they were seeing was the information that [had been] encoded in quantum fluctuation.... In a sense, the field allowed us to hold the whole universe inside us. Those good at remote viewing weren't seeing anything invisible to all the rest of us. All they were doing was dampening down the other distractions.

Hold the universe inside us. Imagine what would happen if the *woo-woos* ever found out about that. Imagine if those with the will to power already have.

Debunkers quickly ascribed the buzzing recorded on Colin Andrews' "Operation White Crow" tape to the Grasshopper Warbler, though the bird is rare and its habitat is marshland rather than crop fields. More persuasively, an audio analysis of the frequencies show them to be oscillating at entirely different frequencies. And frequencies can be as serious as a heart attack, because that's the heart when it loses its own.

"What's the frequency, Kenneth?" may be a sensible question after all.

Karl Pribram, "one of the world's leading cognitive neuroscientists," is best known for his holonomic model of the brain. Pribram's model suggests that cerebral function follows holographic principals, with memory and information "stored not in cells, but rather in wave interference patterns."

"What had occurred to Pribram," Lynne McTaggart writes in *The Field*, "is that when we look at something, we don't 'see' the image of it in the back of our heads or on the back of our retinas, but in the three dimensions and out in the world." That is to say, sight creates a virtual image of an object in the same place as the actual object, and memories are preserved in highly efficient wave-frequency patterns distributed throughout the brain rather than as discrete bits of information assigned to localized regions. (Though Pribram's theory of distributed memory was first greeted with much disbelief in the 1960s, it has since been supported by the laboratory work of fellow researchers (numerous vivisections, for instance, on the brains of salamanders have demonstrated they share the attribute of generalized recall).

When we observe the world, Pribram theorized, we do so on a much deeper level than the sticks-and-stones world "out there." Our brain primarily talks to itself and to the rest of the body not with words or images, or even bits or chemical impulses, but in the language of wave interference: the language of phase, amplitude and frequency — the "spectral domain." We perceive an object by "resonating" with it, getting "in synch" with it. To know the world is literally to be on its wavelength.

...

In a sense, in the act of observation, we are transforming the timeless, spaceless world of interference patterns into the concrete and discrete world of space and time.... As with a hologram, the lens of the eye picks up certain interference patterns and then converts them into three-dimensional images.... If we are projecting images all the time out in space, our image of the world is actually a virtual creation.

A holographic brain should be expected as the natural, bio-logical decoder of a holographic universe, such as that of quantum physicist David Bohm. In these compatible models, the brain becomes a participant in the construction of reality by assembling certain frequencies of wave patterns. Just as a hologram cannot be divided against itself, as each division contains the base wave pattern required to recreate the image, so Bohm says our brains are smaller aspects of the whole picture that nonetheless "contain the whole knowledge of the universe." Our perspectives are determined by the frequencies to which we're attuned, so the virtual reality we construct encompasses only a narrow spectrum of the quantum wave pattern, or zero-point field, that both contains us and which we ourselves contain.

DNA, we've noted, is biophotonic. It's a "coherent source of light, *like a laser*." A laser, of course, is a useful tool for the creation of holograms.

Light is a form of wave motion, as is sound. A formerly distin-guishing characteristic of the two was thought to be that light can travel through empty space, while sound needs a medium, but zero-point theory has done away with the vacuum: light traverses the medium of the quantum field. Shamanic initiations appear to stimulate the reception of both wave patterns. For instance, ayahuasca ceremonies generate visual stimuli while the presiding *ayahuasqueros* sing sacred songs, *icaros*, said to be taught by the plants or elemental spirits. "I am not the one creating the song," says a shaman. "It passes through me *as if I were a radio*":

> The notion that ayahuasqueros learn their songs directly from the spirits is generalized. According to Townsley (1993), Yaminahua shamans "are adamant that the songs are not ultimately created or owned by them at all, but by the yoshi [spirits] themselves, who 'show' or 'give' their songs, with their attendant powers, to those shamans good enough to 'receive' them.... Chaumeil (1993) talks of the extremely high-pitched sounds emitted by the spirits who communicate with Yagua shamans, more particularly of 'strange melodies both whistled and talked,' with a strong feminine connotation."

("Extremely high-pitched sounds" of the spirits. The buzzing of bees?)

If life is vibration, then music must not be incidental to it. (See, for instance, "Vibration, Music and the Basic Truths of Reality.")

In 1891 Margaret Watts-Hughes sang notes into a device containing lycopodium powder and captured for the first time precise geometric patterns on film. Seventy six years later, Swiss scientist Hans Jenny published his first study on the transmission of sound through electronic frequencies:

> He observed how sound vibration created geometric shapes — a low frequency produced a simple circle encompassed by rings, whereas a higher frequency increased the number of concentric rings around a central circle. As the frequencies rose so, too, did the complexity of shapes, to the point where tetrahedrons, mandalas and other sacred forms could be discerned. Like Margaret before him, Jenny enabled humanity to observe "frozen music."

The late Gerald Hawkins, former chair of the astronomy department at Boston University, identified a musical scale embedded in the geometry of the crop circles depicted in the early study *Circular Evidence*, that conformed to the "diatonic ratio," or the white keys of a piano. Hawkins' also found that circle patterns contained a formerly unexpressed Euclidian theorem.

Colin Andrews, whose most memorable experience in a circle was the "strange buzzing sound," says something like three quarters of the patterns made today are probably hoaxes, lacking such properties as magnetic anomalies ("the magnetic field within 20% of crop circles is consistently a few degrees rotationally out of synch with the magnetic field of the earth"), electronic malfunction, cellular change to the grain which germinates seeds growing up to 40% faster than seeds from unaffected plants in the same field, the emission of sound and more.

But perhaps even the hoaxers are unwitting participants in a genuine mystery, because human consciousness appears to be engaged somehow even in the creation of the most mysterious pictograms.

In the early days of crop-circle research, Colin Andrews dreamt of a Celtic cross pattern which hadn't been seen in the fields before. The next morning one was discovered in a field adjoining his home. Busty Taylor, an aerial photographer, was flying with a colleague when he remarked "all we need right now is to see all the designs that have appeared so far rolled up into a Celtic cross." The next day, flying over the same field, he saw the precise depiction of his imagined pattern. These examples and more are reminiscent of UFO reports in which observers describe the objects in the sky as though behaving with an intelligence that is reading their minds.

Researcher Ed Sherwood has found "The Nine" of the Great Ennead of Ancient Egypt — and of Sirius, and Andrija Puharich — represented symbolically in every crop circle season since the early 1980s, when "crop circle seasons" began. He additionally notes that the "contact" of the "White Crow" trilling happened before nine witnesses, on the ninth day of the operation, on the 18th of the month. (For what it's worth, visions of large pyramids surrounded by waves of energy and vibrant colors have been described by "sensitives" while standing in the patterns, as recounted by Eltjo Haselhoff in *The Deepening Complexity of Crop Circles*.)

Laurence Rockefeller spent a fortune — or what might pass as a fortune for the rest of us — on paranormal research, and gave particular attention in his later years to UFOs and crop circles. I think it's always instructive to consider what captures a Rockefeller's interest.

What Dreams May Come

April 28, 2006

Take what you have gathered from coincidence.
— Bob Dylan

I n Dante, Tennessee at about 6:30 on the morning of November 6, 1957, a 12-year old boy named *Everett* Clark opened the door to let out his dog, Frisky. Everett glimpsed a brilliant object sitting in a field about 100 yards away, but was too tired to think much of it and went back inside. Twenty minutes later he returned to call Frisky, and saw his dog standing near the object, along with several other dogs from the neighborhood. "Also near the object," writes Jacques Vallee in *Dimensions*, "were two men and two women in ordinary clothing":

> One of the men made several attempts to catch Frisky, and later another dog, but had to give up for fear of being bitten. Everett saw the strange people, who talked between them "like German soldiers he had seen in movies," walk right into the wall of the object, which then took off straight up without sound. It was oblong and of "no particular color."

Early on the evening of the same day, in *Everittstown* New Jersey, John Tasco went out to feed his dog and saw a "brilliant egg-shaped object hovering in front of his barn," and encountered a dwarfish entity with a pasty face and frog-like eyes dressed in a green suit with shiny buttons and a tam-o'-shanter like cap who said, in broken English, "We are peaceful people, we only want your dog." When Tasco replied that the dog stayed with him, the entity retreated and his pet was found unharmed.

If we have the courage to appear foolish by looking closer, what do we find: two discrete and bizarre accounts from the same day of seemingly thwarted UFO-linked dog-nappings, one early dawn and the other early dusk, one told by a boy named Everett and the other from a town sharing the boy's name. In one the frustrated abductors resembled "German soldiers" but were able to pass through the wall of their craft, and in the other the entity had a leprechaun-like appearance. (Additionally, John Keel writes in *The Eighth Tower* that on the evening of November 6 in 1957 outside Kearney, Nebraska, a fertilizer salesmen named Reinhold Schmidt was given a tour of an oblong craft by German-speaking pilots and a truck driver near House, Mississippi encountered pasty-faced dwarfs who "babbled in a language he couldn't understand.")

Vallee adds, "the stories quoted in this connection verge on the ludicrous. But to pursue the investigation further leads to horror. This is a facet of the phenomenon we can no longer ignore."

Maybe the synchronicities are the point. Perhaps they're little tells by the universe that say, *Pay attention to the fabric here, because you're a part of it.*

John Keel documents many similar winks in *The Eighth Tower*. In the mid-1960s, unrelated people who shared only the surname "Reeve" became subjected to frequent, and statistically aberrant, visitations of the phenomenon. A man named Alvis Maddox was one of the victims of the collapse of the Silver Bridge in Point Pleasant, West Virginia, a tragedy that signaled the climax of the Mothman flap. Three months later, a deputy sheriff in Texas named Alvis Maddox was involved in an otherwise unrelated and widely published UFO sighting. The weirdness of Point Pleasant, West Virginia was followed by sightings in Point Pleasant, New Jersey.

Keel writes:

> The law of synchronicity has created a fascinating statistical anomaly that suggests that witnesses are not accidental but are actually selected. In fact, the deeper you penetrate into this business, the more obvious it becomes that very little chance is involved. The sightings follow preset geographical and time patterns. In the seemingly chance contacts they often carry out repetitive actions that almost seem rehearsed.

Did the entities allegedly encountered by Clark and Tasco *really* want their dogs? There is an almost comic futility about their attempts, reminiscent of the seemingly intentional failures of the phantom clowns and phantom social workers to abduct children in the 1980s. They were demonstrations. Naturally we'll want to ask *Of what*, but perhaps that's not a meaningful question here. Perhaps it's the fact of demonstration and its attendant synchronicities and not its content that is most significant, because it's a manifestation in the mundane world of a normally hidden order of reality and congruity. At least it can be said that the demonstrations *are for us*, and that the patterns exist in order to draw our attention. Patterns like those in the fields emulating the standing waves of a voidless, holographic universe percolating with energy.

We likely know by our experience of them that synchronicities don't pertain only to borderland experiences. However, they do all lead us to borderland issues of human consciousness.

In 1906 Carl Jung found a young patient diagnosed as paranoid schizophrenic staring out of his ward window at the sun, moving his head from side to side. Jung asked him what he was doing, and the man explained he was watching the sun's penis, and moving his head, it moved as well, and caused the wind to blow. Several years later, as Michael Talbot recounts in *The Holographic Universe*, Jung read a translation of an ancient Persian religious text that consisted of a "series of rituals and invocations designed to bring on visions":

> It described one of the visions and said that if the participant looked at the sun he would see a tube hanging down from it, and when the tube moved from side to side it would cause the wind to blow. Since circumstances made it extremely unlikely that the man had contact with the text containing the ritual, Jung concluded that the man's vision was not simply a product of his unconscious mind, but had bubbled up from a deeper level, from the collective unconscious of the human race itself.

Perhaps madness may be said to be close to genius, or the psychotic to the mystic, because certain mental illnesses disable our holographic readers, leaving a paranoid schizophrenic with an innate sense of the interconnectedness of things, but without a way of interpretation, and so a crippling ego confusion settles in.

But collectivity is not a trait of merely the unconscious mind, since one of its common aspects is also our everyday synchronicities: the little moments that tell us we're not observers of the universe set apart from it but its engaged components; and that our thoughts and even our dreams are not thought and dreamt in isolation. (In the 1960s and '70s Dr. Montague Ullman's Dream Laboratory at Brooklyn's Maimonides Medical Center generated extraordinary data suggesting a test subject's dreams could be influenced by the psychic effort of someone unknown to them concentrating on an image in another room.

For instance, in one series of tests the target picture was Chagall's *Paris Through the Window*: a "colorful painting depicting a man observing the Paris skyline from a window. Certain unusual elements stand out very clearly: a cat with a human face, several small figures of men flying in the air, and flowers sprouting from a chair."

Results from the test subject's Third Dream Period:

I was walking. For some reason, I say French Quarter .... And I was walking through different departments in a department store ... talking with a group of Shriners that were having a convention. They had on a hat that looked more like a French policeman's hat, you know the French ... I said French Quarter earlier, but I was using that to get a feel ... of an early village of some sort.... It would be some sort of this romantic type of architecture-buildings, village, quaint.

Fifth Dream Period:

The memory I remember is a man, once again walking through one of these villages, these towns. It would definitely be in the nineteenth century. Attire. French attire. And he would be walking through one of these towns as though he were walking up the side of a hill above other layers of the town.

An excerpt from the subject's notes of associative material:

The thing that stands out is the dream where I described the village .... It's a festive thing ... the Mardi Graish type .... Well, the area must be — I mean, just basing it on the costumes and all — the nineteenth century. Early nineteenth century ... either the Italian or French or Spanish area.... A town of this area ... It would be of the ... of this village type.... Houses very close covering the hills.

Not much has come of this research because psi is still a foreign language, sounding like gibberish, to much of the scientific establishment. Perhaps more profoundly, the empowering implications of human paraconnectivity are something not to be encouraged by forces which mean to keep us divided, dejected and impotent.

Frederick Taylor Gates was a businessman and philanthropist who helped the Rockefellers spend their money and steered John D. Jr. towards a life-long interest in education. In his *1906 Occasional Letter No. 1*, a publication of the General Education Board, a philanthropy he co-created with the Rockefellers to allegedly "support higher education and medical schools in the United States, and to help Black schools in the South," Gates and Rockefeller had their own dreams:

> In our dreams ... people yield themselves with perfect docility to our molding hands. The present educational conventions fade from our minds, and unhampered by tradition we work our own good will upon a grateful and responsive folk. We shall not try to make these people or any of their children into philosophers or men of learning or men of science. We have not to raise up from among them authors, educators, poets or men of letters. We shall not search for embryo great artists, painters, musicians, nor lawyers, doctors, preachers, politicians, statesmen, of whom we have ample supply.
>
> The task we set before ourselves is very simple ... we will organize children ... and teach them to do in a perfect way the things their fathers and mothers are doing in an imperfect way.

Dr. Walter Freeman, President of the American Board of Psychiatry and Neurology in 1948 whose assembly-line ice-pick procedure lobotomized Frances Farmer, didn't like his dreams. Having scared himself with a nervous breakdown brought on by overwork, he took up the habit of at least three capsules of Nembutal every night to induce dreamless sleep. In the 1950s he wrote that lobotomies "made good American citizens" out of "schizophrenics, homosexuals, and radicals."

Public philosopher Jane Jacobs died Tuesday morning at 89. She's best remembered today for her "Silent Spring" of urban planning, *The Death and Life of Great American Cities*, but someday it may be for her last book, *Dark Age Coming*, published in 2004. About its subject Jacobs wrote:

We in North America and Western Europe, enjoying the many benefits of the culture conventionally known as the West, customarily think of a Dark Age as happening once, long ago, following the collapse of the Western Roman Empire. But in North America we live in a graveyard of lost aboriginal cultures, many of which were decisively finished off by mass amnesia in which even the memory of what was lost was also lost.

Mass amnesia, striking as it is and seemingly weird, is the least mysterious of Dark Age phenomena. We all understand the harsh principle: "Use it or lose it." A failing or conquered culture can spiral down into a long decline, as has happened in most empires after their relatively short heydays of astonishing success. But in extreme cases, failing or conquered cultures can be genuinely lost, never to emerge again as living ways of being. The salient mystery of Dark Ages sets the stage for mass amnesia. People living in vigorous cultures typically treasure those cultures and resist any threat to them. How and why can a people so totally discard a formerly vital culture that it becomes literally lost?

Mass amnesia, like a Dark Age, can be intentionally induced. Ice picks are effective as a tool of forgetting, but even Dr. Freeman when up to speed could only lobotomize one at a time. There are more efficient methods for a mass culture that by its nature may be catastrophically amnesiac. Though there's so much we don't need to forget, because we've never learned the plenum we contain.

"The Empire never ended," wrote Philip K. Dick. But he also added, "Against the Empire is posed the living information." The patterns, synchronicities, cryptograms and codes that are forever creating the universe, and us with it, because that's the stuff of which we're made.

The Empire never ended. But we're not finished, either.

In the Air

May 1, 2006

> *Oh if there's an original thought out there, I could use it right now.*
> — Bob Dylan

One thing this blog has taught me is the fallacy of original thought. Or I suppose, to sharpen the point and turn it on myself, I mean the fallacy that my own thought might be original. A comment to Friday's post, for instance:

> In one of Colin Wilson's works ... he speaks of certain cases of people with brains that are largely fluid, covered over with a thin layer of cortex. While most people with this condition are severely retarded, there are known instances of such people showing normal or above normal intelligence. Wilson goes on to speculate on the idea of the brain not as an organ of thought, but as some sort of receiver for thought that arises outside of the body. The idea's an odd one, yet in many ways attractive for the number of loose ends it ties up.

I haven't read that from Wilson but I'm familiar with the study he cites, and it's been helping to inform for me a concept of the brain as a receiver of non-localized consciousness. It seems conducive to a holographic model, and it could contribute to an understanding of a number of psychic and even religious phenomena such as mind-reading, possession and reincarnation. (For example, perhaps rather than evidence for rebirth, a child's memories of a past life are the result of ego confusion brought about by signal error. Or, to use the radio jargon that's appropriately spooky for this metaphor, when a "strong signal [is] in the proximity on the low bands, it will cause cross-modulation and create a 'ghost' signal.")

I still think it's a good idea, though I no longer think it's my own. And a good thing, too. Because perhaps the actual fallacy here is not original thought, but *independent* thought.

I was just thinking that. Maybe we don't need to *put our heads together*. Maybe instead, we need to imagine our skulls as durable cabinets protecting the circuitry that receives the signals pulsing all around us.

When ideas come of age they're simply *in the air*. Inventors and great minds, suddenly and seemingly independent of each other, appear to tap into the same ineffable thoughtstream. Great artists are often recognized by the clarity of their manifestations of universality. In Martin Scorsese's *No Direction Home*, singer Liam Clancy says about Bob Dylan that "it wasn't necessary for him to be a definitive person – he was a receiver – he was possessed," while producer Bob Johnson says Dylan's work isn't to Dylan's fault or credit: "He's got the holy spirit about him – you can look at him and see that."

If we're potentially co-authors and participants in ideas that are "out there," then perhaps we can also intuit and anticipate the *bad* ideas that come of age to work mischief. Because it doesn't always take a secret lodge or a Grove cabin for dark elements to *conspire together*; it only requires a compatibility of unspoken means and motive, up and down the chain of unaccountability. Once the pieces are in place, the commands needn't be explicit and top-heavy and the conspiracy needn't even be self-conscious. For instance, I don't think for a moment that Tony Blair "gave the order" for the murder of David Kelly, though I can well imagine that, on hearing the news, Blair immediately recognized the hand of statecraft and perhaps even his own numb complicity.

Maybe this is what accounts for the 9/11 synchronicities of *The Lone Gunman* pilot. Rather than Chris Carter being tipped off, perhaps he tapped in.

Many of us have been intuiting spoilers to the story arc of the Iraq War for years: The death squads and black ops creating untenable chaos, sectarian strife and intentional failure to the bogus "mission" of democracy, with the objective of generating the "regrettable inevitability" of partition. "Civil War" was talked up, because the End Game for Iraq was always division into impotent colonial Bantustans. We just knew it.

It seems like the End Game has arrived, because suddenly partition, which "just months ago was largely dismissed as a fringe thought," is now being described by the usual suspects in the *Pravdas* of this empire as being the "surest — and perhaps now the only — way to bring stability to Iraq." And just as the *Washington Post* chimes in, Joe Biden shows up in the *New York Times* with an editorial contending that Iraq should be split into three separate ethnographic regions.

If we lack independent thought, then so do they. And if we can see it coming, then maybe we can do something about it before it arrives.

Suspicious Minds

June 6, 2006

I'd had only a Discovery Channel-like familiarity with the work of Rupert Sheldrake when I began considering issues here such as the mysteries of consciousness, DNA and holographic fields, and I've since received much encouragement from readers to get better acquainted. So I'm binging. And I'm thinking how sooner, I'd have gotten to where I am now, if I'd done this years ago.

In *The Sense of Being Stared At*, Sheldrake devotes a chapter to human forebodings and presentiments of disaster. Soon after 9/11, he began gathering dreams and premonitions of the event, 57 in total, many which had been described to friends and family before the attack.

Five nights before 9/11, Manhattan forensic scientist Mike Cherni had "an unusually vivid dream":

> I dreamt that I was a passenger on a commercial jet, seated at a window seat on the left-hand side. The cabin was filled with sunlight, and outside visibility was excellent. I don't remember the beginning of the dream, but I remember a pervasive sense of dread. The passengers and I were deeply concerned about the flight path we were taking; we were flying very low over Manhattan's buildings. I have flown into New York City's three major airports many times and am familiar with the normal approach routes, and this approach was quite out of the ordinary. I also love flying and had had no bad experiences as a passenger or any bad dreams about flying. Yet in this dream I was very frightened about how close we were to the buildings. Many of the passengers were very vocal and shared my concern. I recognized buildings as we flew over them, and it was clear that we were flying directly south over the southern tip of the island. Then there was a tremendous impact and I woke up. This dream disturbed me for days afterward, enough that I described the dream to my wife.

On the morning of Sept 11, Steven Brown dreamed he was "in the stairwell of the World Trade Center with a lot of people trying to get out," while Gina Vigo dreamt "Manhattan was hit by an incredible blizzard. People were running for cover from the fierce gusts of snow and everything was white. Later on, when I saw footage of the falling ash, it was strangely reminiscent." Audrey Parrish dreamed she was in one of the towers when it caught on fire. She escaped by crawling across a glass bridge halfway up into the second tower, "when it too caught fire and burned."

This isn't the bone yard of *Ripley's Believe It or Not*. The stories aren't fabulist amusements which have no bearing on where we find ourselves today. They speak to our deeper nature buried beneath generations of fear-bred ignorance, and reveal intuitive capacities we're expected to deny.

Regarding 9/11 synchronicities such as *The Lone Gunmen*'s March 2001 pilot episode (hijacked, remote-controlled airliners target the World Trade Center to trigger a war for profit), and the Coup's June 2001 CD cover art, (the towers explode near the floors of impact), I contended the artists were not somehow tipped off to the plot, but rather they tapped into the dark frequencies which soon after began troubling the dreams of so many. I'm beginning to wonder whether it will be by recovering our ability to astonish ourselves that we will save ourselves. If we become fully human, then our executioners are finished.

In another case from *The Sense of Being Stared At*, Amanda Bernsohn didn't dream of crashing planes or a burning World Trade Center: "I was walking down a street that was covered in swastikas that were spray painted on the building walls. The Nazis had invaded New York, but I wasn't able to find any people at all."

Sheldrake notes that Bernsohn's dream was of "horror in Manhattan," though it "was not at all like the WTC disaster." About that, perhaps, Sheldrake is wrong.

Mind Over Mind

June 21, 2006

Eden is burning; either brace yourself for elimination,
or else your heart must have the courage
for the changing of the guards.
— Bob Dylan

Maybe I've been reading too many comic books, or maybe too many books that should be comic books. Or perhaps a lot of non-fiction that describes a world most people presume to be fantasy. But I've been thinking lately how it can't be enough to know enough to recognize how strange and perilous our circumstances are, and how wicked the rulers of this age. Because if that's all we're about then it will be *first they came for the communists*-time all over again. Though possibly with the added insult that they won't even be bothered to come for us, because so long as we don't progress beyond analysis and diagnosis to treatment, then our virtual world has no congruity with theirs, and we're nothing but paperless tigers.

"To fight the Empire is to be infected by its derangement." Philip K Dick wrote that in 1978, when it was easy to give up the fight because it appeared already won before it was truly engaged. Americans saw a modest President who wore sweaters in the Oval Office, and who asked small, sensible things of them, such as consumption in moderation. (What they weren't allowed to see was his National Security Advisor "stirring up Muslims" in Central Asia.) And for what it's worth, and it must be something, in every year since there's been a Bush in the White House either by fact or by proxy. And the manifestations of seemingly intractable Empire are promoting in its demoralized opposition a paralytic state of apprehended madness.

So, if we mean to *do something*, how can we avoid Dick's paradox? How can we safeguard ourselves and whatever victories we may win from the viral derangement of Empire? But before we can answer that, perhaps we need to learn of what we're capable. Because the Empire knows, and would rather that we didn't.

A few weeks ago on the RI board, "slimmouse" introduced me to the story of Mirin Dajo, the "inviolable man," whose performances were banned when the sight of his assistant running fencing foils through his body induced a heart attack in an audience member.

Tony Crisp writes that, in 1947,

> A Swiss doctor, Hans Naegeli-Osjord, hearing of Dajo's alleged wild talent, induced him to allow scientific investigation of what happened when he was pierced. In the Zurich Cantonal hospital many people, including doctor Naegeli-Osjord, doctor Werner Brunner, the chief of surgery at the hospital, and a number of other doctors, students, and journalist observed and reported on the experiment. In front of them Dajo stripped to the waist and after spending some time in meditation, had his assistant once more plunge the steel through him. This should have damaged vital organs, but there was no apparent harm, although the witnesses were shocked. Dajo was then asked to allow an x-ray to be taken with the rapier still in place. He agreed, walked to the x ray theatre with the foil still in place. The result of the x-ray undeniably showed Dajo was pierced through vital organs. At a later date Dajo was again examined by scientists in Basel, and this time allowed the doctors themselves to pierce him. Each time there was no apparent harm.

Jack Schwartz was a Nazi concentration camp survivor "who for years had to train himself to endure severe torture and pain." After liberation he "repeatedly astonished dozens of physicians by sticking mammoth six-inch sail-maker's needles through his arms without injury or bleeding."

More on Schwartz:

> Below, Jack Schwartz painlessly — smiling — thrusts a large darning needle through his biceps repeatedly on request for the lab researchers. He was able to stop and start bleeding at will, control his heart rate (stop his pulse), hold lit cigarettes to his arm with no pain, or permanent skin damage. The cigarette burns ranged from simple red marks to blisters on different occasions. With 72 hours all trace of burns disappeared. Although he had been doing these kinds of demonstrations for years, the researchers remarked that "The skin on Jack's arm is as smooth as a baby's." All of his puncture "wounds" closed

immediately, and were completely healed and completely invisible between 24 and 48 hours.

Michael Talbot, in *The Holographic Universe*, uses examples of multiple personality disorder to demonstrate how consciousness, even when fragmented within the same individual, creates its own physical states. Medical conditions possessed by one alter may not be shared by another. Dr. Bennett Braun of Chicago documented a case in which all but one of a patient's sub-personalities were allergic to orange juice: "If the man drank orange juice when one of his allergic personalities was in control, he would break out in a terrible rash. But if he switched to his nonallergic personality, the rash would instantly start to fade and he could drink orange juice freely." Psychiatrist Francine Howland had a dissociative patient arrive for an appointment with an eye completely swollen shut from a wasp sting. She immediately booked him an appointment with an ophthalmologist, but in the meantime, as he was in severe pain, and since one of his alters was an "anesthetic personality" who felt no pain, she had the anesthetic alter become dominant. The pain stopped immediately, and the swelling was gone by the time the ophthalmologist could examine him an hour later, who saw no need for treatment and sent him home. The following day, after the anesthetic personality had relinquished control, the swelling and pain returned, and he again visited the ophthalmologist, who later called Howland for an explanation. "He thought time was playing tricks on him," she said. "He just wanted to make sure that I had actually called him the day before and he had not imagined it."

Trauma-inducing altered states of consciousness, and dissociative personalities exhibiting compartmentalized functionality even on the biological level — where have we seen this before? The Empire's mind-control work has always been about more than zombie creation. It's been about activating dormant, and heightened, human capacities in its service. The "Monarch" subjects were not treated like royalty, but like butterflies: emergent creatures with novel powers, who were told to be proud of their status and their new flesh. For example, survivor Kathleen Sullivan describes "Theta" programming as "thought energy":

I just knew it as magnetic-type energy from the individual to do a number of different things that they were experimenting with, including long-distance mind connection with other people — even in other countries. I guess you would call it "remote viewing" — where I could see what a person was doing in another state in a room or something like that. It was both actual programming and experimentation. Because what they did — they kept it encapsulated in several parts of me, several altered states. It was a lot of training, a lot of experimentation.

Sullivan notes that this level of programming went beyond remote viewing, to projecting mental energy in attempts to kill others at a distance. Fort Bragg's "goat lab" was also training ground for psychic killers, according to Jon Ronson's *The Men Who Stare at Goats*. At least one Green Beret, Michael Echanis, is said to have had success, though former psychic spy Glenn Wheaton told Ronson that Echanis's own heart suffered sympathetic damage. "Everything goes with a cost, see?" said Wheaton. "You pay the piper."

And so we're back to Dick's paradox. The Empire is mad, and we don't want to share in its madness and recreate its enslavements in our opposition to it. But it's made our consciousness part of its dominion, and it exploits our ignorance of ourselves ,and our power to maintain us in a state of false weakness. We shouldn't want to stop hearts with a burst of psychic energy — that's what *they're* about — but we should know that, however unlikely, it's possible that we could. And then we should try to do something better.

Chant Down Babylon

June 23, 2006

> *Men see their dreams and aspiration*
> *Crumble in front of their face*
> *And all of their wicked intention*
> *To destroy the human race.*
> — Bob Marley

M aybe more Yippie, and less Hippie?

Yesterday on the RI board, "Johnny Nemo" remembered Abbie Hoffman saying "There were all these activists, you know, Berkeley radicals, White Panthers ... all trying to stop the war and change things for the better. Then we got flooded with all these 'flower children' who were into drugs and sex. Where the hell did the hippies come from?"

The Yippies were trickster revolutionaries, who staged shamanic acts to advance social transformation. They led thousands to the Pentagon in 1967 to attempt its levitation. They crashed the galleries of Wall Street to shower money on the trading floor. They ran a pig for president. But the decade, in America's memory, belongs to the Hippies.

The misty-eyed nostalgia has created bitterness and confusion over how members of the Grateful Dead can also be members of the Bohemian Grove. Before Neil Young's change of heart, there was dismay at his support for Ronald Reagan and at his "Let's Roll" jingoism. And there's the resistance I still feel within myself to the consideration that Hunter S. Thompson may have been up to some pretty weird shit with some disturbed company, even though Michael Aquino is also a fan, and Thompson said in 2003 that he didn't "hate Bush personally. I used to know him. I used to do some drugs here and there."

But where the hell did the hippies go? They entered into power, and the institutions of selfishness, because *If it feels good, do it* is a philosophy of life that doesn't shy from power, because it needs power to feed the habit.

The Sixties, at least as romantically recalled, is one of the most debilitating things that ever happened to progressive America. A mass, Dionysian movement for social justice became co-opted and debased into bacchanalian self-indulgence, and was called a triumph. In *Breaking Open the Head*, Daniel Pinchbeck tells the story of Robert, who one day in the Sixties consumed three Fly Agarics with some friends. To their disappointment, nothing seemed to happen. Until he went to the kitchen to grab a beer:

Come we go chant down Babylon one more time

I took out the beer, turned around, and across the kitchen there were three huge mushrooms staring at me — a five foot tall, a four foot tall, and a three foot tall mushroom. The mushrooms were red and yellow and they had little eyes and little mouths. They looked just as solid and real as me or you.

Robert and the mushrooms stared at each other, until the largest asked, "Why did you eat us?" Robert thought, and then replied, "I was just following my dream."

Pinchbeck writes,

The mushrooms conferred with each other. Finally they seemed satisfied by his answer. "But are you prepared to follow this path?" the tallest Fly Agaric asked. Robert answered, intuitively and without hesitation, "Yes I am." Whereupon the mushrooms vanished. Fifteen years passed before Robert realized that the path he had agreed to follow was plant shamanism.

(Unknown at the time to Robert, Paul Devereux writes in *The Long Trip* that "the spirits of the mushrooms might appear to the individual and converse with him directly.... The number seen depends on the number of mushrooms consumed.")

A friend of Robert's who also ate Fly Agarics received a similar visitation, and was also asked, "Why did you eat us?" But he answered, "I was trying to get high." The mushrooms told him, "Well, if you ever do this again, we're going to kill you."

That was America in the Sixties, and that was its choice, and these are the consequences. And it was more than just the mushrooms talking. At almost every turn in the culture and the counterculture, the easy and the selfish were chosen over the hard and the common. Not surprising. But America and the wider world still await a vanguard to take the harder paths into sacred space that lead to sacrifice and social transformation. It's a lot to ask, but that's how Babylon gets chanted down.

The Top of My Head

October 28, 2005

For what's left of our religion I lift my voice and pray:
May the lights in The Land of Plenty
shine on the truth some day.

— Leonard Cohen

When the U.S. Declaration of Independence was signed on the second Dog Day of the summer of 1776, the Sun was conjunct Sirius, a star of unrivalled significance to ancient Egyptian mystery religions, esoteric Freemasonry and New Age UFO cults. (Remember Alice Bailey's teaching that the ancient mysteries were received from the "Great White Lodge on Sirius," and that initiation into Earthly orders such as Freemasonry is merely preparatory for "admission into the greater Lodge on Sirius.") In 1846, the date for the laying of the cornerstone of the Washington Monument was chosen to again coincide with the passage of the Sun over Sirius, this time while the Moon was in Virgo. Its dedication ceremony saw Sirius rise over the Capitol building, as Jupiter auspiciously assumed the Moon's position, thus evoking the motto of the Seal of the United States, "Favor our daring undertaking": *Audacibus annue coeptis*, Virgil's invocation to Jupiter, the God. Regarding the great obelisk, David Ovason writes in *The Secret Architecture of Our Nation's Capitol* that it is a "mystery, involved in some of the deeper mysteries of Masonic symbolism." It "represents, from almost every viewing point in the city...a triangle hovering against the skies."

"We are touching upon mysteries which are so extraordinary that they seem to be beyond belief," Ovason adds. "Yet one need only look to the skies, and the records of stellar events, to realize that they are absolutely true."

It shouldn't need to be said, but it seems that everything must be said these days: the existence of mysteries is *not necessarily* an evil. Mysteries themselves merely evidence things hidden, *occulted* from general sight, and suggest there are supra-mundane forces to the world that show their hand to us, the uninitiates, in riddles. The architects and heirs of America's mysteries don't always shy from claiming their credit. The forward to Ovason's "fascinating and well-researched" study of Washington's secret fetish for Egypt's Old Kingdom, and perhaps things older, is provided by C. Fred Kleinknecht, 33rd degree Sovereign Grand Commander of the Supreme Council, 33rd degree (Mother Council of the World), Southern Jurisdiction, USA.

"I'm seeing something that was always hidden," says Jeffrey Beaumont, early in *Blue Velvet*. "I'm in the middle of a mystery and it's all secret." Let's be honest, like Jeffrey: there can be a thrilling novelty to the process of discovery, even if we don't discover what the secret is, but merely that there is a secret. Even, sometimes, once we learn the secret, and find it nauseates and dizzies us. (Amusement rides, too, are about disorientation. Some get their kicks instead from metaphysical and parapolitical scares.) It was only later, when the mystery was recognized as not a vicarious amusement but a threat to life and sense of self, that it stopped being a thrill.

How do we recognize mystery's power? I think it's something like how Emily Dickinson recognized poetry:

> If I read a book and it makes my whole body so cold no fire can ever warm me, I know that is poetry. If I feel physically as if the top of my head were taken off, I know that is poetry. These are the only ways I know it. Is there any other way?

Felt the top of your head come off lately? There's a poetry to this mystery we're in. That's not to say it's a thing of beauty; merely that there's an *authorship*, a manicured landscape of meaning. *An intelligence at work*. Materialists and coincidentalists who lack the semiotic skillset will see neither signs nor patterns; just random moments strung together by our imaginations. But C. Fred Kleinknecht says, "As above, so below."

Edgar Cayce, America's "sleeping prophet," was a Christian and Freemason whose entranced alter claimed to have been a high priest of Egypt named "Ra Ta." Ra Ta predicted an American Golden Age based upon the principals of Freemasonry, linked to the projected opening of a hypothesized "Hall of Records" beneath the Sphinx at the end of the 20th Century. Cayce seems to have been a better psychic diagnostician than he was a prophet, but his influence had a long reach. Cayce advised Woodrow Wilson — two biographers claim he was summoned to Washington to advise on the creation of the League of Nations — the meeting arranged by head of the Secret Service, Colonel Edmund Starling. Starling came from Hopkinsville, Kentucky, and Cayce was born on a farm just outside Hopkinsville and resided in the town until a young adult.

(Does Hopkinsville ring another bell of American weirdness? The "Hopkinsville Incident" of August 21, 1955: a farmhouse, just outside the Kentucky town, besieged by shining, seemingly nickel-plated mischievous entities. Is there a connection? Maybe, though maybe no more than America is a weird place, and some American places are weirder than others.)

What do we do about the poetics of mystery? Sometimes we construct our own. At least that's how I understand the self-discrediting work of Tom Flocco, Sherman Skolnick and others. Flocco's recent "exclusive" fantasies — Barbara Olson arrested! French intelligence kill Israeli terrorists in NYC subway! Bush orders Fitzgerald fired! — is "conspiracy theory" as poetry slam: associative narratives to compete with the official stories, all of them wholly unhinged from reality. Such writers are not disinfo agents so much as they are fabulists, and no matter how often they are proven wrong they will still find a readership, because they promise emotionally satisfying resolution. As in a fable, all loose ends are tied. And like a fable, it all happens without our intervention. All we need do is watch it unfold, though only in our minds.

Poetry can help us understand our situation, if we don't, as Flocco appears to have done, mistake it *for* our situation. I can't speak for Emily Dickinson, but one poem that took the top of my head clean off this year was the film adaptation of Frank Miller's *Sin City*.

Dominating the city's religious and political life are two brothers, a Cardinal and a Senator. The family is respected, and protected, acting above the secular and divine laws they administer. The Roark dynasty harbors serial killers, pedophiles, cannibals. The marginalized characters who challenge their authority doom themselves by doing so, though they leave small victories that survive them. Is this America? No, just something like it. Maybe more than Frank Miller knows. Maybe not as much as I think.

"What the hell do *you* know?" Cannibal Cardinal Roark asks Marv, the monster of vengeance. Marv replies, "I know it's pretty damn weird to eat people." In the end, the esoteric meaning — the consumption of souls — is irrelevant. It is simply *pretty damn weird*. And wrong.

As Senator Roark tells the good cop Hartigan, as Hartigan lies in hospital, wounded and framed for having protected a young girl from Roark's predatory son:

> Power doesn't come from a gun, or a badge. Power comes from lies. Once you got everybody agreeing with what they know in their hearts ain't true you got 'em by the balls.
>
> There's what, maybe, 500 people in this hospital? I could pump you full of bullets right now and I wouldn't even be arrested. Everyone would lie for me. Everyone who counts. Otherwise all their own lies, everything that runs Sin City, it all comes tumblin' down like a pack of cards.

Those who know things go deeper, weirder and darker than Scooter Libby know the cards haven't tumbled yet. Those who don't have yet to see the deck.

"It's all in the egg"

April 13, 2005

My observation of the Universe convinces me that there are beings of intelligence and power of a far higher quality than anything we can conceive of as human; that they are not necessarily based on the cerebral and nervous structures that we know, and that the one and only chance for mankind to advance as a whole is for individuals to make contact with such beings.

— Aleister Crowley

First, a few examples of what I'm talking about, before I try talking about it.

Copper Medic

In his book *Confrontations*, Jacques Vallee devotes a chapter to "Copper Medic," what he describes as his favorite case of UFO visitations. He writes that "what attracted the interest of local ufologists wasn't so much the repeated sighting of a small, egg-shaped UFO on the Chapin's property as the strange material they claimed to have recovered at the site."

It's not the strange material which attracts my interest, but the description of the UFO. In the first incident from 1969 the Chapins, who were then in their mid-'60s, had just killed a rattlesnake. Jane Chapin was going to photograph the body "when she suddenly saw something behind the tall grass, among the trees":

She thought it was a trailer, then realized it was oval, about the size of a VW Beetle. It appeared cream-colored to her. Clint, who saw it from a different perspective, thought it was gray. Both saw how the object lifted up, paused for a brief moment, then disappeared at amazing speed. An oval depression, smaller than the object itself, was found in the ground, as if a large weight had rested there.

The Chapins had several more encounters over the years, sometimes losing consciousness, vomiting and urinating, when they would be hit by an "invisible barrier" radiating waves of heat. Their last encounter was in 1980, shortly before Clint's fatal heart attack. Jane wrote Vallee about it:

We were looking at a road that had been cut through our property and we turned to go down the road, west, and there was a skinny thing in the road, and his egg was not 25 feet from us ... and he took four steps toward us and my hand fell on my gun and he turned around and walked back. He was in a gray suit, and he left no print or prints of the egg. Clint could not move either ... the thing vanished, then the egg went up in the air and turned west, and we both looked at the back of the egg and it opened like a horse trailer door. He was four-foot tall and skinny, maybe 90 pounds. I don't know what he wants ... well, maybe he will take me to where Clint is.

One of the local investigators reported, of one appearance, that the object "rose up off the ground a few feet, then took off like a shot up the canyon, swaying but not striking small trees as it went." But Jane Chapin admitted to Vallee she had lied: the object had flown off *into* the trees, passing *through* them as though they didn't exist. When he asked why she hadn't told that to the local investigators, she replied, "I could see they wouldn't believe me if I told them the truth. They were such nice people. I didn't want to shock them."

Lonnie Zamora

Zamora's sighting is one of the most famous in UFO literature. On April 24, 1964 Zamora, a police officer in Socorro, New Mexico, investigated a sudden, loud roar from an unpopulated gully. "I could see dust fly up," he recalled. "I thought there was something that night have blown up, since there's a dynamite shack over there." He drove his patrol car to the top of a hill to check it out. About a half mile away, he saw a white object that appeared from the distance to be a car turned upside down, and two figures who looked to be four feet tall. Zamora radioed he was going to investigate, and drove a bumpy road on which he temporarily lost sight of the object. He stopped on a Mesa, got out and looked down.

In the gully about 20 feet below him, the "thing" sat silent. The two figures had disappeared. Zamora advanced closer.

"It was egg-shaped with one end, which I figure was the front, sort of tapered," Zamora says. "It was white and smooth, with no windows or openings of any kind. It was sitting on legs about four feet tall and seemed to be about the size of a car."

A sudden roar from the "egg" almost deafened Zamora. Thinking it might explode, the officer turned and ran for some bushes. Glancing back, he saw the object rise straight up. He dove into the bushes and covered his head, then peeked up.

"There was no noise," he says. "It was about 20 feet off the ground, just hovering. There were markings in red letters about a foot high on the side. It looked like a crescent with a vertical arrow pointed upward inside the crescent and a horizontal bar beneath that."

When State Policeman Sam Chavez arrived on the scene, he and Zamora entered the gully, and found a smoldering mesquite bush and six imprints in the ground where the "egg" had rested. Zamora's character was judged unimpeachable, and there was no credible accusation of a hoax. He also made no claims for what he had seen. Three years later he told a reporter, "I'd like to know what the hell it was. *I wouldn't say it was from space or from here either*. If it's a new plane, it sure is good. All I know is I saw the thing, and that's it."

Levelland and White Sands

On the night of November 2, 1957 near Levelland, Texas, independent witnesses repeatedly saw oval and elliptical objects near roadways. One witness was "Sheriff Weir Clem, who was searching the roads as a result of earlier reports and saw a reddish oval cross the road, illuminating the pavement." Within a few hours of the Levelland reports, "an Army jeep patrol at White Sands, N.M., reported an egg-shaped UFO that descended to a point about 50 yards above the bunker used during the first atomic bomb explosion, and a major wave of UFO sightings continued for 2-3 weeks."

The Worcester Egg

Early morning February 3, 2000, Georgina Wells saw an "extremely bright," yellow-glowing egg shape from her bedroom window. It began a slow descent, seemed to land out of sight, and then "came back into view and was really bright again and shot off into the sky and vanished. I have never seen anything go that fast before." Perhaps the most exceptional aspect of this report is that

Wells claims a helicopter was monitoring it the entire time. "I stood up and watched it," Wells says. "It was not a police helicopter with its spotlight as there was no light-beam."

So what's with all the eggs?

There are many more examples. (And not just of the exterior appearance of UFOs. Abductees often describe rounded, milky interiors.) Still, I don't want to get carried away with this. Some UFOs, after all, have also been called "cigar-shaped." If Freud had been a UFOlogist, I expect he would have said that *sometimes a cigar-shaped UFO is just a cigar-shaped UFO.* But in the popular imagination, UFOs are principally "disc-shaped." And to speak of discs evokes *manufacture*, as though they were cobbled together with nuts and bolts, even if those nuts and bolts are cast from exo-terran metals. So analogies are important in themselves, because they can restrict or liberate our assumptions of the true — as opposed to the black budget — phenomena.

What's more, regarding UFOs as egg-like also may render less mysterious some of their observed, bizarre attributes. For instance, on numerous occasions, UFOs have been seen dividing into several equal-sized and identical parts, and recombining into a single unity. It beggars our understanding how a manufactured craft could be engineered to accomplish such feats, and perhaps just as significantly, what the purpose would be. However, we do see something like it in the natural world, in something as commonplace as cell division. But we may not think to look there if we get hamstrung by the paradigm that UFOs, if they exist at all, must be spacecraft. We'll be more likely to see correspondences in nature if we adopt the analogy of an egg, rather than a "disc."

And there may be something more.

Back to Crowley

Remember Lam, and Aleister Crowley's "Amalantrah Working"? Using sex magick with his partner and psychic sensitive Roddie Minor, Crowley claimed to have opened a dimensional portal, through which passed Lam, whose portrait appears an archetypal grey, though Crowley drew him "from life" in 1918, many years before the greys entered our cultural consciousness. Before Lam appeared, Minor channeled messages from a spirit-wizard called Amalantrah, who told Crowley to "find the egg." Ian Blake, who has much of interest to say about Crowley, Lam, and the egg metaphor here, writes that "one of the earlier versions of the Amalantrah Working ended with the sentence, "It's all in the egg." During the final surviving version of this Working, in reference to a question about the egg, Crowley was told: "Thou art to go this way."

Kenneth Grant, Crowley's last student, who was given the portrait, is author of *The Lam Statement*. Grant's purpose was to "regularize and to examine results" of contact with Lam, by "entering the Egg of Spirit represented by the Head." As Blake writes, "in the late 1980s ... Grant allegedly received 'strong intimations' to the effect that Crowley's portrait of Lam "is the present focus of an extraterrestrial — and perhaps trans-plutonic — energy which the OTO is required to communicate at this critical period."

The Typhonian OTO, which follows Grant's teachings, "is concerned with effective transmissions and communications from 'outerspace' for the purpose of opening Gateways. The Typhonian 'deities' denote specific operations of psycho-physical alchemy which involve essences or elixirs secreted (thrown out and/or considered unclean) by the human organism."

And we should note that the purpose of Jack Parsons' "Babalon Working" was a *birth*. Using Enochian sex magick and his "elemental" partner Marjorie Cameron, Parsons was intent on collapsing our reality by introducing into it the incarnation of "Babalon." ("Wicked" in the angelic language said to be given Elizabethan John Dee.)

In a letter to Crowley, quoted in *Sex and Rockets: The Occult World of Jack Parsons*, he wrote "For the last three days I have performed an operation of birth, using the air tablet, the cup, and a female figure, properly invoked by the wand [penis], then sealed up in the altar. Last night I performed an operation of symbolic birth and delivery."

And from his poem, "The Birth of Babalon":
What is the tumult among the stars that have shone so still till now?
What are the furrows of pain and wrath upon the immortal brow?

Why is the face of God turned grey and his angels all grown white?
What is the terrible ruby star that burns down the crimson night?
What is the beauty that flames so bright athwart the awful dawn?
She has taken flesh, she is come to judge the thrones ye rule upon.
Quail ye kings for an end is come in the birth of BABALON.

Is it any more bizarre than the thought of extraterrestrial spacecraft, to consider that Crowley and Parsons may have succeeded, the portal widened, and the ritual birth represented by egg-like manifestations? Well, yes, because it presumes the efficacy of magick, which is a big leap for most of us. But perhaps, even though it's more bizarre, it's also more likely.

One final thought. Lonnie Zamora reported seeing "markings in red letters about a foot high on the side. It looked like a crescent with a vertical arrow pointed upward inside the crescent and a horizontal bar beneath that." To those who regard UFOs as nuts and bolts spacecraft, perhaps these markings would be regarded as the designation of an extraterrestrial authority. Their "flag." But it's quite anthropomorphic to presume aliens would think in such terms.

If we consider ritual magick, the symbol resembles a "sigil," used for the invocation of angelic and demonic entities. I haven't searched yet for a crescent with a vertical arrow within it and a horizontal bar beneath it. But I wonder what the implications would be if one were found.

If You Go Out In the Woods

October 22, 2005

Your father's gone a-hunting.
He's deep in the forest so wild.
And he cannot take his wife with him.
He cannot take his child.

— Leonard Cohen

N ear Cisco Grove, California on the night of September 5, 1964 Donald Schrum, a 27-year old employee of a local missile production plant became separated from his two bow-and-arrow hunting companions. As dusk approached he took shelter in a tree, lashing himself to a branch with his belt. After settling in, Schrum — identified only as "Mr. S." in the files of the U.S. Air Force's Project Blue Book — saw three objects in the darkening sky, a rotating and protruding light affixed to each that emitted "cooing" noises. Mr. S. thought they were rescue helicopters, searching for him, so he climbed down the tree and set signal fires. It was then, he realized they were *not* helicopters.

They were three somethings, [I can find no description of the appearance, other than "strange looking" and "different than anything he'd seen before"], shining beams of bright white lights, and they were circling his location. As he watched them descend, from beneath two of them, two smaller objects were delivered to the ground. Soon after he lost sight of them, he heard a loud crashing in the underbrush, and frightened, climbed to the lower branches of a tall pine tree.

Dr. J. Allen Hynek picks up the story in *The Hynek UFO Report*:

> He thereupon witnessed two humanlike individuals approaching his signal fires. They were garbed in silvery collarless suits, had unusual

protruding eyes, and communicated to one another via an unintelligible cooing noise. According to Mr. S., they were trying to dislodge him from his tree position when a third "alien," described by Mr. S. as a "robot," appeared on the scene. Mr. S. fired some arrows at the "robot" but failed to distract or divert any of the strange individuals. [Another account reports that when he finally hit the robot, "there was an arc flash and the robot was knocked backwards."] Then he tried lighting parts of his clothing on fire and throwing it at them to frighten them away. The individuals had violent reactions, and at the same time their craft began to ascend upwards, emitting a vapor which caused him to black out.

Schrum regained consciousness in the early dawn, found his companions and told them what had happened. Later, he told his father-in-law, who persuaded him to talk to authorities. Hynek mentions that the Air Force report notes "Mr. S." appeared "stable and consistent in telling his story," though it explained the alleged sighting as "psychological." The Air Force kept the tape of Schrum's narrative, as well as one of the arrows he had fired at the robot.

Hynek adds:

The story of a bow-and-arrow hunter, held at bay high in a tree, setting flame to parts of his clothing and tossing them down onto the heads of his assailants until he was half-naked, passing out because of strange fumes emitted by "aliens," is certainly hard to believe, *unless one considers it within the framework of the whole parade of stories similar to it.*

It's a story that belongs to traditional folklore: the hunter who wanders off into strange woods and experiences enchantment. To our degraded understanding, enchantment sounds *cute* and *quaint* and *precious*, when it can be as frightening as a fairy tale.

Hynek's book was published in 1977 and I read his account of the Schrum case for the first time last Thursday, and what it most recalled for me was the "chupa" flap of the early 1980s, centered upon the small, remote town of Parnarama in northern Brazil. Jacques Vallee researched the cases, traveling to Parnarama to interview witnesses and survivors (at least five people were said to have died from close encounters), and the results were published in his 1990 book *Confrontations*.

(By the way, last Spring, Jeremy of *Fantastic Planet* wrote a terrific piece entitled "Ultradimensional Terror and You" which used the chupas as a springboard into an exploration of the Twin Peaks mythology as a "ready-made semiotic set within which to discuss the possibility of ultradimensional entities invading our 'Reality' and essentially having their way with us.")

Vallee writes that the chupas were usually described as small "boxlike UFOs equipped with powerful light beams" which flew over "the wooded areas and the river valleys at night. *All of the victims in Parnarama were deer hunters who had climbed into trees during the night*, as is frequently the case in that part of Brazil." Unless someone in Parnarama had gotten hold of *The Hynek UFO Report*, and the people conspired to punk Vallee and others, I find that an interesting fact.

In most cases, the chupas flew above the treetops and shone their beams toward the earth. They were said to make a humming sound, "like a refrigerator or a transformer," and did not appear large enough to contain a human pilot.

From *Confrontations*:

> The hunting technique used in the region is unique: the hunters climb ten to fifteen feet into the trees, then spend the night in a hammock waiting for deer or other game. They take a flashlight with them to spot the animals.

> A theory among local people is that the chupas are attracted by the flashlights, come over the hammocks, and strike the victims with their concentrated beam. However, I found little consistency in the descriptions of the beam itself. One witness compared it to an electric arc. On an interview tape another witness said he remembered a "bad smell" like an electrical odor (ozone?) and saw a blinding light, with pulsating colors inside....

> Several people reported being exposed to the chupas in late 1982 as they were lying in their tree hammocks.... They had lost their previous vitality. A 43-year-old man who "used to be afraid of nothing" now lives in constant fear. He is "scared of things that are not part of my experience."

After being struck by a chupa beam, victim Dionizio General "came rolling down the hill. For the following three days he was insane with terror; then he died." Another, Abel Boro, screamed as the light engulfed him. A friend ran to the Boro house to get his family, but Abel was dead, his body white, by the time they arrived. (It might be presumed that the isolated locals would leap to the explanation that chupas were spirits of the woods, but Vallee notes a local rumor that chupas were "American prototypes" stealing their blood.)

What are some points of congruity between the Schrum incident and the "chupas," and what might they suggest?

• The victims were hunters who bedded down in tall trees.

• Schrum's UFOs and the chupas behaved as though drawn by fire and flashlight.

• They emitted strong beams of light and similar sounds (a "cooing" and a "humming").

• Their actions appear intended to terrorize, even to death.

• The extraterrestrial hypothesis again offers the least satisfying explanation.

Think of the apparent futility of Schrum's *whatevers*, shaking the tree all night with the apparent purpose of dislodging him. *Apparent.* Because like the Hopkinsville monsters, who besieged a farm house all night long but never threatened to enter, if they'd really wanted him out of that tree, they could have had him. But *they weren't trying*. Not really. Like the Flatwoods Monster, and "Mothman," and others, it just meant to say "Boo." Like Fungus the Bogeyman, their job is to give us a good scare. (Though, as the chupas tell us, if they scare us to death that's our problem.) Why? I like how Jeremy put it: fear is "the porterhouse steak of garmonbozia," and garmonbozia is *Twin Peaks*-speak for the intense human emotions upon which vampiric entities feast.

One more hunter's story, this from Patrick Harpur's **Daimonic Reality**.

Carl Higdon, a 40-year old mechanic, was hunting elk in Wyoming's Medicine Bow National Park on October 25, 1974, when he decided to try a part of the woods little explored by hunters. Higdon came upon a group of five elk, and put his gun to his shoulder and fired.

Harpur writes:

> Something strange happened. The sound of the shot was curiously muffled and the bullet seemed to travel so slowly that Carl was able to

watch it in flight. It fell to earth some 15 to 20 meters in front of him. It was completely crushed. Amazed, Carl picked up the bullet and put it in his pocket. Then, turning at the sound of a branch cracking, he saw a very tall man standing about 20 meters away in the shade of a birch. This man, or whatever he was, had yellow skin, bristling straw-colored hair, and was wearing a black costume.

He approached Carl and said, surprisingly, "How you doin'?" — to which Carl replied: "Pretty good." "Are you hungry?" asked the stranger. "Yeah. A little," said Carl. The man tossed him a package containing four pills, telling him to take one, which would last him for four days. Carl did take one, whereupon the man asked if Carl would like to go with him. "I guess," said Carl, and for the first time he saw a transparent illuminated "cubicle."

Carl embarked, noticing two other figures clad in black and five elk in a cage. They traveled to what the stranger called his "planet," but Carl was not allowed to leave the vehicle. Returning to the forest, Carl was dropped out of the cubicle onto rocky

ground, near an unknown cow trail. He followed it, and came to a truck stuck in the mud, and used its CB radio to call for help. It turned out to be his own pick-up, which he had not recognized. When police arrived they found him "distraught, red-eyed, tearful, and (like the medieval near-death visionary, Alberic, who could not remember his mother) unable even to recognize his wife, who had come with them. He could only repeat the story of the pills and the men in black."

A wild tale, and like all such tales, impossible to verify. Yet his bullet was in his pocket where he'd placed it, folded like a glove. And to ask *But was it real?* is likely to miss the point. Fungus the Bogeyman returned to a home and family after a good night's scare. To what, and to whom, do these entities return? Does the yellow man in the black uniform ever say "Honey, I'm home?" Are there factories assembling the bizarre and ungainly robots of Schrum's and many others accounts? Why is there so little standardization of craft, and why are there so many different kinds of entities? Religion and occult lore have more to say in this regard than exopolitics, because these things are manifesting themselves *for us*.

Higdon might not have been terrorized, but he was drained, left a blubbering mess, like so many who encounter the Other. The Otherworld, too, has those who play good cop/bad cop. So long as they feed.

"I wish that hadn't happened"

December 9, 2005

What good am I if I know and don't do,
If I see and don't say, if I look right through you?
— Bob Dylan

J ack Houck is a retired defense consultant who spent 42 years with Boeing Aerospace as a systems consultant. He is also a "researcher of paranormal phenomena," who has been throwing "psychokinesis parties" for 25 years.

Houck dates his interest in the paranormal to the mid-70s, when he learned of Stanford Research Institute's remote-viewing program, and was encouraged by SRI's Harold Puthoff and Russell Targ to conduct his own experiments. The results persuaded Houck of the reality of remote viewing and the significance of psi research, and ever since he has been instructing thousands around the world, many in defense industries, "how to use the power of your mind" to perform PK feats such as metal bending. Including, yes, spoons.

Here Houck describes his "first PK Party":

[W]e were sitting in a circle and I had passed out my grandparents antique silverware — it has all been dedicated to science now. There was a lot of giggling and laughter because I do not think people believed that this was really going to happen. I don't think that I thought it was going to happen either. However, I was testing this conceptual model and had to follow through with the experiment. All of a sudden a four-teen-year-old boy had the fork he was holding begin to have the head slowly fall over. He started screaming and yelling; he jumped up out of his chair. That got everyone's attention so that everyone in the room saw the fork bending over. As I looked around the room, everyone's eyes were huge as they stared at this boy's fork. I like to call this an instant, belief system change. All of a sudden, other people found that the silverware they were holding became soft in their hands. They later described it as if the metal became a little warm and felt like putty in their hands. It seems to lose its structure for a few seconds. The metal stays soft for between five and thirty seconds. Here they were, finding what is normally nice hard silverware becoming soft and structureless in their hands. Most of the people in the room then began to wildly bend up the silverware. They were screaming and yelling, and this was a real peak emotional event occurring in my living room. In the middle of all this pandemonium I reached back to my dining room table and grabbed the big steel rod, handed it to the fourteen-year-old boy and said, "Bend this!!" He looked at me and said, "I can't do that." Then I said "Don't ever say can't — that is like putting a block in your mind." He agreed to try and started rubbing his hand up and down the steel rod. After about five minutes I again heard him yelling. He was jumping up and down in the middle of the living room. With no more force than simply moving his hands while holding the rod over his head, he bent that rod into a 270-degree turn. The next day I rushed over to the Sears store and bought all the rest of the rods that size in their bin and took them into the laboratory. We had the head metallurgist try to physically bend one of the similar rods. He was a big man, about 200 lbs. He was not able to bend the rod until he finally bent it over his knee, using all his might — red-faced and all. Seeing the difference between the young man doing it with no apparent effort at the PK Party, and the big metallurgist using a tremendous effort to bend it physically, really impressed me.

Retired Major General Albert Stubblebine, then commanding officer of the U.S. Army Intelligence and Security Command (INSCOM), was an attendee of Houck's parties, and was so impressed he added it to the itinerary of a retreat for senior INSCOM staff officers at a conference facility near Leesburg, Virginia. Jim Schnabel tells the story in his book **Remote Viewers**:

Someone handed out spoons and forks, and Stubblebine gave a short talk on how it was done, and then 25 to 30 colonels and generals stood around holding these eating utensils and staring at them, waiting for something to happen.

At one point, a somewhat skeptical colonel turned his head to say something to a colleague, and as he did, his fork suddenly drooped into a ninety-degree angle. Everyone looked at him and his fork, at which point the fork bent back up, then down again, and finally settled into an angle of about forty-five degrees. The colonel whose fork it was put the thing down, shaking his head, evidently unsettled. He was a Christian, and later would denounce the entire thing as the trickery of the devil.

"I wish that hadn't happened," said the colonel.

I don't think there can be true comprehension of how America got *here* from *there*, without assuming that sentiment has been often thought and voiced in the halls of the cryptocracy.

Psychokinesis should be only a mild offense to the psyche of someone raised with the conventions of either mainstream faith or anti-faith, and I don't mean to suggest that spoonbending is the work of the devil. But other things colonels and Christians have found themselves mixed up in could certainly be described as such. Mind control, for instance. Think of brainwashing and hypnotism in the alleged service of national security: of being able to take a life in your hands and make of it an experimental marionette like Candy Jones, or a programmed patsy as Sirhan Sirhan almost certainly was. I have to think that somewhere in the beta-testing of human subjects, consciences were appalled at the successes — *"I wish that hadn't happened"* — but because success was the only condition, just as with an unwise black magician, the work continued, and was refined. Subjects became younger, methods became harsher to better imprint more elaborate and deviant programming. *And I really wish that hadn't happened.*

We should be able to see how this happens. Acting against one's conscience in a relatively small matter can set up a logic which justifies actions more terrible in order to see the "pay off" for the first offense. And the way is eased, naturally, in a military culture where private conscience is expected to stand down for "national security." (Though over time that mask has slipped, and it has become simply what it is: horror and high crime.)

I may be wrong, but I doubt there are great wizards in the Pentagon. I imagine, instead, a bunch of sociopathic punks playing with the *Necronomicon* and thinking they have the power, seeing *something* about it seems to work but not understanding why, or how that could be a bad thing. Meanwhile, the silent witnesses and conflicted perpetrators mutter to themselves, "I wish that hadn't happened."

Correspondence and Sanctuary

November 27, 2005

"No hay banda! There is no band. It is all — an illusion!"
— *Mulholland Drive*

I was thinking last week about the other Bob Woodward, and that started a train of thought which hasn't yet come to a complete stop.

The other Bob Woodward is the young man who's bizarre plea for political asylum in a Vermont church the morning of December 2, 2001 was met with a hail of police bullets and a circuitous ambulance trip to the hospital — three miles in 40 minutes — that conspired to take his life, though Woodward, armed only with a pocket knife, had threatened no one but himself. (He'd said he would rather die than be tortured.)

I won't repeat the story here that's well told at justiceforwoody.org, but let's note these things:

• Woodward worked with mentally disabled children, and told the congregation so.

• He claimed he had been receiving threats of torture and death from federal agents, apparently for his environmental activism.

• He said "I'll never rail against the Bush Administration again, or the military or any of these other things. I just can not leave here, I am in danger."

• Some of what he said sounds impossibly bizarre, though he made his most bizarre and disturbing remarks lying in his blood on the floor of the church sanctuary. For instance, "The CIA killed Jeb Bush." A police officer replied, "Well, Jeb Bush isn't dead yet." Woodward answered "No — the *other* Jeb Bush."

I can't assess Woodward's claims. (Though "Neighbors maintain they saw two men, apparently government agents, visit his apartment Saturday evening.") I don't even know them. He was extremely agitated that Sunday, desperate for witnesses with whom to share his story and tell why his life was in imminent danger, but once he had them it appears he didn't know where to begin. And I think that's something to which everyone who has gone down a rabbit hole, no matter which one and no matter how far, can relate.

To me, the lesson of Woodward's tragedy is obscured by the question, How do we begin telling people what we've learned, and what we suspect, without sounding crazy? Where do we start? And how can we before we find ourselves in similar desperate circumstance?

Perhaps we need to resign ourselves to sounding mad to most people. I expect that to many still comfortable with the established paradigm, whether we're talking about assassinations or MK-ULTRA or UFOs, it's all just different degrees of paranoia. There's a steep learning curve to secret history, and without knowing some of it our talk of present and future mysteries will sound like gibberish. CIA, aliens and mind control: isn't that the usual constellation of delusion?

And yet we need to admit there are such things as madness and delusion, and avoid the corresponding conceit of the so-called, and sometimes rightly so, fringe: just because it's *out there* doesn't make it right.

And it's often complicated, especially off the High, Weird End, when genuine correspondences are also mad.

More than the account of odd sightings of a strange flying creature with glowing red eyes, John Keel's *The Mothman Prophecies* is a record of an eruption of all manner of occult/trickster phenomena in West Virginia in the mid-sixties. Animal mutilations, poltergeists, mechanical voices on telephones, UFOs, monsters and "Men in Black."

In late October 1966, on one of his regular pre-dawn strolls, Leonard Elmore of Duncan Falls, Ohio, came upon a "strange building." He was only two blocks from his house, but he had never before seen the L-shaped structure that "looked like a galvanized iron shed" sitting in a large field. He walked a little closer to get a better look, and saw no windows or doors. He was overcome with a sense of dread, which he could not explain later, and began to turn back. It was then, Elmore claims, that he "distinctly heard a normal male voice" come from inside the structure, saying "Don't run ... don't run." When he returned soon after, it was gone.

Keel writes:

> When he showed me the field I was perturbed to find that it was right next to the Duncan Falls Elementary School. An unusual number of sightings and Fortean events seem to be concentrated around schools and the largest percentage of witnesses consists of children between the ages of seven and eighteen. Another statistical oddity is that *the majority* of the adults who claim their autos were pursued by UFOs or monsters *are schoolteachers, especially teachers specializing in abnormal children* — the very bright or the mentally deficient. [emphases added]

Remember the phantom clowns and social workers? During the Mothman flap, homes in the Ohio Valley of West Virginia were visited by phantom census takers, who were also chiefly interested in the numbers and ages of children.

The *other* Bob Woodward, we've noted, worked with mentally disabled children. I'm not saying he was being hounded by monsters or UFOs. I'm simply saying there is, it seems, a *correspondence of interests* among the human and inhuman monsters of our study. So perhaps it doesn't matter a great deal *what* exactly was hounding him. (The correspondence extends further: alien entities are always passing on dire warnings of environmental calamity, just as Woodward was warning the congregation.)

And here's something else.

Keel also writes that UFOs and bizarre entities "all appear to have the ability to ferret out human females during their menstrual period." He also notes that "the phenomenon has an almost pornographic preoccupation with our mating practices."

Now, consider the mission of the "Typhonian Ordo Templi Orientis," the branch of the OTO founded by Aleister Crowley's purported spiritual heir Kenneth Grant:

> The Typhonian OTO is concerned with effective transmissions and communications from "outerspace" for the purpose of opening Gateways. The Typhonian "deities" denote specific operations of psychophysical alchemy which involve essences or elixirs secreted (thrown out and/or considered unclean) by the human organism. Its formula is that

of the XI° involving kalas that are entirely absent from the masculine organism.

Grant's Typhonian OTO is principally concerned with "opening Gateways." The Gateway through which, Grant holds, Lam entered Crowley's world. (Concerning the Babalon Working of Jack Parsons and L. Ron Hubbard, Grant has written that "Parsons opened a door and something flew in.") These dark entities Grant likens to the "Old Ones" of H.P. Lovecraft, whom he regards as a "natural adept."

Crowley's XI° degree of the OTO pertained to anal intercourse: the sex magickal meaning of the Eye of Horus. The XI° degree of Grant's Typhonian OTO "is based on intercourse during menstruation and is considered by some as the true reversal of the IX°, i.e. being a part of the same cycle. It is regarded that Crowley was unaware of the true formula as the Typhonian XI° involves specific *kalas* that are entirely absent from the masculine organism."

So there's John Keel, scratching his head at how manifestations of UFOs and alien entities seem linked to menstruation, and an occult order of sex magic concerned with "opening Gateways" which, for its final degree, entails ritual intercourse during menstruation.

It's crazy. But as crazy at it sounds now, just imagine trying to explain it to a church congregation as police snipers take aim.

For myself, I worry about my writing becoming nothing but morbid entertainments, like evangelical tracts that decry the Devil and his ways and then indulge the reader's unadmitted fantasies with details of the dark worship. I worry that maybe I'm compounding distraction and a sense of futility. Most of all, I worry that I'm right. Even a little. And again, for a number of reasons.

I've begun logging unusual phone calls. Frequent untraceable silences, odd beeps, industrial noise and strange voices. Maybe, as most mothers might say, I just read too much. Maybe I simply have a lousy phone line. But I'm starting to keep a record nonetheless.

Our car was broken into the other night. Other than some change it seems that nothing was stolen. Not exactly high drama in the big city. It happened before, when the world was more or less recognizable. Still, for a moment I had that feeling in the pit of my stomach, and couldn't help but wonder.

I get that feeling sometimes looking at how IPs of frequent visitors to the blog resolve to defense agencies and installations, and such concerns as Mitre Corp, Booz Allen Hamilton, Dyncorp, NASA, Lockheed Martin, Los Alamos and Brown Brothers Harriman. But I can't know who's on the other end, or why. The military-industrial-financial complex is just that, and it's foolish to presume that everyone in its employ is *in on it*. Some may just be looking for a glimpse of a bigger picture drawn from an alternate map. Some may want something else. Hundreds of hits from the Pinkerton division devoted to government computer security suggests something else. Perhaps that they *want* me to know they're watching. *And why on Earth would they want to do that?*

Paranoia's the Black Lung disease of miners down the rabbit hole. Once you obsess that they're out to get you, they've got you. Often, I would think, without their even knowing it.

Perhaps that's what got Woody shot. There are lots of good minds out there broken by the evil of the world. And there's something about the Bush family that brings it out in people. The Web is littered with exquisite examples.

But of course, they *are* out to get us — aren't they? Certainly they mean to stop us from stopping them, and will use any means necessary to do so. But short of that, maybe not. They may even want us to do our thing, and stoke the paranoia, because that suits them just fine.

There's an aspect of the UFO phenomenon that I find very suggestive of this, though I don't know whether it's possible anymore, after the Will Smith movies, to have a serious discussion about "Men in Black." Still, I'd like to give it a shot.

The usual interpretation of these bizarre encounters is that of threat. Cryptic and dreadful warnings are spread to UFO witnesses to "keep quiet" about what they saw and what they know, even if they saw little and know even less. Yet the threats never appear to be carried out. As with the phantom clowns, social workers and census takers, the sense of menace is delivered, but that's the end of it.

John Keel's *The Mothman Prophecies* and Jacques Vallee's *Confrontations* record accounts of "Men in Black" visitations so strikingly similar, they perhaps provide keys to understanding the nature of the phenomenon.

Keel tells of a tall man with pointed features and "thyroid" eyes, wearing an ill-fitting and out of fashion black suit, sat in a booth at a New York City restaurant in the summer of 1967 and said he wanted something to eat, but could be no more specific than "food." The waitress brought a steak, which he stared at for a long while, then picked up his knife and fork and observed the other patrons. He did not know how to use the utensils. The waitress watched him fumble for a while, and then showed him how to cut the steak and spear it with his fork. She asked him where he was from. He answered, "Another world." Hardly the actions and words of someone whose mission is dissuading people from an interest in UFOs.

In May of the same year, a figure identifying himself as "Major Richard French" of the U.S. Air Force entered the restaurant of a Mrs. Ralph Butler in Owatonna, Minnesota. French had an olive complexion and pointed features, and dark hair that was much too long for an air force officer, Mrs. Butler thought. He was dressed in civilian clothes that seemed brand new. Butler saw the soles of his shoes, and they were absolutely unscuffed. Otherwise, he appeared unexceptional until he complained about an upset stomach, and Butler brought him some Jello.

"Did you ever hear of anyone — especially an air force officer — trying to drink Jello?" Butler asked. "Well, that's what he did. He acted like he'd never seen any before. He picked up the bowl and tried to drink it. I had to show him how to eat it with a spoon."

One of Vallee's investigations in *Confrontations* takes him to Happy Camp, a small lumber town near Mt. Shasta in Northern California. In the fall of 1975 a rash of UFO sightings, entity encounters and abductions rattled the community, which already had a Fortean reputation for Sasquatch spotting and "local legends about the Puduwan, strange beings with paranormal powers." (And as in Roswell and Point Pleasant and Hopkinsville and similar towns across America, the Chamber of Commerce sees a buck to be made in the legacy of weirdness. The lead story of the latest edition of *Happy Camp News* is "Bigfoot Video Cameras Are Down.") In one bizarre incident, five disparate witnesses claim to have been led from a foggy canyon, in confusion, onto a craft by beings which spoke to them about the Bible. Their next conscious memory was, unaccountably, driving down the mountain singing an old Gospel chorus. Vallee writes that he finds it "interesting that the hymn they were singing was 'There is Power in the Blood of the Lamb.'"

Vallee continues:

> The Happy Camp events encompass abductions, suffocating fog, large birds, small beings with welder helmets, chases by jets, poltergeists [and] gravity anomalies.... But it would not be complete without its own Man in Black episode.
>
> Thus I was almost relieved to learn how, early in 1976, a stranger who had never been seen in town happened to stroll into Lois's Cafe. Helen and Pat [two contactees] were there, quietly having dinner at different tables.
>
> All conversation stopped when the man came in. He ordered a steak dinner but *proved unable to use a knife and fork*, and eventually left without paying, a sure way to be remembered by the local people. Pat told me that he had pale skin and "oriental" eyes. He wore a bizarre sort of shirt and no coat, although it was the middle of winter. He smiled constantly at people in a strange, forced grimace. Among the peculiar things he did during his extraordinary dinner was a brave *attempt to drink Jello out of his glass*. [emphases added]

Keel's and Vallee's restaurant stories are separated by eight years and thousands of miles. If it were virtually anyone but Keel and Vallee telling them, I would presume them to be hoaxes or urban legend. But they conduct their own investigations on site, rigorously avoid leading witnesses, and are skeptics in the best and proper sense of the word.

Such incidents are typically described by observers of the phenomenon as "slip ups." Keel writes that "a few, like Richard French, almost pulled off their capers without drawing attention to themselves. But in nearly every case there was always some small error, some slip of dress or behavior."

Perhaps, instead, we ought to consider that there is a correlation between effect and intention. These aren't slip-ups. These are *displays*. Rather than dissuade people from thinking and talking about UFOs, they encourage speculation and breed paranoia. Many witnesses hadn't thought much about their sightings, or told many people, until visited by odd figures who say "we know what you saw" and warn them not to speak of it. Instead of turning attention away from the phenomenon, these characters draw attention to it. Just like UFOs, which act as though they *want* to be seen rather than not, the "Men in Black" make spectacles of themselves. Why?

"Men in Black," when they appear to be men at all — some outstanding encounters describe comically robotic figures — are often said to have ruddy or olive complexions and "oriental" or "thyroid" eyes, speak in "sing-song" voices and walk in a halting manner as though out-of-sync with our reality and strangers to our time and space. Keel says they often claim to be representatives of the "Nation of the Third Eye."

This is one of those many times when I've believed I've had an original idea, only to find it's already on the table: perhaps what we call the "Men in Black" are entities manifesting themselves as representatives of Shamballa, the Great White Lodge of Sirius linked to Tibet and Eurasian mythology. (Also see this post, and these two threads, for recent studies of the significance of Shamballa and Eurasian mythology to modern apocalyptics such as Richard Heinberg.) I would suggest, though, the possibility that this appearance is assumed not because it reflects reality, but because these are tricksters adapting to the contours of belief of elite occultists, whose energies call them forth.

Perhaps this is why they often assume the guise of government agents, or are mistaken for such, because they are mimicking their occult human complement. They also share an interest in inducing paranoia, even as they make a pretense at doing the opposite.

There are things of which we *should* be afraid, but we can be smart about it. Paranoia is fear bred in ignorance, which only serves the interest of the would-be rulers of the world. Paranoia is *not knowing what we're up against*. As weird as things get, if we can see it coming then we may in a position, and on our feet, in order to do something about it.

Down the Scole Hole

December 26, 2005

It's gettin' dark, too dark for me to see
I feel like I'm knockin' on heaven's door.

— Bob Dylan

In the post "You can't go home again" we looked at borderland experiences described by veterans of military and intelligence sponsored remote-viewing programs. In passing I mentioned the Scole Experiment: a five-year exercise in contact with disincarnate entities, based in the cellar of an English farmhouse (coined the "Scole Hole"), that saw similar psi phenomenon under exceptionally controlled circumstances. Just as scientists at Lawrence Livermore saw seemingly holographic and "almost comically stereotypical," images of eight-inch UFOs flit about their laboratory, so the Scole team "witnessed a miniature UFO flying around the cellar where we held our sessions." Reading Grant and Jane Solomon's *The Scole Experiment*, I see there's more. One of the independent researchers who sat in on the Scole sessions was Russell Targ, co-founder of Stanford Research Institute's remote-viewing program.

The phenomena recorded in the Scole sittings was unusually rich and obtained under protocols anticipating the objections of skeptics. There was channeling of course, as well as spirit voices, noises, dancing lights, levitations and physical manifestations of alleged spirits. Also "apports" — the inexplicable materialization of dozens of objects onto the session table, including an original pristine copy of the *Daily Mail* from January 4, 1944 and a tiny gold disc with hieroglyphics, "the source of which has not yet been identified." And remarkable captures on audiotape, photographic film and video.

Photographic experiments included independent investigators initialing and placing unopened and unexposed film in a sealed tub, sitting with the tub at a session, and then overseeing its development. Results included the imprinting of poetry, esoteric symbols and diagrammatic instructions to improve the transmissions.

The video experiments began in May 1997, and were dubbed "Project Alice" because they involved an arrangement of mirrors before a camera "to capture moving images sent from the spirit world," write the Solomons. (Mirrors have long been used as an aid to receiving visions from other realms. John Dee's obsidian mirror, used by his scryer Edward Kelly in his Enochian work, is on display in the British Museum.)

For most of the experiments, the camera sat on its tripod in the dark positioned before two mirrors. At the end of the sessions the team often saw that the camera had repeatedly and impossibly zoomed in and out on its own accord, and the tapes contained weird scenes, smiling faces, vibrant colors and hints of body parts moving across the screen in a red light. One tape showed a pink and gold line running horizontally down the screen, which pivoted to reveal it was a square shape on edge. As it rotated, it was seen to contain an image. According to the Scole team, "this was a very clear view of an animated inter-dimensional friend, whose features, to say the least, were not exactly as our own." They called their new friend "Blue." His screen capture is the classic "grey alien.". There are also pyramids in another spirit transmission, presumably some etheric vista.

Speaking of pyramids, some of what the alleged spirits of Scole had to say sounds remarkably similar to what "the Nine" — the supposed Great Ennead of Ancient Egypt — have been saying through various CIA-sponsored mediumships since 1952. That the purpose of our material lives is "to come to Earth for the experience," for instance. "Manu," described as a "powerful and extremely spiritual guide" who was always the first to speak, and who claimed to have "enjoyed many incarnations" including one in "what you now call South America," anticipates a "great awakening in many ways":

> What we do is part of that plan. There are cosmic, pulsating energies coming to the Earth all the time. Everything is evolving, nothing stays still. At this time in his evolution, man is ready for these energies to come upon him and give him what he is thirsting for. So we shall give him the refreshing rain of knowledge, that he may drink from these waters, that he may know of his own spiritual self....
>
> First we must reach out to man's higher aspect and then filter down to his everyday life and the choices he makes. Only that way will

change come about.... As you think of the people of this Earth, and the very Earth itself, so you help to activate these ancient vibrations that are coming forward at the moment. The age is right for this to happen.

The Scole Experimental Group assumed that the entities with which they made contact were spirits of the dead, curious themselves to make contact, who formed a complementary team on the other side. The researchers assumed they were who they said they were, because of the benign nature of the contact, and the fact that some channeled voices would transmit messages from loved ones containing information only the contactee could possibly know.

That's a lot to assume. I can think of two other explanations, besides a hoax, for the same phenomenon. For instance, perhaps the contactee influenced events by subconsciously transmitting the private knowledge to the medium. (It's difficult to describe the margins of innate human psi and the occult, because even occult workings demand a willing human partnership. Perhaps a genuine medium would also be sensitive to incarnate spirits.) Also, many UFO contactees describe having their minds read. Maybe something similar is going on when a "spirit" claims to be someone familiar to the contactee and backs it up by sharing private information.

The Scole team traveled to California and demonstrated their results in nine separate sessions. One was a "scientists session" for NASA and representatives of Stanford University. The Scole team did not know who was going to attend or where the session would be held, and before the demonstration began the scientists searched the room, a basement gymnasium. A Native American materialized during the session, dancing and chanting, and drums which were mounted high on the wall began to beat. Then familiar spirits appeared, calling some of the scientists by name though their identities were unknown to the Scole team, and explained to the group that the area was an ancient sacred site, and the peoples who had lived there long ago were influencing the session.

"Interestingly," the Solomons write, "some of the astrophysicists later started a group of their own."

In its report on its five-year project, the Scole Group commented that:

Our understanding of what Manu told us is that humanity has consciously or unconsciously been sending out a signal asking for help for our world for some time and that many loving beings have heard our plea. They are now coming in response to our request to aid us in any way they possibly can. It seems that the many dimensions are bound together with the common thread of love. This love transcends all other things. What a truly wonderful notion that is.

Well, that's one way to look at it. Another is that there are supra-mundane entities as interested in opening gateways into our reality as there are humans keen on opening channels into theirs, and willing to say and do anything to achieve it. I suppose it would be wrong to presume them all to be Lovecraftian nightmares, but it may be more prudent then throwing open the door and saying "Welcome, brother."

I like this advice from Emmanuel Swedenborg, so I'll quote it again:

When Spirits begin to speak with a man, he must beware that he believes nothing they say. For nearly everything they say is fabricated by them, and they lie: for they are permitted to narrate anything, as what heaven is and how things in the heavens are to be understood, they would tell so many lies that a man would be astonished.

The Scole spirits say the crossing is getting easier, and more people will begin to see them and understand their own spiritual lives. Maybe. Or maybe, it's a cookbook.

Full Spectral Dominance

January 14, 2006

You could go down to the canyon,
piss away this incarnation,
but just remember that you pay for what you get.
— Bruce Cockburn

s I said in an earlier post, I'm finding the correspondences between boundary experiences a fascinating and instructive study. And an aspect that almost always appears present, whichever boundary is breached, is the electrical. Perhaps not surprisingly so, since the electric is also an irreducible aspect of physical life. It's not only *out there*, but it's *in us*. (In other words I suppose, *wherever you go, there you are*.) Our brains are not just grey *matter*; they also carry a frequency. And it seems, or so we're told, when we tune it just so, we can pick up other stations of reality's broadband.

It's what Bob Monroe was talking about, as he detailed his 40-year astral travelogue. Monroe developed a technique he called "hemi-sync" for inducing altered states of consciousness by entraining the brain towards certain frequencies. In the early '80s, INSCOM officers and the military's remote viewers were visiting Virginia's Monroe Institute every few weeks for it's five-day "Gateway Lifeline" program to hone their paranormal skills, though for their sake it was given the less squishy title of "Rapid Advancement Personal Training." (Monroe's military-intelligence connections might have been a birthright: it is said that his father was James Monroe, Executive Director of the CIA's mind-control cut-out the Human Ecology Society.)

Monroe's first book, *Journeys Out of the Body*, includes a number of diary entries from the late '50s and early '60s which recount his early experiences with astral projection before hitting upon hemi-sync. For instance:

11/5/58 Afternoon

The vibrations came quickly and easily, and were not at all uncomfortable. When they were strong, I tried to lift out of the physical with no result. Whatever thought or combination I tried, I remained confined right where I was. I then remembered the rotating trick, which operates just as if you are turning over in bed. I started to turn, and recognized that my physical was not "turning" with me. I moved slowly, and after a moment I was "face down," or in direct opposition to the placement of my physical body. The moment I reached this 180-degree position, there was a hole. That's the only way to describe it. To my senses, it seemed to be a hole in a wall which was about two feet thick and stretched endlessly in all directions.... I felt that if my vision were good enough I could probably see nearby stars and planets.

Monroe spends weeks cautiously exploring the hole. He reaches in a hand, and is astonished when a hand takes his and shakes it. He hears his name called, and voices exclaiming "Come here quick! Look!" On one occasion he puts his hand through and feels something sharp dig into his palm, "like a hook, and it dug in more deeply when I tried to withdraw it." On another, his hand feels as though it's been thrust into "electrically charged hot water."

Finally, "gathering courage, I pulled myself through in a sweeping rush, just as a swimmer might pull himself through a hole under water. "What followed were a series of experiments "that were remarkable in their consistency of data, and defied any historical explanation." (Also, we ought to say, defying corroboration.) Monroe found, on repeated visits, a "physical-matter world almost identical to our own," though with weird details askew. (There were no electrical devices, and even the smallest car had a "single bench seat that will hold five to six people abreast.") He could travel in this realm he called "Locale III" largely undetected, ghost-like. What's more, he found he could "possess" the body of an inhabitant, and directly experience life in Locale III.

(I know the fallacy of interpreting the next thing I read by the last thing I've read. Still, I can't let it pass how much Monroe's description of pulling himself through the hole reminds me of the account from Skinwalker Ranch of the "tunnel" alleged to have appeared before the pair of NIDS researchers, and the black humanoid which was seen to hoist itself out and walk away.)

During an early passage of discovery in the realm, Monroe noticed something suddenly fly past him. "I turned just in time to see it heading for the wall and the hole. I was afraid for some reason that this was something that would go through and try to enter my body." Maybe so. In the early '80s, an alleged spirit named Miranon, picked up somewhere outside our space-time, "seemed actually to possess Bob Monroe one day... speaking through him like a spirit through a medium," writes Jim Schnabel. "Miranon still possessed Bob fairly often" when military personnel were frequent visitors to the Institute. Monroe was so taken by the Seth-like pronouncements of his astral friend that he named a pond on the property "Lake Miranon."

Monroe died in 1995, and Skip Atwater became the Institute's Director of Research. From 1978 to 1988, Atwater served as the Operations and Training Officer for the U.S. Army Intelligence remote-viewing program.

Journeys Out of the Body also records visionary alleged "precog" side effects Monroe experienced during his early astral experiments. They are usually *dread*ful with strange menace and futility:

11/5/61

I am standing alone outside my house.... I see a group of aircraft emerge from the cloud cover, just above it. They approach, and I note that they are not typical aircraft or rockets.... They are not like any airplanes I have seen before. No wings are visible, and each machine is gigantic.... Each is shaped like the head of an arrow, V-shaped ...

6/12/63

Gasoline is unavailable, electric power has been shut off. there is a great sense of fatality among everyone. It doesn't seem to be the product of atomic war, and there is no concern as to radioactive fallout. There is principally a feeling of doom and the breakup of civilization as we know it due to something momentous having taken place, a factor beyond human control.

Monroe adds, "I hope some of them *are* hallucinations."

Dr. Albert Hoffman, the "father of LSD," but perhaps better described as its midwife, turned 100 a few days ago. Like so many other things we trip over this fraught century, lysergic acid diethylamide first appeared in Nazi-dominated Europe, and first through dreams and intuition.

Hoffman was looking for compounds that induced muscle contraction. After synthesizing LSD and testing it on animals to no useful effect Hoffman's research moved on. But strangely, he began to dream repeatedly about its molecular structure, and was gripped by a "peculiar presentiment" that compelled him, five years later, to resynthesize the compound and ingest it intentionally.

"In the annals of science," Daniel Pinchbeck writes in **Breaking Open the Head**, "it is notable that many scientific insights first appear in dreams and visions":

> The German chemist Friedrich Kekule, for instance, dreamt of a snake with its tail in its mouth, and understood that the molecular structure of benzene was a closed carbon ring. The French mathematician Jules-Henri Poincaré, during a sleepless night, saw mathematical symbols colliding until they coalesced into equations. These intuitive levels of insight, whether scientific or artistic, function like the prophetic dreams of shamans.... Hoffman's discovery of LSD was that kind of insight — a flash from a deeper order of the self or, perhaps, from outside the self entirely.

How did the Amazonian shamans come to discover their complex psychoactive compound of ayahuasca? They say the plants taught them in dreams. And intuition seemed to lead to the synthesis of DMT in 1931, nearly 20 years *before* it was discovered to be a naturally occurring alkaloid in plants. (It wasn't until 1972 that it was found to be an endogenous compound, produced by the human brain.)

Pinchbeck records his ceremonial ingestion of ayahuasca:

> The hallucinations started to deepen into a realm that I could not recognize, that I lack language to describe. I found myself wandering across a shimmering space with beings that never stopped changing — porcupine-quilled, tusked, multitongued, amoebic, but even those words are only approximations of entities that could be compared to the darker imaginings of H.P. Lovecraft. The shaman and the elders seemed to be inhabiting this space with me. Glowing in the light cast

by the fire, their features seemed animated by an almost nonhuman intensity. They sang, their words unintelligible, to these creatures, interacting with them, in mystical communion. It seemed that this was the goal of the ayahuasca ceremony, the arrival point. These were "the heavenly people."

The scene is similar to that described by Robert Monroe in *Journeys Out of the Body* of a hellish layer close to our mundane reality, through which he would pass while projecting his astral self, which felt like bait above "a gray-black hungry ocean where the slightest motion attracts nibbling and tormenting beings." He writes that "it is easy to conclude that a momentary penetration of this nearby layer would bring 'demons' and 'devils' to mind as the chief inhabitants." It also recalls the hallucinatory witness to shapeshifting in some accounts of mind-control survivors.

DMT frequently induces similar visions of interstellar voids, hungry insectoid intelligences and abduction scenarios indistinguishable from those of UFO encounters, including alien intercourse. Here "Rex" describes his controlled injection in Dr. Rick Strassman's *DMT: The Spirit Molecule*:

When I was first going under there were these insect creatures all around me. They were clearly trying to break through. I was fighting letting go of who I am or was.... They were interested in emotion. As I was holding on to my last thought, that God equals love, they said, "Even here? Even here?" I said, "Yes, of course." They were still there but I was making love to them at the same time. They feasted as they made love to me.... The thought came to me with certainty that they were manipulating my DNA, changing its structure.

Strassman ended his clinical studies of the drug in part because he gave serious weight to the warning of a "highly intuitive" friend who told him she saw "evil spirits hovering around you. They want to come through this plane, using you and the drugs."

If there *are* many dimensions beyond, or behind, those we normally inhabit, it would seem by the congruity of experience that there are a variety of means to their unlocking. Yet all of them — occult workings, remote viewing, astral projection, UFO abductions and shamanic chemistry — share the trait of inducing altered states of consciousness. And something else they share is the abiding, deep attention of military intelligence. At this point, someone's likely to mention the "holographic universe" and its alleged implication that "nothing is real." Perhaps instead it means that *everything* is real, including the "imaginal realm" described by French Islamic scholar Henry Corbin in his 1972 work, *Mundis Imaginalis*:

> Upon returning [from a mystical vision] the beholders of this world are perfectly aware of having been "elsewhere": they are not mere schizophrenics. This world is hidden behind the very act of sense perception and has to be sought underneath its apparent objective certainty. For this reason we definitely cannot qualify it as being imaginary in the current sense of the word, i.e., unreal or nonexistent. [It] is ontologically as real as the world of the senses and that of the intellect [perceived by] the "psychospiritual senses."

Psychologist Kenneth Ring talks of "the shamanizing of modern humanity" in his book *The Omega Project,* which studies the commonality of Near-Death Experience and UFO encounters. Ring writes that "we could be in the beginning stages of a major shift in levels of consciousness that will eventually lead to humanity's being able to live in two worlds at once — the physical and the imaginal." He believes that NDEs and UFOs, like the mystical and visionary states found in shamanic ritual, may be adventing at this time as an evolutionary aid towards the development of "latent capacities for imaginal perception."

I'm not sure I agree with Ring's rosy conclusions drawn from the evident thinning of the veil. I wonder instead whether a nexus of powerful parties on both sides of the portal with investments in *control* are conspiring to *exploit* gateways, the result of which may mean a near blunt-force stunting of the development of human consciousness.

I know this is highly speculative, but it's one of those crazy thoughts I have when I look up and see grids in the sky where there were none before, and marvel at the calculation behind our conspicuous dumbing down. What is it about us that is being *suppressed*, and who most profits by it?

"The Great Satan"

February 24, 2005

A Priest and a Bishop

promise to come back down to Earth again soon, and talk of run of the mill concerns like bogus wars, plagues and the End of the World. But first things, before Last Things.

For instance, have you heard the one about the Toledo priest? It's not a joke, except maybe to those who think ritual abuse is the domain of hysterical women and their suggestible children. And I guess that would be most people.

From Sunday's *Toledo Blade*:

DARK ALLEGATIONS ARISE AMID PROBE OF NUN'S SLAYING
Authorities expand investigation to claims of ritualistic sex abuse

For Toledo police, it was a rare assignment: Search an abandoned house on the edge of a cornfield in western Lucas County where people reportedly took part in ritual abuse ceremonies.

...

The search of the decrepit, wood structure last year was a sign the investigation of the Rev. Gerald Robinson was moving beyond a murder case.

No longer was the probe focusing solely on the man accused of killing Sister Margaret Ann Pahl, but was expanding into a new direction: accusations that children were molested and raped by priests in ritual services.

...

Four women told detectives about being abused between the late 1960s and 1986 during cult-like ceremonies involving altars and men dressed in robes, the accusers told *The Blade*. "I've had nightmares about this since I was a child," said one woman, who asked not to be named. "I didn't think anyone would believe me."

Noted forensic expert Henry Lee has been retained to examine the physical evidence of the 25-year old slaying, which police are still calling a "ritual" killing "because of the circumstances surrounding the crime, including the way her body was found: lying face up with an altar cloth draped over her torso, her body posed to appear like she was sexually assaulted." A "deliberate" pattern of stab wounds is said to resemble a cross.

Awful, but why should we care here, and can we please get back to bashing Bush? All in good time.

Then there's the one about the two Bishops. Or perhaps, just one.

Let's go back to Johnny Gosch for a moment, about whom we wrote here with respect to the Gannon/Guckert fiasco. In the first chapter of Noreen Gosch's self-published book about her son's abduction, *Why Johnny Can't Come Home* (released November, 2000), she writes of a visit from a young man, George Paul Bishop, who went by "Paul," and who was associated with the CIA:

> Within six months of the kidnapping, a young man identifying himself as Paul Bishop contacted me by phone. He told me an international kidnapping/pornography ring had taken my son. I asked, "How do you know that to be true, can you prove it!" He replied, "I work for a government agency which is investigating pedophile organizations. And there are indicators in your case that suggests your son was taken by such an organization. We feel he is being used for pornography and prostitution." All clues were pointing to the kidnapping being organized and not that of a "lone criminal." I found it difficult to believe and accept that my son could have been targeted by such an organization.

> ...

> Paul Bishop, CIA Asset, made another short trip to Des Moines, July 31,1984. It was at this time, he reported the name of the man who was the "spotter," Sam Soda, in Johnny's kidnapping.... Sam was not too cooperative, became annoyed with Bishop, asking him to leave his office. There is indication today that these two individuals knew each other prior to this time. Before Paul left Des Moines, he created a very intricate map of the crime scene, indicating time sequence of each aspect of the kidnapping. Paul dated and initialed the map using GPB (*George Paul Bishop*).

> ...

> During this time, I had also been working with Senator Grassley from Iowa; he had been particularly helpful in facilitating with the FBI. Many times Paul Bishop would call me from Senator Grassley's office. When finished speaking with me, he would hand the phone to one of

Grassley's aides who I was familiar with. That convinced me Paul was an accepted visitor on the hill in Washington.

...

Senator Specter asked Paul Bishop of his relationship to the case, to me, and did he know this to be true. Paul indicated he was an investigator and that every word of my testimony was accurate. Paul remained by my side during the hearing; answering questions asked by Senator Specter: these were the only words he spoke. This struck me as very unusual but then I had never been in this arena before to observe how a CIA man would conduct himself. At no time did Paul ever identify himself as CIA during the hearing or afterward during the interviews with the Washington press. He withdrew from the view of the cameras.

Now consider this story, from Fairfax Virginia, February 2, as the Gannon story was starting to unravel:

POLICE ARREST TWO ON CHILD PORN CHARGES

A complaint about excessive comings and goings of teenage boys at a Chantilly house led, this week, to the arrest of two Fairfax County men for child pornography offenses.

Richard Evans, of Annandale, and *George Bishop*, of Chantilly, who co-manage a literary Web site, were both arrested by Fairfax County Police on Friday, Jan. 28.

Police started investigating Bishop, 46, after they received a complaint that he was allegedly inviting teenage boys to come to his house, to drink alcohol and to take illegal narcotics.

For what it's worth, according to this, Mrs. Gosch has seen the photo of the arrested Bishop, *"and it is him. No doubt about it."*

Writing years earlier, she wondered whatever happened to the young CIA asset, who used to call her "mom":

He was a young person in his twenties and I sometimes wonder, *had he been used in some manner by the very element that took my son? Was he sent here to share with me the threads of truth, which would unfold later? It was years before the CIA was revealed as a part of this problem* of missing children in our country and the world. [emphases added]

A Globalized and Sheltered Disorder

The White House call-boy scandal opens the door on some strange places. But it would be wrong to call all the places "America." Consider a few from recent years:

BRITAIN:

ALLEGED PEDOPHILES HELM BLAIR'S WAR ROOM

Counterpunch, January 29, 2003

A child-sex scandal that threatened to destroy Tony Blair's government last week has been *mysteriously squashed and wiped off the front pages* of British newspapers. Operation Ore, the United Kingdom's most thorough and comprehensive police investigation of crimes against children, seems to have *uncovered more than is politically acceptable at the highest reaches of the British elite*. In the 19th of January edition of *The Sunday Herald*, Neil Mackay sensationally reported that *senior members of Tony Blair's government were being investigated for paedophilia* and the "enjoyment" of child-sex pornography:

"*The Sunday Herald* has also had confirmed by a very senior source in British intelligence that at least one high-profile former Labour Cabinet minister is among Operation Ore suspects. The Sunday Herald has been given the politician's name but, for legal reasons, cannot identify the person.

"There are still unconfirmed rumors that another senior Labour politician is among the suspects. The intelligence officer said that a 'rolling' Cabinet committee had been set up to work out how to deal with the potentially ruinous fall-out for both Tony Blair and the government if arrests occur."

The Blair government has responded by imposing a comprehensive blackout on the story, effectively removing it from the domain of public discussion. Attempts on the part of this journalist to establish why the British media has not followed up on the revelations have met with a wall of silence. Editors and journalists of *The Times, The Daily Telegraph, The Guardian, The Independent, The Sunday Times, The Observer, The Sunday Telegraph, The Daily Mail, The Daily Express, The Mirror, The Sun*, the BBC, Independent Television News and even *The Sunday Herald* have refused to discuss the matter. [emphases added]

CALL TO LIFT VEIL OF SECRECY OVER DUNBLANE

The Guardian, February 14, 2003

Campaigners yesterday called for a review of the 100-year secrecy rule imposed on some documents seen by the inquiry into the Dunblane killings which were never made public.

The move comes after the Scottish cabinet this week instructed Scotland's most senior law officer to look again at the 100-year ban placed on a police report on Thomas Hamilton, who murdered 16 primary schoolchildren and their teacher.

There have been allegations that the lengthy closure order was placed on the report after it linked *Hamilton to figures in the Scottish establishment*, including two senior politicians and a lawyer.

...

There has been much speculation about the identity of the politicians in the report. It is known that in June 1996 Michael Forsyth, then Scottish secretary and MP for Stirling, congratulated Hamilton on running a boys' club in Dunblane. [empahsis added]

BELGIUM:

Ritual abuse, pedophilia, murder, and the charge of a government cover-up

The Telegraph, August 17, 2001

Five years after the bodies of four murdered Belgian girls were discovered at houses owned by the paedophile Marc Dutroux, the father of one of them has accused the country's police and justice system of a cover-up ensuring that his trial has still not begun.

The claims by Paul Marchal, father of An Marchal, who was 17 when she disappeared in 1995, echo what many Belgians now privately believe: that *Dutroux and his paedophile ring had connections with high-ranking members of the establishment* in Belgium.

In a country that is becoming inured to corruption in public life, the theory of a cover-up is now increasingly accepted as the real reason why the Dutroux case has yet to come to court. [empahsis added]

Belgium's X Files

BBC, May 2, 2002

There appears to be *a steel veil drawn over the facts at the highest level* and no one is prepared to expose those involved in this blatant cover-up.

...

The official answer is that a series of hysterical conspiracy theories forced investigators to search for paedophile networks, which didn't exist. But for observers of this debacle, that's exactly what didn't happen. Far from being investigated, *leads pointing to a network seem rather to have been blocked or buried*. [emphases added]

More from David McGowan:

Adding further fuel to the fire, as a *Los Angeles Times* report revealed, were claims by "a highly regarded children's activist, Marie-France Botte ... the *Justice Ministry is sitting on a politically sensitive list of customers of pedophile videotapes*." The same report noted, "The affair has become further clouded by the discovery of a motorcycle that reportedly matches the description of one used in the 1991 assassination of prominent Belgian businessman and politician Andre Cools. Michel Bourlet, the head prosecutor on the pedophile case, meanwhile, has publicly declared that the investigation can be thoroughly pursued only without political interference. Several years ago, Bourlet was removed from the highly charged Cools case, which remains unsolved."

...

Outrage continued to grow as more arrests were made and evidence of high-level government and police complicity continued to emerge. One of Dutroux's accomplices, businessman Jean-Michel Nihoul, *confessed to organizing an 'orgy' at a Belgian chateau that had been attended by government officials*, a former European Commissioner, and a number of law enforcement officers. A Belgian senator noted, quite accurately, that *such parties were part of a system* "*which operates to this day and is used to blackmail the highly placed people who take part.*" [emphases added]

PORTUGAL

PORTUGAL ROCKED BY CHILD SEX SCANDAL

Allegations that a child sex ring has been operating out of state-run children's homes in Portugal for decades has prompted intervention by President Jorge Sampaio.
BBC, May 29, 2003

The developments sparked an outcry in Portugal, particularly when it was reported that a former president and several government ministers, as well as the police, *knew of the allegations as far back as the early 1980s but failed to take action.*

"Faced with the horror that so many children, who were entrusted to us to be educated and cared for, were victimised, it is necessary to declare here that the president is certain that the guilty will be severely punished," President Sampaio said in a speech.

The latest high-profile arrests are of men publicly accused of sex abuse by former children of Casa Pia, Portugal's largest network of homes for troubled children.

Casa Pia first made the headlines following allegations that an employee at the institution allegedly *helped wealthy child molesters* to meet young boys in his care for over two decades. [emphases added]

CHILE

Chilean elites caught in child porn ring
Boston Globe, Jan 12 2004

VALPARAISO, Chile — Congresswoman Maria Pia Guzman is a strait-laced conservative who has suddenly and unexpectedly become an outcast at the Congress building here. Sometimes her follow legislators murmur an insult when she comes within earshot: "Witch!"

Guzman did not unleash the sex scandal now rocking Chile's political and social elite, a sordid tale centered around a millionaire businessman and some runaway teenagers.

But she did *publicly link a handful of congressmen and senators to the case*, suggesting some of her own political allies might be involved in an alleged ring of prostitution and child pornography. And for that, some of her fellow legislators will not forgive her.

When she gets in an elevator with other congressmen, they often step out. "There is a very strong psychological warfare going on," Guzman said in an interview in her Valparaiso office. Lighting a cigarette, she added: "Before this case, I had stopped smoking." [emphasis added]

MEXICO

Mob In Mexico Burns Two Federal Agents Alive
AP, November 24, 2004

MEXICO CITY — A crowd angry about recent child kidnappings cornered *plainclothes federal agents taking photos of students at a school* on Mexico City's outskirts and burned the officers alive, the latest example of mob justice in a country beset by corrupt police and high crime.

...

The violence began in the early evening, when locals collared three men staking out a school in the San Juan Ixtlayopan neighborhood. *The area has been tense since two youngsters disappeared and were feared kidnapped* from the school. Some in the crowd appeared to believe the agents were kidnappers. When asked about complaints that authorities had failed to respond to demands to investigate the disappearances, Figueroa said a full schedule had prohibited federal authorities from concentrating on the case. [emphases added]

The National Security State's Left-Hand Path

But let's leave sex for a moment, to talk about magic. Before we talk about both.

We've already engaged in some high speculation with respect to the hidden hand of Aleister Crowley in the occult subtext of the National Security State. Perhaps, *just perhaps*, Crowley's "Amalantrah Working" had succeeded in creating a dimensional portal, through which the prototypical "Grey," whom he called Lam, crossed. And that the "Babylon Working" of his American adepts, Jet Propulsion Laboratory's Jack Parsons and L. Ron Hubbard, created a breech, initiating the modern "UFO" phenomenon.

To this understanding, the UFO phenomenon does not demonstrate extraterrestrial contact. It demonstrates a *summoning*.

And we should note here that if there is *any* credence to this, then behind the modernity lie the "Enochian entities" of the Elizabethan spiritualist Dr. John Dee, who was "almost certainly a prime mover in the 'Illuminati' and 'Rosicrucian Brotherhoods' of that time, which played a central role in the birth of modem science."

Let's consider this UFO case, from July 6, 1959. Major Robert Friend, the acting chief of "Project Blue Book" at Wright-Patterson Air Force Base, was asked to travel to Washington to evaluate a discovery of Naval Intelligence. Two officers had traveled to Maine the month before, to meet a woman "who claimed to be in contact with extraterrestrials":

The officers met the woman and watched her enter a trance and become a "communications link." The woman sat mesmerized. Only her arm from the elbow down moved. It scribbled out meaningless circles interspersed with legible letters. They spoke questions to which answers appeared within the scribbling. The answers indicated they were coming from a kind of space patrol leader named "AFFA."

According to the officers a number of unverifiable answers were offered to such questions such as, "What is the population of Jupiter?" Among other things, AFFA said he and his men were part of an inter-solar-system police force investigating atomic tests on Earth. But more interestingly, the Navy intelligence men posed questions incompatible with her education of technical understanding- questions like "What is the length of the Uranus ' day?" and "What is the distance between Jupiter and the sun at Jupiter's apogee?" "Her" answers were correct, the two incredulous investigators later reported to Friend.

About 2 p.m. July 6, 1959, at a secret government office concealed on the top story of a garage at 5th and K St., N.W., Washington, D.C., *one of the two commanders, just back from Maine, went into a trance during which he wrote messages which indicated they were from an individual named "AFFA."* AFFA's origin: planet Uranus.

Another Navy intelligence and a civilian intelligence officer were present.

...

Among the more interesting interchanges later reported to Friend were the following:

Q. It's very interesting that we are talking with someone that we can see, but can we have proof of your existence?

A. What kind of proof do you want?

Q. Can we see you or your craft?

A. When do you want to see?

Q. Now.

A. *Go to the window.*

All the intelligence people went to the window, where they saw a UFO fly by (i.e.) not stationary) a short distance away. As they later told Friend it was saucer shaped and brighter around the perimeter than in the center.

The confusion that followed ended the communication with AFFA. [emphases added]

Of interest to us here is the fact that "AFFA" is a word in the "angelic" Enochian language given Dee by the entities which had contacted him in the 17th Century. "AFFA" means "*nothing*," or "*empty*."

Jacques Vallee has contributed much to an understanding of the deceptive, tricksterish characteristics of UFO contact; its irrationality; and its continuity with folkloric phenomena of ages past. When people have expected angels or faeries, they have recorded contact with entities claiming to be the same. When human consciousness came to accept extraterrestrials as a more plausible conduit of supra-human contact, then entities began identifying themselves as visitors from Venus, Uranus, Zeta Reticuli or wherever.

Crowley reintroduced Enochian magic to modern followers of the "left hand path" of spiritual dissent while with the Hermetic Order of the Golden Dawn. He rearticulated it when he was initiated into the Ordo Templi Orientis.

Crowley's occult signature is "sex magick." Depending on the desired effect, it may be practiced autoerotically, with a partner, or multiple partners. It is always ritualized. The "workings" of Crowley and Parsons were founded in this principle. (In Parson's record of the Babalon Working, when he writes "invocation of wand with material basis on talisman," he is describing masturbation and ejaculation. In *Sex and Rockets: the Occult World of Jack Parsons*, John Carter describes it as a "symbolic fertilizing of Parsons' desire through a very literal application.")

It may sound silly, and almost quaint. To the materialist, all magical thinking is, at best, no more than that. But let's turn to Crowley's *MAGICK in Theory and Practice*, and it sounds neither:

> But the bloody sacrifice, though more dangerous, is more efficacious; and for nearly all purposes human sacrifice is the best.
>
> The animal should therefore be killed within the Circle, or the Triangle, as the case may be, so that its energy cannot escape. An animal should be selected whose nature accords with that of the ceremony — thus, by sacrificing a female lamb one would not obtain any appreciate quantity of the fierce energy useful to a Magician who was invoking Mars. In such a case a ram would be more suitable. And this ram should be virgin — the whole potential of its original total energy should not have been diminished in any way. For the highest spiritual working one must accordingly choose that victim which contains the greatest and purest force. *A male child of perfect innocence and high intelligence is the most satisfactory and suitable victim.* [emphasis added]

It's worth recalling here, that in the first part of my interview with mind-control survivor Kathleen Sullivan, she describes the religious practices of her abusers and handlers as those "promoted by Great Britain's Aleister Crowley. Those practices are especially bestial and dangerous — especially for children." And that her father, her "primary mental programmer and tormentor, was big into the teachings and practices of Aleister Crowley."

By the Second World War, Crowley was already an asset of British intelligence. According to Gerald Suster's *The Legacy of the Beast*, it was on Crowley's advice to the Director of Naval Intelligence that Winston Churchill adopted the V-sign, as a symbolic counter to the swastika, and the "thumbs up," which signaled not only victory, but sexual magic.

Imagine what must have been swept up by the Allies at war's end, in Project Paperclip. Not only Nazi science, but the esoteric knowledge of Himmler's *Ahnenerbe*, the Nazi Occult Bureau.

From Michael Fitzgerald's *Storm-Troopers of Satan: an Occult History of the Second World War*:

Hardly an occult theory escaped the attention of the Nazis, especially in Himmler's Occult Bureau and the German navy. It cannot be stressed too often that the world as perceived by the Nazis was a magical cosmos. As such, anything which could assist them in their aims of world domination through magical means was eagerly grasped. And in every case, where the choice existed between a positive and negative symbol, the Nazis opted for the negative, evil version. In this respect they demonstrated their consistent adherence to a conscious and deliberate Satanism, an attempt to establish a religion of blood and destruction.... Probably at no time in recent history has the world come closer to falling under the domination of a group of initiates serving consciously Satanic ends.

Now consider this: if Paperclip brought together the esoteric knowledge of "left-hand path" Anglo and Germanic secret schools in the "fight against communism," how would we recognize it today?

And let's just suppose — and I'll grant it's a *big* suppose, even in this context, and even with such supporting evidence as exists, since it beggars not only our credulity but our decency —

that there *is* an international network of pedophilic elites. The question ought to be, why? Can it really all be attributed to the indulgence of forbidden desires? Or could it have an esoteric dimension — might it be about power? And not in the usual, true sense of power in abusive relations. I mean, in the esoteric sense. The Crowleyan sense. The sense of *sex magick*.

Er..."Fidelio"?

Well. Welcome to my scary mind.

I'm beginning to feel a bit like a down-market version of the Tom Cruise character in *Eyes Wide Shut*, who went looking for a good time and found instead an Illuminati sex ritual. I know the code that got me in; I just don't know the code that can get me out.

I didn't expect to find myself here, entertaining the "I"-word. I mean, *come on*; could this be something like the world: a populace mollified on sucker faiths like the "New Age" Maitreya and a Moonified Christianity, while pedophilic Luciferians, allied to transdimensional tricksters, practice Crowley's law of "Do what thou wilt"?

The final word to Jacques Vallee. In *Masters of Deception*, he writes that when alleged communication with UFO occupants "touches on political subjects, [it] tended to emphasize totalitarian images. Vorilhon, for instance, reports he was told that democracy was obsolete. Raymond Bernard was instructed to expect a 'reversal of the old values.'"

Could it be?

Shhh — it's supposed to be a secret.

Egg Hunt

April 14, 2006

But the eating — it filled him with white light.
— *Sin City*

Father Gerald Robinson, in the docks, looks like Henry Lee Lucas's dumber brother. In the collar of a priest, which he wore for decades, he's the sort of man responsible parents might entrust with their children. But he's the Toledo priest belatedly facing trial for the 1980 ritual murder of a nun, Sister Margaret Ann Pahl. She was found, strangled and stabbed to death, in the sacristy of the chapel of Mercy Hospital, an altar cloth draped over her torso and her body posed lewdly to suggest she had been sexually assaulted. Her chest was punctured by nine stab wounds, forming a "deliberate" pattern of an inverted cross.

Today, Good Friday, is Gerald Robinson's 68th birthday. Margaret Ann Pahl was murdered on Holy Saturday. Her 72nd birthday would have fallen on that Easter Sunday. And Robinson's trial begins this Monday. A curious alignment of remembrance this long weekend.

Robinson was an early suspect and failed a polygraph test — he later admitted having lied when he'd said he'd heard the murderer's confession — but the case was cold until a number of women began to speak freely about having endured, as children, rape and ritual abuse in "cult-like ceremonies involving altars and men dressed in robes." Beneath the robes were Toledo clergy, and one of them, allegedly, was Gerald Robinson. ("I've had nightmares about this since I was a child," said one survivor. "I didn't think anyone would believe me.") Then, following the discovery of blood transfer patterns linking Robinson to the murder, he was arrested.

Again, it will be interesting to see how the ritual aspects of the murder and the ceremonial abuse of children get played by an embarrassed prosecution and a defense eager to capitalize on the seeming, bloody absurdity of it all.

Robinson retired from the priesthood in 2004, but his bishop has granted him permission to wear the collar in the courtroom. He wouldn't have stood a chance otherwise.

The Devil You Know

May 4, 2006

> *They're whispering his name*
> *through this disappearing land*
> *But hidden in his coat*
> *is a red right hand.*
>
> — Nick Cave

Nineteen-year-old Italian Benjamino Evangelista emigrated to the U.S. in 1904 and changed his name to Benny Evangelist. Two years later he began having ecstatic visions — "my own views and signs," he said, "that I see from 12 to 3 A.M." — and they lasted for 20 years. He wrote it down in one of America's many "received" books, which he titled *The Oldest History of the World Discovered by Occult Science in Detroit, Michigan*. The first volume, self-published in 1926 and out-of-print until September 2001, left the history at the time of Noah.

It was the only volume Evangelist lived to complete. On the morning of July 3, 1929, he was discovered slumped in the chair of his home office, his severed head at his feet and the floor littered with copies of *The Oldest History in the World*. Upstairs, his wife Santina was found hanging across the bed, only sinews connecting her head and neck, and clutching in one hand their murdered 18-month old son Mario. In another room lay the butchered remains of their three other children, Angelina, Margaret and Eugenis, ages seven, five and four.

The *Detroit Free Press* of July 5, 1929 ran a story headlined "Massacre of 6 in Cult Family Baffles Police":

> Evangelist was a man of mystifying history on the religious side of his life. More than 20 years ago he founded the "Union Federation of America," a weird religious theory in his own somewhat warped mind, and, having been "appointed by God," he wrote the "bible" of that faith.

...

Several pieces of women's undergarments, each tagged with the name of its owner, police point out, reveal that the so-called mystic indulged in practices of "voodoosim," or devil worship. Such garments, "voodooism" has it, can lead to the finding of a missing person, when they are properly handled by one versed in the mystic arts of that belief.

...

"Evangelist, no doubt, was insane," Father [Francis] Beccheniu said [who was to bury the family the following Saturday], "Of that I am sure, although he was shrewd and seemed to have quite a lot of intelligence in other matters. Mrs. Evangelist was more of a fanatic than her husband on the subject of religion, and she did not display the intelligence revealed by him.

"I do not believe Evangelist was sincere in practicing the creed he had established. Rather, I believe he founded the mysterious cult with all of its weird props and practices, with the sole idea of making money."

The previous day's breaking story of the murders adds color regarding Evangelist's cult:

Eight or ten wax figures, each hideous and grotesque to the extreme, and each presumably representing one of the "celestial planets," were suspended on the altar in a circle by wires from the ceiling. Among them was a huge eye, electrically lighted from the inside, which Evangelist referred to in his bible as "the sun."

The walls and ceiling of this "religious sanctum" were lined with light green cloth, which bulged out in places like the walls of a padded cell. In a window of the basement, which was on a line with and visible from St. Aubin avenue, a large card bore the words: "Great Celestial Planet Exhibition."

Evangelist and his family undoubtedly were killed while the "prophet" was in his office after having "read the signs" from the celestial bodies, for his bible states that he "saw them from 12 to 3 a. m."

It was the worst mass murder in Detroit's history. Theft was not a motive; valuables were untouched. And it remains unsolved today.

What's the point of rehashing such a tragic though long-cold case? The trance-like authorship of the text, the occult aspect of the crime, the media's inadequacies, the singular brutality, "baffled" police and the impotence of justice: *it's America*. It always has been America.

Another cold case, this from Sonoma California, but only 20 months old: "Tantalizing clues in pair's slaying" read the headline in yesterday's *San Francisco Chronicle*. Sheriffs have released evidence — a sign of some desperation — from the murder scene of a young engaged couple killed camping on a beach in hope of comparing "our evidence to people's suspicions," says Lt. Dave Edmonds. The evidence includes pictures of devil faces carved or burned in nearby driftwood and enigmatic journal pages in several different hands mentioning leprechauns and the tooth fairy and containing text like, "At the Driftwood Inn, alone again, outside of myself and placid as hell."

The two murder victims were shot in the head, likely at close range while they slept. There was no sign of a robbery: "None of the couple's belongings, including Christian literature and camping gear, had been disturbed." Reverend Chris Cutshall, father of victim Lindsay, age 22, says "We have no idea at this stage whether these drawings have anything to do with the case. But we believe their deaths were satanically motivated anyway. These were great kids who were serving the Lord, and they didn't have any enemies other than the evil one."

It's easy to discount such remarks as simply a grieving father finding consolation and meaning in setting his religious template upon his daughter's mysterious death. American evangelicals seem to invite such discounting. And that so many seem to *want* there to be a vast satanic conspiracy, as though one provides an inverted confirmation of the surety of their own faith, makes it easy for those who wish to do so to dismiss allegations of ritual abuse and occult crime as the product of religious hysteria, confusion and ignorance. But the unsolved murders in Sonoma remind me of the still unsolved 1974 murder of student Arlis Perry, found stabbed in a Stanford sanctuary with a tall candle in her vagina and another between her breasts, which in turn recalls the 1980 killing of Sister Margaret Ann Pahl in a hospital chapel, an inverted cross stabbed into her torso, for which Father Gerald Robinson is at last standing trial. (In an interview with the prosecution, "Robinson said he was stunned when he walked into the sacristy and [fellow hospital chaplain Rev. Jerome] Swiatecki turned around and said, 'Why did you do this?' Robinson said he did not know why the other priest pointed the finger at him.") Also, the Sonoma murders were cited by Richard Hamlin in his recent trial, referring to the satanic rituals he claims wife Susan described to him. Many took place, he said, on Goat Rock, close to the murder scene.

Satanic Ritual Abuse and occult crime negate themselves for many progressives who might otherwise now be inclined to believe the worst of Earthly Powers. This is because the charges are a challenge to secularist and reductionist assumptions, and come cloaked in layers of ridicule and the seeming superstitions of the reactionary right, against which they have been struggling all their political lives.

Or let me break it down this way. As a youth I had a fundamentalist conversion experience from which I spent the next ten years recovering. (It's told, as a lie, in my novel *Anxious Gravity*.) I was already of the left, and a conservative faith was not an easy graft, with presumptions of ideology always in my face. But the inner tensions were worse, and eventually things just blew apart. Recovery for me meant jettisoning much of the conceptual and cultural ballast of my faith in order to save its largely ineffable core.

Before I knew any better, "Satanic Ritual Abuse" sounded like a scratchy record from my past that I'd left in my parents' basement when I moved out. It was the ghost of an abandoned paradigm: the fear of a backward-masked planet. But I kept reading, until finally I knew something worse. Worse than the devil I'd known, who had sensational publicists in "anti-cult crusader" Bob Larson and "former high priest" Mike Warnke.

On his ministry broadcasts Larson regularly works up a nice head of froth over Satanism, but privately he's on friendly terms with frequent guests, including Satanist and esoteric fascist Boyd Rice. There's a fascinating interview with Rice here that presents a window on their relationship. Asked whether he thinks Larson is a "repressed Satanist," Rice replies enthusiastically "That's what I'm always telling him! I'm always saying, "Bob, you're Satanic, you're just presenting it in a convoluted way, because you're going on the air and taking advantage of these weak, confused people, and they're giving you their money.""

Meanwhile, Warnke is a manic preacher and "America's number one Christian Comedian" who claims to have led a murderous Satanic cult of 1,500 members in the mid-'60s, yet is almost certainly an abusive and pathological fraud.

The evangelists found a perfect foil in Anton LaVey, who could pass the bucket with the best of them, and obligingly inhabited the caricature of the devil-on-earth right down to the plastic horns and cat suit. But *better the devil you know*, because this devil whom both sides pimped was little more than a Halloween spook, and a figure of titillation at a safe distance for sheltered Christians who liked to receive their vicarious kicks under cover of "testimony."

I expect, for many, Satanic Ritual Abuse is not a serious subject because the devil they know is not a serious figure. Unlike the devil they don't.

There are at least 2,635 place names in America sharing the words *Devil*, *Diablo* or *Diabla*. Loren Coleman writes that "Europeans coming to America were quite taken with the sinister experiences they had or they would hear about from the Native Americans already here, and these colonists started giving the name Devil to all the locations that were tied to unexplainable phenomena." Places like South Dakota's Hill of the Little Devils, which Lewis and Clark were told by plains Indians was inhabited by "midgets" who would kill anyone who approached their "spirit mound." (Clark wrote that the Omahas, Otoes, and Sioux were so afraid that "no Consideration is Sufficient to induce them to approach the hill"); Oklahoma's Devil's Promenade, where generations of glowing, orange orbs have been observed; the barren circle of North Carolina's Devil's Tramping Ground; and the Devil's Highway, Route 666, which links skinwalker accounts to more modern American mythologies of Roswell and the Trinity atomic blast.

An American folly has always been the thought that the nation resides in a "New World." Large numbers of immigrants were drawn to the novelty of America by the prospect of shedding the superstitions of the Old, but Europeans also found ancient wild things of spirit that had not yet been domesticated by generations of dogma and forgetfulness. And because we are also spirit and not altogether perfect and wise, they found perfect and ignorant hosts.

It's been said that Bush's backwash base would still support him even if he ate a baby on television. But he does effectively just that every time he praises the bloody course of his war, which has already claimed a quarter million innocent lives. He's feeding something older than America, a parasitical demon which is also devouring the host, whether he knows it or not.

There *is* a Satanic criminal underground, trading in flesh and guns and drugs, but there is another network underlying it and unconscious of itself. The ritual child abuse of Ponchatoula's Hosannah Church appears unconnected to a broader conspiracy, so how did these seemingly unsophisticated, small-town parishioners come to adopt an ancient, secret tradition of sex magick? Ritual abuse happens in churches in part because that's where ritual happens, and like it or not, humanity appears hardwired for ritual.

When Prescott Bush robbed Geronimo's grave and carried his skull home to Yale as a trophy, was he fully conscious of partaking in a universal warrior cult that finds power in the remains of the worthy dead?

"America is a nation of prayer," said Prescott's grandson last Thursday, asking Americans to "humbly recognize our continued dependence on divine Providence." Someone better acquainted with America said "that god you been prayin' to is gonna give ya back what you're wishin' on someone else."

Single Pervert Theory

August 18, 2006

> *Sometimes I doubt your commitment to Sparkle Motion.*
> — *Donnie Darko*

As much as the media love a good blood feast, it's beginning to slowly back away from the bizarre John Karr. The seeming Manchurian Pedophile is right to say he's not innocent, but he doesn't contain the mystery of the JonBenét Ramsey case, which America is likely never to admit to itself.

In the spring of 1996, months before the Ramsey murder, Karr was apparently attempting to lure children through his "e-mail based crisis feedback program" called Powerwurks. ("All my plans revolve around kids. I am very concerned about the well being of all young people. I'll do anything I can to help find a missing child.") His bogus support group, similar to "Arcadian Fields Ministry," sought to draw kids, at least virtually, into a supposedly "safe and private environment where you can freely and comfortably express your thoughts and feelings on any subject. No subject is banned from discussion. All conversations are strictly confidential and that's a promise!!" (The "thoughts and feelings" Karr meant to encourage was clear from another post on k12.chat.elementary: "Is sex among people under 10 a rarity or common place?")

But Karr's ex-wife, to whom he hasn't spoken since their 2001 divorce, following his arrest for possession of child pornography, says he was with her and their children in Alabama the Christmas of JonBenet's death. And Karr's claim to have drugged and raped the little girl he "loved very much" just doesn't match the autopsy report.

At second glance, Karr appears to be nothing but a dead soul who took the Gary Glitter Adventure Tour, and staring at a Thai jail cell after having lost everything but his perversion, fell back upon his morbid obsession with the Ramsey case as his last advantage. And Homeland Security, for its own reasons, was happy to oblige. Karr may still have some truth to tell, but that depends upon his yet-unverified resume, which alleges he was employed "in some of the most prestigious schools in the United States, working with children from high-profile families" between 1996 and 2001.

Six years ago a different wrinkle was added to the Ramsey story, which America's national media wasn't nearly as interested in reporting. From Boulder's *Daily Camera*, February 25, 2000:

DA PURSUES NEW RAMSEY LEAD

District Attorney Alex Hunter has turned over new information to Boulder police and the FBI that he says could provide a major breakthrough in solving the 3-year-old JonBenét Ramsey murder case.

The information is from testimony and documents provided voluntarily by a 37-year-old California woman who was brought forward by Boulder attorney Lee Hill. The woman said she has suffered a lifetime of sexual and physical abuse, beginning at age 3. Her story, if true, could mean the Ramsey case is tangled in sexual abuse and involves more people than originally thought.

...

Hill, who is a former San Diego County deputy district attorney and former special assistant U.S. attorney and is experienced in investigative work, said, "She is among the most credible witnesses I have ever interviewed." He is representing the woman in her decision to give information to authorities.

The woman has described to police years of sexual and physical abuse in California homes at the hands of adults who stayed at holiday and other parties, after other guests had left for the evening. Then, she said, another "party," one of sexual abuse for the gratification of a select group of adults, would begin.

In talking to detectives, the woman draws parallels between sexual techniques used at these sessions and the physical evidence of garroting that investigators found on the body of JonBenét Ramsey. The woman told detectives she believes JonBenét was killed accidentally when an asphyxiation technique used to stimulate an orgasmic response during a child sex and porno "party" went too far.

The woman told police she knows firsthand about asphyxiation (choking) to produce a sexual response because it had been done to her when she was a child. The woman said in her experience little girls were dressed provocatively and trained to say provocative things, such as, "It's a pleasure to please you."

She told police that when girls did not perform as expected, they were struck on the head. That was because their hair covered the wound. A big night for such "parties" was Christmas night, she said. Over the years, she said, many parties were held then because a large number of cars around a house did not arouse suspicion in the neighborhood and the children had a full week to heal from their wounds before returning to school.

JonBenét Ramsey's death occurred overnight Christmas 1996. The autopsy report concluded she suffered a blow on the head and was strangled.

The woman said she knows the Ramseys through the Fleet White family. She said the godfather to her mother is Fleet White Sr., 86, of California. Fleet White Jr. of Boulder and John Ramsey were close friends until the death of JonBenét.

On March 10 of that year, this story appeared in the *Daily-Times Call*:

MESSAGES WARN THERAPIST TO AVOID FIGURE IN SEX RING

BOULDER — The California therapist who is treating the so-called Mystery Woman in the JonBenet Ramsey murder case has received telephone messages ordering her to stay away from her patient, who has come forward with allegations of lifelong sexual abuse by a ring that includes figures in the Ramsey case.

The five messages were left at the office of Mary Bienkowski over what is believed to be a six-month period. One of the calls appears to be made by one woman and the other four made by a second woman.

The text of the calls follows:

1. (Caller One) "Hello Mary. This is a very interested party in regards to (Mystery Woman's) welfare. (Her) past and her future are of no, of no concern to you. She made an error in judgment when she came to see you and you have caused her nothing but pain and suffering. Her main concern now is her new husband and her family. She has started a life and is going to be moving as far away from you as possible. She belongs with her family and nobody else. She is off limits to you."

2. (Caller Two) "Hello. Leave (Mystery Woman) alone. We take care of our own. Everything. And nothing is any of your business."

3. (Caller Two) "Hello. It's high time that you caught on that (Mystery Woman) doesn't have time for your foolishness. Thank you."

4. (Caller Two) "(Mystery Woman) is going on an extended vacation with her family and while there will seek medical care for her problems. (Mystery Woman) has forgotten more than you will ever know. So."

5. (Caller Two) "Hello. Sticks and stones may break our bones, but words will never hurt us. So leave (Mystery Woman) alone. It's against the law to disturb the peace. Don't forget it."

Bienkowski on Thursday said that when Boulder detectives interviewed her on Wednesday, they questioned "the structure, not the content of her treatment."

Bienkowski said she felt detectives were "looking for ways to invalidate the statements."

On October 13, 1999, the day after the announcement that there would be no charges filed in the Ramsey case following the adjournment of the Grand Jury, Denver journalist and *Panama Deception* Oscar winner Joe Calhoun was given a 23-page file "of such a bizarre nature," he told Constantine, "I was extremely circumspect about regarding it as a collection of genuine documents and confidential memos. I jokingly referred to it to some of my colleagues as *The Blair Witch Project* of the JonBenet Ramsey case. I didn't pursue any of the leads mentioned in the file until recently." What Calhoun had received in October was the story of Belinda Shultz, and her allegations that her son Nicholas had been sexually abused by his father and others at "satanic' sex rituals in Texas and Colorado.

It was only after the "mystery woman," Nancy Krebs, came forward that Calhoun "decided to give it a second look, since the information contained therein seemed to parallel the information the woman was providing Boulder D.A. Alex Hunter and the police. Upon rereading all of the information contained in it, and cross-referencing names, the entire file had more of a flow of information." (Krebs' questioning by Boulder police can be found online.)

The DNA of an unidentified white male is beneath JonBenet's fingernails and mixed with her blood. Whatever guilt the Ramseys may bear in their daughter's death is shared, just as JonBenet was likely shared in life.

It's perhaps easy to see how Belgians, already familiar with the disclosure of its fascist secret army's false flag terror of the Brabant massacres, could admit that Marc Dutroux has friends in high places who also preyed upon their children. After Brabant, what, now, could be inconceivable?

Even at this late date, most Americans aren't there yet.

10. The Old Masquerade

After committing many cruel deeds he died, never knowing what it was to dream.
— The City of Lost Children

Conspiracature

April 12, 2006

When you got nothing, you got nothing to lose.
You're invisible now, you got no secrets to conceal.

— Bob Dylan

Funny, how the public face of the "Satanic Panic" flap was a black-clad Dr. Evil with an Eddie Munster 'do, and its fearless vampire hunter an almost impossibly bumbling everywhere-man of the far right with an FBI backstory. And how the leading proponents for the "disclosure" of *extraterrestrials* have been military careerists or intelligence assets, while the most noisome "researchers" supporting the ET hypothesis have also been disseminators of military disinformation. Or how, suddenly, the loudest voices for "9/11 Truth" are those of former Bush aides and lifelong Republicans, beating the drum for — dig it — no passenger aircraft having struck the World Trade Center.

It's more than just theme and content that evoke *The Outer Limits*. It's our uncritical digestion of dubious information that becomes our fattening hobby. *We will control the horizontal. We will control the vertical.... Sit quietly and we will control all that you see and hear.* If we're open to all channels and lack the discernment to know what we're watching, we're nothing but passive consumers of conspiratainment.

Ritual abusers aren't likely to be the overt occultist and the kid getting his hate on to Black Metal, but the priest in Toledo and the preacher in Ponchatoula; the prominent Nebraskan belting out the national anthem at two Republican national conventions. More often than not, the abuser isn't the self-marginalized outsider of caricature, but the insider: the one who already has power by the world's measure, and who means to gain more of it. But that caricature is too good to let go, and on all sides, because on all sides can be found the allies and the assets of power that encompass and define the discourse. And so the foolish and imprecise caricature becomes the defining image of the crime — likely to become an uncrime — for both those disposed to discount everything and those who eat it all up.

Who profits by the *"You're with us or you're against us"* essentialism of the advocates for the most contentious and spurious speculations on 9/11, and how far does it carry us from the scene of the crime and its high criminals? The pods, the holograms, the missiles, the demolitions: how did we arrive at this familiar position of irrelevance, and who do you think means to keep us here? *Popular Mechanics*, CNN and the great Anglo-American dailies don't shy from drawing straw man caricatures of conspiracy, and then delight in setting them ablaze with all of us supposedly inside like some springtime wickerman sacrifice; yet the meat of the case for criminal intent rots on the offering plate. Why do you think that is, and who do you think might like it like that? The conspirators, who create both a false opposition and a false conspiracy, remain invisible and free to deal more death.

It's a conceit of liberalism to believe knowledge is power, and it's a deceit of the "Information Age" to mistake information for knowledge. Gone missing, for the greater part, is wisdom. Find that, and maybe we find our power.

"Big Brother is watching, so learn to be invisible." That's some advice dished out early on in Grant Morrison's *The Invisibles*. It's a comic book from the mid-'90s, a *knowing* caricature of a guerrilla war waged by the "Invisible College" against an occult elite that Morrison claims was determined by his own abduction/shamanic experience in Kathmandu. It also happens to contain more wisdom about the world than yet another cut-and-paste contending that the hole in Tower Two was too small for a Boeing 767. Art can do that. Even comic art.

A few years ago Morrison said, "Fuck man, I tell you when I was a kid I read Robert Anton Wilson and all this shit and here we are, we're standing here, talking about this shit and it's real!"

If the popular culture — even the popular *alternative* culture — gives us little but caricature, at least we have a good comic book.

Do Like Elvis Did

August 26, 2005

*It will scramble up your head and drag your brain about.
Sometimes you gotta do like Elvis did and shoot the damn
thing out*

— Bob Dylan

I haven't been watching much television recently, but a couple
of weeks ago we had digital cable installed. Now that we
receive FoxNews and MSNBC, I know what American's are
talking about when they talk about Aruba.

There needn't be a media conspiracy here, not beyond the
ones we already know, to account for the obsessive-compulsive
coverage of this summer's showcase disappearances. While the
Bush White House appears to jump the shark — it's falling in
the ratings, but who's going to step up and cancel it? — sympathetic executives naturally counter-program. The networks,
staffed by intelligence assets and owned by oligarchs and arms
peddlers, run instead homespun mysteries to consume the attention and care of the citizen-audience.

(Though sometimes, such stories may serve even as distractions from themselves. I recall tuning out as much as possible
during the saturation coverage of the JonBenet Ramsey investigation. The story, I thought, had no great significance beyond
its own tragedy, and the morbidity of the coverage left me only
depressed and uninformed. I just didn't want to hear it. Now,
from this station down the rabbit hole, I wonder whether I didn't
hear enough. Or perhaps, hear it correctly.)

I found this consideration of the Mystery of the Missing Persons Coverage interesting; that "the most effective kinds of distraction or sublimation are those that echo or harmonize with
the concerns they seek to distract us from."

People *are* disappearing, and not just in Aruba. They're being lifted right off their American feet and bundled off to Homeland gulags. Constitutionality isn't what it used to be, and what
it used to be isn't what it presumed to be. Common sense is

absent, mass demonstrations go unreported, and invisible ballots go missing. So maybe it's perfectly understandable why Americans should be trained to transfer their anxieties to Natalee Holloway or Olivia Newton-John's boyfriend. There, their worries will be rewarded with neither demands nor expectations placed upon them, unlike their political and even parapolitical concerns, which threaten to call people out of their armchairs; even if their worries haven't sharpened beyond a vague sense of dread.

What to do? Like Elvis, you can shoot out the television, but America has left the building. Left behind is an America-shaped void that a lot of people still want to call home, because it plays one on TV.

The Aristocrats

June 19, 2006

> *It's always the same, the name of the game*
> *Is who do you know higher up?*
> — Bob Dylan

Familiar with the joke, and the movie of the joke? It's allegedly the comedian's "secret handshake": a family of vaudevillians visits a talent agent, who's reluctant to take them on because family acts are "too cute." But the act is a litany of scatological and sexual obscenity, often with horrific violence, and the more imaginative the comedian's depiction of the young children's abuse the more successful is regarded its telling. "It's the perfect joke," says Dana Gould. "Just hearing out loud descriptions of giddy shit-covered incest." (Like Otto Peterson's: "then my daughter comes on stage. She's a real sexy 9-year-old. I hit her with an ax handle....") When the family has finished, the agent says "That's a hell of an act. What do you call it?" And the father always replies: "The Aristocrats!"

Get it? The joke's pay-off is the supposed disparity between depravity and nobility. *What could be more absurd* than a family of torture artists, engaging in polymorphous abuse, identifying themselves by a term denoting high social station?

Here's another variation of the joke, as told by Crown Prince Vittorio Emanuele Alberto Carlo Teodoro Umberto Bonifacio Amadeo Damiano Bernardino Gennaro Maria of Savoy:

> Italy is in shock after the son of its last king was arrested as part of an investigation into prostitution and corruption. One of the country's best-known figures, Prince Victor Emmanuel was detained in the north but taken to a jail in Potenza in the south where the probe is based.
>
> His family strongly denies the allegations against the 69-year-old who went into exile with the rest of the country's royals when Italians rejected the monarchy in favor of a republic, in 1946. But the magistrate who signed the arrest warrant for the prince and 12 other men told reporters about what he called *"extremely alarming evidence."*

"I believe I have made a rigorous assessment without taking into account the rank of the person concerned," said Alberto Iannuzzi.

Others detained include Salvatore Sottile, a top aide to the foreign minister in former Premier Silvio Berlusconi's government.

According to media reports, investigators believe Prince Victor Emmanuel had contacts with Mafia clans and was involved in procuring prostitutes for clients of a casino in Campione d'Italia, an Italian enclave on Lake Lugano near the Swiss border.

Implicated in Victor Emmanuel's corruption charges is also his cousin, Bulgaria's former child King: Simeon II, Simeon Saxe-Coburg.

[And on edit, updating with a story from May 29 posted in the comment field:]

POLICE BUST SUSPECTED CHILD TRAFFICKING GANG

A Bulgarian gang of suspected child traffickers has been broken up by police in simultaneous operations in Italy, Austria, Germany and Bulgaria. Police in Italy say dozens of people were arrested in the raids.

Most of the children moved by the gang were from Bulgaria and were between the ages of eight and 13-years-old. They appear to have been sold to the gang by their poverty stricken parents.

Police said some of the children appeared to have been sexually exploited, they had been kept in slave like conditions and they had been used to move drugs and commit crimes. Operation Elvis Bulgaria — co-ordinated by the Italian Carabinieri — involved police forces in Austria, Germany and Bulgaria.

[It's not a great stretch to see the potential of a link between this action of Italian police and the unspecified "extremely alarming evidence" against Victor Emmanuel, which also appears to have a Bulgarian connection.]

Some other knee-slappers of the Italian Prince have included shooting a tourist to death in 1978 (and subsequently acquitted of unintentional homicide), dealing arms for the likes of the Shah of Iran (his son bears the name Reza in honor of Reza Pahlavi), defending Mussolini's anti-Semitic legislation under his father, the last King of Italy, as "not that terrible," and having been a member in good, secret standing of P2, Licio Gelli's criminal fascist Masonic lodge. As was, let's never forget, Berlusconi.

In April 1981, Milan magistrates broke into Gelli's villa and discovered his lodge's membership lists, which read, says Daniele Ganser in *NATO's Secret Army: Operation Gladio and Terrorism in Western Europe*, like a "Who's Who in Italy and included not only the most conservative but also some of the most powerful members of Italian society." Fifty high-ranking officers of the army, for instance, and ten bank presidents. In the subsequent parliamentary commission, Communist member Antonio Bellocchio lamented that "we have come to the definite conclusion that Italy is a country of limited sovereignty because of the interference of the American secret service and international freemasonry." He regretted most commissioners had not followed their analysis to its logical end, but understood why they could not, because then "they would have had to admit they are puppets of the United States of America, and they don't intend to admit that ever."

Even without a joke, even just as a punch line, there remains something anachronistically comic about the aristocrats. They appear about as serious as actors in a heritage fort or pioneer village, recreating the rituals of a long-dead era. Their form is absurd, because their function appears to carry no consequential gravity. Yet they remain apart from us in a privileged world, linked by blood. And not only by the blood in their veins.

Early in Grant Morrison's *The Invisibles* — comic art, and as funny as the End of the World — we read a phone conversation between Whitehall and an occultic assassin. Scion of the ruling class Sir Miles Delacourt, who's favorite recreation is the most dangerous game, cuts the conversation short: "Look, I have a Cabinet ritual to attend, and if it's anything like the last one we'll be up to our knees in blood and spunk for at least the next twelve hours." It could almost be a joke.

A network of fascist Princes and Kings, laundering money, shooting tourists, running guns and elite prostitution rings, is a hell of an act. What do *you* call it?

It's All In the Game

May 25, 2006

North America's getting soft, patron, and the rest of the world is getting tough. Very, very tough. We're entering savage new times, and we're going to have to be pure and direct and strong, if we're going to survive them.

— *Videodrome*

Perhaps you've seen this:

VENEZUELA LAWMAKERS BLAST VIDEO GAME

CARACAS, Venezuela (AP) — A U.S. company's video game simulating an invasion of Venezuela is supposed to hit the shelves next year, but it's already raising the ire of lawmakers loyal to President Hugo Chavez.

...

Pandemic describes *Mercenaries2: World in Flames* as "an explosive open-world action game" in which "a power-hungry tyrant messes with Venezuela's oil supply, sparking an invasion that turns the country into a war zone." The company says players take on the role of well-armed mercenaries.

...

Lawmaker Gabriela Ramirez said "Mercenaries 2" gives a false vision of Chavez as a tyrant and Venezuela as being on the verge of chaos. She said the game could be banned under a proposed law aimed at protecting Venezuelan children from violent video games.

"Pandemic has no ties to the U.S. government," says Greg Richardson, the firm's vice president of commercial operations. That's the sound of hairs splitting. Pandemic Studios is a Pentagon subcontractor through the aegis of the "Institute for Creative Technologies," launched by the U.S. Army in 1998 with $45 million as a go-between with the entertainment and gaming industries. Pandemic is the developer of military training simulations such as *Full Spectrum Command*, commercially available as *Full Spectrum Warrior* for gaming on Playstation and XBox.

("A quantum-leap forward in battlefield simulation" says Game Informer. "Enlist Now" for updates.) "Within days of its release" in 2004, "gamers figured out the cheat code to unlock the Army-only version hidden on the commercial discs, featuring less flashy graphics but smarter opponents." (Gee, how careless can the Army get?)

The Pentagon is co-parenting Pandemic with its unlikely — or possibly inevitable — same-sex sugar daddy: U2's Bono. His Elevation Partners spent $300 million last November to bring the Studio together with Bioware "to create the world's best funded and largest independent game development house." Now there's a cause.

America's New Flesh is machine-scarred from its generational incubation in immersive battlefields which are, like Bono sings, even better than the real thing. Meanwhile, the real thing becomes just another level of play, until you play it, survive it, and return with the Home Version. Diplomacy is never on the table, except as a board game that few young people have the patience to engage. So it has to be Grand Theft Oil, when some "power-hungry tyrant" in Venezuela "messes" with America's petroleum. War is the last option. Play is the first.

Defending *World in Flames*, Pandemic publicist Chuck Norris says "although a conflict doesn't necessarily have to be happening, it's realistic enough to believe that it could eventually happen." Or, as in the words of Brian O'Blivion, "The battle for the mind of North America will be fought in the video arena." It's been fought, and maybe decided, for this generation.

Fairytale of New York

December 7, 2006

You promised me Broadway was waiting for me.
— The Pogues

Funny the things that choke people up. For George H.W. Bush, it's apparently Jeb (though more likely, for the curse-word his family name has become). For me, every December, it's the Pogues' "Fairytale of New York." And if it gets to you, too, you may know that December 18 will mark the sixth anniversary of Kirsty MacColl's death.

MacColl and her family were vacationing in Mexico, where she introduced her sons Jamie and Louie to her love of scuba. After one dive in the protected waters of Cozumel's coral reef, the family surfaced into the path of a 31-foot powerboat that had trespassed into the marine park, traveling at greater than 20 knots.

Then 13 years old, Louie remembers what happened:

She suddenly screamed, "Look out!" and tried to push us out of the way. The boat was already over us — I could see the propellers…. I was swimming in Mummy's blood. I heard Jamie shout, "Where's Mummy?" I screamed that she'd been hit, and to swim the other way and not look back.

Having desperately pushed her sons to safety, MacColl's back was ripped open by the boat's propeller, virtually severing her chest and left leg. "Apparently the paramedic threw up on arriving at the scene," says her mother, Jean. "But two boys have to live with those last memories of their mother for the rest of their lives."

The powerboat was the *Percalito*, and its captain 67-year-old tycoon Guillermo Gonzalez Nova, chairman of mega-chain retailer Comercial Mexicana, one of Mexico's largest companies. Gonzalez Nova's two sons and their families were aboard, and one of the sons is believed to have been at the helm, though the story went that it had been Jose Cen Yam, an illiterate deckhand who had never before piloted the craft. (The MacColl's dive-master, Ivan Diaz, said in a statement to authorities that "After they ran over us, I saw Cen Yam jump forwards from the back of the boat, to the controls.")

Yam, who had trouble on the stand telling his left from his right, was sentenced to serve two years and 10 months, but was allowed to walk free after paying the equivalent of a £61 fine.

In the years since, the Justice for Kirsty campaign has seen a few small victories, but no justice. In May, the Cozumel federal prosecutor was found liable for breach of authority for having failed to register the MacColl appeal as a criminal investigation. And last February, after Bono dedicated "I Still Haven't Found What I'm Looking For" to her memory during a U2 concert in Monterrey, Vincente Fox spokesman Ruben Aguilar felt bound to say "the federal government is following this situation."

And that's where it lies, like so many other modern horrors: the crimes of privilege and crimes of state unpunished, because it is the privilege of state to judge itself and its own.

Warren Commission skeptics were rewarded with the House Select Committee on Assassinations, but when its original chief counsel Richard Sprague signaled that he intended to conduct a genuine investigation, he was promptly replaced by the horrified powers that wanted no such thing. ("I demanded the records from the CIA," Sprague told *Probe* magazine, "and now there was an abrupt refusal, and I subpoenaed them. At that point, [Henry] Gonzales, who was Chairman of the Committee, ordered the CIA, or told the CIA that they need not respond to my subpoena, and fired me, and ordered the U.S. Marshals to come in and remove me from my office.") What they got instead was Robert Blakey, whose hedged presumption of a conspiracy involving organized crime made for a lovely limited hang out. The conspiracy nuts could have their conspiracy, but it was one in which elements of government were wholly absent. (Even when named, and known. For instance, Jack Ruby's mob connections received attention, but his police connections did not. Nor did his anti-communist gunrunning, where criminal conduct and intelligence work became indistinguishable.)

UFOlogists received similar treatment in 1968 with the *Condon Report*: an "independent" inquiry commissioned by the

U.S. Air Force, contracted to the University of Colorado. After years of pressing for an investigation, they were given the appearance of one, led by a man who didn't bother to mask his disdain for the subject.

A memo written in 1966 by project coordinator Robert Low to university officials before the contract was assigned demonstrates what kind of project was intended:

> Our study would be conducted almost exclusively by non-believers who, although they couldn't possibly prove a negative result, could and probably would add an impressive body of evidence that there is no reality to the observations. The trick would be, I think, to describe the project so that, to the public, it would appear a totally objective study but, to the scientific community, would present the image of a group of nonbelievers trying their best to be objective, but having an almost zero expectation of finding a saucer. One way to do this would be to stress investigation, not of the physical phenomena, but rather of the people who do the observing — the psychology and sociology of persons and groups who report seeing UFOs. If the emphasis were put here, rather than on examination of the old question of the physical reality of the saucer, I think the scientific community would quickly get the message.... I'm inclined to feel at this early stage that, if we set up the thing right and take pains to get the proper people involved and have success in presenting the image we want to present to the scientific community, we could carry the job off to our benefit.

9/11 skeptics who shout themselves hoarse for an "independent investigation" should expect any hard-won fruit of their labors to prove just as artificial. So why continue to scream for one?

We don't need another investigation, least of all one conducted, or commissioned, by the few and guilty privileged. There have already been *millions* of independent investigations of 9/11. Some haven't amounted to much, because the investigators have been dazzled by the flash and sleight-of-hand of the Black Lodge's mythmakers. (And though it's great to see David Lynch question 9/11, it's distressing to see him wading about in *Loose Change*'s shallow muck. I believe that being right for the wrong reasons is one of the last and greatest impediments to seeing justice done, because they are reasons which will never convict the guilty, and only sway the gullible.) But in spite of the disinformation, and sometimes because of it, we know enough to make a criminal accusation against elements of the United States government. What we lack is either the law to which they might be subject, or the will to do justice ourselves.

Gonzalez Nova's speedboat entered restricted waters at excessive speed, and after striking Kirsty MacColl, his patsy-deckhand was seen to take the wheel. No more investigation is required. Not for the MacColl family, and not for us. All we need now is justice, and to push our children out of harm's way. Neither happens by polite and patient request.

A Post-November 5th World

March 18, 2006

> *Let me take you by the hand and lead you through the streets of London.*
> *I'll show you something to make you change your mind.*
> — Ralph McTell

It's only a movie. Well no, thank God: *V for Vendetta* is also a graphic novel with a reach that will always exceed Joel Silver's grasp. Still, I won't be one of those people who can't see the screen for his upturned nose at the faithlessness of an adaptation. (Foolish me, I actually expected the destruction of the Houses of Parliament in the opening act, just like on page six.) Because there is a plot point added that means everything to V's story, and ours, post 9/11.

The first chapters of Alan Moore and David Lloyd's *V for Vendetta* were published in 1982. Today, Moore's introduction from the series' first DC Comics run invites thoughts of *you think you've got it bad*:

> It's 1988 now. Margaret Thatcher is entering her third term of office and talking confidently of an unbroken Conservative leadership well into the next century. My youngest daughter is seven and the tabloid press are circulating the idea of concentration camps for persons with AIDS. The new riot police wear black visors, as do their horses, and their vans have rotating video cameras on top.

But Moore knew his dystopic vision had already undershot reality: "Naiveté can also be detected in my supposition that it would take something as melodramatic as a near-miss nuclear conflict to nudge England towards fascism." And here's where the post-9/11 adaptation honors Moore's work by departing from it: the backstory of medical experimentation to which V had been subject is extended to a black ops bio-weapons attack on schools and public transit, leading to the deaths of 100,000 people. Foreign patsies are framed and executed, and the government rewarded with limitless authority in exchange for the promise of security.

Natalie Portman's character, Evey, tells V her father used to say that "artists use lies to tell the truth, and politicians lie to hide it." I think the film becomes genuinely important here, by artfully telling why a government might want to kill its own people. The lies of art serve a hard truth well. The political lies are well told, too, and comically familiar. The laughter they provoke is bittersweet.

Now, with a spoiler advisory, here's where I think the film falters as dangerous art. (At least as *good* dangerous art.)

The climax sees thousands of Londoners converge on Parliament at V's appointed hour. Fine. But *they all look like V*, shod in identical mask, cap and cape. It's reminiscent of the black hoodies of Eminem's *Mosh*. I know it's easier to depict visually, but for the love of all that's anti-fascist, unity doesn't mean uniformity. Hell, abhorrence of diversity is one of fascism's most noxious and prominent traits. So the spectacle of an identically-costumed silent crowd, marching with seeming mind-controlled precision doesn't exactly make my heart shout *"Freedom forever!"*

But even an antifascist of Woody Guthrie's pedigree found himself similarly wrong-footed on occasion. In "She Came Along to Me," first recorded for Billy Bragg and Wilco's *Mermaid Avenue*, Guthrie wrote

> *And all creeds and kinds and colors*
> *Of us are blending*
> *'Til I suppose ten million years from now*
> *We'll all be just alike.*

> *Same color, same size, working together,*
> *And maybe we'll have all of the fascists*
> *Out of the way by then*
> *Maybe so*

Or maybe not, if it takes us all being the same size, kind, color and creed.

The world needs fewer uniforms, even on our side. We ought to be the irregulars.

Lost Girls

August 30, 2006

> *Gimme absolute control, over every living soul,*
> *And lie beside me, baby — that's an order.*
> — Leonard Cohen

Briefly, I'm wondering what to make of Kola Boof. Nearly a quarter of the Sudanese poet's autobiography, *Diary of a Lost Girl*, describes her months spent in Morocco in 1996 as Osama bin Laden's unwilling mistress. Boof has been called a "fraud" (a "pathological liar" according to bin Laden biography Peter Bergen) for her iconoclastic portrait of Osama as a Van Halen-loving, dope-smoking gangbanger, who "rambled on about his favorite TV shows: *The Wonder Years*, *Miami Vice*, and *MacGyver*." (Bergen and other authorities also assert that bin Laden was not in Morocco in 1996, though the same authorities also say little, or merely repeat bin Laden's own denial, concerning his reported visit to a Dubai hospital in July 2001, where he met with the CIA station chief and Saudi royals.)

Where the Boof story is getting attention these days it's usually played for laughs, on account of bin Laden's supposedly comic infatuation with Whitney Houston. But there's something much more interesting. From an excerpt in September's *Harper's* magazine: "He said the U.S. government was made up of 'fanatical crusaders' and that *he'd once worked as a mind reader and trained secret agents for the CIA.*"

Now, Boof *could* be a fraud, though her revelations about bin Laden's secret life are no more bizarre than Amanda Keller's about Mohammed Atta, or Leola McConnell's about Bill Bennett, or Cathy O'Brien's about Dick Cheney, or so many other women and men — and girls and boys — about so many other devout jihadists and born-again crusaders. The behavior is always shocking, but it should no longer be surprising. No man's a hero to his valet, and neither is he a saint to his mistress or sex slave. If we mean to pierce the public veil we need to hear them out. (Or as Boof says, "in any mansion...it's the maids and the 'whores' who know the most. Trust me.")

And we should also consider the possibility that, even if Boof had been Osama's mistress and he told her such things, he may not have been telling her the truth. Perhaps he thought it a good line, to *impress the ladies* with his connections. But his connections didn't need embellishment, and "mind reader" strikes me as an unlikely fabrication.

Either Boof is lying, bin Laden was bullshitting, or they're both telling the truth. And the implication of that — of Osama having been a psychic spy and a trainer of agents for the CIA — has much more gravity than his "paramount desire" for Whitney Houston. But it's not as funny, so don't hold your breath for the headlines.

Jackson 5.0

March 11, 2006

So I work in that same beauty salon, I'm chained to the old masquerade
The lipstick, the shadow, the silicone: I follow my father's trade
— Leonard Cohen

Michael Jackson may be another example of a celebrity distraction which, upon examination, reveals more about our society's moral condition than a tabloid could imagine. Almost certainly more than it would dare to describe.

Yesterday, Jackson was ordered to close Neverland for having failed to pay the ranch's 47 employees their salary or insurance since the end of 2005. Unfortunate for the unpaid staff and the abandoned llamas, but no surprise. He's moved on since his acquittal, like Gary Glitter did after his 1999 conviction, having departed last June for a Bahrain "vacation" from which he's yet to emerge. ("For the people working at Bahrain's malls, the person covered head to toe in a black veil, gloves and glasses appeared to be a rich, doting Saudi mother.... But why would a woman wear a man's shoes? Why the bodyguards? And why did the person's fluid movements seem so familiar?")

Last week's real Jackson story ran in the *New York Daily News*, under the snappy banner "Creepy dad was root of all clan's woe, singer sez." The singer was brother Jermaine, and the claims were based on the projected outline for his abandoned "tell-all" family story.

Reading that Joseph was a nightmare of a father and sexually abusive towards his daughters is not exactly a "stop the presses" moment. What's new is this:

> Jermaine even suggested his father may have set up Michael to be somehow victimized by older men.
>
> He tells how his father would have Michael join in at late-night hotel room meetings with "important business people," and wondered whether "something happened" to Michael at those sessions.
>
> He said he sensed something was wrong because Michael would be sick for days after. "What was Joseph doing?" Jermaine wrote.

This lifts the Jackson family horror show to a whole new order of dysfunction, one that sees parents network with power and trade their children for privilege. This should be a motif familiar to anyone acquainted with the literature of mind control and ritual abuse survivors: the father and first controller, passing his child-victim up the social ladder of abuse in return for status, protection and reward. All that's missing is the element of occult terror. Or maybe not: "LaToya also described being awakened in the night by Joseph wearing a "monster mask."

Perhaps we can take more from this than the suspicion that the Jackson clan had gotten with *the program*. Perhaps rather the point is that the program exploits pre-existing conditions for abuse which are more common than most suspect. (This is how I tend to think of Ponchatoula's Hosanna Church.) Yet we shouldn't discount the suspicion, either, particularly given some of Michael's paranormal interests and peculiar associations. His close friendship with SPECTRA contactee and channeler of the Nine, Uri Geller, for one instance. (Jackson was Geller's best man in 2001 when he and his wife renewed their vows, the same year Geller is said to have been reactivated as a psychic spy.) His entourage included a "personal magician."

Even if you wanted to, you won't be reading Jermaine's account now. Like every Jackson sibling who's tried to break from Joe, he's climbed down, returned to the fold and scrapped the book, apparently on the strength of Michael's threats to sue. Previously, Michael has given cause for family observers to attribute his grotesque body dysmorphia to a dread of resembling his father. Yet there they were at Jackson's trial last year, hand in hand.

In the big picture Michael Jackson means not very much. But his little picture may be more newsworthy than the news suggests.

Married to the Octopus

December 11, 2006

It can kill from any distance, but you never see it strike.
— T-Bone Burnett

For a long while I resisted the Diana story by the same solipsistic rationale Noam Chomsky resists John Kennedy's: she was inconsequential *to me*. (As John Judge assesses Chomsky's verdicts on the murders of Kennedy and King, "it's just a function of how much you liked the guy whether he was done in by coincidence or not.") I still find her so, but her slightness of gravity is misleading, because her life and possibly her death were no more about her than my judgment of either should be about me.

If little else is certain beyond the seldom-acknowledged fact that Dodi Fayed was the nephew of Adnan Khashoggi, then the late admission that the U.S. Secret Service "was bugging her calls in the hours before she was killed" establishes beyond doubt that this was a person of interest to actors who should be persons of interest to us. It's the kind of disclosure that is usually processed by an incurious media as a fact "that will only fuel conspiracy theories," without asking even the most cursory questions that the new evidence begs, like why were the Americans bugging Diana, for how long before her fatal crash had they been doing so, and is it plausible, as alleged, that they were doing this without a nod and a wink from MI6?

Sometimes you can tell a conspiracy by the high grade of disinformation that accrues about it, including the number and quality of shadowy "renegade insiders" eager to step up, speak out and muddy the waters. For instance, *former* MI6 officer Richard Tomlinson claimed both driver Henri Paul and photographer James Andanson, whose white Fiat purportedly struck

Diana's death car before it lost control, were employed by his agency to spy on the celebrity couple. (Paul of course died in the crash, and Andanson was found dead in the woods three years later, an apparent suicide.) *Former* CIA agent Oswald LeWinter tried to sell to Mohammed Al Fayed apparently forged documents spelling out in big, block letters an alleged DIA-MI6 assassination plot. And it may even be true, but to showcase the truth within the framework of a lie is to strip its consideration of credibility. (Regarding LeWinter, Al Fayed's attorney Mark Zaid told CNN six years ago that he "was responsible for disseminating a lot of the — what's been deemed disinformation about [the October Surprise]. He has shown up in allegations that Swedish Prime Minister Olof Palme was murdered. He has shown up involving allegations of the bombing of Pam Am 103, and then he showed up in this latest endeavor of his. He is quite a man of mystery.")

Another man, and another mystery, though perhaps the same conspiracy, was George Smith:

> I lost my job, my house, my wife and children because it all became too much for me…. Today I feel under great stress again because the establishment is mounting a campaign against me. They are very powerful and privileged and have lots of money to pay lawyers to prevent me from telling the truth.

Former soldier, and footman and valet to the royals, Smith claimed to have been raped by Prince Charles' close aide Michael Fawcett (Fawcett and Charles, said Smith, were lovers). Diana interviewed Smith and taped his allegations years before they became public — such as they did — though what happened to the tape "became a matter of considerable controversy" upon her death. In a comic act of self-policing, the Prince's senior staff investigated Smith and found his claims without merit and forced his resignation. And then, less than two years after the story broke, Smith was dead of an "unknown illness."

Diana herself was dead three years after composing a letter to her former butler, Paul Burrell, in which she said "this particular phase in my life is the most dangerous. My husband is planning 'an accident' in my car; brake failure and serious head injury." (A few weeks before the crash, the Mercedes had been stolen from the garage of the Ritz Hotel. "Police recovered the car but found that its instrumentation had been tampered with," Kenn Thomas writes in *The Octopus*. The limo was then recon- ditioned. LeWinter's likely hoax document notes this, stating that the car was "rebuilt to respond to external radio controls.")

Lord Stevens has "been assured" that the 39 classified documents detailing Diana's final conversations "did not reveal anything sinister or contain material that might help explain her death." To put it another way, those who clandestinely bugged Diana have given their word there is nothing suspicious on the tapes they refuse to release, and that's good enough for the head of Scotland Yard's "exhaustive" inquiry.

Celebrity can blind us to the thing itself, particularly when beauty and youth are weighted with great wealth and genera- tional power. (Paris Hilton's circle of rich and pantiless fem- bots is almost enough to make "elite mind-controlled sex slave" go mainstream.) That Di and Dodi meant nothing to me only means that I had no reason to wish them dead. Others, I can't speak for.

Fatally Beautiful

February 09, 2007

> *She was born in the back of a thirty-four Ford*
> *And raised in a foster home.*
> *Her guardian made sexual connection with her*
> *Before she was even grown.*
>
> — T-Bone Burnett

Jay Leno said that politics is just show business for ugly people, which makes me wonder what business Jay Leno thinks he's in. But he's not half-wrong, though the truth must be uglier than he could imagine.

Sensational celebrity deaths are sometimes more than distractions, especially when the fame is all about sex and money, because that's so much of what power is about. Just ask George H.W. Bush. It may be impolitic to whisper about the underage callboys paying his White House a midnight visit, but we're allowed to have a chuckle at his tapping Teri Hatcher's ass. ("Frisky for an 82-year-old, ain't he?" Nyuk, nyuk.)

Anna Nicole Smith's money came from J. Howard Marshall, who came from Yale and American oil, so you can imagine how his bloodline would be anxious to hold onto it. He served as special counsel to Standard Oil during the early war years, when the company was still trading with Germany and in open collaboration with IG Farben. (About which Judge Charles Clark ruled that "Standard Oil can be considered an enemy national.") Marshall went on to take a large stake in Koch Industries, a major financier of far-right interests.

I won't bother to speculate here about Smith's death, other than to note the legitimacy such speculation is popularly accorded, which is broadly denied theorizing about similarly suspicious deaths which befall Leno's ugly people. What interests me is that we ought to consider sometimes the fate of the rich and beautiful without worrying we're getting suckered into a pop culture edition of Trivial Pursuits.

Smith was a Marilyn Monroe knock-off who traded up, and over-the-top, in her own commodity. And Monroe, more than most beauties, knew something about the entrancement of power. And yet her death stands outside the standard corpus of conspiracy literature. Perhaps because her significance is devalued by her celebrity. But more likely because in death, as in life, she poses a threat to the Camelot mythos.

I don't think we need to choose. And if it's true, then we should say both that the Kennedy assassinations were High Crimes of State and that Monroe's was an assisted suicide.

She died of barbiturate overdose — beside her naked body was found an empty bottle of Nembutal — and yet her stomach was empty. John Miner, a deputy DA who attended the autopsy, witnessed a small amount of liquid, but as Donald Wolfe notes in *The Assassination of Marilyn Monroe*, "we did not detect any sign that would indicate it contained any heavy drugs or sedatives." The examiner's report reads that "a smear made from the gastric contents and examined under the polarized microscope shows no refractive crystals," which is inconsistent with ingestion of a large amounts of barbiturates. Coroner Thomas Noguchi requested analysis of Monroe's kidneys, stomach, urine and intestines, which would have revealed how the barbiturates had entered her system. The laboratory samples disappeared. Miner remarks, "in the entire history of the LA County coroner's office there had never been a previous instance of organ samples vanishing."

A week before her death, Monroe spent a weekend at Lake Tahoe's Cal-Neva Lodge as a doped-up plush-toy of owners Frank Sinatra and Sam Giancana. Later, friend Ralph Roberts said Monroe described it as a "nightmare," and that she'd felt more like a prisoner than a guest. Photographer Billy Woodfield, who'd worked with both Monroe and Sinatra, told Wolfe that Sinatra gave him a roll of film from the weekend to develop: "In his darkroom the photographer was shocked to see that the photos were of an unconscious Marilyn Monroe being sexually abused in the presence of Sam Giancana and Sinatra. Marilyn had been drugged in order for the compromising photos to be taken." Woodfield advised Sinatra to burn them.

FBI electronic surveillance of Giancana corroborated the account. Agent Bill Roemer remembers a conversation, after Monroe's death, between Giancana and Johnny Rosselli:

The conversation was muted, but what I had gleaned was that Giancana had been at Cal-Neva ... with Sinatra and Marilyn the week before she died. There, from what I had been able to put together, she was involved in an orgy. From the conversation I overheard, it appeared she may have had sex with Giancana. Rosselli said to Giancana, "You sure get your rocks off fucking the same broads as the brothers, don't you?"

The weekend over, Marilyn flew back to LA and entered her limousine barefoot, "out of it — a mess."

Suddenly, what's so far-fetched about "presidential models"? Or did you think this just happened in the movies?

Little School of Horrors

May 15, 2007

And says, "How does it feel to be such a freak?"
And you say, "Impossible," as he hands you a bone.

— Bob Dylan

He stopped doing it years ago, because if he hadn't he'd have killed himself or someone else by now, but New York artist Joe Coleman used to blow himself up. As "Professor Mamboozo" — either his geek avatar or, as he described it, a raging spirit that would take possession of his body — Coleman would arrive uninvited at the house parties of strangers, provoke a confrontation and ignite the mass of firecrackers he'd strapped to his body. In the confusion, smoke and fear he would slip away before police arrived. When Mamboozo debuted on New York's avant-garde art scene in a 1981 performance at the Kitchen he also rolled in bloody meat, bit the heads off live rats and pressed a shotgun against the forehead of the woman who had booked him and asked, "How'd you like the show?" The traumatized crowed was an audience no more, Coleman having yanked them out of their art house detachment through horrification ritual and the sudden shock of their own possible, imminent death. ("I told them as hard as I could without killing them," Coleman told *Re/Search* in Pranks.)

I thought about Coleman the other day when I read of the teachers of an elementary school in Tennessee who convinced their sixth graders a gunman was attacking, and repeatedly told the hysterical children it wasn't a drill.

One hooded teacher pulled on a locked door, "pretending to be a suspicious subject," and another told the students there had been a shooting, and that they were to lie on the floor in the dark and keep quiet. Twenty kids started to cry and tremble and beg for their lives. Some held hands.

"I was like, 'Oh my God,'" said 11-year old Shay Naylor. "At first I thought I was going to die. We flipped out — I was freaked out. I thought it was serious."

School officials cite "poor judgment," but it's a prank worthy of Joe Coleman. *They told them as hard as they could without killing them.* And when Coleman would lead his classrooms beyond endurance and up to the edge of their own oblivion, he didn't do it simply because he was an artist, but because he also had visceral contempt for his audience and all of humanity. "You say the man who hates his fellow man is the problem," he wrote in a poem/rant. "But they ain't the problem. You're the problem. The sexual deviant, the murderer, the serial killer, the taker of human life is the cure. You're the problem...."

Teachers and staff may tell themselves and the parents of their charges that it was an exercise in preparedness, but it takes a special antipathy for an adult to terrorize a child, even when they have already told themselves they're terrorizing the children for their own good. And this is often what children brutalized by ritual cult abuse and trauma-based mind control *are* told: that it's for their own good, and that it will transfigure their minds and flesh into something which mundane experience is incapable of producing. As perhaps other teachers in another small town told themselves and their nursery age children, before they drugged and raped them and forced their participation in candle-lit ceremonies.

Naggingly, there *is* transfiguration in trauma, and it can be communicated through both art and ritual. Coleman calls himself an "alchemist — I'm trying to transform base emotions into a kind of gold." Together, art and ritual are the nucleic acids of religion, which intends to remanifest naive states unknown to us in our current nature, whether that means union with the divine, with our deeper selves, or with something else. (I hadn't heard the term before I typed it, but I now see "remanifest" is one of the "Aeon-supporting Words" of the Temple of Set.)

The artist and the priest are often tormented by what's missing; by the absence of God and the silence of spirits. But Chesterton, writing of Yeats' "concrete mysticism," said it was "not abnormal men like artists, but normal men like peasants, who have borne witness a thousand times to such things. It is the farmers who see the fairies. It is the agricultural laborer who calls a spade a spade, who also calls a spirit a spirit." It has been those most connected to the Earth who have also found the invisible, visible. Modern life made even the Earth invisible.

Now that Earth is recognized to have fallen into crisis worthy of a super-villain, and everyone in the "developed world" is seeing green and increasingly experiencing the trauma of a life out of order, we shouldn't be surprised if we start to see stranger things, again, as though for the first time.

The *New York Times*, reviewing a retrospective of Joe Coleman's paintings last September, wrote that, "in a startlingly prophetic vision of his from 2000 the twin towers burn."

Prophetic, but maybe not all that startling.

Principalities and Powers

May 18, 2007

> *Well, God is in heaven and we all want what's his,*
> *But power and greed and corruptible seed*
> *Seem to be all that there is.*
>
> — Bob Dylan

You know Jack Kirby? Even if you don't, there's an old, rare interview with him online worth watching. Because Kirby, like few others, helped shape America's popular imagination. Which is, perhaps disturbingly so, the universe in which we often find ourselves.

"Everybody else had their gods," he asked. "What are ours?" Kirby made comic books, but he made them out of myth and religion. He found Galactus in the Bible, and Silver Surfer became his fallen angel. And though the costumes and the muscles may look absurd, his source materials were that which have made and broken civilizations. Which arguably, right there, is another absurdity.

All right then; but what's that to do with Jerry Falwell, and why is he reminding me so much now of the "Madman from Sudan," Abdullah the Butcher?

Well, Abdullah the Butcher is actually Larry Shreve from Windsor, Ontario. He runs a rib and Chinese food joint outside Atlanta now, though at 70 he still wrestles. He's older than Kirby's Captain America, who also was someone else when he set aside his cowl and shield. Shreve's said to be a nice guy outside the ring, but inside he'll still fuck you up.

"Who are our evil gods?" asked Kirby. To many on America's liberal left, Falwell was one. He was the christofascist nightmare who was to mandate prayer and criminalize abortion. Falwell's religion was a modern, Anglo-American dispensationalist cult befitting a comic book — Jack Chick was his Jack Kirby — and it was an angry shout to secular and pluralist America: *You're going down!*

Through seven years of Bush and many years before, Republicans have spent Falwell's support as electoral capital, and Democrats have held it up as a scary lightning rod to animate their own base. But Falwell's dead, and the *Handmaid's Tale* remains a fiction. (Though a fiction within the meta-fiction of contemporary America.) Perhaps, after all, he was more Larry Shreve than Galactus.

To liberal and progressive Americans, Falwell has been *the man you love to hate*. And he sure knew how to put on an entertaining show. ("The pagans, and the abortionists, and the feminists, and the gays and the lesbians" were responsible for 9/11? That's some conspiracy theory.) But Falwell was not the force he pretended to be, nor the power most begging for contention. Falwell was, in the end, another asset of Sun Myung Moon, whose influence upon the life of America's elite remains largely unsuspected and invisible. Thirty years ago, the Congressional Investigation of Korean-American relations reported:

> During the investigation, the subcommittee found it very difficult to obtain reliable information about the extent to which Moon industries were involved in weapons production and sales. The Moon Organization has self-proclaimed goals of controlling political and secular institutions and a strident ideology which envisions the formation of a "Unification Crusade Army." Moon's speeches foresee an apocalyptic confrontation involving the united States, Russia, China, Japan, and North and South Korea, in which the Moon Organization would play a key role. Under these circumstances, the subcommittee believes it is in the interest of the United States to know what control Moon and his followers have over instruments of war and to what extent they are in a position to influence Korean defense policies.

Falwell was a wrestler in a ring, but if that's all you saw you were missing the best part.

License to Spin

September 8, 2006

> *Now at midnight all the agents and the superhuman crew*
> *Come out and round up everyone that knows more than they do.*
>
> — Bob Dylan

Have you seen the "revelation" that Anderson Cooper interned for the CIA during his sophomore and junior summers away from Yale? "Soon after" his post-graduate time in Hanoi studying Vietnamese, says the *Radar* report, "Cooper apparently gave up his Bond fantasy to pursue a career in journalism."

Bond fantasy. You hear that a lot from people who either don't know better or who know much worse. Sure, there are plenty of whoring dipsomaniacs on the company payroll, but I bet even James Angleton's car didn't have an ejector seat. Most so-called intelligence work — and especially that of media assets — is better suited to a cubicle than a jetpack.

The Bond conceit has been played by hooked-up lone-nutter Gus Russo, who says his initial skepticism of the Warren Report "was fueled by the naiveté (perhaps it was the arrogance) of a seasoned teenager who had read all the James Bond novels. I knew about spies, and fake defectors, and sharpshooters, and patsies. The government couldn't fool me!" As soon as he'd finished consulting on Oliver Stone's *JFK*, Russo began speaking highly of an up-and-coming debunker named Gerald Posner, and in a 1993 symposium in Chicago he shocked fellow researchers by ridiculing the notion that Oswald was associated with U.S. intelligence. "How many of you think Oswald was some kind of James Bond?" he asked. "I thought this was an oddly posed question," writes investigator Jim DiEugenio. "Nobody had ever reported Oswald owning an Aston-Martin, or leading an army of underwater scuba divers in a spear-gun fight, or employing all kinds of mechanical gadgetry to disarm his enemies. Far from it." Oswald was simply too marginal and unstable a character to be a player, claims Russo, ignoring the fact that it's on the margins that the unstable characters get played. (Though in recent years he's refined his position to allow that Oswald actually did figure in a conspiracy. A communist conspiracy.)

Cooper, of course, has more of the Bond, or Blofeld, about him than Oswald. Never has a patsy been both a Vanderbilt (and though most of the family squandered their inheritance, mother Gloria did alright for herself) and a Yalie. "Yale has influenced the Central Intelligence Agency more than any other university," says historian Gaddis Smith, "giving the CIA the atmosphere of a class reunion." The spy slang "spook" initially referred to a member of a Yale secret society. (See also "Spooks in Blue" and "For God, Country, Yale and the CIA" by the *Yale Daily News*.)

Cooper's internships nearly two decades ago don't imply that he's "on the payroll." But the payroll isn't very long. It's the *assets*, not the agents, that predominate in the media, and his summer work is a strong indicator of affinity: something the Agency would not be inclined to forget as it follows the progress of his career, even as Cooper's viewers remain in the dark.

This is something to be remembered by 9/11 truthseekers who are ready to settle instead for heroes, and uncritically embrace longtime intelligence veterans as sudden "converts" and spokespersons. Like 28-year CIA analyst William Christison, whose "Stop Belittling the Theories About September 11" was widely astroturfed last month. His leading points, that an "airliner almost certainly did not hit The Pentagon" and "controlled demolition" brought down the towers, are the most contentious and speculative and least profitable arguments that can be made for 9/11 complicity. As with "former Bush insider" Morgan Reynolds' *triple-dog-dare-ya* that there were no planes at the World Trade Center either, more sensible observers need to ask why *certain* people with *certain* backgrounds are advancing *certain* positions, rather than be gratified that persons of a *certain* stature are saying something, *anything*, even when it's wrong or uncertain or foolish.

"Heeeere's Justice!"

January 25, 2005

T
ry to imagine Jay Leno devoting an entire *Tonight Show* to Dr. Peter Dale Scott, and to the topic of Dick Cheney's possible complicity in the attacks of 9/11. Or maybe David Letterman conversing for an hour with Dr. Nick Begich, co-author of *Angels Don't Play this HAARP*, on the weaponization of the ionosphere.

Because as bizarre and unlikely as those scenes would be, 37 years ago this month, Johnny Carson spent 50 minutes with New Orleans District Attorney Jim Garrison — and millions of Americans — on the subject of the state-sanctioned murder of John F. Kennedy.

Audio files of Carson's Garrison interview can be downloaded from the Internet, but a big note of caution: distortion makes them all but unlistenable. If anyone knows of better quality samples (or even better, video), please let me know.

Considering today's total absence of serious mainstream dialogue regarding controversial subjects, the first thought that might come to some of us is *Man, the past rocked!* Well no, it didn't, regardless of how tempting it is to succumb to ill-founded nostalgia whenever we can rightly say *Man, the present sucks!* The awful truth is that America's media was compromised then as well, and riddled with Intelligence assets doing Mockingbird journalism. (See, for instance, James DiEugenio's essays regarding the obstruction of the Garrison investigation and the exposure of Jim Phelan in *The Assassinations.*)

In its favor, the media wasn't yet *so* dumbed-down and concentrated in the hands of a few defense contractors. And on that account, Garrison was able to tell a prickly and incredulous Carson:

> The function of the Warren Commission was to make the American people feel that the [JFK assassination] had been looked into so that there would be no further inquiries, so that the American people would not find out the involvement of elements of the Central Intelligence Agency, so that they would think the matter was closed.

Carson was uncomfortable with Garrison's material, and his performance so querulous and off-key that NBC issued a press release that said "the Johnny seen on TV that night was not the Johnny we all know and love. He had to play the devil's advocate, because that makes for a better program." Apparently Johnny was furious at the apology, and vowed Garrison would never be on his show again.

Not that there was much chance of a return visit, anyway. Carson and NBC had to be shamed by *Tonight Show* guest Mort Sahl into extending an invitation in the first place.

As Garrison tells it, in *On the Trail of the Assassins*:

> The articulate satirist, who was spending an extended period of time in New Orleans helping the office in a variety of ways, was well aware of my problems communicating with the people through the news media. Even the simplest press conference involved a process of "translation," so that what came out in the media never seemed to be precisely what I had said. Sahl, being in show business, had access to places I did not, like the Johnny Carson show. One night when he was on the program, the conversation drifted to the subject of the assassination and my investigation. Suddenly Sahl turned toward the audience and asked if they did not think Carson should invite me to be a guest on the show so that I could explain my side of the case. The response was so demonstrably affirmative that it left Carson and the network with no alternative. A few days later I received a telegram of invitation, which I promptly accepted.

Sahl is one of my favorite undersung heroes of the Sixties, for having spent the capital of a successful career in the Quixotic pursuit of justice for the murderers of America.

That strikes me as the trajectory of an honorable man.

There's an interview with Sahl a couple of months later in 1968, before the epochal one-two of Dr. King and Robert Kennedy, that is as prophetic as anything I've read from that time:

> ARGO: Why is the truth behind the assassination of President Kennedy the last chance of America for its survival?
>
> SAHL: Because the evidence developed by District Attorney Garrison indicates that *certain people had to take President Kennedy's life in order to control ours.* In other words, as Richard Starnes of the *New York World-Telegram* said, the shots in Dallas were the opening shots of World War III. There's been a great change in this country since Kennedy. *I'm afraid a great deal of our hope was interred with his remains.*

> ...

> ARGO: What would you say are the roots of this whole era?

SAHL: *Fascism. It started with the death of Roosevelt. They moved in and they negated every treaty we made with every world leader who didn't fit the fascist/militarist mold.* We went back on our word. As David Schoenbrun says very well, "I am not a dissenter for saying this. Those who betrayed American policy are the dissenters." We've gone back on the dream of national independence and we were the model for the rest of the world. Then when they followed our model, we attacked them for it. Shameful. No one has a right to stain the American flag. And unfortunately, we have people in this country who did it. *If America goes, it will surely be an inside job.*

...

ARGO: Why is the trial that Mr. Garrison's pursuing really the trial of the American people?

SAHL: Because we have to decide. *Once the neo-fascists became bold enough to slay the President on the street, they showed their hand.* They showed how arrogant they had become. Now it's a question of symptom. That crime was a national symptom. *If we can turn our back on that, we will pay a terrible price.* That will be the end of this democracy. As a matter of fact, it's been dying since Kennedy's death. We have to cleanse our soul. It's much the same as the French when they regained their national honor, not by framing Dreyfus, but by admitting that they did.

ARGO: What does Garrison mean: "The key to the whole case is through the looking glass. Black is white; white is black"?

SAHL: He means that the first thing the government did when the President was killed was to ratify his death and to appoint a group of honorable men to initial a fraudulent report. To eventually say there is no fourth bullet, even though there's a fourth bullet hole. The man was shot at from three sides, but there was only one side. In other words, the government decrees it is so. And that eventually the government may be forced to form a Ministry of Truth which will rule there was no John Kennedy, if it becomes convenient. That's what he means. When Lyndon Johnson says to us, as an example, "We have to continually keep up brush fire wars to protect the peace." Well, that's Orwell. War is peace, and peace is war, and love is hate. *And you finally sell it just that way: the contradiction. And you do it by making the American people mad because those are the mouthings of a madman. We can be driven mad; it's the same virus that bit the Germans.* [emphases added]

RIP, Johnny Carson.

And Mort Sahl, where have you been?

11. The Kingdom Is Opening Again

Nobody knows what's coming down.
But it's coming down.

— T-Bone Burnett

Planet of Lost Children

July 7, 2006

But between you and me they were really dupes of the Wicked King
Who wanted to rob the children of their dreams.
— T-Bone Burnett

When I was a young boy, before I could have a hand in my room's decoration, there was a strange piece of art hanging on the wall opposite my bed. It was a copper-like bas-relief, about a foot high, of a stereotypical Chinese laborer, grinning in mid-stride. When the door was open, I couldn't see it from my bed.

I thought about it a lot. I wondered whether, behind the door and out of sight, he was still striking the same pose. I began to imagine another life for him, and other purposes. I thought, when I would leave a messy room and return to find it tidy, it must have been the man on the wall picking up after me. (When I shared the theory with my mother she was understandably annoyed that I hadn't first considered that it might be her.)

Now the thing is, on at least one afternoon, while I lay on my bed, I *saw* this figure as a life-sized man, step out from behind the door and stare at me. (He waved.) And I accepted this, since I'd already imagined more for him, and he seemed kindly enough. And of course, I was just a child.

I hadn't thought of this for many years, because like so many wonders it just didn't *fit*, and it didn't *do anything* for me now. But then I thought about tulpas, "imaginary friends" and the naturally altered states of children, and how they have always been regarded as totems of strong magic. And at last it did something.

Explorer and initiate Alexandra David-Neel introduced to the West the Lamaist practice of thought-form creation in her book

Magic and Mystery in Tibet. She writes, regarding her own efforts at tulpa creation:

> Besides having had few opportunities of seeing thought-forms, my habitual incredulity led me to make experiments for myself, and my efforts were attended with some success. In order to avoid being influenced by the forms of the lamaist deities, which I saw daily around me in paintings and images, I chose for my experiment a most insignificant character: a Monk, short and fat, of an innocent and jolly type.
>
> I shut myself in tsams and proceeded to perform the prescribed concentration of thought and other rites. After a few months the phantom Monk was formed. His form grew gradually fixed and lifelike looking. He became a kind of guest, living in my apartment. I then broke my seclusion and started for a tour, with my servants and tents.
>
> The Monk included himself in the party. Though I lived in the open, riding on horseback for miles each day, the illusion persisted. I saw the fat tulpa; now and then it was not necessary for me to think of him to make him appear. The phantom performed various actions of the kind that are natural to travelers and that I had not commanded. For instance, he walked, stopped, looked around him. The illusion was mostly visual, but sometimes I felt as if a robe was lightly rubbing against me, and once a hand seemed to touch my shoulder.
>
> The features which I had imagined, when building my phantom, gradually underwent a change. The fat, chubby-cheeked fellow grew leaner, his face assumed a vaguely mocking, sly, malignant look. He became more troublesome and bold. In brief, he escaped my control. Once, a herdsman who brought me a present of butter saw the tulpa in my tent and took it for a living lama.
>
> I ought to have let the phenomenon follow its course, but the presence of that unwanted companion began to prove trying to my nerves; it turned into a "day-nightmare." Moreover, I was beginning to plan my journey to Lhasa and needed a quiet brain devoid of other preoccupations, so I decided to dissolve the phantom. I succeeded, but only after six months of hard struggle. My mind-creature was tenacious of life.

(Also, and mentioned previously here, Philip K. Dick talks about tulpas and Disneyland, and a supposed ghost in Greenwich Village resembled "the Shadow," the fictional creation of the deceased author whose house it "haunted.")

Now, with respect to imaginary friends, in "Baby Center's Ask the Experts" a mother writes:

My four year old has an imaginary friend called Cheeney who is 16 and lives in England (apparently). Strange seeing we live in New Zealand i.e. the other side of the world. Sometimes what she comes out with scares me too, but mostly I just put it down to an active imagination, and she certainly has that! Sometimes my husband does get annoyed holding the car door open for a long time so all her "friends" can come out. He has even closed the door on a few — oops!

Of course, so long as the imagined friend remains unexperienced by others, there is not much to concern us here. As David-Neel wrote regarding her tulpa, "There is nothing strange in the fact that I may have created my own hallucination. The interesting point is that in these cases of materialization, others see the thought-forms that have been created."

For what they may be worth, here are a couple of recent and possibly relevant posts on the "Unexplained-Mysteries" forum which similarly elevate the mystery.

From "chaoszerg":

When i was a child my mom and dad apparently heard a voice talking to me while i was asleep at the time i had a imaginary friend so this frightened my mom because of the voice so we moved and it never happened again.

And "ShadowLady":

When my little brother was between the ages of 3 and 6, he had an imaginary friend named "Bill." I actually heard my brother talking to his "friend" and then his "friend" answering back. We had all kinds of weird things happen in our house and we always blamed Bill. My brother is 24 now and he still swears that Bill was real, that he could see him and hold conversations with him. FREAKY!

Finally from *I Used to Believe* ("the childhood beliefs site"), this contribution from "Frances Ames":

I was a very lonely little girl when I was 5 years old and lived on Toronto Island at Hanlan's Point. I wished real hard for some new friends, my age, to play with when we all went to the beach, a few hundred yards from our house. An old man came and said here is 2 friends for you to play with. They will grow as you grow. They will stay with you as long as you don't tell anyone their names. Well, I was so happy. I would build things in the sand and they would too. I used to talk to them and my mother would pester me and asked who I was talking with. I finally told mom who they were. Dingus and Tardar. They went away and never came back. My 5 yr. old cousin saw them too. He let me know that after we became age 60. He told me the old man's name was Pookie. True story.

In *The Field*, Lynne McTaggart writes that EEG studies of the brains of children under five show that they "permanently function in alpha mode — the state of altered consciousness in an adult. Children are open to far more information.... In effect, a child walks around in a state of a permanent hallucination." Alpha waves appear to bridge the conscious and the subconscious. For much of our waking adult life, we don't have a decent bridge.

If childhood is a naturally liminal state, then perhaps much of what's called High Magick amounts to the attempt to recreate its conditions. (*You say Tulpa, I say Imaginary friend.*) Or in other words, a subset of occult science may amount to the recovery of power nascent to childhood. And what, I wonder, does this have to say about the child victims of mind control and ritual occult abuse?

The Predator Class

August 09, 2006

> *There'll be phantoms.*
> *There'll be fires on the road*
> *and the white man dancing.*
> — Leonard Cohen

In the middle of his September, 2004 address to the UN General Assembly, making the case that America's purpose is to "build a better world beyond the war on terror," George Bush had this to say:

> Because we believe in human dignity, America and many nations have joined together to confront the evil of trafficking in human beings. We're supporting organizations that rescue the victims, passing stronger anti-trafficking laws, and warning travelers that they will be held to account for supporting this modern form of slavery. Women and children should never be exploited for pleasure or greed, anywhere on Earth.

It was a rare *where did that come from* moment during one of Bush's more lucid performances. And while it's appropriate to place the exploitation of children in the context of the "war on terror," he was disingenuous about what that place should be. Consider this BBC story from July 5, 2000:

Wanted Israeli diplomat flees Brazil

Police in Rio de Janeiro say an Israeli diplomat suspected of belonging to an international child pornography ring has fled Brazil and returned to Israel.

The Israeli diplomatic mission confirmed that its vice-consul, Arie Scher, had flown home at the request of the Israeli government, which it said had ordered an investigation into the allegations.

Police want to question him in connection with pornographic pictures and videotapes of young children found in the home of a Hebrew language teacher arrested on Tuesday.

The children were pictured and filmed at the diplomat's house.

Police said the pictures had been published on the Internet with the apparent aim of attracting foreign paedophiles to Rio de Janeiro.

Scher was to resurface five years later, when he was appointed Israel's new consul to Australia replacing Amir Laty, a spy who was himself expelled for seducing diplomats, defense specialists and journalists "in the hope of cultivating young women with access to government secrets."

That sex is a tool of espionage should not be much of a story, though it should, at least *be* a story. Despite its glamorization and parody in film, whoring for intelligence remains largely invisible and unacknowledged. Remember August 2004, when New Jersey Governor Jim McGreevey resigned on account of a relationship with former Israeli naval lieutenant Golan Cipel, the man he had named his state's homeland-security czar? Speculation that Cipel may have cultivated the affair as an intel op was duct-taped over as both "anti-gay" and "anti-Semitic," by American liberals on the usual forums who pretended to have never heard the name Pussy Galore.

But "international child pornography" is a sex crime of a different order. And Scher's Australian placement and support from his Foreign Office, which rejected the accusations against him as "terribly exaggerated," suggest kiddie porn wasn't a *Blame it on Rio* personal indiscretion, but rather something that came with the job; much like the human-smuggling scandal out of the U.S. embassy in Azerbaijan that saw Ambassador Reno Harnish shuffled sideways to an environmental posting engaged in the "fight against bird flu."

A question to consider is why someone like Scher, who in his previous posting was apparently engaged in the covert pursuit of luring foreign pedophiles to his host country, would be considered an appropriate appointee for the position of consul to Australia.

I came upon a butcher. He was slaughtering a lamb.
I accused him there with his tortured lamb.
He said, "Listen to me, child, I am what I am,
and you, you are my only son."
— Leonard Cohen

In February of last year, the same month diplomat/child pornographer Arie Scher was named Israel's consul to Australia, Shaine Moore was found dead in his Adelaide home, ten days after he was reported missing. On March 18, 2005, South Australia Police declared his suspicious death a "major crime" and "suspected murder," while withholding results of the post mortem for "operational reasons." (This past Monday, David Richard Fraser pleaded not guilty to Moore's murder.)

Moore had been an informant in investigations conducted by the office of Peter Lewis — at the time, South Australia's parliamentary speaker — into an alleged murderous elite circle of pedophiles, which counted as a member at least one prominent state politician. He was the second informant to be murdered. (The first, Robert Woodland, was found "bashed to death last December [2004] in Adelaide's south parklands. His murder is unsolved.") By April 2005, two more would be killed. ("Pedophile link to 4th murder.") The same month, the South Australian government forced Lewis' resignation from the office of speaker, and the same day it "took the extraordinary step...of introducing legislation to the Lower House which would limit parliamentary privilege by preventing media outlets from naming any MP or public official allegedly involved in sexual misconduct, even if he is identified in Parliament."

In his resignation speech, Lewis said:

> The most outrageous thing of all, which disturbs me most about the information which has come in to my office is not the matter of paedophiles in South Australia's parliament but what appears to be the related and organised activities of those paedophiles in high public office — that is, the judiciary, the senior ranks of human services portfolios, some police, and MPs, across the nation, especially within the ranks of the Labor Party.... Paedophiles of the kind to which I am referring here are the most gracious and beguiling of people in the community and are able to manipulate the opinions of others and attract their favorable attentions more effectively than most. It is not surprising that we find them in the jobs and roles of leadership. Their guile and cunning enable them to conceive of ways to organise their activities so that they are almost impossible to prevent, detect and prosecute.

Since the days of laundering Southeast Asian drug money through such shells as the Nugan Hand bank, Australia has been a significant hub in the global nexus of organized crime and intelligence, supporting a national class of elites whose allegiance is not to the nation-state, and whose morality is unbound by law. On the single occasion Australia's blind allegiance — almost literally blind, with respect to the NSA's installation at Pine Gap — was challenged, during the government of Gough Whitlam, the CIA helped engineer Whitlam's fall. Australia is that important.

The Australian outback, like the American desert, is an ancient and unorganized space that was a stage for strange displays to its original human inhabitants, who regarded their home as shared with wild spirits that were themselves inhuman. And like the American desert, the outback has become a "proving ground" for other strange displays, those of deep black technologies that don't appear to be of this world even when they are, and a host to persistent rumors of occult twists to the story of military intelligence. *Location, location, location.*

Australia and Great Britain were the only members of note in George Bush's "coalition of the willing." Perhaps we should consider Australia's alleged ring of pedophiles holding "high public office" — a "wild" allegation that saw four informants murdered — alongside the suppressed revelations of Britain's Operation Ore, that senior members of Tony Blair's cabinet are suspected pedophiles and consumers of child pornography. Perhaps the "special relationship" of the major coalition partners has been bonded by more than blood, and the glint of madness that's come to Blair's eyes in recent years has revealed its method.

Born in Time

September 26, 2006

You're comin' thru to me in black and white
When we were made of dreams.

— Bob Dylan

You've seen the story of the presidential doodles. There are many odd and revealing examples, such as G.H.W. Bush's "any more dead ones?" (ABC News says his sad and teary face "gives the note a bit of melancholy, or maybe humor," appropriately ambiguous for a man of shimmering surface and black depths), but the one perhaps receiving the most notice hasn't even been reproduced online. It's a page from John F. Kennedy, on which he's written, repeatedly, "9-11," and underscored the word "conspiracy" next to it.

Paul Joseph Watson wondered whether this was some kind of "inside joke" or a "hat tip to the 9/11 truth movement" before concluding, "one thing's for sure — it's weird." I'd say rather that two things are certain: it's both weird, and it's not.

ABC explains the numbers, without accounting for the word "conspiracy," by saying that "It turns out that was the tally of a committee vote, not a foreshadowing of the Sept. 11, 2001, attacks." But that's a misapprehension of foreshadowing, which always carries within it a duality, referencing both a prosaic explanation and a supra-prosaic that is revealed only in hindsight. If this were, say, a Richard Condon novel and not living history, and so foreshadowing just a literary device, there would be no dispute that Kennedy's doodle fit the definition. It's disputed now because people object to the impression that we may be the characters instead of the authors of our lives.

Kennedy's doodle didn't "predict" 9/11 any more than The Coup's cover art or *The Lone Gunmen*'s pilot episode, but all three are suggestive of a grander conspiracy — the grandest — that encompasses all of human history. I'm talking about the conspiracy of consciousness. That by encoding the narrative of history with artful gestures of interpretation — the things that make us go *hmmm* — consciousness conspires to bring us to comprehension.

Consider for a moment the familiar JFK and Abraham Lincoln coincidences, how their stories seem to enfold, and unfold, one another. Such details as Lincoln's election to congress in 1846, JFK's exactly 100 years later, and each entering the presidency 14 years after that; Lincoln's having a secretary named Kennedy, and Kennedy's a secretary Lincoln, and each being succeeded by a man named Johnson; both were shot in the head on a Friday, Lincoln by a man with three names born in 1839 who fled a theatre to a warehouse, while Kennedy's alleged three-named gunman, born in 1939, fled a warehouse to a theatre; "Kennedy" and "Lincoln" each contain seven letters, and John Wilkes Booth and Lee Harvey Oswald, 15 — you know the list, and how it goes on.

Of course, a grab bag of coincidence a century apart should defy the conventions of even the loosest conspiracy model. But in a holographic model, things change. It is consciousness — not individual consciousness, but the collective consciousness of all life — that draws locality and temporality out of the wave pattern of higher vibrations that form the holographic universe, and constructs the space and time setting for our life narrative. And consciousness *is* a storyteller, employing literary devices such as foreshadowing as well as metaphor in our waking curiosity and dream state, while some astral project and remote view, and as plant shamans, with heads full of snakes, explore innerspace via such gateways as DMT and ayahuasca.

JFK didn't "plan" 9/11, or have "inside info" as I've seen some Amazing Randiesque skeptics sarcastically assert. But repeating patterns, even across centuries or great distances, may still evidence a conspiracy. But the better kind: one of undifferentiated consciousness provoking us within the continuum towards greater reading comprehension.

Perhaps to help it write a happier ending.

> *Time marches on, time stands still.*
> *Time on my hands, time to kill.*
> *Blood on my hands, and my hands in the till*
> *Down at the 7-11.*
> — Warren Zevon

Time Out of Mind

I've always been dismayed by the thought of reincarnation, so its unlikelihood has always been a comfort. Which is why it saddens me to consider that oblivion may have been as much wishful thinking as paradise.

But if the occult is on the table in these times then we need to talk about this, too, since reincarnation is the "great fundamental doctrine" of the Mystery Schools, as Dion Fortune writes in *Sane Occultism*. And more to the point, the emerging holographic model in which our minds are seen to both extend beyond our material bodies, and to have emerged from a common consciousness, provides the theoretical construct in which reincarnation becomes scientifically credible, if not inevitable.

Before we go much further, let's recall again the congruities of boundary experience, which are all manifested in part by higher frequencies of electro-magnetic vibration. Remote viewing may be regarded as a subset of astral projection, or out-of-body experience, while an OBE could be called a Near-Death Experience before its time. And the phenomenology of NDEs is remarkably similar to that of UFO encounters, as detailed in Dr. Kenneth Ring's *The Omega Project*. And cords of each lead us to Fortune's fundamental doctrine.

Psychoactive research, too. In Rick Strassman's *DMT: The Spirit Molecule,* he recalls the chill along his spine when he noted for the first time that it takes 49 days from conception to the first signs of the human pineal gland, the same span recorded in the Tibetan *Book of the Dead* from death to reincarnation. (Forty-nine days is also the time of gender differentiation.) Strassman contends that endogenous DMT, produced in the pineal near death, may act as a "scout" for the non-corporeal realm.

Strassman writes:

> As we die, if near-death experiences are any indication, there is a profound shift in consciousness away from identification with the body. Pineal DMT makes available those particular non-embodied contents of consciousness. All the factors previously described combine for one final burst of DMT production: catecholamine release; decreased breakdown and increased production of DMT; reduced anti-DMT; and decomposing pineal tissue. Therefore, it may be that the pineal is the most active organ in the body at the time of death....

> *The consequence of this flood of DMT upon our dying brain-based mind is a pulling back of the veils normally hiding what Tibetan Buddhists call the bardo, or intermediary states between this life and the next. DMT opens our senses to these betwixt states with their myriad visions, thoughts, sounds and feelings. As the body becomes totally inert, consciousness has completely left the body and now exists as a field among many fields of manifest things.* [emphasis added]

Bruce Moen — who received his training in altered-state projection at the Monroe Institute — describes in his book *Voyages into the Unknown* OBEs spent as a "first responder" guiding the shocked dead of Oklahoma City towards the souls' "reception center." He notes he saw a Monroe associate, named Rebecca, doing the same, "her arms spread out in love...providing a portal," and that they acknowledged each other with smiles. Later, in this world, by telephone, they compared notes. ("Oh Bruce, the babies" were her first words.)

Reincarnation was the core tenet of Robert Monroe's philosophy, which he said he learned over decades of astral travel. Remember his "I/There"? Monroe taught that the self we know is merely the fragment of the "Total Self" which is currently living a physical life. The total self is a cluster of many beings who each live many lifetimes. (Since Monroe's death in 1995 Skip Atwater, former Operations and Training Officer of the U.S. military's remote-viewing program, has served as the institute's Director of Research.)

Where Life and Death are Memorized

Dr. Joel Whitton is a Toronto psychologist who, in 1972, participated in the "Philip" experiment, which allegedly created a fictional ghost by the power of a group's applied will (not unlike making a tulpa). In the decades since he has researched reincarnation, and his 13-year work with 30 individuals is published in the book *Life Between Life*.

Of Whitton's subjects, Michael Talbot writes in *The Holographic Universe* that many "gave uncannily accurate historical details about the times in which they had lived":

> Some even spoke languages unknown to them. While reliving an apparent past life as a Viking, one man, a 37-year-old behavioral sci-

entist, shouted words that linguistic authorities later identified as Old Norse. After being regressed to an ancient Persian lifetime, the same man began to write in a spidery, Arabic-style script that an expert in Near Eastern languages identified as an authentic representation of Sassanid Pahlavi, a long-extinct Mesopotamian tongue that flourished between A.D. 226 and 651.

Perhaps we should ask now, if we are confident that the subjects are not inventing a past life, can we assume that they are always recalling one? There are endless signals in the super-hologram. Could it be that, when tuning in the higher vibrations, their brains-as-receivers instead pick up the cross-talk of disembodied consciousness? Rather than a transmigration of souls, this would mean a certain entanglement. *Possibly*. Entanglement could account for certain manifestations of mental and spiritual illness, including "possession." But the distinction may be chiefly rhetorical if we all partake of the same consciousness, and it fails to account for the alleged physical footprint of past lives upon the present.

Dr. Ian Stevenson, head of the Department of Psychiatric Medicine at the University of Virginia School of Medicine, published an article in 1993 entitled "Birthmarks and Birth Defects Corresponding to Wounds on Deceased Persons." He found that 35% of children who claim to recall past lives bear a birthmark or defect they attribute to a wound suffered in an earlier incarnation.

Stevenson writes:

The cases of 210 such children have been investigated. The birthmarks were usually areas of hairless, puckered skin; some were areas of little or no pigmentation (hypopigmented macules); others were areas of increased pigmentation (hyperpigmented nevi). The birth defects were nearly always of rare types. In cases in which a deceased person was identified the details of whose life unmistakably matched the child's statements, a close correspondence was nearly always found between the birthmarks and/or birth defects on the child and the wounds on the deceased person. In 43 of 49 cases in which a medical document (usually a postmortem report) was obtained, it confirmed the correspondence between wounds: and birthmarks (or birth defects). There is little evidence that parents and other informants imposed a false identity on the child in order to explain the child's birthmark or birth defect. Some paranormal process seems required to account for at least some of the details of these cases, including the birthmarks and birth defects.

Talbot notes that Stevenson has escorted many children to the locales of their past lives, and observed them effortlessly navigate what should have been strange neighborhoods as they "correctly identified their former house, belongings, and past-life relatives and friends."

Interestingly, and contrary to the presumptions of religion, Stevenson and most NDE researchers find no evidence of "retributive karma" or judgment of "sin" or uncharitable conduct. Talbot writes that Stevenson has found that:

> ... although a person's material conditions can vary greatly from one life to the next, their moral conduct, interests, aptitudes, and attitudes remain the same. *Individuals who were criminals in their previous existence tend to be drawn to criminal behavior again;* people who were generous and kind continue to be generous and kind, and so on. From this Stevenson concludes that it is not the outward trappings of life that matter, but the inner ones, the joys, sorrows, and "inner growths" of the personality, that appear to be most important.

But wait: "inner growth" would appear to include criminality — *be all the bastard you can be* — as there is neither judgment nor reward beyond that which we make for ourselves. And accordingly, ancient, evil souls would be inclined to re-manifest once again as dark actors and vectors of calamity, though perhaps more skilled for having incorporated the lessons of many lifetimes.

By this perspective, reincarnation sheds its religious ardor and becomes all about experiment. But whose?

Cold Irons Bound

Late one evening in October, 1973, at 2,500 feet and good visibility, the crew of an Army Reserve helicopter flying from Columbus to Cleveland saw a red light to the west, heading south. Initially, it was taken to be an F-100 out of Mansfield, though Richard Dolan writes in *UFOs and the National Security State* that the airbase later confirmed there were no aircraft in the area. Abruptly, the light changed direction and headed directly towards them. Captain Lawrence J. Coyne, with 19-years-flying experience, tried to radio an airport but found his communication equipment had failed. He then sent his craft into a dive to 1,700 feet as the light drew close, stopping dead directly in front revealing a cigar-shaped, metallic body with a small dome on top. One crewman thought he saw windows. The red light was shining on the front of the object, a white light on the side and a green on the bottom. The object then positioned itself above the helicopter and remained stationary for 10 seconds, flooding the cockpit with green light before continuing west. As it departed the helicopter radio returned to working order. Oddly, the altimeter showed them to now be at 3,500 and climbing, yet the stick for descent still pointed down and Coyne had not attempted to ascend.

Witnesses on the ground included a family of five driving below on a rural road, who saw both object and helicopter and the green light. Another witness, Jeanne Elias, was in bed watching TV and put a pillow over her head at the sound of the diving helicopter. The noise woke up her 14-year old son and the green light bathed his bedroom.

Resolute debunker Philip Klass said the crew must have misidentified a meteor, and that the witnesses on ground had to be lying.

The crew received peculiar attention in the aftermath. Captain Coyne received a call from the Department of the Army, Surgeon General's Office, inquiring whether he had since had any "unusual dreams." He reported a particularly lucid dream of an out-of-body [OBE] experience.

Richard L. Thompson, in his concordance of UFO accounts and ancient Vedic texts entitled *Alien Identities*, quotes Sgt John Healey, one of the helicopter crewmen:

> As time would go by, the Pentagon would call us up and ask us, Well, has this incident happened to you since the occurrence? And in two of the instances that I recall, what they questioned me, was, number one, have I ever dreamed of body separation, and I have — I dreamed that I was dead in bed and that my spirit or whatever was floating, looking down at me lying dead in bed ... and the other thing was if I had ever dreamed of anything in spherical shape. Which definitely had not occurred to me.

The Pentagon frequently called Captain Coyne with similar questions, and would inquire after all the crew members. *"One wonders,"* writes Thompson, *"who in the Pentagon might be interested in the UFO/OBE connection."*

Perhaps this is a good place to reintroduce the egg imagery common to UFOs and the soul, and occult workings meant to open portals and birth a new aeon. Whitley Strieber writes in *Transformation* that his visitors told him, *"We recycle souls."*

Death Is Not the End

The idea of Alex Proyas' *DarkCity* came in a recurring childhood nightmare, of darkly clad, vampiric "strangers" playing God to a somnambulant people. One day you may be a subway driver; the next, an investment broker, and you were to never remember you'd been anything else. The subjects were treated with indifference, and though sometimes they would be given a good life it was incidental to the benefit of the hidden strangers, who fed upon their emotions. A good film, that would make a crummy blueprint for eternity.

Because here's the rub: If Charles Fort is correct, and we're "property," the lease may not expire with our mortal body. If reincarnation *is* a fact, then its purpose is not likely a benefit to us, insofar as "us" has any sensible meaning. If non-human intelligence is fabricating spiritual phenomena in this world, what is to prevent it from doing the same in the next? If criminal souls do return to this existence and, by their nature and by the system that rewards it, so often rise to cruel power, then who would benefit more than hungry spirits that feed upon the traumas they inflict? And might some occult traditions exist in order to pass on the knowledge of the perseverance of the soul in order to maintain earthly power from grave to grave?

Time, they say, will tell.

Necromocracy

October 14, 2006

> *Across history, other nations had gone insane. Other movements had been evil or tried awful wizardries. But none perpetrated murder with such dedicated efficiency. The horror must have been directed not so much at death itself, but at some hideous goal beyond death.*
>
> — David Brin,*The Life Eaters*

When I was taught history in high school, Athens was a favorite historical analogue for the United States. Both were considered accidental empires and, for the most part, benign necessities of their dangerous times. For America, this was the period of its so-called *soft* power (even though its application often felt hard as hell away from home), but Mossadegh and Allende could tell you better. The self-celebrating mythology of America's global reach was always democratic, and its extended aspects — its colonies, though they would never be called such — were assumed to be dependencies by choice. America's Athenians were regarded as individuals, and its military the champion of an individual's liberty. Unlike the *Evil* Empire of the Soviet Union, whose subjects and armed forces were thought more comparable to the severe and undifferentiated Spartans.

But in wartime, and in a time of re-mythologizing war, America's mythmaking undergoes a radical makeover to favor Sparta and the 300 of King Leonidas. It's too tempting a story to resist, because no matter its overwhelming might, it seems that for the good of its soul America must also, at least in its fiction, regard itself as the underdog. (You could perhaps sense something of this in the relish with which supporters of the Iraq war recounted America's "abandonment" by its traditional allies and the United Nations. "Going it alone" never felt so good.)

A new film treatment of the Battle of Thermopylae, *300*, will be released early next year, and it looks like just the ticket to introduce the legend of Sparta to America's popular culture of perpetual war. Particularly appropriate, since Persian arms are once again the perceived enemy, and the few who stand against them now are Rumsfeld's 150,000. (And that reminds me: do you remember reading how, "in the summer of 2001, when security agencies were regularly warning of a catastrophic attack by al-Qaeda, Defense Secretary Rumsfeld's office 'sponsored a study of ancient empires — Macedonia, Rome, the Mongols — to figure out how they maintained dominance,' according to the *New York Times*"?) This latest, and most extreme version is based upon the work of graphic novelist Frank Miller, of the admirable *Sin City*, but who is also an unabashed propagandist for the White House shooting script. His next project is *Holy Terror, Batman!* in which bin Laden targets Gotham City and the Dark Knight "kicks al-Qaeda's ass."

An inspiring defeat is sometimes worth more to a military and its masters than a sure victory, just as allowing an attack to happen can be of greater long-term benefit than its prevention, and through the centuries the blood of 300 soldiers has probably nourished a thousand campaigns. Perhaps, recalling this post, some of the same soldiers, over and over again. General George Patton was persuaded he was one, as dramatized here ("I fought in many guises, many names. But always me.")

Reincarnation aside, there's a certain necromancy here, in romanticizing the deaths of those long dead in order to stir the living to want to join them. A similar working was accomplished with the 3,000 dead of 9/11 who, though representing many nations, after death all somehow became alchemical Americans. Not only by the *Let's Roll!* stage-management of their unoffered sacrifice were many thousands more inspired to enlist, die and suffer grievous injury, but their blood is deemed sufficient to cover that of 655,000, and the murderers of Iraq and their enablers still enjoy untroubled sleep.

Call it what you want, but that's some strong magic.

I have to question whether there is an evil force in the world and whether or not I have been influenced by it.
— Jeffrey Dahmer.

Much like Gilles de Rais, the sixteenth century Hungarian Countess Elizabeth Bathory is notorious for tearing apart young children to satisfy her sex-magical appetite. Her taste was for girls, more than 600 of them, and she was able to consume so many of them because it was only late in her career that she turned her desires to the daughters of her own kind. Down the hill, beneath her castle, villagers had "often claimed to have heard screams emanating from within this place, and they spoke of disappearing girls and of murder, but no one had dared approach the regal, 50-something countess until now. Word had come to the king that she had kidnapped or killed nine girls *from good families*."

Naturally she'd had help. Servants and hirelings were employed in abduction and torture, including Elizabeth's own childhood nurse Ilona Joo, who admitted to having killed 50 girls by her own hand. Some claimed to have been forced to act against their will, and some others instructed their mistress in black magic. ("Thorko has taught me a lovely new one," she wrote her husband, Ferencz Nadasdy. "Catch a black hen and beat it to death with a white cane. Keep the blood and smear a little of it on your enemy. If you get no chance to smear it on his body, obtain one of his garments and smear it.")

Twenty-one judges tried Bathory and her accomplices, though in deference to her station she was accused of simple criminal acts, while her common help faced the more scan-

dalous charges of vampirism, witchcraft and occult ritual. They were convicted and tortured, then beheaded or burned alive, but Bathory was again protected by her class and its cognitive dissonance at the atrocities of nobility. She did not even receive a formal decision of guilt, but was under "castle arrest" for the rest of her life, its entrances and windows walled up except for food and circulation. The court declared a life sentence suitable so she could "find time to repent."

Four hundred years later, Bathory remains one of pop culture's favorite monsters, and her name evocative of decadent aristocrats playing at sex and death. Yet her husband, who predeceased her by ten years before the revelation of her crimes, died with even more blood on his hands, but is remembered as something else.

In 1578 Nadasdy became the chief commander of Hungary's armies in its war against the Turks, who called him "the Black Prince" on account of both his bravery and his cruelty. (For instance, It's reported that when his troops captured the village of Urmisz he instructed that its priest be beheaded and its women and children raped and burned alive.) Nadasdy was notorious for his imaginative methods of torture, which he shared with his apprenticing wife, but his "excesses" were on the battlefield against Muslim invaders and their allies, rather than in the comfort of home against his "own kind," and that's a distinction that is usually enough to tell a national hero from a homicidal maniac.

The sixteenth century seems so long ago we might as well be talking of a different planet and a different species, but we're not, and it's still us. If we had film from the time to view, rather than oil paintings and engravings, we'd recognize ourselves more readily. (Elizabeth's uncle was the famous Stephen Bathory, King of Poland, who hosted occultist-spy John Dee and his scryer Edward Kelly on their visit to the continent. Dee's Enochian magick, relaunched into the world by Aleister Crowley, is so established in the backstory of our culture that it's a key plot point of the "Lonelygirl15" saga, arguably YouTube's greatest viral phenomena.) We should also recognize ourselves from much more distant times. The fossil record of modern humans begins 196,000 years ago. From that point until now, there is nothing that physically distinguishes us from our prehistory. About 50,000 years ago, with the flourishing of art, adornment and symbolic representation, our ancestors' interior lives begin to look familiar. It's all sex and death, which is to say, religion. And if it's primitive, then so still are we.

From a statement of Vietnam war veteran Sgt. Larry J. Cottingham, January 24, 1973: "There was a period when just about everyone had a necklace of ears but as the men were wounded they thought it was bad luck and got rid of them. Scalps were a kick for a time also but there were lice in the hair and they got rid of those too and it didn't last long." Those were modern American boys, adorning themselves like "savages" with fetishes made from the flesh of the enemy.

In New Orleans, a young veteran of Iraq, Afghanistan and Katrina named Zackery Bowen left a five-page suicide note and jumped off a bridge after dismembering his girlfriend and cooking her head and legs in the apartment they shared above a voodoo shop. His victim-lover, Addie Hall, came to national attention last year for flashing her breasts to police cars. ("Female survivors of the storm were urged by government rescuers to flash their breasts in order to receive help in Katrina's immediate aftermath.") Friends of Bowen say he "displayed both pride and bitterness" over his experience of war. ("Somewhere overseas there had been an incident concerning a child that weighed heavy on him, said Donovan Calabaza, another bartender at Buffa's, 'but we really didn't get into it.'" Other times Bowen "would grow angry and distraught...talking of how the government [had] 'messed him over.'")

In little more than three years in Iraq, there are more than 600,000 dead who shouldn't be. As with the victims of most serial killers, they remain unnamed and unmissed except by their loved ones, and the occasional justice allegedly undertaken on their behalf means persecuting the odd accomplice rather than the perpetrator. The logic of madness that compels the maniac to kill is the same that drives the maniac state towards mass murder and genocide. The more dead by their hand, the more power they accrue, and it's not a simple equation of slaying one's enemies. It's about the alchemy of turning lives into spent fuel.

The Clown at Midnight

September 6, 2006

Nobody laughs at a clown at midnight.

— Lon Chaney

More people than ever are ready to believe it's midnight in America, and not many of them think there's anything funny about it. But when was the last time you noticed the hands on the clock move? How long has it been midnight?

In *The Secret Doctrine*, Helena Blavatsky writes that "occult philosophy teaches that even now, under our very eyes, the new Race and Races are preparing to be formed, *and that it is in America that the transformation will take place*, and has already commenced." In 1888 America still seemed like a vigorous novelty that might give something new and good to the world, rather than one of its weirder places of ancient dark that could pull it down to hell. Blavatsky was optimistic about the New Race that America was begetting. She presumed that the transformation involved the elevation of consciousness, which would lift all life with it. Generations later, I think we can say it hasn't quite worked out that way.

"Fascism is the supreme expression of religious mysticism," states Wilhelm Reich in *The Mass Psychology of Fascism*. "It transposes religion from the 'otherworldliness' of the philosophy of suffering to the 'this worldliness' of sadistic murder." Pasolini knew that, too, and showed us he did with *Salo*. ("Our guide restored the divine character of monstrosity thanks to reiterated actions. That is to say: rites.")

Fascist mysticism is at the same time relentlessly materialistic, and its "New Race" attained by dominating matter which includes the masses, which are just meat to enact the will of the leadership. The Nazi New Man owed so much to American eugenics, the shadow it casts in 21st century America is more of a homecoming. (Anti-fascism may be back in style in Washington, though just the style, as Bush's handlers shift again the terms of conflict to now suggest America is at war with "Islamofascists." Or, *I know you, are but what am I?*)

Animals are turning up mutilated in Louisiana's Tangipahoa Parish, home of the Hosanna Church Satanic sex cult, whose black-robed elders drew pentagrams on the floor of the "youth hall," raped children and forced them into bestiality. Yesterday, Baton Rouge television reported that Tangipahoa Sheriff's detectives were investigating the "killing of three cats, a dog and a horse; and the mutilation of another dog and two horses." All had their throats slashed by a sharp blade, and there are no suspects or leads. The Sheriff's office notes, with supposed reassurance, that the mutilations and slayings "do not appear to be ritualistic." (The Hosanna Church also practiced the mutilation and sacrifice of cats, though since prosecutors are determined to whitewash occult intent right out of their case, some may contend there was no ritualistic intent there either.)

No one *told* these people to do this. I don't believe Pastor Louis Lamonica and the rest of his suburban congregation-cult were programmed to ritually assault children, or even that they are necessarily connected to a wider, and deeper, network of devil-worshipping pedophiles. It seems to be inchoate knowledge among those who seek power in dark places that the defilement of the innocent, particularly children, makes for strong magick. Just as disbelief seems the natural defense posture of those who are preyed-upon.

Maybe it's *always* been midnight in America. It's simply taken a clown in the White House to alert Americans to their missing time. If so, what should we expect a minute past?

In July 2005, Colin Campbell's newsletter of the Association for the Study of Peak Oil and Gas published an argument for Social Darwinism by William Stanton entitled "Oil and People." Stanton called those who couldn't *grok* the necessity of extreme population reduction "sentimentalists," and argued that human rights needed to be replaced by "cold logic." They have had their day, wrote Stanton:

> Individual citizens, and aliens, must expect to be seriously inconvenienced by the single-minded drive to reduce population ahead of resource shortage. The consolation is that the alternative, letting Nature take its course, would be so much worse.... When, through old age, accident or disease, an individual becomes more of a burden than a benefit to society, his or her life is humanely ended. Voluntary euthanasia is

legal and made easy. Imprisonment is rare, replaced by corporal punishment for lesser offences and painless capital punishment for greater.

Cold logic and mystical, sadistic murder. In a good and necessary cause, we'll be told. And not a word about the magick.

Unconscious Kingdom

October 10, 2006

The writing on the wall, come read it, come see what it say.
— Bob Dylan

This narration opens Lars von Trier's *Riget* ("The Kingdom"):

The Kingdom Hospital rests on ancient marshland where the bleaching ponds once lay. Here the bleachers moistened their great spans of cloth. The steam evaporating from the wet cloth shrouded the place in permanent fog. Centuries later the hospital was built here. The bleachers gave way to doctors and researchers, the best brains in the nation and the most perfect technology. To crown their work they called the hospital The Kingdom. Now life was to be charted, and ignorance and superstition never to shake the bastions of science again.

Perhaps that arrogance became too pronounced, and their persistent denial of the spiritual. For it is as if the cold and damp have returned. Tiny signs of fatigue are appearing in the solid, modern edifice. No living person knows it yet, but the gateway to the Kingdom is opening once again.

When the gateway opens, what comes through are phantom ambulances, the undead, child ghosts — etheric manifestations that affront the materialist reductionism of the Kingdom's staff, who believe their beliefs represent the highest expression of humanity's ascent from superstition. But their rationalism is finally ineffectual to support their pinched worldview against the chthonic onslaught — much like the real-life experience of the Livermore Laboratories scientists who found they "couldn't go home again" — and turned to despised ritual, trance and voodoo-like sacrifice in order to meet and bargain with the otherworldly elements that had erupted in their world.

But the message of *The Kingdom*'s preamble is that the otherworld is what our world was before it was our world. That is, that we are inheritors of strange and ancient lands. Our ancestors, the first inheritors, knew; but for the better part we have forgotten. Though not all, and some perhaps not the best of us.

Our fully-human forefathers who lived before history left ubiquitous traces of their inner lives on cave walls and rock faces. Remarkably, across enormous distance and time the imagery remained conspicuously familiar, and religious. From all inhabited continents, and from the Upper Paleolithic to traditional cultures which until our own time contributed in isolation to the collective body of sacred art, we find the same recurring abstract geometric patterns, and similar depictions of shapeshifters in various stages of transformation. (It's interesting to note how now, after the "end" of history, the shapeshifter figure occupies again the shadows of our consciousness at the borderland of worlds. A recent example is the pseudo-documentary "Brandon Corey Story," a slick piece of disinfotainment that exploits our authentic apprehensions by fabricating evidence upon legitimate suspicions.)

Graham Hancock devotes much of his recent *Supernatural* to cave art, with particular attention paid to the finding of paleoanthropologist David Lewis-Williams, that its imagery appeared to be the language of universal trance states:

> At some stages of the visionary experience subjects in laboratory tests report seeing displays of specific kinds of abstract geometrical patterns. What is interesting is the evidence that such patterns are universal and culture-free. Once we have entered a state of consciousness that has been altered deeply enough — itself a universal neurological capacity for the human race — it seems that everyone, everywhere experiences visions containing very much the same combinations of patterns and shapes.

Whether achieved by the ingestion of psychoactive drugs, spirit dancing or some other ritual, the trance-state of a shaman is essentially the same phenomenon regardless of time and place, as it is an unequivocally human event. Displays of geometric patterns are often followed by scenes of hybrid animals and impressions of great and alien intelligence, leading to the message the shaman sought to carry back to his people from the spirit world. If Lewis-Williams is right, then much cave art is an iconography of these altered states, and perhaps traditional cultures' own attempt at their interpretation.

I think this is important as well as interesting, because despite our modern and post-modern embarrassment, the spirit realm — and *whatever* we may mean by that — has spoken to humanity since before we had words to respond. That so many now live as though spirit didn't exist doesn't mean that spirit isn't still talking to us. If we don't again raise spirit to consciousness, then we have no discernment regarding this bug in our ear, loudly buzzing. (Also, I believe this to be important because caves may not only be our heritage but also our inheritance; if not literally, then quite possibly near enough.)

The German soldiers in Afghanistan who desecrated human remains by securing a skull on their vehicle's towing winch, and the one who held it next to his penis for a trophy photograph — is this learned behavior? The ritualized pederasty found around the world, from ancient times to the present — how have disparate cultures come to the same religious sex practice? These are deeply buried things that are rarely brought to consciousness. Which is why I believe characters like Gilles de Rais and Elizabeth Bathory merit some attention, and why art has attributes that may inform us more about our predicament than plodding Reason.

> *Nobody knows what's coming down,*
> *but it's coming down.*
> — T-Bone Burnett

Getting back, in a roundabout way, to this and the walls of our cave, I've been thinking of eyelash mites. Familiar with them? They're familiar with us. They're burrowed head-down in our pores, gripping our follicles with their tiny claws, binging on oil and dead skin cells. Untold generations have known nothing but our noses, brows and eyelashes, where they're as good as top of the food chain. But even when we know they're there, we don't have cause to think much about it.

They're familiar with us — they live on us, in every sense — but they don't *know* us. How could they? Even if they were raised to self-awareness and could comprehend their immediate circumstance and of what their world consisted, they would still lack our imperfect frame of reference. They wouldn't know what we know, let alone what we don't know. And how much don't we know?

I've always found it difficult to conceive that a third of the static on a television set tuned to an unallocated channel is cosmic radiation. I mean, *it's in my home*. How can something so familiar do something so incredible? I know TVs, radios and other electronic devices pick up "stray electromagnetic waves," but it doesn't seem right somehow that the same instrument on which I can watch another *Seinfeld* rerun also presents the decaying of photons from our universe's roiling moment of creation.

Remember the Scole Experiment? Grant and Jane Solomon's book includes testimony from Scole witness Dr. Ernst Senkowsky, who writes:

> Throughout history, "mediums" in "trance" states have expressed "transinformation" and performed "transcommunication" through speech or automatic writing. Since the 1950s, all types of electronic apparatus (audio-tapes, video tapes, radios, telephones, TVs, computers) have been used in this field. Each piece of apparatus constitutes the final link in a hypothetical translation chain. They delivered messages from no-where into now-here and allowed dialogues with otherwise hidden "virtual transpartners" or "communicators."

Anyone slightly curious about the Scole material will likely already be familiar with EVP, "Electronic Voice Phenomenon, " and have heard some of the recorded samples here. Some see, in the video experiments, little people akin to Terrence McKenna's "self-transforming machine elves" of DMT.

From last year's post about Scole:

> The video experiments began in May 1997, and were dubbed "Project Alice" because they involved an arrangement of mirrors before a camera "to capture moving images sent from the spirit world," write the Solomons. (Mirrors have long been used as an aid to receiving visions from other realms. John Dee's obsidian mirror, used by his scryer Edward Kelly in his Enochian work, is on display in the British Museum.)
>
> For most of the experiments, the camera sat on its tripod in the dark positioned before two mirrors. At the end of the sessions the team often saw that the camera had repeatedly and impossibly zoomed in and out

on its own accord, and the tapes contained weird scenes, smiling faces, vibrant colors and hints of body parts moving across the screen in a red light. One tape showed a pink and gold line running horizontally down the screen, which pivoted to reveal it was a square shape on edge. As it rotated, it was seen to contain an image. According to the Scole team, "this was a very clear view of an animated inter-dimensional friend, whose features, to say the least, were not exactly as our own." They called their new friend "Blue." His screen capture is the classic "grey alien" on the top left of this post. The pyramids on the right are from another spirit transmission, presumably some etheric vista.

The Scole group's Robin Foy tells the Solomons that "some of the researchers within the transcommunication network say they are regularly receiving messages from the spirit world via their telephones, computers and fax machines," and speculates about the possibility of an "interdimensional Internet": "computers are based on semi-conductors and the spirit scientists [at Scole, experiments were made on "both sides" to facilitate communication] often told us that these semi-conductors, like germanium and silicon, have important properties that allow the bridges between dimensions to be crossed."

Our cave walls are now flat screens, and perhaps not everything that appears on them can be accounted for by our own hands and imagination. That is not to assume they are also portals for "departed spirits," which is the claim of the disincarnate intelligences (if that is what they are). Perhaps something else is going on.

UFOs are also an electromagnetic phenomenon, though of a much higher order of strangeness than our television sets. But what should we make of the congruities between the wiring of our societies and the explosive flaps of "flying saucers" and "alien" sightings? Compounding the mystery Dr. Kenneth Ring, in *The Omega Project*, has tabulated an inclination towards "Electrical Sensitivity Syndrome" in subjects who have had either a UFO encounter or a Near-Death Experience. Nearly half of the former and a quarter of the latter agreed with the statement, "I found that electric or electronic devices more often malfunctioned in my presence than I remember being the case before." (Only a fraction of control groups agreed.) A 53-year old radio station manager named Hazel Underwood told Ring that "after the [UFO] 'incident' I was able to literally 'cut off' a 1,000 watt radio transmitter." A 43-year old administrator with a history of abduction experiences said "I am extremely sensitive to high frequencies.... I have continual problems with cars and the electrical systems (like trunk releases automatically popping open, radios full of static...electronic anomalies within the home."

A 36-year old woman, a survivor of a Near Death Experience, wrote,

> Dr. Ring, I have a difficult time as many computers malfunction and lights will blow out when I walk under them. This has happened for years, and I tried to ignore that this was happening. I simply cannot wear a watch for long before it breaks down. I went to...a department store and walked in front of their brand new computer and it quit working. When I held up a fluorescent light bulb in my hands the entire bulb lit up, like it was turned on. It seemed like there was a lot of static electricity.

Alleged entities advising the use of electronic devices as gateways; the electromagnetic effects of close encounters; Electrical Sensitivity Syndrome in both UFO contactees and Near Death survivors: what frame of reference do we have to account for all this, and can it be possible to find one that does from our mundane perspective?

Which reminds me of eyelash mites, and this perspective shift:

> Bed mites have one mission and one mission only, they are intent on eating you alive every single night that you crawl into bed to go to sleep. And their plan is foiled every single morning when your alarm wakes you up because God, in his infinite wisdom, cursed them with mouths too small to feasibly consume all of you in an eight-hour period.
>
> But don't believe for a second that they aren't trying. Because they are.

"When twilight dims the sky above"

November 21, 2006

Where it intersects the space at hand, this shaman with the hoops stands
Aligned like living magnetic needle between deep past and looming future.
— Bruce Cockburn

Since I began to regard "High Weirdness" and associated UFO phenomenon with new eyes — which means ever since I discovered Jacques Vallee, and digested the first volume of Richard Dolan's UFO's and the National Security State — I've wondered about Brazil.

Around the world, numinous moments of contact with an "alien Other" may provoke inspiration or dread, but almost never do they occasion the injury or death of the contactee. Bizarre entities may threaten, but there's also often an unaccountable futility to their threat. The Hopkinsville siege, for instance, which followed upon a UFO sighting, where clawed, bug-eyed creatures seemingly impervious to gunfire spent a night repeatedly approaching a farmhouse and terrifying the family within, yet were unable or unwilling to broach the feeble doors or windows. Donald Schrum's similar experience nine years later in California, though hounded by very different entities after witnessing an apparent UFO land nearby while on a hunting trip. Schrum spent a night in a tree fending off three strange, awkward figures by tearing off strips of his clothing, setting them on fire and throwing the smoking remnants down upon them. The "men in black," "phantom clowns" and "phantom social workers" which make great demonstrations of intimidation and menace while also showing an inability to make good on it. When injury does occur to a contactee, as it did to Betty Cash of the Cash-Landrum encounter, the injuries are usually incidental and not with intent.

Brazil is different. In Brazil, UFOs maim and kill with purpose and intelligence. Do you remember the "chupas," refrigerator-sized barrels or boxes skimming roofs and treetops, shooting concentrated beams of radiation at hunters and villagers? Vallee has traveled to the region and interviewed survivors and witnesses. One doctor he spoke to had seen no fewer than 35 patients, all telling the same story of being struck by beams of intense white light and exhibiting similar burns and symptoms of dizziness, headaches, numbness and anemia. Vallee writes in *Confrontations* that:

> Nobody has ever ridiculed these people. Their intelligence has never been insulted by the pundits of the *New York Times* or the arbiters of rationalism of *Le Monde*. They speak in simple, direct ways about what they saw. The admit to being scared, and when they speak about illness and death it is in the same calm, even voice with which one speaks about the reality of all the mysteries around us.

In the same book Vallee tabulates claims of UFO-related deaths, and excluding those that can be deemed accidental, every individual fatality is Brazilian.

Former skeptic turned UfOlogist Bob Pratt, who died a year ago today, spent the last 25 years of his life investigating the subject. His investigations often led him to Brazil. (Some of Pratt's original research may be read online). Brent Raynes records part of a conversation with Pratt in his book *Visitors from Hidden Realms*:

> What intrigues me more than anything else is that some UFOs in Brazil have been very aggressive, perhaps even hostile. They have terrorized many people, they have injured more than just a few, and they have left others dying.
>
> Nearly every case in my book UFO Danger Zone shows the harrowing effect an encounter can have in Brazil. They include injuries, deaths, levitations, attempted levitations, and people being zapped by beams of light from UFOs. And there is nearly always terror.... Sometimes people weren't safe even in their own homes because beams of light from UFOs would pierce tile roofs as if they didn't exist, and burn someone inside.

In 1981 Pratt saw the wounds of Claudiomira Rodrigues, who told him that three years before she was awakened by a beam of light shining through her window. Raynes notes that "Outside she could see, from the chest up, what looked like a man in a diving suit, but his eyes seemed unusually small. She said he had an instrument that resembled a pistol. Aiming it in her direction it shot a beam three separate times.... [leaving] three small pinpoint scars in a triangular pattern on the upper right side of her chest."

So what are we witnessing here? Is the discrepancy between the manifestations of UFO phenomenon in Brazil and elsewhere a socio-cultural artifact, or could something else account for it? Answering that question may go some way towards answering the more fundamental questions about the nature of the phenomenon.

And here's something that may inform our inquiry:

What is the South Atlantic Anomaly?

The Earth is surrounded by a pair of concentric donut-shaped clouds called the Van Allen radiation belts which, like magnetic bottles, store and trap charged particles from the solar wind. They are aligned with the magnetic axis of the Earth, which is tilted by 11 degrees from the rotation axis of the Earth, and are not symmetrically placed with respect to the Earth's surface. Although the inner surface is 1200 — 1300 kilometers from the Earth's surface on one side of the Earth, on the other they dip down to 200 — 800 kilometers. Above South America, about 200 — 300 kilometers off the coast of Brazil, and extending over much of South America, the nearby portion of the Van Allen Belt forms what is called the South Atlantic Anomaly. Satellites and other spacecraft passing through this region of space actually enter the Van Allen radiation belt and are bombarded by protons exceeding energies of 10 million electron volts at a rate of 3000 'hits' per square centimeter per second. This can produce 'glitches' in astronomical data, problems with the operation of on-board electronic systems, and premature aging of computer, detector and other spacecraft components.

More here on the effects of the Anomaly:

Random glitches affect humans as well. Since the days of Apollo 11, astronauts in space have reported seeing random flashes of light — with their eyes closed. These flashes are believed to be caused by energetic particles striking sensitive areas of the retina. In a recent experiment, astronauts aboard the Mir wore detector helmets to help researchers correlate the number of reported flashes with the measured particle flux. If the flashes increased when Mir entered the South Atlantic Anomaly, then protons would be revealed as the likely cause; if not, then heavy ions (which appear in equal amounts inside and outside the proton belt) would be indicated. The frequency of the flashes increased in the Anomaly, but only slightly, suggesting that protons alone are not responsible, but neither are heavy ions.

So it seems that the South Atlantic Anomaly may well have a few more surprises in store.

Credible UFO reports frequently mention the demonstration of highly electro-magnetic properties. ("The radar displays went completely blank and the gyro was spinning very rapidly, as if a strong magnetic force was present," Raynes quotes retired Admiral Jorge Martinez, former Chilean Chief of Naval Operations, regarding one instance in which he'd witnessed a UFO emerge from the ocean.) Could Brazil's anomalous UFO encounters be accounted for by the coincident anomaly in the Earth's geomagnetic field? Could the unique hostility they exhibit in the country be attributed to the relative concentration of radiation over the region? In which case, elsewhere, their aggression might somehow be held in check by more efficient geo-magnetism.

UFOs, we've noted previously, are also very common images to Amazonian ayahuasca ceremonies. Perhaps unsurprising, because we, as well, are electromagnetic; even biophotonic. So perhaps when we approach an answer to the UFO phenomenon, we'll approach an answer to that of our own.

"Do You See What I See?"

December 14, 2006

If a space ship touched down
In my yard I would run
Right towards it, yelling,
"Greetings, let's go have some fun!"
— Arthur's Songbook

On the evening of September 27 in the village of Premanon during France's seriously weird year of 1954, a 12-year old named Raymond Romand stepped out of his farmhouse and immediately saw in the yard an apparent humanoid entity "as tall as a door, and shiny, like a wardrobe with a mirror."

It approached Raymond and gently touched him, and he fell to the ground terrified. His nine-year old sister Janine and two other children, who had followed him outside to play, now saw it too. The entity moved away, and Raymond, encouraged by the presence of others, began throwing stones as it left. One sounded as though it struck something metallic. The entity left the yard for a downhill pasture, where the children observed it enter an object they described as a "ball of fire," which soon ascended into the sky.

The children knew their parents and their community well enough to realize this was something best kept to themselves. But the next day at school Raymond told a friend, who told others. When it was overheard by a teacher she called the police. At the spot of the "ball of fire," officers from Saint Claude and Les Rousses found four triangular indentations in the ground and a clearly defined area of compression 12-feet in diameter with grass heavily flattened, like a pinwheel, in a counterclockwise fashion. "In addition," Jacques Vallee writes in *Challenge to Science*, "a pole fence had been grazed and the bark of a pine tree was scorched five feet above the ground."

But to me, the most interesting aspect of the story is the reaction of Raymond's mother:

> Throughout this investigation, Mrs. Romand displayed a very strange attitude. She seemed deeply shocked by the whole affair and reluctant to let the interview take place. She refused to believe that Raymond might have seen something. A very pious, devout woman, she stated plainly that "flying saucers" and "Martians" could not exist and that she would rather believe that an evil spirit, or the Devil himself, was prompting her son to lie.... A newspaper reporter who went to Premanon and spoke to the woman remarked that her home was probably one of the few places in France where the subject of "flying saucers" had never been discussed at the dinner table. The children themselves never used the term "saucer" or "Martian." They said and repeated that they had seen a "ghost." The idea of a "flying saucer" was started by the adults in Premanon.

To Mrs. Romand it became of paramount importance, both for her family's reputation in the community and her until here were unchallenged assumptions of the way things were, that her son must have made the whole thing up. Think about that for a moment, and you may see what a common response it is to information that transgresses our base-beliefs. Sometimes, the consequences of admitting certain realities are thought to be so grave, we would rather believe a loved one a lunatic or a liar for testifying to them.

But Raymond and the children didn't change their story. Tthey had seen, what they had seen, and the best reference they had for it was not the "flying saucers" of adults' presumptions but rather vaguely (and so perhaps most accurately), a "ghost." Raymond was punished for his resistance to admitting a lie, and was confined to the house until the episode was behind them and normalcy restored.

Edward Ruppelt, director of Project Blue Book, came to respect the ineffability of the UFO phenomenon, yet he also said "next to the 'insufficient data' file was a file marked 'C.P.' This meant crackpot. Into this file went all reports from people who had... inspected flying saucers that had landed in the United States." To this, Vallee remarks that if "we do not refuse to study the UFO as an aerial object, we cannot logically refuse to study it when it has reported to have landed." Furthermore, "we cannot dispose of the sightings made by pilots, customs officers, and railroad engineers, people who are not prone to go berserk, by saying that they have 'merely' had hallucinations or invented a science fiction story."

We all have our meta-narratives about Life, the Universe and Everything by which we interpret events and perceive trends. We need them if we aspire to critical thought, but we also ought to be conscious of them and of what they represent: they're the mental scaffolding which supports our modeling of the world, they are not the world itself. And so they need to be flexible, and we need to be humble enough to reconfigure them when necessary according to new evidence and fresh insight. If not, we can find ourselves in rabbit holes of our own making that resemble nothing so much as *The Princess Bride*'s battle of wits. (*"Truly you have a dizzying intellect." "Wait 'til I get going!"*)

With respect to UFOs, it's a fairly common parapolitical conceit to subsume the entire phenomenon to mind control, and relegate everything that doesn't fit, Ruppelt-like, to the crackpot file. Such absolutism regards the paranormal as a competing and even threatening meta-narrative: if UFOs and "aliens" have been hoaxed and employed as screen memories, then that's regarded as the depth of their reality. No further investigation is required nor considered beneficial.

The Litvinenko story provides an interesting example of competing meta-narratives. The current Kremlin line is that the former spy was not assassinated, but rather unintentionally poisoned by polonium-210 he was peddling to al Qaeda, for use as the trigger for a nuclear bomb. It's fascinating to watch this digested by some in the West who, if told a similar tale by the White House, would probably respond *How gullible do they think we are?* Polonium makes an unlikely choice of poison, unless the assassination was also a myth-making exercise to suggest the Chechens had the bomb. In any regard, answering the rhetorical *Cui bono?* is not so easy, unless you want to be a Wallace Shawn about it.

Senator Tim Johnson's critical illness is another. Could it be an assassination attempt? Naturally; it always could be. But let's keep our hypotheses in an open hand, and not a balled fist, especially at this early date. Otherwise our theorizing can lapse into soap opera every bit as unreal, though with the appearance of reality, as "Lonelygirl15"'s flight from a Thelema-like cult. (Besides, Johnson's no Paul Wellstone, whom Dick Cheney threatened with "severe ramifications" for voting against the war. And to think the Republicans need another body in order to control the agenda, is to mistake parties for partisanship and the Washington consensus for representative democracy.)

And regarding 9/11, "inside job" for some means making the hijackers disappear altogether, so Daniel Hopsicker's ongoing investigation into Mohamed Atta's deep political *demimonde* will be dismissed as a "distraction," "disinfo," or a threat best disregarded. Their mental scaffolding has become a fetish, and is incapable of innovation or correction.

We need nimble minds about this stuff, and to always be ready to erect new scaffolding when the old no longer serves us well. When we see a ghost, perhaps we ought to say we've seen one, even if we don't believe in them.

12. Paging Mr. Badthing

Call it intuition, call it a creeping suspicion.

— Nick Cave

No Guru, No Method, No Teacher

February 28, 2007

> *Thanks for the information: "Never give a sucker an even break"*
> *When he's breaking through to a new level of consciousness.*
> *There always seems to be more obstacles in the way.*
>
> — Van Morrison

How to "Question Authority," when it's Authority telling us how to question it?

The year 1956 saw the launch of the first "Disclosure Project," a model for those that followed. The National Investigations Committee on Aerial Phenomena, or NICAP, was a civilian lobby group which called for an end to the U.S. Air Force's embargo on its UFO data. By the mid-50s America already had a number of UFO organizations, but NICAP was to become the largest, and most aggressively dedicated to ending official secrecy.

For an organization with such an outré mandate, and supposed civilian composition, it boasted a lot of heavy brass. As Richard Dolan details in his *UFOs and the National Security State*, three U.S. admirals sat on NICAP's first board: Rear Admiral Delmar Fahrney, former head of the Navy's guided missile program; Vice Admiral Roscoe Hillenkoetter, first director of the CIA; and Rear-Admiral HB Knowles. Another early board member was Bernard Carvalho, who soon headed up its membership committee. Researcher Philip Coppens notes that Carvalho "was often used as the go-between for private companies owned or run by the CIA, such as Fairway Corporation, an airline company used by the heads of the CIA." If all that wasn't spooky enough, NICAP's first Vice-Chairman was White Russian émigré Count Nicolas de Rochefort who incidentally, and unknown to earnest Chair Donald Keyhoe, served as a member of the CIA's psychological warfare staff.

At the Agency, Rochefort answered to Colonel Joseph Bryan. In late 1959 Bryan, representing himself only as an Air Force officer, approached Keyhoe and asked to see his "really hot cases." Keyhoe, on his guard, refused. Bryan then made a series of public statements about the off-world aspects of the phenomenon, criticizing official secrecy. Keyhoe was finally put at ease, and Bryan too joined the board.

Now, what do you think became of NICAP, and the state of American UFOlogy, for having all these impressive insiders "onboard"?

In 1962 NICAP was at its most popular, and appeared close to surprising success. "In February," Dolan writes, "a plan was germinating among congressmen to end UFO secrecy using a statement by Roscoe Hillenkoetter, by far NICAP's most prestigious member." Keyhoe was instrumental in mapping a strategy with sympathetic congressmen for opening the government's records, and it was understood Hillenkoetter's reputation was the key to getting a serious hearing on the floor. Before Keyhoe could visit the Vice Admiral to plan their next steps, Hillenkoetter announced his resignation from NICAP, stating that he had no intention of proceeding with either an investigation or a statement to Congress, and that the Air Force was "doing all it could" with respect to UFOs. The organization, and Keyhoe, took a huge credibility hit from which neither would ever recover.

By the end of the decade, Bryan had engineered Keyhoe's dismissal and replacement by an outsider named John Acuff, who had formerly served as executive director of the intel-connected Society of Photographic Scientists and Engineers (SPSE). Acuff's management, says Dolan, was either wholly inept or deliberate sabotage: he ended Keyhoe's subcommittee system, told regional members to operate independently and discouraged cooperation, declared all data to be NICAP proprietary knowledge, which could not be freely disseminated, and criticism of government UFO policy was no longer permitted. Acuff was succeeded by Alan Hall, a "former CIA covert employee for 30 years," as noted in 1979 by *The New York Times Magazine*. NICAP, which Nick Redfern in his *On the Trail of the Saucer Spies* calls "the one organization more than any other that had caused major headaches for officials when it came to the UFO controversy," finally folded the following year. Redfern adds that "some would argue that the downfall of NICAP had been the ultimate intent of the CIA from the beginning," though Colonel Bryan's son contends that "my father's unswerving, outspoken faith in UFOs...was, I felt, something of an embarrassment.... I do not believe it was the sort of public position an agent would take whose covert goal was to smother interest in UFOs."

On the other hand, you can squeeze the life out of a thing if you embrace it hard enough.

I remember the giddy buzz a couple of years ago, when Morgan Reynolds became the first figure who could be called a "Bush insider" to step up as a "9/11 Truth" advocate, and not the most humble one at that. His splashy Web site and his speaking engagements quickly carried him to the forefront of the "movement's" second wave of leadership — which, unlike the first, is largely consumed by specu- lative issues of controlled demolition (Reynolds wrote that "WTC demolition is truth inviolate"). It was then that his theories became increasingly bizarre and his conduct particularly divisive and fractious. Now, the planes them- selves were hoaxes, and the build- ings demolished by "directed energy" beam weapons. Among those signing on to Reynolds' theories was David Shayler, "former MI5 agent turned whistleblower", who alleged last Sep- tember that "The only explanation is that they were missiles surrounded by holograms made to look like planes." (*The Sunday Times* smartly remarked, "are we sure this isn't an MI5 agent posing as Shayler in an attempt to discredit him?")

Bill Christison, a 29-year CIA Veteran and former director of the agency's Office of Regional and Political Analysis, has writ- ten that "An airliner almost certainly did not hit The Pentagon. Hard physical evidence supports this conclusion.... The North and South Towers of the World Trade Center almost certainly did not collapse and fall to earth because hijacked aircraft hit them.... These first two points provide the strongest evidence available that the 'official story' of 9/11 is not true." Retired Major General Al- bert Stubblebine, former director of the U.S. Army Intelligence and

Security Command and military patron of remote viewing, now says "I look at the hole in the Pentagon and I look at the size of an airplane that was supposed to have hit the Pentagon. And I said, 'The plane does not fit in that hole.' So what did hit the Pentagon? What hit it? Where is it? What's going on?" And Paul Craig Roberts, Assistant Secretary of the Treasury in the Reagan administration and former Associate Editor of the *Wall Street Journal*, writes "I will begin by stating what we know to be a solid incontrovertible scientific fact. We know that it is strictly impossible for any building, much less steel columned buildings, to 'pancake' at free fall speed. Therefore, it is a non-controversial fact that the official explanation of the collapse of the WTC buildings is false."

What credibility is lent Roberts for having served under Reagan, or for having been in *The National Review*'s radical right stable? ("In their hatred of 'the rich,'" Roberts has also written, "the left-wing overlooks that in the 20th century the rich were the class most persecuted by government. The class genocide [in communist societies] of the 20th century is the greatest genocide in history.") Before "9/11 Truth," Reynolds was calling for the rolling back of U.S. labor regulation, claiming that a minimum wage contributes to unemployment. To those who argue Left and Right are false dichotomies perhaps it doesn't matter, and such characters merely represent the Truth Movement's "Big Tent." But to those who see in 9/11's outline a brutish war of the wealthy few upon the world's many poor, perhaps it should matter a great deal.

Is it a sign of health that such figures have elbowed their way to the front? If he were still alive, we could ask Donald Keyhoe. What should we make of their laser-like focus upon Pentagon missile theory and demolition? Is it confirmation that the movement is on the right track, or that it's gone off the rails and is being led further afield? Why are none of them apparently interested in talking about, say, Norman Mineta's testimony before the 9/11 Commission ("Do the orders still stand?"), and its excision from the commission's video archive and published record? Why are insiders not to be trusted, and their authority rejected, until they begin telling us what some of us want to hear? Then, suddenly, they become guileless figures in the know who do again what they did before: lead us.

Is it the future yet?

March 24, 2005

Something tells me, maybe, yes? It must be hard to tell for those who had expected to live the Jetsons' life. *Where are my domestic robots? Where is my flying car?* But I don't think we'll be getting flying cars. Not *us*.

After a lull of, say, 30 years or so, things are suddenly coming at us too fast to process. Though processing, at this stage, should be nearly superfluous. We should recognize what is coming if we recall, say, 30 years ago, having heard such words as, *"If present trends continue, in 30 years ..."*

If you care for a glimpse of your Future, Imperfect, read three Terry Schiavo-free stories from the past few days:

WORRIES SWELLING OVER OIL SHORTAGE

In the space of a couple of hours last week, crude oil prices hit a record $56 a barrel, President Bush fretted publicly over world oil shortages and the Senate voted to open an Alaskan wildlife refuge to drilling.

...

When oil production stops rising to meet growing demand, it "will result in dramatically higher oil prices, which will cause protracted economic hardship in the United States and the world," a team of Energy Department consultants warned in a report last month.

"The challenge of oil peaking deserves immediate, serious attention if risks are to be fully understood and mitigation begun on a timely basis." [emphasis added]

OPEC SAYS IT'S LOST CONTROL OF OIL PRICES

OPEC ministers meeting in Iran Wednesday will be grappling with a problem they haven't confronted in the cartel's 45-year history. In the past, OPEC tried to cool overheated prices by pumping more when supplies got too tight. But most OPEC producers say they're already pumping as fast as they can. And despite the high cost of a barrel of crude, world demand shows no signs of slowing.

...

"OPEC has done all it can do." Qatar Oil Minister Abdullah al-Attiyah said. *"This is out of the control of OPEC."* [emphasis added]

OIL COULD GUSH TO $100

That's the view from analysts who may have considered that prospect a long shot just a few months ago. And to be sure, some still think that's a stretch from the current $55 level, short of a major disruption like a terrorist attack.

But momentum is gaining for a view that sees rising crude prices as more than a temporary spike due to speculation or terrorism fears. If that's true, New Yorkers can expect to be socked for items from gasoline and heating oil to rent and groceries.

"It [$100 oil] is totally realistic within a year or two," said Stephen Leeb, who tracks oil for his own investment firm.... "I don't think $100 is even a big deal," Leeb said. His long-term projection? Try *$250 a barrel in six to nine years.* [emphasis added]

But wait: the price of a barrel of oil dipped below $55 dollars this week, so it can't be that bad. No; actually, it's worse. Because the price dropped on the strength of U.S. crude inventories, not on account of global production, which is destined only to fall. And anything that keeps energy consumers from confronting their inevitable powerdown is a very bad thing indeed.

Canada increased its proven oil reserves some 3,600 percent in 2003 by, for the first time, including the synthetic crude from Alberta's tar sands. Suddenly, Canada had 180 billion barrels of oil, the second largest on paper, after Saudi Arabia's own over-stated reserve. A good thing? No, and again, worsening a bad situation. Because the meaning of "cheap oil" is not principally found in the cost at the pump, but in the energy efficiency of the oil's extraction: the Energy Return on Invested Energy (EROIE). Cheap oil, at its cheapest, which we're well past, meant up to 100 times the energy returned on investment. In *The Party's Over*, Richard Heinberg quotes geologist Walter Youngquist on the tar sands, saying "it takes the equivalent of two out of each three barrels of oil recovered to pay for all the energy and other costs." Tar sands extraction, by any measure, is extremely costly, not least because extracting the oil requires massive amounts of fresh water. Within a few decades, we may find such a use for fresh water to be madly extravagant.

Peak Oil is real, and it's here, and it's bad. Mike Ruppert may say that's the end of the story. And he may be right. But I wonder if, *just maybe*, that's where it starts to get interesting. And I don't mean in a good way.

So, is that it, then?

If it is, then we ought to get to get acquainted with Easter Island.

Read *The Lorax* lately? That's the short history of Easter Island. To transport and erect their Moai — the huge figures carved from volcanic rock — the Polynesian *Oncelers* deforested their tiny, remote home of its palm trees, which held together the fragile soil and provided shelter for 25 species of nesting seabirds. They'd arrived on the island around 900 A.D.; just 600 years later agriculture was failing, poultry was off the menu, cannibalism was introduced, and there was no wood left to build boats with which to escape. By 1872, the population had fallen to just 111, from approximately 20,000.

In this February interview, Linda Moulton Howe asks Dr. Jared Diamond, author of *Collapse: How Societies Choose to Fail or Succeed*, whether we face a global Easter Island event. He thinks the odds for catastrophe are auspicious:

DIAMOND: In the past, societies that had not many people and with rather simple technology still managed to destroy their environments. For example, Easter Island with maybe 20,000 people with just stone and wooden tools they did manage to deforest the island and so doing, they destroyed their society. It took them 850 years to do it. Today, though, (on the Earth), we don't have 20,000 people. We have 6.5 billion and we have bulldozers and nuclear power, so we're far more people and far more potent and destructive technology. We can destroy our environment much faster than the Easter Islanders. In fact, there are many parts of the world that have gotten de-forested within half a dozen years, or within a few decades. That's what makes our present situation serious.

HOWE: Why do you think that global warming and all of the potential consequences does not rise globally above politics and become a world priority to solve because it will affect everyone?

> DIAMOND: It's a problem of what is called *"creeping normalcy."* It's not something that exploded like the Pinatubo Volcano in the Philippines, nor like September 11, 2001. Instead, the temperatures get a little warmer and then a little colder and then warmer and then colder. It's been gradually creeping along and there hasn't been a moment in which someone said, "My God, it's 10 degrees warmer this year. We've got to start doing something."

That's the reason why it has taken 30 years for essentially every knowledgeable climatologist to agree that global warming is a serious problem, and that people are the cause of it. It's also why it's taken 30 years to get all, except the last two governments, to agree about its importance.

The "cheap oil" of the Easter Islanders was their wood. It made possible transportation and industry, and its disappearance had unexpected and dire consequences across the culture, and drove it to extinction. If that's all we have — *if no powers have made provisions for what's to come next* — then the lights are going out on global civilization.

Quite possible. And given what we have before our eyes much of the time, most probable. But I wonder about what's behind some eyes, and also about what we're permitted to see some of the time. And it's not wishful thinking.

"A science-fiction world"

In a July 2001 interview, Bob Dylan said "We are living in a science-fiction world where Disney and Disney's science-fiction have won. This is the real world. Science-fiction has become the real world, whether we realize it or not."

And, *just maybe*, that world is becoming *Zardoz*.

Remember? Zardoz is the name of the flying stone god of the 23rd Century "Exterminators," who believe themselves to be the rulers of the world. One of their number — Sean Connery, in a red leather thong — catches a ride in the big head, and discovers Zardoz is just a techno-magickal device of social control for the world's true masters, a somewhat Luciferian sect of elites called the "Eternals." ("Zardoz," of course, proves to be a corruption of *The Wizard of Oz*, which, coincidentally, is frequently named by mind control survivors as a triggering device in Monarch programming.)

MSNBC made a case for the *Zardoz* scenario, with this report from last September:

"FLYING TRIANGLE" SIGHTINGS ON THE RISE

They have become legendary in UFO circles. Huge, silent-running "Flying Triangles" have been seen by ground observers creeping through the sky low and slow near cities, and quietly cruising over highways.

The National Institute for Discovery Science, or NIDS, has cataloged the Triangle sightings, sifting through and combining databases to take a hard look at the mystery craft. Based in Las Vegas, NIDS is a privately funded science institute with a strong research focusing on aerial phenomena. The results of their study have just been released, and lead to some *unnerving, puzzling conclusions.*

The study points out: "The United States is currently experiencing a wave of Flying Triangle sightings that may have intensified in the 1990s, especially towards the latter part of the 1990s. The wave continues. *The Flying Triangles are being openly deployed over and near population centers*, including in the vicinity of major interstate highways."

...

The NIDS study emphasizes that the flying of these vehicles may be *more in harmony with an attempt to display or to be noticed.* There appears to be little or no attempt to hide. That finding has led to a modification of an earlier NIDS hypothesis that the Triangles are covertly deployed Defense Department aircraft. [emphases added]

I know: "black triangles" could describe many conventional, or *near* conventional, aircraft developed by U.S. defense contractors. But these triangles are different: huge; silent; capable of sudden changes in speed and direction; able to hover and accelerate at seemingly impossible velocities.

And as the NIDS study finds, rather than a shielded black ops project, the pattern of sightings is more suggestive of *"an attempt to display or be noticed."* Then there are the vivid, flashing lights which, after reading this witness, makes me wonder whether they are intended, at some point, to have a *psychotropic* effect:

... size of object based in part on the hugeness of the strobing *"cop car gumball" banks of lights....* [It] looked like it was on a dreamy pleasure cruise ...very quiet ... just a low humming ... and *strobing bizarre red/clear/blue huge banks of lights. This thing was so psychedelic flashy,* I couldn't believe I was standing there alone watching it. I knew it was for real when I saw my dog looked up at it. [emphasis added]

Another funny thing about these black triangles: even though they've been seen by tens of thousands, intercepted by air force fighters, tracked on radar, photographed and videotaped, *it's intellectually suspect to mention them.* So they are excised from the realm of things that might matter, and consigned to Fortean novelty. "Black triangles" have become the "black helicopters" shorthand for the *au courant* debunker of the "paranoid style." Never mind that both are real.

From a Las Vegas television news report on "Top Secret Black Triangles":

[T]he airspace over Belgium was repeatedly violated by huge unidentified black triangles. Ten thousand witnesses saw them. Several were photographed. The Belgian Air Force dispatched F-16s to intercept and destroy the unknown intruders, but the triangles *performed maneuvers that seem virtually impossible.* [emphasis added]

Dr. Colm Kelleher said, "They launched on several occasions top of the line military aircraft against these things and they were left in the dust. One minute they're overhead, and the next they're over the horizon."

Here is a good resource for the remarkable 1989-1990 triangle "flap" over Belgium, and here is an account of how it started:

[T]he Belgian flap began in November of 1989. The events of November 29 would be documented by no less than thirty different groups of witnesses, and three separate groups of police officers. All of the reports related a large object flying at low altitude. The craft was of a flat, triangular shape, with lights underneath. This giant craft made not a sound as it slowly, fearlessly, moved across the landscape of Belgium. There was free sharing of information as the Belgian populace tracked this craft as it moved from the town of Liege to the border of the Netherlands and Germany. Two F-16s were ordered to intercept and identify this phenomena, and one of the jet's radars locked the object in. It appeared as a small diamond on the pilot's screen. *The pilot reported that only a few seconds after locking on the target, the object began to pick up speed, quickly moving out of radar range.* An hour-long chase ensued, during which time the F-16s picked up the strange craft's signal two additional times, only to see it fade from view. The triangular craft seemed to be playing a cat and mouse game, and finally was lost in the night lights of Brussels. *The pilots of the fighters reported that the UFO had made maneuvers at speeds beyond the capability of their technology, and once the radar showed the craft almost instantly drop from 10,000 to 500 feet in 5 seconds.* [emphases added]

Analysis of Belgian radar data from a March 30, 1990 sighting can be found on this page, and below is a graph of the triangle's performance. Altitude in thousands of feet is measured on the left, Heading (degrees) and speed (knots) on the right, and elapsed seconds on the bottom. The red line is altitude, the green heading, and the blue speed.

Here's an account from 1996 of six British troopers encountering a black triangle while on night moves. ("It really did my head in") For what it's worth, under hypnosis, a soldier recalled American forces acting in concert with it. ("Tell me what you can see now, Mark." "A Yank...") And reportedly, according to a "top BBC executive," British media has been silenced with a "D-Notice" on the subject of Black Triangles:

The executive, who cannot be named, is the former producer of a very popular BBC science programme. He told one of our team that the black triangle "craft," first witnessed by hundreds in the Hudson Valley region of the United States [(mid-1980's), then by thousands in Belgium (1989-90) and more in Britain], has been "heavily D-Noticed" by the Government. For this reason the BBC will not be reporting on the enigmatic craft, no matter how many witness reports they receive.

According to the former science programme producer, the reason the Government has seen fit to slap a restrictive notice on reporting of the Triangle is because -so far as the Government has secretly informed the BBC- the craft is part of a new secret military project, and as such must be protected under the secrecy laws.

If this is the case, however, it surely begs the question: *If the so called Black Triangle is a secrety military aircraft, then what is it doing hovering over residential areas and frightening people half to death? Something somewhere simply does not add up.* [emphasis added]

Another apparent "triangle" is the famous "Phoenix Lights" (which, despite the name, was viewed on a nearly 500 km course from Arizona to Nevada March 13, 1997). The lights were not discreet UFOs in formation, but arrays of lights about the edges of a single, black, wedge-shaped craft. Witnesses could discern the shape of a massive black craft as it occluded the stars overhead.

Six points regarding the Phoenix Lights from a press release of the National UFO Reporting Center, prepared by Peter B. Davenport:

1. Perhaps thousands, or tens of thousands, of witnesses on the ground witnessed at least one object pass and/or hover overhead which they described as being huge, gigantic, or unimaginably large. Many of the witnesses reported that they had the impression that *a Boeing 747 could land on the back of the object* they had just witnessed pass overhead their location.

2. Most witnesses described the object as being generally triangular in shape, with anywhere from five, to "many, innumerable," lights on the leading edge of the object. Some observers reported that the pattern of lights consisted of three lights clustered near the "nose" of the object, with one light on each of the trailing tips of the triangle. Other individuals reported an object that appeared to have seven large lights equally spaced along its leading edge.

3. *The object apparently was capable of very rapid flight*, probably even supersonic flight, although *few witnesses reported any sound emanating from it.* The object was reported heading generally to the southeast over Henderson, NV, at 1855 hrs. (Pacific), and was next reported heading to the south in the vicinity of Paulden, AZ, approximately 22 minutes later at 2017 hrs. (Mountain). Within approximately one minute of the sighting in Paulden, the object was reported from the vicinity of Prescott Valley, AZ, roughly 30 miles to the south. The object then appeared over Phoenix, where it is reported to have hovered for 4-5 minutes in the vicinity of the intersection of Indian School Road and 7th Avenue.

4. The object passed through the airspace of Sky Harbor Airport, where it was *witnessed by air traffic controllers* in the airport tower,

and where it also was *reported via radio by at least one commercial flight crew*. They reported via radio that the object was passing directly overhead their aircraft, which was on the ground preparing to depart Sky Harbor. The object reportedly did not appear on radar, and it did not communicate via either radio or transponder.

5. From the Phoenix area, the object reportedly proceeded generally south toward South Mountain, continuing southeast toward Tucson, AZ, along Interstate 10. One family, driving northwest toward Phoenix on Interstate 10 near Casa Grande, AZ, reported that the object remained above them for an estimated 1- 2 minutes while they were driving at approximately 80 miles per hour. *The object was so large above them that the family's two children in the back seat of their station wagon simultaneously could see the opposite "wing tips" of the object out both the left and right passenger windows.*

6. The National UFO Reporting Center received a telephone call approximately seven hours after the incident from a person who identified himself as an airman stationed at Luke Air Force Base, located 20 miles to the west of Phoenix. The individual reported that the U. S. Air Force had launched two F-15c fighter aircraft from Luke AFB, and that one of the aircraft had "intercepted" a gigantic object over the intersection of Indian School Road and 7th Avenue. It was also reported by this individual that the *onboard radar of the intercepting fighter had suddenly gone to a condition of "white noise,"* and that the lights on the anomalous object simultaneously had suddenly dimmed in unison and disappeared from the pilot's sight. [emphases added]

Eye in the sky?

So what'll it be: Easter Island, or *Zardoz*? Either way, a Dark Age, though the former comes without the sham sky-god of techno-magickal social controllers. So maybe we should hope for Easter Island. Maybe we should reconsign the black triangles to the realm of Fortean novelty, where they can exist, *sort of*, but not matter. Maybe that would be a less dark prospect, and we can try to squirrel away some wood while we can, to maybe carry us to another island someday.

To a practitioner of ritual magic, the triangle "is the area in which the spirit appears and is compelled to obedience," writes Lon Milo DuQuette in *The Illustrated Goetia of Aleister Crowley*.

"The almost infinite metaphysical virtues of a triangle make it a perfect device to confine and control that which has never been confined and controlled by you."

Should we survive what we'll need to survive, we may be alive to see either the end of our Moai culture, or the beginning of something worse, if our Immortals have been preparing, covertly, for a post-carbon world after all. But unless we start shouting now, and do more than shout, I doubt we'll have much say in the matter.

Be seeing you?

No time to think

May 30, 2005

The magician is quicker and his game is much thicker than
blood,
and blacker than ink.
And there's no time to think.
— Bob Dylan

Most people who give any thought to UFOs won't — and even self-described "UfOlogists" can't — devote the kind of energy and attention to the study of the phenomenon that it actually merits. As in many pursuits, there really isn't much money to be made on the serious end of things. (If you want to perpetrate hoaxes, create a new religion or dumb down the data for mass consumption, that's another matter.) There's no "UfOlogy" career path; it's an all-amateur effort, squeezed in around the edges of peoples' ordinary lives.

This puts the public at a huge disadvantage, because powerful forces have been at work for a long time to confuse and deceive us by manipulating the phenomenon. And some of these forces are even human.

As ever, the disinformation itself makes an important study, because it's as worthwhile to know what they want us to think as it is to know the truth. And there, beneath the official denials, are several layers of deception that mean to direct the public towards the presumption of extraterrestrial origin. I've written much on why I believe this is as unsatisfying to the data as swamp gas, and that we should be highly suspicious of the silence of the military-occult complex to the occult characteristics of the phenomenon. Those who suggest occult provenance are marginalized, even on the margins, as was Lord Hill-Norton, former UK Chief of Defense and a UFOlogist of high repute, who formed an organization in 1997 called UFO Concern to warn of their "Satanic nature."

The disinformation is chiefly divided between two main narratives. In one, the government is suppressing the healing technologies and spiritual teachings of benevolent space brothers, who mean only to save us. In the other, they mean to eat us. Elaborate castles in the air — or rather, enormous bases underground — have been constructed, in which humans and their Reptilian allies are said to sometimes conduct horrible genetic experiments, and other times battle each other in *Starship Trooper*-like shoot outs. For instance, the legend of the joint U.S.-alien Dulce base appears to have had its origin in the disinformation campaign waged against researcher Paul Bennewitz, and then — the hallmark of brilliant disinfo — to have taken on a life of its own, perpetuated by hoaxers and the credulous.

UfOlogist Bill Moore, author of the first books on Roswell and the Philadelphia Experiment, admitted to having been part of a U.S. Air Force disinformation campaign against Bennewitz, in return for access to classified material. Moore's main contact Richard Doty, who also "befriended" Bennewitz, was trained in disinfo and psychological warfare. The campaign was successful: it drove Bennewitz so paranoid that he had to be institutionalized for a time, and the disinfo which nearly drove him out of his mind is alive and well on the Internet. (The sad episode is well told in Greg Bishop's *Project Beta: The Story of Paul Bennewitz, National Security, and the Creation of a Modern UFO Myth.*)

And note: if there is no U.S.-alien base under Dulce that doesn't mean nothing weird is going on out there. In fact, the legend arose and took hold to explain the weirdness that remains unexplained, the cattle mutilations, for instance, which according to the disinformation were for genetic experiments. Yet one would think an advanced race of space travelers would have genetic technologies at least as advanced as ours, which would not require such gruesome and wasteful methods. Rather than for science, the mutilations appear to be more for ritual purposes. And for another instance, there's the matter of many sightings of UFOs around Dulce, some seen to actually penetrate the surface. Though no opening into the Earth was seen, one was presumed, and then an underground base is just one assumption away. But if UFOs are hyperdimensional, rather than extraterrestrial, we should expect them sometimes to pass unobstructed through solid matter, and there are many other examples of similar observations from around the world. (In "It's all in the egg" I wrote how Jane Chapin had initially lied to investigators, and told them that the object flew over the trees though she had seen it pass through them as though they didn't exist, because "I could see they wouldn't believe me if I told them the truth.") If the *genuine* phenomenon is hyperdimensional, there's no need to presume the objects need to access hidden doors and underground garages.

Also, there is a kind of disinformation which actually creates the events, and suggests *we ain't seen nothin' yet*. And let's keep an eye on"Prophet Yahweh.")

About four in the morning on November 26, 1979, in the French town of Pontoise, three friends in their mid-twenties named Franck Fontaine, Salomon N'Diaye El Mama and Jean-Pierre Prevost, were loading up an old station wagon with jeans and sweaters to sell at a market. Fontaine was startled by a luminous object, larger than the full moon, descending behind a nearby building. He pointed it out to his companions, and decided to get a closer look in his car.

Jacques Vallee, in **Revelations: Alien Contact and Human Deception**, tells what happened when Salomon and Jean-Pierre, who saw a large ball of fog engulf the car, approached it:

> The found the car on the right side of the road with its parking lights on. It was indeed surrounded with a large ball of whitish fog around which three or four smaller spheres were moving. These spheres entered the large ball, which itself was absorbed into a cylinder that flew off into the sky at a very high speed.

> Dumfounded in the face of the phenomenon, they were unable to react while the manifestations were taking place. Eventually they rushed toward the car. Franck had vanished.

The two, frantic, called the police, who arrived about 30 minutes later. (The first officer on the scene reported that Franck's car was surrounded with very thick fog, and a witness in a nearby apartment, suffering from insomnia, corroborated the story of bizarre luminescent displays at the time of Fontaine's disappearance.) Unsurprisingly, their story was not taken seriously, and under harsh interrogation were accused of perpetrating a hoax, and even of killing their friend. That is until exactly one week later, on December 3 at 4:20 am, when Salomon's doorbell rang.

Vallee again:

> When the bell rang in the apartment, Salomon got up in his pajamas, opened the door and confronted the man every cop in France had been hunting for the last seven days. Franck Fontaine was confused and angry. Why did Salomon go back to bed when they should already be on their way to the market? Where was Prevost? And what would they do about the car, which was missing? Obviously it had been stolen with everything it contained.
>
> Salomon started crying, hugged his friend, and told him everything was all right: the station wagon was in the parking lot, and a whole week had elapsed! Confused, Franck had to acknowledge that he had a beard of several days' growth.... He stared wordlessly out of the window while Salomon sprinted down the road to get Prevost.... They showed him the front-page headlines, which were printed about him in every newspaper in France.

Fontaine had no idea what had happened to him, though he began to remember drifting in and out of consciousness for a long time, lying in a laboratory on top of a machine. Along the walls were tall cabinets and blinking lights and dials, and signs in a language he couldn't read. Often, floating above him, were small luminous spheres, and he heard soft voices which seemed to emanate from the spheres, speaking to him about the perils of the Earth, and the projected date of their official contact with humanity.

Fontaine wanted to forget the whole affair and resume a normal life. He refused hypnosis, saying enough people already thought he was crazy. A hypnotist named Daniel Huguet, who may have been contracted by French intelligence, turned his attention to Prevost. Under hypnosis Prevost recalled having been contacted by an entity named Haurrio during Fontaine's absence, who told him that he should start a cult of UFO believers, to trust the extraterrestrials and save their own lives and spare the world. Haurrio said the group would be used as the kernel of a new civilization.

Prevost claimed to have been given a date, of August 15, 1980, when the extraterrestrials would being revealing themselves. Hundreds gathered near the site of Fontaine's abduction, and left disappointed. Three years later he was given another date, and still the aliens stood him up.

What was going on?

In *Revelations*, Vallee writes that the investigation led to the French military and technological establishment. An associate researcher of Vallee's got the story in a Parisian safe house on November 14, 1980, from a "Mr. D.," whose full name Vallee knows, who was on the staff of the Service Technique des Engines Tactiques at the French Ministry of Defense.

From the exchange:

"Will you tell me what the disappearance of Franck Fontaine was all about?"

"We refer to the operation as an Exercise of General Synthesis. A highly-placed personality has done detailed planning for it." [He mentioned the name of a cabinet member with vast connections to the world of high technology.]

"How many people were in the know?"

"No more than ten to fifteen, all at a high enough level to establish what sort of manipulation was justified under the state secrets rule."

"What were your objectives?"

"The operation was structured around military, scientific, and political goals. It was purely national and had no impact beyond our borders."

"What happened to Fontaine?"

"We put him to sleep and he was kept under an altered state of high suggestibility."

"Were you also using the media? Did you have wider objectives?"

"I cannot answer your question. But *if this operation had been completed, the next phase would have been far worse*."

"Why are you telling me all this?"

"I have my own reasons."

"Aren't you afraid I will publish this interview?"

"Anything you publish will simply be denied."

[emphasis added]

Vallee adds:

Franck's recollection of being inside some sort of laboratory, lying on top of a machine, and going in and out of consciousness for a week, is consistent with the idea that he spent that time in some secret service facility such as the "hospitals" where defectors and suspected spies are interrogated.... All the events that happened to Franck are well within the state of the art.

And I would add that Fontaine's laboratory is evocative of that described by survivors of trauma-based mind control.

This kind of disinformation is a very lengthy strip-tease of dry runs and beta testing. But for what purpose? What information was gleaned by the abduction of Fontaine, and Prevost's inducement to create a UFO cult? What would have been the "next phase," which would have been "far worse"?

Whatever the answer, someday the beta testing will be completed, and the real show will begin.

Take time to think. And don't take your eyes off the magician.

Space Cadets

January 9, 2006

An article last week in *The Scotsman* claimed an "extraordinary 'hyperspace' engine that could make interstellar space travel a reality by flying into other dimensions is being investigated by the United States government." The theory is to create an intense magnetic field that would provide gravitational thrust:

> Also, if a large enough magnetic field was created, *the craft would slip into a different dimension*, where the speed of light is faster, allowing incredible speeds to be reached. Switching off the magnetic field would result in the engine reappearing in our current dimension.
>
> The U.S. Air Force has expressed an interest in the idea and scientists working for the American Department of Energy — which has a device known as the Z Machine that could generate the kind of magnetic fields required to drive the engine — say they may carry out a test if the theory withstands further scrutiny.
>
> Professor Jochem Hauser, one of the scientists who put forward the idea, told *The Scotsman* that if everything went well a working engine could be tested in about five years.

Such an article can't help but make me think of Nick Cook's *The Hunt for Zero Point*. Cook's odyssey began at *Jane's Aviation Weekly*, when someone anonymously dropped a 1956 clipping on his desk with the headline "The G-Engines Are Coming." In many respects, the 50-year old article was not unlike that in last week's *Scotsman*: "in the United States and Canada, research centers, scientists, designers and engineers are perfecting a way to control gravity — a force infinitely more powerful than the mighty atom. The result of their labors will be antigravity engines working without fuel — weightless airliners and space ships able to travel at 170,000 miles per second."

The article from '56 states that the research is supported by the Glenn L Martin Aircraft Company, Bell Aircraft, Lear and several other U.S. firms. It quotes Lawrence Bell as saying they are "already working" on canceling out gravity. The head of Advanced Programs and VP in charge of the "G-Project" at Martin Aircraft, George S. Trimble, adds that manufacturing a gravitational field drive "could be done in about the time it took to build the first atom bomb."

Cook almost tossed it in the wastebasket, because almost as soon as such reports appeared in the mid-sixties it seemed as though they'd never existed. The research either never happened, was discontinued, or went deep black.

Cook, picking up the thread of a possibly deeply-guarded military-industrial secret, began by tracking down Trimble. He asked his media contact friend at Lockheed Martin, Daniella Abelman, to see if Trimble was still alive, and ask him if he'd be interested in an interview. Cook didn't tell Abelman why he wanted to talk. She called back soon after, and said that Trimble was alive and retired in Arizona. "Sounds hard as nails, but an amazing guy. He's kinda mystified why you want to talk to him after all this time, but seems okay with it. Like you said, it's historical, right?"

"Right," Cook said.

Abelman called back a few days later. "Separated by an ocean and five time zones," Cook writes, "I heard the catch in her breathing."

"It's Trimble," she said. "The guy just got off the phone to me. Remember how he was fine to do the interview? Well, something's happened. I don't know who this old man is or what he once was, but he told me in no uncertain terms to get off his case. He doesn't want to speak to me and he doesn't want to speak to you, not now, not ever. *I don't mind telling you that he sounded scared* and I don't like to hear old men scared. It makes me scared. I don't know what you were really working on when you came to me with this, Nick, but let me give you some advice. Stick to what you know about; stick to the damned present. It's better that way for all of us."

The familiar name of Hal Puthoff, formerly of Naval Intelligence and the NSA, then director of Stanford Research Institute's Remote Viewing program on behalf of the CIA and DIA, turns up midway through *The Hunt for Zero Point*. Puthoff has been doing theoretical work for NASA on the zero-point energy field since the early 1970s. (Before meeting, Cook had doubts he was acting wisely. "Did I really want to declare my interest in antigravity to a man who had clear connections to the intelligence community?") Cook probed him gingerly: Did Puthoff know of forms of aerospace travel, perhaps in the "black" world, whose principals contravened the laws of physics or our understanding of aerodynamics?

He sucked the top of his pen, giving the question a lot of thought before responding. "I've certainly talked to people who claim that something is going on," he said, pausing to add: "I would say the evidence is pretty solid."

When asked to choose which of five avenues proposed by NASA's Breakthrough Propulsion Physics program stood the greatest chance of success, Puthoff selected without hesitation the perturbation of space-time through antigravity.

Cook left the interview with the impression that Puthoff meant to indirectly communicate that tangible results had already been achieved. There is much more direct evidence in *The Hunt for Zero Point* to support such an assumption. And as Cook suggests, "if antigravity had been discovered in the white world, then someone, somewhere had to be perfecting it — maybe even building real hardware — in the black."

Was there an antigravity Manhattan Project about which now the general public is finally being fed the theory? I think it would be more astonishing if there wasn't. For one thing, there have been too many reliable sightings of discoid craft being piloted or repaired by seemingly ordinary men in military uniforms, and even baseball caps. (Though as I've made clear in other posts, I don't believe the relatively prosaic explanation of nuts and bolts black-budget craft can account for the genuine UFO phenomenon. If humans can already build craft capable of slipping into other dimensions, then the veil is exceedingly thin, and presumably may be crossed in the opposite direction.) And for another, it makes an awful sense. I suggested last March that our "Immortals" have been preparing — covertly, and for a long time — for a post-carbon world. One that may not include most of Earth's population.

If the G-Engines are coming, they've probably already arrived. And they're not meant for the likes of us.

Is that your final A.N.S.W.E.R.?

September 25, 2005

And he just walked along, alone, with his guilt so well concealed.
And muttered underneath his breath, "Nothing is revealed."
— Bob Dylan

Another march on Washington, and more grumbling about A.N.S.W.E.R.'s performance.

Much of the noise comes from embarrassed moderates, who are new to the demonstration game and are simply not that demonstrative. Others suggest A.N.S.W.E.R. engages in bait and switch: draw mass numbers with the cause of Iraq and then use the platform to catapult the propaganda, including wedge issues bound to alienate sizeable contingents of the crowd, and serves to categorize a generalized anti-war movement in terms of Stalinist caricature.

Now, I don't have a problem with radical politics. Those *are* my politics. And I do believe that mass events are good occasions to wisely shed light upon the interconnections of injustice. What I have a problem with is Ramsey Clark. I don't trust him. And so, I must have a problem with A.N.S.W.E.R. I don't trust it, either.

A.N.S.W.E.R., established by Clark's International Action Center, shows a national, organizational savvy in securing police permits and outclasses and outspends all popular opposition groups in America. (Though there's no transparency regarding the source of its funds.) While the Iraq War is its rallying cause, A.N.S.W.E.R. was founded, presciently, on September 14, 2001, even before the "War on Terror" was officially launched, even rhetorically.

Why don't I trust Clark? If LBJ's former Attorney General was ever going to win my trust, he would have repudiated his handpicked Clark Panel, its medical professionals linked to the intelligence community, and its findings a whitewash of John F. Kennedy's incomplete and adulterated autopsy records. He would have apologized to history and America's thwarted justice for stating just days after the murder of Dr. King, and even before a suspect was in custody, that "all of our evidence at this time indicates that it was a single person who committed this criminal act." Years later in *The Nation*, after his radical makeover, Clark said James Earl Ray should not be given a new trial, but rather his case ought to be studied by a government panel. As Lisa Pease asks in *The Assassinations*, "Did Clark really think the government, which produced the Warren Commission and the House Select Committee on Assassinations (HSCA) and failed to reveal the truth about either the Martin Luther King case or the Kennedy assassination, should have been given a chance to bamboozle us yet again?"

The American Left of Chomsky and Cockburn and *The Nation* will never touch these matters of conspiracy. So Clark is largely untouched by his legacy of abetting three of the most egregious miscarriages of modern justice — John, Martin and Bobby — which, uncorrected, have brought America to this point of low comedy and great horror.

If your intent is generational warfare, you had better give some forethought to stage managing your opposition. As you turn up the pressure, you need to ensure people can vent some steam. It makes them feel better. Like they've done something.

The Coincidence Theorist's Guide to 9/11

Sunday, August 15, 2004

Happy coincidenting!

That governments have permitted terrorist acts against their own people, and have even themselves been perpetrators in order to find strategic advantage is quite likely true, but this is the United States we're talking about.

That intelligence agencies, financiers, terrorists and narco-criminals have a long history together is well established, but the Nugan Hand Bank, BCCI, Banco Ambrosiano, the P2 Lodge, the CIA/Mafia anti-Castro/Kennedy alliance, Iran/Contra and the rest were a long time ago, so there's no need to rehash all that. That was then, this is now!

That Jonathan Bush's Riggs Bank has been found guilty of laundering terrorist funds and fined a US-record $25 million must embarrass his nephew George, but it's still no justification for leaping to paranoid conclusions.

That George Bush's brother Marvin sat on the board of the Kuwaiti-owned company which provided electronic security to the World Trade Center, Dulles Airport and United Airlines means nothing more than you must admit those Bush boys have done alright for themselves.

That George Bush found success as a businessman only after the investment of Osama's brother Salem and reputed al Qaeda financier Khalid bin Mahfouz is just one of those things - one of those crazy things.

That Osama bin Laden is known to have been an asset of US foreign policy in no way implies he still is.

That al Qaeda was active in the Balkan conflict, fighting on the same side as the US as recently as 1999, while the US protected its cells, is merely one of history's little aberrations.

The claims of Michael Springman, State Department veteran of the Jeddah visa bureau, that the CIA ran the office and issued visas to al Qaeda members so they could receive training in the United States, sound like the sour grapes of someone who was fired for making such wild accusations.

That one of George Bush's first acts as President, in January 2001, was to end the two-year deployment of attack submarines which were positioned within striking distance of al Qaeda's Afghanistan camps, even as the group's guilt for the Cole bombing was established, proves that a transition from one administration to the next is never an easy task.

That so many influential figures in and close to the Bush White House had expressed, just a year before the attacks, the need for a "new Pearl Harbor" before their militarist ambitions could be fulfilled, demonstrates nothing more than the accidental virtue of being in the right place at the right time.

That the company PTECH, founded by a Saudi financier placed on America's Terrorist Watch List in October 2001, had access to the FAA's entire computer system for two years before the 9/11 attack, means he must not have been such a threat after all.

That whistleblower Indira Singh was told to keep her mouth shut and forget what she learned when she took her concerns about PTECH to her employers and federal authorities, suggests she lacked the big picture. And that the Chief Auditor for JP Morgan Chase told Singh repeatedly, as she answered questions about who supplied her with what information, "that person should be killed," suggests he should take an anger management seminar.

That on May 8, 2001, Dick Cheney took upon himself the job of co-ordinating a response to domestic terror attacks even as he was crafting the administration's energy policy which bore implications for America's military, circumventing the established infrastructure and ignoring the recommendations of the Hart-Rudman report, merely shows the VP to be someone who finds it hard to delegate.

That the standing order which covered the shooting down of hijacked aircraft was altered on June 1, 2001, taking discretion away from field commanders and placing it solely in the hands of the Secretary of Defense, is simply poor planning and unfortunate timing. Fortunately the error has been corrected, as the order was rescinded shortly after 9/11.

That in the weeks before 9/11, FBI agent Colleen Rowley found her investigation of Zacarias Moussaoui so perversely thwarted, that her colleagues joked that bin Laden had a mole at the FBI, proves the stress-relieving virtue of humour in the workplace.

That Dave Frasca of the FBI's Radical Fundamentalist Unit received a promotion after quashing multiple, urgent requests for investigations into al Qaeda assets training at flight schools in the summer of 2001 does appear on the surface odd, but undoubtedly there's a good reason for it, quite possibly classified.

That FBI informant Randy Glass, working an undercover sting, was told by Pakistani intelligence operatives that the World Trade Center towers were coming down, and that his repeated warnings which continued until weeks before the attacks, including the mention of planes used as weapons, were ignored by federal authorities, is simply one of the many "What ifs" of that tragic day.

That over the summer of 2001 Washington received many urgent, senior-level warnings from foreign intelligence agencies and governments - including those of Germany, France, Great Britain, Russia, Egypt, Israel, Morocco, Afghanistan and others - of impending terror attacks using hijacked aircraft and did nothing, demonstrates the pressing need for a new Intelligence Czar.

That John Ashcroft stopped flying commercial aircraft in July 2001 on account of security considerations had nothing to do with warnings regarding September 11, because he said so to the 9/11 Commission.

That former Chief Investigative Counsel for the U.S. House Judiciary Committee David Schippers says he'd taken to John Ashcroft's office specific warnings he'd learned from FBI agents in New York of an impending attack – even naming the proposed dates, names of the hijackers and the targets – and that the investigations had been stymied and the agents threatened, proves nothing but David Schipper's pathetic need for attention.

That Garth Nicolson received two warnings from contacts in the intelligence community and one from a North African head of state, which included specific site, date and source of the attacks, and passed the information to the Defense Department and the National Security Council evidently with no effect, clearly amounts to nothing, since virtually nobody has ever heard of him.

That FBI Special Investigator Robert Wright claims that agents assigned to intelligence operations actually protect terrorists from investigation and prosecution, that the FBI shut down his probe into terrorist training camps, and he was removed from a money-laundering case with a direct link to terrorism, sounds like yet more sour grapes from a disgruntled employee.

That George Bush had plans to invade Afghanistan on his desk before 9/11 demonstrates only the value of being prepared.

The suggestion that securing a pipeline across Afghanistan figured into the White House's calculations is as ludicrous as the assertion that oil played a part in determining war in Iraq.

That Afghanistan is once again the world's principal heroin producer is an unfortunate reality, but to claim the CIA is still actively involved in the narcotics trade is to presume bad faith on the part of the agency.

Mahmood Ahmed, chief of Pakistan's ISI, must not have authorized an al Qaeda payment of $100,000 to Mohammed Atta days before the attacks, and was not meeting with senior Washington officials over the week of 9/11, because I didn't read anything about him in the official report.

That Porter Goss met with Ahmed the morning of September 11 in his capacity as Chairman of the House Permanent Select Committee on Intelligence has no bearing whatsoever upon his recent selection by the White House to head the Central Intelligence Agency.

That Goss's congressional seat encompasses the 9/11 hijackers' Florida base of operation, including their flight schools, is precisely the kind of meaningless factoid a conspiracy theorist would bring up.

It's true that George H.W. Bush and Dick Cheney spent the evening of September 10 alone in the Oval Office, but what's wrong with old colleagues catching up? It's also true that George HW Bush and Shafig bin Laden, Osama's brother, spent the morning of September 11 together at a board meeting of the Carlyle Group, but the bin Ladens are a big family.

That FEMA arrived in New York on Sept 10 to prepare for a scheduled biowarfare drill, and had a triage centre ready to go that was larger and better equipped than the one that was lost in the collapse of WTC 7, was a lucky twist of fate.

Newsweek's report that senior Pentagon officials cancelled flights on Sept 10 for the following day on account of security concerns is only newsworthy because of what happened the following morning.

That George Bush's telephone logs for September 11 do not exist should surprise no one, given the confusion of the day.

That Mohamed Atta attended the International Officer's School at Maxwell Air Force Base, that Abdulaziz Alomari attended Brooks Air Force Base Aerospace Medical School, that Saeed Alghamdi attended the Defense Language Institute in Monterey merely shows it is a small world, after all.

That Lt Col Steve Butler, Vice Chancellor for student affairs of the Defense Language Institute during Alghamdi's terms, was disciplined, removed from his post and threatened with court martial when he wrote "Bush knew of the impending attacks on America. He did nothing to warn the American people because he needed this war on terrorism. What is ... contemptible is the President of the United States not telling the American people what he knows for political gain," is the least that should have happened for such disrespect shown his Commander in Chief.

That Mohamed Atta dressed like a Mafioso, had a stripper girlfriend, smuggled drugs, was already a licensed pilot when he entered the US, enjoyed pork chops, drank to excess and did cocaine, was closer to Europeans than Arabs in Florida, and included the names of defense contractors on his email list, proves how wily the radical fundamentalist Muslim can be.

That 43 lbs of heroin was found on board the Lear Jet owned by Wally Hilliard, the owner of Atta's flight school, just three weeks after Atta enrolled — the biggest seizure ever in Central Florida — was just bad luck. That Hilliard was not charged shows how specious the claims for conspiracy truly are.

That Hilliard's plane had made 30 round trips to Venezuela with the same passengers who, always paid cash, that the plane had been supplied by a pair of drug smugglers who had also outfitted CIA drug runner Barry Seal, and that 9/11 commissioner Richard ben-Veniste had been Seal's attorney before Seal's murder, shows nothing but the lengths to which conspiracists will go to draw sinister conclusions.

Reports of insider trading on 9/11 are false, because the SEC investigated and found only respectable investors, who will remain nameless, and no terrorists, so the windfall profit-taking was merely, as ever, coincidental.

That heightened security for the World Trade Center was lifted immediately prior to the attacks illustrates that it always happens when you least expect it.

That Hani Hanjour, the "pilot" of Flight 77, was so incompetent he could not fly a Cessna in August, but in September managed to fly a 767 at excessive speed into a spiraling, 270-degree descent and a level impact of the first floor of the Pentagon, on the only side that was virtually empty and had been hardened to withstand a terrorist attack, merely demonstrates that people can do almost anything once they set their minds to it.

That none of the flight data recorders were said to be recoverable even though they were located in the tail sections, and that until 9/11, no solid-state recorder in a catastrophic crash had been unrecoverable, shows how there's a first time for everything.

That Mohamed Atta left a uniform, a will, a Koran, his driver's license and a "how to fly planes" video in his rental car at the airport means he had other things on his mind.

The mention of Israelis with links to military intelligence having been arrested on Sept. 11 videotaping and celebrating the attacks, of an Israeli espionage ring surveilling DEA and defense installations and trailing the hijackers, and of a warning of impending attacks delivered to the Israeli company Odigo two hours before the first plane hit, does not deserve a response. That the stories also appeared in publications such as Ha'aretz and Forward is a sad display of self-hatred among certain elements of the Israeli media.

That multiple military war-games and simulations were underway the morning of 9/11 – one simulating the crash of a plane into a building; another, a live-fly simulation of multiple hijackings, taking many interceptors away from the eastern seaboard and confusing field commanders as to which was a real hijacked aircraft and which was a hoax, was a bizarre coincidence, but no less a coincidence.

That the National Military Command Center ops director asked a rookie substitute to stand his watch at 8:30 am on Sept. 11 is nothing more than bad timing.

That a recording made Sept 11 of air traffic controllers describing what they had witnessed, was destroyed by an FAA official who crushed it in his hand, cut the tape into little pieces and dropped them in different trash cans around the building, is something no doubt that overzealous official wishes he could undo.

That the FBI knew precisely which Florida flight schools to descend upon hours after the attacks should make every American feel safer knowing their federal agents are on the ball.

That a former flight school executive believes the hijackers were "double agents," and says about Atta and associates, "Early on I gleaned that these guys had government protection. They were let into this country for a specific purpose," and was visited by the FBI just four hours after the attacks to intimidate him into silence, proves he's an unreliable witness, for the simple reason there is no conspiracy.

That Jeb Bush was on board an aircraft that removed flight school records to Washington in the middle of the night on Sept 12th demonstrates how seriously the governor takes the issue of national security.

To insinuate evil motive from the mercy flights of bin Laden family members and Saudi royals after 9/11 shows the sickness of the conspiratorial mindset.

Le Figaro's report in October 2001, known to have originated with French intelligence, that the CIA met Osama bin Laden in a Dubai hospital in July 2001, proves again the perfidy of the French.

That the tape in which bin Laden claims responsibility for the attacks was released by the State Department after having been found providentially by U.S. forces in Afghanistan, and depicts a fattened Osama with a broader face and a flatter nose, proves Osama, and Osama alone, masterminded 9/11.

That at the battle of Tora Bora, where bin Laden was surrounded on three sides, Special Forces received no order to advance and capture him and were forced to stand and watch as two Russian-made helicopters flew into the area where bin Laden was believed hiding, loaded up passengers and returned to Pakistan, demonstrates how confusing the modern battlefield can be.

That upon returning to Fort Bragg from Tora Bora, the same Special Operations troops who had been stood down from capturing bin Laden, suffered an unusual spree of murder/suicides, is nothing more than a series of senseless tragedies.

Reports that bin Laden is currently receiving periodic dialysis treatment in a Pakistani medical hospital are simply too incredible to be true.

That the White House went on the anthrax medicant Cipro September 11 shows the foresightedness of America's emergency response.

That the anthrax was mailed to perceived liberal media and the Democratic leadership demonstrates only the perversity of the terrorist psyche.

That the anthrax attacks appeared to silence opponents of the Patriot Act shows only that appearances can be deceiving.

That the Ames-strain anthrax was found to have originated at Fort Detrick, and was beyond the capability of all but a few labs to refine, underscores the importance of allowing the investigation to continue without the distraction of absurd conspiracy theories.

That the anthrax case is now closed following the timely overdose of the unindicted Dr Bruce Ivins means there's one less loose end for us to worry about.

That the FBI reportedly offered his son a $2.5 million dollar reward and "the sports car of his choice" if he would turn evidence against his father, demonstrates how certain they must have been that they had the right man.

That Republican guru Grover Norquist has been found to have aided financiers and supporters of Islamic terror to gain access to the Bush White House, and is a founder of the Islamic Institute, which the Treasury Department believes to be a source of funding for al Qaeda, suggests Norquist is either naive or needs a wider circle of friends.

That the Department of Justice consistently chooses to see accused 9/11 plotters go free, rather than permit the courtroom testimony of al Qaeda leaders in American custody looks bad, but only because we don't have all the facts.

That the White House balked at any inquiry into the events of 9/11, then starved it of funds and stonewalled it, was odd, but since the commission didn't find for conspiracy it's all a non-issue anyway.

That the 9/11 commission's executive director and "gate-keeper," Philip Zelikow, was so closely involved in the events under investigation that he testified before the the commission as part of the inquiry, shows only an apparent conflict of interest.

That commission chair Thomas Kean is, like George Bush, a Texas oil executive who had business dealings with reputed al Qaeda financier Khalid bin Mafouz, suggests Texas is smaller than they say it is.

That co-chair Lee Hamilton has a history as a Bush family "fixer," including clearing the elder Bush of the claims arising from the 1980 "October Surprise", is of no concern, since only conspiracists believe there was such a thing as an October Surprise.

That FBI whistleblower Sibel Edmonds accuses the agency of intentionally fudging specific pre-9/11 warnings and harboring a foreign espionage ring in its translation department, and claims she witnessed evidence of the semi-official infrastructure of money-laundering and narcotics trade behind the attacks, is of no account, since John Ashcroft has gagged her with the rare invocation of "State Secrets Privilege," and retroactively classified her public testimony. For the sake of national security, let us speak no more of her.

That, when commenting on Edmonds' case, Daniel Ellsberg remarked that Ashcroft could go to prison for his part in a cover-up, suggests Ellsberg is giving comfort to the terrorists, and could, if he doesn't wise up, find himself declared an enemy combatant.

That the 9/11 Commission dismissed any inquiry into the hijackers' financing with the single line that an answer to who bankrolled the attacks would be "of little practical significance" suggests they wanted to focus instead on what was really important.

That Norman Mineta has testified to Dick Cheney's presence in the Presidential Emergency Operations Center before the impact of Flight 77 (which doesn't accord with Cheney's own timeline), a Cheney aide asking as the plane was just 10 miles out "Do the orders still stand?" and the Vice President snapping back "Of course the orders still stand, have you heard anything to the contrary!?" could have referred to anything. After all, there was a lot going on.

That Mineta's testimony was omitted from the Commission's report means only that it was already a long enough book. That it was scrubbed from its video archives means it must not have been worth watching in the first place.

That George Bush agreed to testify before the Commission only in the company of Dick Cheney, without taking an oath, with no recording devices, and only one staffer permitted to take notes which were not to be made public, dispels the canard that you can't take him anywhere.

That Donald Rumsfeld called Flight 77 a "missile" within three days of the launch of the first website promoting the "Pentagon missile theory" misdirection is nothing more calculating than another "Rumsfeldism."

That just as skepticism of the official story began breaking into mainstream awareness, a former Bush administration official such as Morgan Reynolds and a former MI5 officer like David Shayler joined the movement and laid claims to lead it, asserting the radical theory that no planes whatsoever were used in the attacks, means nothing other than they're entitled to their opinion.

That the military intelligence unit known as Able Danger identified Mohammed Atta and other hijackers as al Qaeda assets as early as 1999 was a one in a million shot. That it then lost its funding was an unfortunate though unavoidable consequence of budgetary concerns.

That al Qaeda was a de facto ally of NATO in the Kosovo campaign shows that you can't always choose your friends.

That Kosovo has since become a critical transit hub into the West for Afghan heroin demonstrates the need to redouble our efforts at nation building.

That Daniel Pearl was lured to his death by Mohammad Atta's bagman and double agent Omar Saeed Sheikh while Pearl was investigating the relationship of al Qaeda to Pakistani intelligence, proves nothing more than the inherent dangers of travel abroad.

That Wolfgang Bohringer, one of Atta's closest associates in Florida and subject of an FBI terror alert after his intention to start a flying school in the South Pacific became known, was released from custody after telling authorities he worked for the CIA, doesn't mean he meant that CIA.

I could go on. And on and on. But I trust you get the point. Which is simply this: there are no secrets, an American government would never accept civilian casualties for geostrategic gain, and conspiracies are for the weak-minded and gullible.

That's that ...

13. All American Monster

They say, "Everything's all right."
They say, "Better days are near."
They tell us, "These are the good times."
They don't live around here.

— Warren Zevon

Bless the beasts and children

June 23, 2005

We shall see that at which dogs howl in the dark, and that at which cats prick up their ears after midnight.

— H.P. Lovecraft

For a while there, back in the 1980s, some extremely High and Outside news began intruding into mainstream consciousness: Satanic Ritual Abuse, crop circles, alien abduction and cattle mutilation became *newsworthy*. If permitted to continue as subjects for serious inquiry, consensus reality might have begun to groan under its contradictions, and for some there would have been Hell to pay.

It wasn't hard to spin the story — actually, spin the public — that there was nothing to see, and that those who saw *something* were fools or charlatans. Most people were happy to accept any reason not to take the reports seriously. What they most wanted to hear was the reassurance that the weirdness was "debunked," and the world really was as normal as their own experience of it.

So the "False Memory Foundation" was born in 1992, declaring a "syndrome" where one didn't exist, in order to lay to rest "Satanic Panic." Never mind that nearly half of the declassified files obtained by John Marks, author of *The Search for the Manchurian Candidate*, documented CIA interest in the occult, nor that the Foundation's Board was composed of scientists whom the CIA had contracted to conduct mind-control research.

And so, "Doug and Dave" appeared in 1991, claiming they had made all the crop circles in southern England since 1978, some 2,000, with planks and string. Though they were unable to recreate them for the media, or produce the anomalies associated with genuine circles, it didn't matter: To most people who had lifted their eyes for a moment out of the ordinary, they'd seen what they needed to stop paying attention: all circles had been debunked, because two pub crawlers had fessed up. Never mind that their story was traced "to a company in Somerset that carries out research on top secret military projects."

Alien abduction, typically of UFO material, was made to disappear in plain sight by being absorbed into the Military-Entertainment Complex. It was *"X-Files* stuff," and so not a serious subject. Accounts were ascribed to the faulty memories of hysterics. Never mind that not all memories were "recovered," and not all victims hysterical. And never mind the existence of credible, independent witnesses, physical evidence and corroborating phenomenon.

Not much effort was devoted to debunking cattle mutilation. The rural setting of the crimes made it easy to convince sophisticated city-dwellers — who never see a living cow let alone one mutilated — that it was all the work of natural predators, copycat punks or disease. Never mind that ranchers knew better, nor that it never went away.

Two weeks ago, Ray Riguidel found the mutilated carcass of a 10-year old cow in his pasture. One eye, one ear, its udder and sex organs were missing. There were no tracks or footprints. There was no blood.

"I've heard about it before, but it never really sunk in," Riguidel said. "But it's sunk in now. It's real."

George Larre, who lost a cow to a similar mutilation five years before, added, "If you haven't seen it, I wouldn't expect anyone to believe it. But if you really see one for yourself, and you understand what coyotes will do, you know it's not predators. Some people say it's from up above, and I don't know. I'm not going to say it is or it isn't. But when you see absolutely no clues and no reason, you really have to wonder."

A friend recommended that Riguidel call Fernand Belzil, a plain-speaking local rancher who has been investigating mutilations for eight years and makes modest claims for his findings. Belzil's interest in the phenomenon "snowballed" after visiting his first mutilation site, "and it's been one hell of a deal ever since. It kind of just opened up a can of worms." Belzil doesn't presume to know what's going on. As for UFOs, he says

"I guess I believe...but I'd sure like to see one first. We're naïve to believe we're alone in this universe, but I guess that's just my opinion."

Some samples of Belzil's research, drawn from his Web site:

June 6, 1999, near St Paul, Alberta

As you will see by the picture, half the nose area was cut out, one eyelid was removed, another one-inch deep cut about an inch long just below the left eye. The penis & scrotum were removed. The oval cut on the stomach was 16 by 12 inches and it looked like a surgical cut. The flesh where it had been skinned showed no signs of teeth marks or any other abnormality.... The rectum area was cut out in a triangle shape.... There was no blood anywhere.

June 15, 2002, Veteran, Alberta

A beef Hereford cow was found mutilated in a clump of trees lying on her back with the 4 legs sticking upward. I only have 2 other cases that were found on their back. This is a very strange case. The branches of the trees above her were broken. It appears to have been dropped there. The tongue was removed, the flesh on the jaws neatly incised, ear and eye also removed, and no blood. Notice the surgical incision of the neck area.

May 15, 2003, near Derwent, Alberta

I was called out to a farm about 35 miles south of St Paul, near a town called Derwent. There I was shown a 2-day-old male lamb that had been mutilated. It was found inside a corral that had a solid board, 4-foot high fence surrounding it to keep out predators.... There was a perfectly round incision found between the hind legs in the udder area, no teeth marks and no sign that a knife had been used. There were no burn marks on the skin in that area. The rectum was cut out. At the lower part of the rectum incision the tail had a neat V-shape cut (under part of the tail) that went back about 2 inches. Very odd. The intestines were taken out through the rectum and piled a foot and a half behind the lamb. Both eyes had been removed, the lower jaw had been broken and the right side of the skull appeared smashed.

Theories, as they usually do, abound, and generally conform to investigators' other presumptions.

Linda Moulton Howe has been studying cattle mutilations for nearly a quarter century. In 1980, before it became unthinkable to do so, and after Governor Richard Lamm of Colorado declared mutilations to be "one of the greatest outrages in the history of the western cattle industry," adding "it is no longer possible to blame predators for the mutilations," CBS aired her investigative documentary *Strange Harvest.* Howe's belief is that bovine tissue's similarity to that of humans offer aliens a means to relatively benignly sample the effects of environmental pollutants. (Howe has the courage to examine disreputable subjects, but too often I find her conclusions distressingly credulous.)

Budd Hopkins believes cow eggs are being harvested to serve as hosts for transgenic alien-human cloning. That much more than eggs are taken, that his advanced extraterrestrials should be expected to have developed a less wasteful and attention-getting methodology, and that more than cows are mutilated (as above, in Belzil's account of a two-day old lamb), don't seem to enter into his calculations, because he's already weighted the equation to come out "extraterrestrial."

My presumption, as usual, is towards an occult explanation. (Remember the calf mutilation associated with the murder of Father Alfred Kunz, who was exposing ritualized pedophilia in Wisconsin's Catholic Church, and the canine sacrifices of the Process Church.) Which isn't to say it's always *wholly* human. Because the phenomenon appears to fall in a grey zone of significant convergence of both human cultic practice and UFO activity.

Perception of what's going on would undoubtedly shift if the cattle were cats, and the ranches city blocks. Sometimes they are, as in this 1995 account from Kelowna, B.C., which begins with a woman looking out her kitchen window and seeing "two brilliant lit cigar shaped objects moving slowly over the apple trees, at about thirty or forty feet of height":

As they scoured the area the objects bathed the orchard in blue light and in the woman's words "seemed to be looking for something." The craft then began to slowly move from the back of the orchard and headed in the direction of the house. They now stopped directly next to the house over a garage addition and shone down white beams of light. Even stranger, the witness described the lights as broken up, "like a white line down the highway."

It is here where high strangeness enters the picture. The woman said that in retrospect a thought that passed through her mind during the sightings was her concern for the cats.

Neighborhood cats would often congregate in the garage and this was now where the lights were "searching." The objects then "turned off" and left. The next day over a dozen cats in this area of Kelowna were missing and were never seen again.

Last fall our hotline received a call from a fellow in Burnaby who said that he witnessed, along with his brother, a dark shadowy figure run in front of them as they stood in the driveway of their home one rainy night. More disturbing, all three of his cats were gone. Oddly enough, the man said he witnessed the same dark figure as a young boy not far from the area. At that time the shadowy-shape ran into a bush.

The Kamloops area of B.C. was also privy to a rash of half cat mutilations as well, with a dozen or so cats mysteriously cut up. Same show, no blood, no muss, no apparent fuss and again, never a sign of struggle, no fur strewn about and no spilled blood.

Someone is doing something with our cats. Since the early nineties UFOBC has been aware of the "Half Cat" mystery on the Lower Mainland. At this time the mutilated cats first showed up in Vancouver's West Side. In these instances cats had been sliced in half with great precision and then somehow drained of their blood (exsanguination). Never a drop to be found, with no stains at all on the remaining feline carcass (in these cases, half carcasses).

In the Surrey area last fall half cats started showing up again. I talked to two women who were unfortunately "victims of the circumstance." Living about three or four miles apart, both women found their own cats' remains. In the first case one of the woman was off to do some banking, oddly enough she said that morning she took the long way to the bank, and to her shock found her dead cat. It was placed to appear to be coming out of a manhole cover in the middle of the road. The woman pulled over and saw that it was her own cat cut in half. Like other cases the other half was nowhere to be found . As is the way, the culprit seemed to want his work to be noticed. The other unfortunate young woman found her cat in the alley behind her house. Devoid of all blood, showing no signs of struggle and once again cut in half. Perfectly! The SPCA is sticking to their guns that these are coyote attacks. Out of ignorance or in order to quell any panic, I don't know but that's their story and they're sticking to it!

It was with great surprise when I fell upon a similar story of half cats in upstate New York in a town called Lee which is close to the Hudson Valley. However, the "coupe de grace" came when I was thumbing through an old *Fate Magazine* recently and discovered that the Half Cats have also surfaced in Gulf Breeze (Florida), Plano (Texas), Fall's Church (Virginia) and St Louis (Missouri). In Fall's Church twenty cases were reported alone, with slightly less than that number showing up in St Louis.

No one is suggesting aliens are experimenting on cats. In an urban environment, upon house pets, the cultic aspect of the phenomenon comes into sharper focus. Yet here, too, we have a UFO associated with the event.

So perhaps, instead of mutilations for a scientific purpose these are ritual killings, perhaps for the magick of the blood sacrifice or simply the induction of terror into the world. Regardless, the reason for the killing *is* the killing. Certainly the thought of cultists in cahoots with their bloodthirsty gods is not as comforting a hypothesis as aliens studying tissue samples to gauge environmental pollutants, but to me it's the explanation which makes best, unfortunate sense of the evidence. That it's a strange explanation is of no account, because whatever the explanation, it *must* be a strange one.

Jacques Vallee writes in *Messengers of Deception* that "the symbols attached to the UFO phenomenon are the primary images of life: blood, death, sex, time, space and sky":

What are the organs taken by the mutilators? The eyes, the ears, the tongue and the genitals: that is, the organs concerned with communication and reproduction. The culprits deserve credit not only as good surgeons, but also as good psychologists.

Should we note the common feature of cored rectums, and that, according to Aleister Crowley, the anus denotes the Eye of Horus? Should we be thinking, sacrifice?

Father Alfred Kunz, 68, was a popular Wisconsin priest who, with Fathers Malachi Martin and Charles Fiore, had been compiling evidence of Satanic ritual abuse and pedophilia in the Roman Catholic Church. His body was found the morning of March 4, 1998, face down in a pool of his blood, his throat slashed. The case remains unsolved.

All three priests received death threats, and all three are now dead. According to William H. Kennedy, author of *Lucifer's Lodge: Satanic Ritual Abuse in the Catholic Church*, the "threats increased when conclusive evidence emerged of Milwaukee Archbishop Rembert Weakland's operation of a network of pervert priests who were

sexually abusing parishioners." (Weakland was forced to resign in a sex scandal in 2003.)

And then there's the calf mutilation.

From *The Las Vegas Weekly*'s "The Devil and Father Kunz":

> According to police reports, it happened between 10 p.m. March 2 and 4 a.m. March 3 at a farm less than 15 minutes away from St. Michael — nearly the exact time frame of Kunz's murder the next day. The caged animal's throat was slit, but, unlike Kunz, its genitals were sliced off. The farmer told police it was probably the work of a cult in the area.

The calf's throat was slashed, its blood drained into a milk pail and congealed into about an inch at the bottom. It also had its hind legs cleanly cut through at the pelvis. Its legs "were cleanly, almost professionally cut off," said the young man, named Wagner, who found the calf at about 7:30 A.M. on his father's farm on Schneider Road. "You would have to know what you were doing." Its hind legs were nowhere to be found.

Six weeks after Kunz's murder, according to *The Las Vegas Weekly*, Malachi Martin "swore he had inside information that the killing was the 'signature' work of 'Luciferians,'" and that "'what Luciferians resent is interference with someone they regard as theirs.'" Presumably, someone like Archbishop Weakland.

Martin died of a stroke induced "by a fall as he prepared for an exorcism. From his hospital bed shortly before his death, Martin insisted during a check-in call from an associate: 'No, I did NOT fall. I tell you, my legs were pulled out from under me!'"

There are a lot of hungry things out there. And not all of them are coyotes.

Bad medicine

December 29, 2005

This subject's still taking shape for me, which is fine, because it's partly about shapeshifting. And that isn't to say it's about Reptoid Shapeshifters from Outer Space, because it isn't, except maybe to reframe that subject instead as a dark slice of pure Americana. Because I'm thinking, rather, about Navajo witchcraft: the "bad medicine" of, let's call them, "left-hand path" medicine men. Specifically, *yee naaldooshi*: the "skinwalkers."

Anthropologist Dan Benyshek of the University of Nevada-Las Vegas, quoted in Colm Kelleher and George Knapp's *Hunt for the Skinwalker*:

> Skinwalkers are purely evil in intent. I'm no expert on it, but the general view is that skinwalkers do all sorts of terrible things — they make people sick, they commit murders. They are grave robbers and necrophiliacs. They are greedy and evil people who must kill a sibling or other relative to be initiated as a skinwalker. They supposedly can turn into wereanimals and can travel in supernatural ways.

I find it interesting that the initiation fee of killing a close relative is similar to the blood price exacted for admittance into high Satanic circles, and also the generational sacrifice of one's own children to ritual bondage and mind control.

Then there's John Perkins, the National Security Agency-recruit and author of the favorite liberal limited hang-out *Confessions of an Economic Hitman*, who is also the author of *Shapeshifting: Shamanic Techniques for Global and Personal Transformation*, and leads workshops on the subject. Here's Perkins, in an interview with "Spirit of Maat":

> For definitional purposes we can talk about Shapeshifting occurring on three different levels:
>
> The first is cellular, and that is when a person of an indigenous culture shapeshifts into a plant or animal, or in our culture when a cancer grows in someone and then miraculously disappears.

The second level is personal Shapeshifting. That is when we decide to transform our personality — and usually that means becoming more of what we most expect in ourselves. It might mean when a person honors themselves as a good writer or a better dancer or politician. It could also mean transforming an addiction.

...

During the process of writing the book Shapeshifting, I found that many people had the opinion that cellular shapeshifting, where people become jaguars and plants, was important years ago for indigenous peoples and cultures that had to escape from enemies in the forest, or hunt down buffalo and other animals — but was not important in this day and age and probably doesn't occur anymore.

I disagree. I have seen a lot of very significant cellular Shapeshifting around the world. There are lamas in Tibet who fly across mountains and melt snow with the heat of their bodies, and shamans in the Amazon who become jaguars, and people in this country who miraculously get cured of cancers. I think cellular Shapeshifting is very important, because when we cellular Shapeshift, we realize that we really are one with everything.

Shapeshifting is not just Perkins' metaphor for adaptation and personal transformation. He believes — he claims to have *witnessed* — shapeshifting on a cellular level.

What am I trying to say? This is what I'm trying to say: we don't need to look to Alpha Draconis to find a *culture* of shapeshifting. Shapeshifting is as American as Cowboys and Indians, and even more so than Cowboys. Regardless of what we think about the subject, even if we say *this cannot be so it can't be true*, a living culture which holds such things both possible and essentially evil is indigenous to the United States, and in particular to the western lands which have seen so much bad medicine of late, from Los Alamos to Jack Parsons and UFOs. And then there's the New Age shamanism of the NSA's Perkins.

Doug Hickman, a New Mexico educator, says in *Hunt for the Skinwalker* that "the Navajo skinwalkers use mind control to make their victims do things to hurt themselves and even end their lives." Again, we've seen this before. Survivors of covert ritual abuse/mind-control programs often need to have self-destruct alters reintegrated into their core personalities so they do not

harm or kill them-
selves once the pro-
gramming has been
detected. I find such
similarities more in-
teresting, and possi-
bly more important,
than speculation as

to whether human-to-animal shapeshifting is literally possible.

There's a ranch in Utah said by a local tribe to be "in the path of the skinwalker." After an embarrassment of weirdness terrorized its new owners in the mid-1990s — UFOs, boxy "chupas", cattle mutilations, orbs, anomalous entities and more (their first day, the family was visited by an oversized wolf that attacked a calf and could not be killed or even brought down by a point-blank barrage, whose tracks simply ended in the mud) — the property was purchased by a mysterious Las Vegas multimillionaire named Robert Bigelow, rumored to have CIA ties. "Another rumor has it that the death of his son several years ago brought about his passionate interest in the paranormal."

Perhaps the strangest and most provocative aspect to the story is that of the "orange structure" which often appeared low in the ranch's western sky and was allegedly viewed by all members of the Gorman family on dozens of occasions. (The family name is actually Sherman, but they're pseudonymously identified in Colm Kelleher and George Knapp's *Hunt for the Skinwalker*). It was nearly perfectly round, though it appeared flattened rather than spherical. (It's appearance changed according to the angle at which it was viewed. On one occasion of its appearance Tom Gorman, the father, was driving off of the property, and approached it from the side. As he did, it seemed to thin-out until it was undetectable, as if it were two-dimensional. Though even that doesn't do justice to the strangeness, since it could not be seen from the opposite direction.)

When he observed it through binoculars long after the sun had set, Tom claimed he could see, in the middle of the orange mass, "another sky." A blue sky, while the ranch's sky was black. Kelleher and Knapp write that "Tom felt like it could have been a tear or a rent in the sky about a mile away, and through the rent he could see a different world or perhaps a different time.... For Gorman, this was a rare glimpse into what might actually be happening on his property."

On two particular nights while Tom observed the orange structure its "other sky" was not visible; its center instead had the appearance of multiple layers of an onion that receded from him. As he watched, he saw a "fast-moving black object that was silhouetted perfectly against the bright orange background." It was moving rapidly through the center of the structure and soon exited, silently, into the Utah night sky, where Gorman soon lost sight of it.

This almost beggars credulity, and so it should. But such extraordinary sights are not unknown in the American west. A family of ranchers named Bradshaw had a two-year brush with high weirdness near Sedona, Arizona in the early '90s, including encounters with glowing orbs, poltergeists, cattle mutilations and strange humanoids. They also claimed to witness a similar "structure" in the sky that appeared to serve as a gateway between different realities. (The Bradshaws' story is told in a book entitled *Merging Dimensions: The Opening Portals of Sedona*.)

A similar uncanny event was reported to have occurred the night of August 25, 1997, after the ranch had been purchased by Robert Bigelow. A pair of researchers with Bigelow's National Institute for Discovery Science (NIDS), identified as "Jim" and "Mike" in *Hunt for the Skinwalker*, were sitting silently on the edge of a bluff in the middle of the night, monitoring a pasture. At one point Jim climbed down into the field to meditate, as he had found that meditation sometimes "activated the phenomenon." A couple of hours later atop the bluff, at about 2:30 A.M., Jim's eye caught a faint, yellow light on a track through the field, about 150 feet bellow. As he watched it brighten, he gestured to Mike. They both watched, and it grew bigger as well as brighter. Jim took out his camera and Mike his night-vision binoculars. The light appeared positioned above the ground, rather than situated upon it. Mike whispered, "It's a tunnel. Not just a light."

And then: "Jesus Christ — something's in the tunnel! Oh, my God. There is a black creature climbing out. I see his head. It has no face. It's on the ground. Oh my God, it walked away." Mike reported it to be huge — maybe six feet tall and 400 pounds. Shortly thereafter, the yellow circle dimmed, shrunk and vanished.

After 15 minutes and no further sighting, the pair climbed down to the track. At the spot where the "tunnel" had appeared, there remained only the strong, pungent smell of sulfur. Jim's film showed the smudge of yellow light, but nothing more.

On four different occasions NIDS asked a number of well-respected remote viewers, most of whom had been employed by "Project Stargate," to independently engage in blind targeting of the ranch. That is, they were given no information about what they were to be looking at, or expectations about what they might find. They were given a random coordinate and asked to describe events associated with it. One, identified only in *Hunt for the Skinwalker* as "one of the most uncannily accurate remote viewers alive today" (a frequent description of Joseph McMoneagle), produced a "near exact" sketch of the ranch, identifying features, as well as a spot in the southwest corner of the property which he said harbored a "disturbing" energy. In a later test, another viewer was asked to provide impressions of a daytime calf mutilation. According to Kelleher and Knapp, he sensed that a robotic drone had carried it out, and that it might have been of "interdimensional origin." He also added that the drone "had some connection" to the U.S. military. Other viewers also suggested some inexplicable military involvement with a foreign and frightening Other. They had impressions of uniformed men in dark sunglasses and naval tattoos, and inhuman entities speaking an unknown language.

Consistently and independently, the remote viewers expressed feelings of "dread, nervousness, darkness and death" associated with their blind targeting of the property.

Pointedly, the phenomenon became more fleeting after NIDS began its investigation. There were observations of paranormal events — orbs, cattle mutilations, weird entities — but they did not have the frequency noted by the Gormans, and over the years of investigation the weirdness essentially dried up. Kelleher and Knapp make an interesting observation, one I've made here previously about the nature of similar encounters with the weird:

> Was there something now missing from the engagement? Perhaps it was the level of emotion that the Gorman family had provided in spades but was missing from the scientific team. The stress level in the family was unbelievably high. It was palpable. The Gormans did not interact with the phenomenon because they wanted to; they simply had no

choice. In contrast, the NIDS scientific personnel were there by choice. They carried with them an attitude of cool detachment. There was almost an aggressiveness in the pursuit of the phenomenon that may have psychologically turned the tables, assuming of course that a consciousness was involved.

It seems nearly a maxim that weirdness of this high order seeks out those who don't expect it and are therefore less prepared to cope with it. Again, it's the "garmonbozia" principle: fear is a favorite delicacy at the feast of intense human emotions.

And what can we make of the suggestion of military involvement. The Gorman family and area residents noted strange mechanical noises and hums from beneath the ground. The same has been said of Dulce and other sites, supporting for some the claims of a vast network of underground military-alien bases. (I've written previously why I consider that to be disinformation.) Yet the indigenous peoples of the region tell of having heard the same noises underfoot for generations, since before there was a United States. So what is it? If there's something down there, it's been there a long time.

There does appear to be a thread in need of untangling which connects the U.S. military, high weirdness and Native American tradition and land, particularly sacred sites. The San Luis Valley of Colorado for instance, where Maurice Strong and his then-wife built their "Valley Of the Refuge Of World Truths," is a holy place for many indigenous nations, including the Navajo. There's Indio's Cabazon Indian Reservation, notorious for Casolaro's Octopus and now also the trial of Richard Hamlin. (Hamlin's father-in-law Sidney Siemer, whom he accuses of ritually abusing his wife Susan, "freely admits" having worked there in the 1980s during the time of Wackenhut and PROMIS. Before she recanted her testimony, Susan claimed to remember her father subjecting her to mind-control torture in an Indio warehouse.)

Dread, nervousness, darkness and death. That's some pretty heady stuff to tap into. The skinwalker ranch makes a fine spooky story, but if it and stories like it describe genuine phenomena then we should be more than spooked. We should be alert as well. Because maybe it also informs our estimate of the situation. Maybe it can help us understand who is trying to tap into what, and why.

Confessions of an Economic Shape-shifter

August 24, 2006

They sentenced me to 20 years of boredom
For trying to change the system from within.
— Leonard Cohen

There's a school of liberal American thought — one that serves a gated community — that says John Perkins' *Confessions of an Economic Hit Man* is about as deep as it gets. If there *is* a conspiracy, so that mindset goes, then it goes *this* far: the cheating of nations of their inheritance by persuading their rulers to take on massive developments contracted to U.S. industry, paid for by enormous loans, that in turn become the weapon of indebtedness to buy a government's allegiance. The story Perkins tells in *Hit Man* is that of the privateering ruin of the world, coordinated by the deniable aegis of covert statecraft, and it's good as far as it goes. But it's not Perkins' only story.

Perkins has written other books about his time spent in the wild places of the world, but they're the kind of books likely to embarrass the reader who thinks *Hit Man* is tell *all*. He's taken ayahuasca and seen the holy anacondas; discovered the power of dream and learned principles of shapeshifting from the shamans. In fact, "he is currently working with several major corporations to introduce the concepts of shapeshifting and tribal wisdom into the highest levels of executive thinking."

Now, whatever *that* may mean (and it may include such dispiriting "transformations" as Bono's equity firm buying 40%

of Forbes magazine, which may make his persona more skin-walker than shapeshifter), Perkins doesn't intend shapeshifting to be understood as pure metaphor. (Though presumably, when he describes the CIA's "jackals" who are called in to perform the wet jobs, it's just a figure of speech.) He means, literally, shape-shifting: that it can entail authentic, cellular change.

Perkins' esoteric knowledge may not be known to the casual reader of Hit Man, but the State Department, in its page "Identi-fying Misinformation," draws attention to Perkins' other titles in order to scare away the faint of mind. Alluding to *The World Is As You Dream It*: "shamanistic techniques from the Amazon and Andes," the anonymous flunky writes: "As to whether Perkins was acting at the behest of the U.S. government, the world is not "as he dreams it." Higher up the food chain, where people are known to "create our own reality" and "other new realities, which you can study, too," opinions may differ.

Perkins offers some personal accounts of cellular transforma-tion in his book *Shapeshifting*, the most dramatic drawn from 1994 when a friend, Sarah, was stricken with a deadly virus. Infectious fluid filled her chest cavity such that her heart and lungs were obscured on x-rays. At Thanksgiving, doctors warned her husband William that she was unlikely to survive until Christ-mas. William had traveled to Ecuador with Perkins and shared his interest in shamanism; Sarah did not. But close to death, she invited him to visit and talk, and then asked if he could use shamanism to heal her. Eventually agreeing, he asks Sarah to lie down and lights a candle by her bed. Fanning her with branches, he "called on Kitiar, Viejo Itza, and several other shamans to as-sist me. I asked Pachamama to do whatever was appropriate." And then:

A tiny ball appeared. The size of a marble, it materialized like a sort of hologram of light near her heart. The thought intruded that it was just my imagination. Quickly I chased this thought away and returned to being the observer. The ball grew larger, to the size of a Ping-Pong ball; it had a bluish hue. It was not like a solid object; it appeared more fluid, and seemed to vibrate. It moved slowly around her chest cavity. I had the feeling that it was searching for something. I also had the feeling that I should try to enter it; however, something told me to be wary and to re-sist this temptation. I shook the branches more forcefully over her body. As I did so, the ball's color changed to a deeper blue, a color approaching black, then it sprouted two branches of its own, which it waved in unison with the rhythm of mine.

Its branches spread and flattened until they became wings. The ball had shifted into the shape of a bat.... It darted about, then swooped through her torso, and I understood that it was drinking up fluid that threatened her life. Again, this came to me in the form of a knowing, like intuition, or a thought that we are sure is correct yet do not understand how we know it. Then the bat lifted up out of her body, flew directly past me and to the open window behind me. Perched on the windowsill facing outside, it made spastic, jerking motions. I realized with a start that it was regurgitating the fluid it had extracted from Sarah.

The next day Sarah had a radiology appointment which confirmed that a "measurable portion" of the fluid had vanished. The radiologist was surprised, and Sarah's cardiologist told William "Sometimes these things happen." Perkins repeated the healing sessions three times in the next week, after which Sarah had another examination. The fluid had completely disappeared. Her doctors, their confidence shaken, recommended she travel from Florida to Minnesota's Mayo Clinic for another round of tests, which when complete confirmed that an unexpected healing had occurred.

Perkins recounts other brushes with what could be called either high weirdness, or perhaps more charitably, elevated energies; an evening in the Amazon, for instance, stepping into a clearing and seeing "a blue light flash high up in the top of the canopy. And again. Then it rose out of the forest — a vibrating globe of blue light":

Then another light appeared. This one seemed to materialize out of thin air. The two hovered side by side. Like huge balls of energy, they moved closer to me and then flashed quickly away, disappearing behind the thick wall of the rainforest trees.

These aren't stories which most Amy Goodman-progressives are going to want to hear. But since they are told with the same conviction, by the same insider whom they delight to cite as a source for how the world really works, perhaps they should pay them some attention, and accord a similar measure of respect. Maybe then they'd learn the world's workings go also very deep, and strange.

Under the Red Sky

January 10, 2007

> *Let the bird sing, let the bird fly.*
> *One day the man in the moon went home*
> *and the river went dry.*
>
> — Bob Dylan

Sometimes, like these times, the world appears strange even in newspapers.

Thousands of birds fall dead from the sky in Australia and dozens litter the streets of Austin Texas; New York City is bathed again in a mysterious stench, and again authorities assure residents it's harmless, though they don't know what it is and are no longer even trying to find out; multiple reports of fireballs, rock falls, strange lights and UFOs (one in Iran today, and a dramatic flap two years ago, a report which the BBC illustrates with a photograph of Venus) compound the sense that's no longer nonsense: that the sky really *is* falling. (The O'Hare UFO story became the *Chicago Tribune*'s most read article online, ever.) Weather patterns are breaking down and reconstituting in alarming ways, winning deathbed conversions from climate-change skeptics. And perhaps most incredible of all — or it would be, if it represented something like a departure from script — the White House is about to escalate the war in Iraq and likely thereafter engage Iran, inviting a Stalingrad scenario upon U.S. forces in the Middle East.

War-making may seem too familiar and explicable to be rightly considered alongside the bizarre phenomena that are usually relegated to "news of the weird" irrelevance because they don't fit rational narratives. But there has often appeared to be a symbiosis of war and the weird, as though one helps to manifest or memorialize the other in this world, and perhaps somewhere else.

In folklore around the world, ghost stories are largely the domain of dead soldiers. Hawaii's Night Marchers, the *huaka'i po*, are said to be the torch-bearing spirits of slain warriors. Legends of Ireland's fairy folk tell of them waging war in the skies. Foo fighters were drawn to military aircraft. And ancient battlefields and their graveyards are among the most fraught locations on Earth for paranormal activity.

"Wherever there has been great suffering, people are always seeing strange things," says Edward Tinney, former historian and chief ranger at Chickamauga-Chattanooga National Military Park. Chickamauga, like many Civil War battlefields, has seemingly been imprinted with the shadows of lives lost. Phantom cannons and drums are heard, and holographic representations of dead soldiers — "ghosts," commonly called — have been witnessed performing endless loops of routine. Most curious, Chickamauga is reportedly also home to a skinwalker-like shapeshifter known as "Old Green Eyes." Tinney describes an encounter one early morning in 1976 with a figure "wearing a long black duster, with shaggy, stringy, black, waist-length hair":

> From the man's body language, Tinney feared he was about to be attacked, so he crossed to the other side of the road, he said. When the man became parallel with Tinney he turned and smiled a devilish grin, and his dark eyes glistened. Tinney said he turned to face the man and began to back-pedal, as his companion did as well. At that moment, a car came down a straightaway in the road, and when its headlights hit the apparition it vanished, he said.

On another battlefield, in the summer of 1969, three GIs were on guard duty near Da Nang in South Vietnam. Two years later one of them, Earl Morrison, told investigator Don Worley what they had seen:

> And all of a sudden, I don't know why we all three looked out there in the sky and we saw this figure coming toward us. It had a kind of glow and we couldn't make out for sure what it was at first. It started coming toward us real slowly. And all of a sudden we saw what looked like wings, like a bat only it was gigantic compared to what a regular bat would be. After it got close enough so we could see what it was it looked like a woman. A naked woman. The color — she was black.
>
> Worley: Her skin was black?
>
> Witness: Right, her body was black, her skin was black, the wings were black, everything was black. But it glowed. It glowed in the night, — kind of a greenish cast to it.

487

Worley: You mean she glowed or there was a glow around her?

Witness: There was a glow on her and around her. Everything glowed. Looked like she glowed and threw off a radiance. And we saw her arms toward the wings. They looked like a regular molded arm with the hand and fingers and everything, but they had skin from the wings going over. And when she flapped her wings it didn't make any noise there at first. It looked like her arms didn't have any bones in them or anything because they were limber just like a bat. She started going over us and we still didn't hear anything. She was right straight up and when she got over top of our heads she was maybe 6 or 7 feet up.

Worley: What did you guys do, — just stand there?

Witness: We couldn't do anything — we didn't know what to do. We just froze. We just watched what was going over cause we couldn't believe our eyes.

Worley: Nobody went into panic, dove for the bunker?

Witness: No, we just looked because ...

Worley: Nobody fired at her?

Witness: No, it's amazing what you would do under certain circumstances. And we just looked at it. We couldn't believe it because we had never seen anything like this before in our lives....

Let's note here how often bizarre phenomena are ascribed to "outer space," when often it's simply because the events seem so *out there*. When we speak of anomalous sightings in the sky, we're referring to *aerial* objects, not objects beyond our own atmosphere. And with respect to war-making's interface with the weird, let's recall that Mothman's "nest" was an abandoned World War II munitions plant.

All of this is to suggest that war and conflict create fissures through which things can slip, the nature of which remain unknown to us, other than to say they don't appear to belong to this world. On the other hand, if we're talking about energies that desire egress into our world — or perhaps rather, our consciousness — then perhaps they don't simply wait for cracks to appear; they help to create them, and enter into co-dependence with the human actors who can create the disruptive conditions conducive to their manifestation.

According to West Salem, Wisconsin's *Coulee News*, a 53-year-old Native American and his 25-year old son were driving on Briggs Road the evening of September 26, when a figure the size of a man with a 10 to 12-foot leathery wing span flew at their windshield and up into the sky. "The creature had pronounced ribs, human-like legs with claws for toes and arm-like appendages tipped with claws. The creature's eyes glowed yellow, and the face had a snarling expression, with rows of sharp teeth." To the older witness, "the creature seemed hungry. It also seemed angry to have been seen and gave an unearthly howl as it flew out of sight."

Both witnesses are said to have become violently ill after the sighting, and the father remained ill for a week afterwards. The son was so shaken by the encounter that he won't speak of it, and the father will only because he wants people "to know what is out there," though "he believes *the more he talks about it, the more power it gives the creature*." I find this an intriguing construction. Not because, conversely, our ignorance might empower us, but for the man's intuition that this was not a flesh-and-blood creature, but an entity of thought-form.

Just a few years ago, much of the weird in the Western world appeared to be drying up and blowing away on the wind of mockery. That it's returned, along with war, may be more than a coincidence of psychology.

Index

Symbols

300 (movie) 405

A

A Beautiful Mind 146
Abelman, Daniella 452
Acuff, John 432
Ahmad, Mahmoud 50, 459
al-Attiyah, Abdullah 436
al-Bayoumi, Omar 74
Albini, Luciani 23, 25
al Hazmi, Nawaf 74
Alien Identities 403
Allende, Salvador 405
al Mihdhar, Khalid 74
Al-Qadi, Yassin 64-66
Al Suqami, Satam 167
Amazing Randi 256
Amir, Yigal 55-57, 394
Analog 244
Anashim 56
Andanson, James 370, 371
Andrews, Colin 255, 258, 261, 262
Angels Don't Play this HAARP 383
Antonio, Jose 181, 183, 184, 200, 207, 252, 357
Anxious Gravity 341
App, Austin 92
Applewhite, Marshall 148
Aquino, Michael 112, 113, 153, 154, 193, 217, 258, 279
Arlington County After-Action Report 5
Artaud, Antonin 231, 235, 236
Ashcroft, John 66, 67, 458, 464
Asner, Ed 167

Assassination of Marilyn Monroe, The 374
Assassination of Robert F. Kennedy, The 28
Assassinations, The 383, 455
Atta, Mohamed 50, 75-79, 167, 168, 366, 426, 459-462, 465
Atwater, Skip 318, 400

B

Baggio, Sebastiano 25
Bailey, Alice 226, 285
Balco, Method 92
Baltimore Sun 61
Banco Ambrosiano 456
Baptista, Antonio 252
Barbie, Klaus 43, 44
Barnes, Harry G 179
Bathory, Elizabeth 406-408, 415
Bathory, Stephen 408
BBC 45, 81, 255, 328-330, 393, 441, 486
BCCI 93, 134, 456
Beaumont, Jeffrey 286
Beccheniu, Francis 339
Begala, Paul 67
Begich, Nick 383
Bell Aircraft 451
Bellant, Russ 78
Bell, Lawrence 451
Bellocchio, Antonio 357
Belzil, Fernand 470-472
Benedict XV 212
Bennett, Bill 366
Bennewitz, Paul 446
ben-Veniste, Richard 461
Benyshek, Dan 477
Berezovsky, Boris 48, 52
Bergantino, Joe 64, 65
Bergen, Peter 366
Bergman, Ingmar 137
Berlusconi, Silvio 24, 356
Bernard, Raymond 336

Bernsohn, Amanda 273, 274
Bigelow, Robert 479, 480
bin Laden, Osama 16, 17, 61,
    65, 366, 367, 406, 456,
    458, 462, 463
bin-Laden, Salem 456
bin Laden, Shafig 459
Bishop, George 327
Bishop, Greg 446
Bishop, Paul 326, 327
Blair, Tony 328, 396
Blair Witch Project, The 347
Blake, Ian 293
Blakey, Robert 361
Blame it on Rio 394
Blavatsky, Helena 29, 237, 410
Blood, Jack 83
Blowing Up Russia 46, 49, 51
Blue Velvet 286
Bobby (movie) 50
Body Electric, The 257
Boeche, Ray 171, 172
Bohemian Grove 279
Bohm, David 172, 260
Bohringer, Wolfgang 79, 465
Bohr, Niels 256
Bono 359, 361, 483
Boof, Kola 366, 367
*Book of Coming Forth By Night,
    The* 154
Book of the Law, The 240-242
Booth, John Wilkes 398
Booz Allen Hamilton 308
Borjesson, Kristina 44
Bourlet, Michel 330
Bouverie, Alice 225
Bove, Adamo 19
Bowen, Zachary 409
Bradshaw (family) 480
Bradshaw, Linda 238
Braun, Bennett 277
Breaking Open the Head 231,
    280, 319

Breitweiser, Kristen 76
Brin, David 405
Bronfman (family) 223
Bronner, Michael 62
Brown, Aaron 82
Brown Brothers Harriman 308
Brunner, Werner 276
Bryan, Joseph 432
Brzezinski, Zbigniew 8-10, 99
Buffet, Warren 49
Burnett, T-Bone 370, 373, 387,
    389, 415
Burrell, Paul 371
Bush, Barbara 48
Bush, George W. 8, 10, 35, 37,
    38, 42, 47, 54, 65, 66,
    81, 91, 98, 100, 101,
    122, 127, 131, 155,
    192-194, 236, 237, 245,
    274, 279, 287, 304, 326,
    351, 353, 380, 382, 393,
    396, 410, 433, 435, 456,
    457, 459, 460, 465
Bush, George H.W. 24, 25. 48.
    49, 78, 91, 110. 113.
    123. 234. 254. 364,
    377, 403, 459
Bush, Jonathan 74, 456
Bush, Marvin 456
Bush, Neil 48
Bush, Prescott 343
Butler, Steve 460

C

Calhoun, Joe 347
Calvi, Roberto 25, 27
Cameron, Marjorie 293
Campbell, Colin 411
Campbell, Gordon 45
Caradori, Gary 150
Carbajal, Ruben 46
Carreira, Maria 251
Carson, Johnny 387-390

Carter, Chris 270
Carter, John 334
Carvalho, Bernard 431
Case Closed 20
Casolaro, Danny 11, 72, 482
Castiglioni, Francesco Saverio (Pius VIII) 26
Castro, Fidel 21, 45, 85
Cave, Nick 235, 338, 429
Cayce, Edgar 286, 287
Central Intelligence Agency (CIA) 10, 11, 21, 25, 29, 30, 40, 41, 43, 44, 45, 47, 49, 50, 51, 61, 70-72, 74, 75, 77, 78, 84, 86, 93, 95-97, 100, 101, 105, 108-110, 114, 116-118, 122, 123, 134, 135, 140, 147, 149, 152-154, 160, 177, 186, 197, 215-220, 223, 224, 250, 258, 304, 305, 313, 316, 326, 327, 361, 366, 367, 371, 381-383, 396, 431-433, 452, 456, 457, 469, 479, 484
Chagall, Marc 266
Chalker, Bill 196
Chamish, Barry 55-57
Chaney, Lon 410
Chapin, Clint 289, 290
Chapin, Jane 289, 290, 447
Chaplin, Charlie 18
Charleston Post and Courier 169
Chavez, Hugo 121, 127, 144, 291, 358
Chavez, Sam 291
Cheney, Dick 10, 54, 65, 68, 81, 84, 95, 96, 127, 237, 366, 383, 426, 457, 459, 464, 465
Cherkasky, Michael 72
Chertoff, Michael 64-68
Chicago Tribune 486

Chick, Jack 380
Chomsky, Noam 55, 370, 455
Christian, Jonn 28
Christison, Bill 433
Christison, William 382
Churchill, Winston 335
Church of Satan 154
Cipel, Golan 394
Circular Evidence 255, 261
Clancy, Liam 270
Clark, Charles 373
Clark, Everett 186, 263
Clark, Ramsey 454
Clem, Weir 291
Clinton, William J. 48, 250
Cockburn, Alexander 55, 169, 316, 455
Cockburn, Bruce 419
Cohen, Leonard 37, 51, 162, 195, 229, 242, 285, 295, 366, 368, 393, 394, 483
Coleman, Joe 376-378
Collapse: How Societies Choose to Fail or Succeed 437
Collins, Denis 80
Committee for the Scientific Investigation of Claims of the Paranormal (CSICOP) 14, 15
Complete Guide to Mysterious Beings, The 199
Condon Report 361
Confessions of an Economic Hitman 477
Confrontations 141, 151, 289, 296, 297, 308, 309, 420
Constantine, Alex 215, 347
Cook, Fred J. 147
Cook, Nick 92, 451
Cooper, Anderson 381
Cooper, Cary 36
Coppens, Philip 431
Corbin, Henry 321

Corn, David 168
Corso, Phillip 7, 8, 10
Cosmic Serpent: DNA and the Origins of Knowledge, The 245
Cosmic Triggers Vol. I 235, 240, 244
Cottingham, Larry J. 409
Coulee News 488
Coup (musical group) 273, 397
Coyne, Lawrence J. 403, 404
Crane, Peter 219
Crick, Francis 245, 247
Crisp, Tony 276
Crowley, Aleister 124, 125, 172, 175, 189, 190, 233, 237, 240-243, 289, 292-294, 306, 307, 332, 334-336, 408, 443, 475
Cruise, Tom 213, 214, 233, 336
Cult of Lam 193
Curtis, Don 219
Curtis, Stephen 48
Custer, Jerrol F. 161
Cutshall, Chris 340

D

Dahmer, Jeffrey 406
Daily Camera 345
Daily Express 328
Daily Mail 312, 328
Daily Telegraph 328
Daimonic Reality 298
Dajo, Mirin 276
Dames, Ed 215
Dancing Naked in the Mind Field 196, 197
Dan, Uri 55
Dark Age Coming 267
DarkCity 404
Da Silva, Jose Antonio 181-184, 188, 190, 200

Da Silva, Luiz Inacio Lula 71
Davenport, Peter B. 442
David, Dennis D. 160
David-Neel, Alexandra 389, 391
Davis, Erik 201
Davis, Kathie 198
Dawkins, Richard 140
Day After Roswell, The 7, 8
De Almeida, Avelino 209
Death and Life of Great American Cities, The 267
De Bonis, Donato 25
Dee, John 181, 233, 293, 313, 332, 333, 408, 416
Deepening Complexity of Crop Circles, The 262 333, 334, 414, 422
De Rais, Gilles 406, 415
De Rochefort, Nicolas 431
Detroit Free Press 338
De Vaca, Cabeza 465
Devereux, Paul 281
Diamond, Bernard 29
Diamond, Jared 437
Diary of a Lost Girl 372
Diaz, Marisol 188
Di Savoia, Vittorio Emanuele Alberto Carlo Teodoro Umberto Bonifacio Amadeo Damiano Bernardino Gennaro Maria 359
Dickinson, Emily 286, 287
Dick, Philip K 242, 243, 268, 275, 390
DiEugenio, Jim 381, 383
Dimensions 181, 186, 211, 237, 263, 480
DMT: The Spirit Molecule 185, 320, 399
Dolan, Richard 179, 188, 402, 419, 431, 432
Donahue, Aaron C. 155

Dongo, Tom 238, 239
Dozier, James 153
Dr. Mary's Monkey 20
Drug Enforcement Agency (DEA) 43, 44, 50, 72, 461
Dulles, Allen 92, 93, 109, 115-120
DuPont (family) 92, 223
DuQuette, Lon Milo 443
Dutroux, Marc 329, 330, 347
Dylan, Bob 5, 12, 18, 23, 26-28, 33, 35, 45, 80, 83, 89, 116, 129, 133, 139, 145, 156, 167, 198, 213, 216, 231, 263, 269, 270, 275, 301, 312, 323, 351, 353, 355, 376, 379, 381, 397, 413, 438, 445, 454, 486
Dyncorp 308

E

Echanis, Michael 278
Edge of Reality, The 201
Edmonds, Dave 340
Edmonds, Sibel 67, 73, 84, 464
Eichmann, Adolph 177
Eighth Tower, The 264
Eisenberg, Dennis 55
Eisenhower, Dwight 146
Elgin, Duane 220
Eliash, Sarah 55
Ellsberg, Daniel 464
Elmore, Leonard 305
Eminem (Marshal B. Mathers III) 365
Emmanuel, Victor 355, 356
Evangelista, Benjamino 338
Evans, Richard 327
Expendable Elite 160
Eyes Wide Shut 336

F

Fahrney, Delmar 431
Falwell, Jerry 379, 380
Fantastic Planet 297
Farley, Dick 227
Farmer, Frances 267
Favish (family) 92
Fawcett, Michael 371
Fayed, Dodi 370, 371
Fayed, Mohammed Al 371
Federal Security Service of the Russian Federation (FSB) 38, 46, 47, 50, 51
Fedorak, Bohdan 92
Ferrie, David 20-22, 149
Field, The 249, 258, 259, 392
Financial Times 38
Fine, Glenn 67, 74
Fiore, Charles 475
Fitzgerald, Patrick J. 80, 81, 287
Fitzgerald, Michael 335
Fitzsimmons, Robert & Charlene 10
Flocco, Tom 287
Flying Saucer Review, The 182
Fontaine, Franck 447-450
Fonzi, Gaeton 46, 93, 152
Forbes 484
Fort Bliss 12, 13
Fortune 10
Fortune, Dion 399
Fox, Vincente 361
Foy, Robin 218, 417
Franco, Francisco 24
Frasca, Dave 75, 458
Fraser, David Richard 395
Freas, Kelly 244
Freeman, Walter 267
French, Richard 309, 310
Friend, Robert 332
From Psyops to MindWar: The Psychology of Victory 112-115, 153

Full Spectrum Warrior 358

G

Galdau, Florian 92
Gannon, Jeff 110, 127, 147, 326, 327
Ganser, Daniele 357
Garrett, Joseph 209
Garrison, Jim 11, 21, 149, 150, 383-385
Gasser, Roberto 44
Gates, Frederick Taylor 267
Gehlen, Reinhard 93
Geller, Uri 243, 244, 369
Gelli, Licio 24, 25, 27, 356, 357
George, Charles Philip Arthur (Prince Charles) 371
Giancana, Sam 374, 375
Gill, William 162-164
Giordano, Al 143
Giuliani, Rudy 72, 170
Glass, Randy 84, 458
Glenn L Martin Aircraft Company 451, 452
Glitter, Gary 344, 368
Globe and Mail 50, 100
Goddard, Jean-Luc 18
Goizueta, Roberto 85
Gómez, Luis 43
Gonzales, Henry 361
Goodman, Amy 485
Gosch, Johnny 149, 326
Gosch, Noreen 326
Goss, Porter 459
Gould, Dana 355
Grand Chessboard, The 10
Grant, Kenneth 124, 125, 193, 237, 239, 293, 306, 307
Grant, Ulysses 125
Grassley, Chuck 326, 327
Grateful Dead 279
Great Dictator, The 18
Greenfield, Allen 241-243

Greenwell, Russell 157, 158
Grey, Barry 9, 332
Grimorium Verum 243
Guardian 328
Guarino, Phillip 24
Guthrie, Woody 365
Gutierrez, Alfredo 44
Guttenberg, Steve 151
Guyatt, David 24
Guzman, Maria Pia 331

H

Haaretz 53
Hair of the Alien 196
Hall, Alan 432
Hamill, Pete 91
Hamilton, Lee 62, 308, 329, 464
Hamlin, Richard 341, 482
Hancock, Graham 414
Hancock, Larry 11, 414
Happy Camp News 309
Harner, Michael 247
Harper's 366
Harpur, Patrick 298
Haselhoff, Eltjo 262
Haslam, Edward 20-22
Hatcher, Teri 373
Hauer, Jerome 72
Hawkins, Gerald 261
Healey, John 403
Heavenly Lights 15, 251, 253
Heinberg, Richard 436
Heiner, Kent 160
Hellyer, Paul 8
Hence, Kyle 62
Henschel, Peter 70
Higdon, Carl 298, 300
Hillenkoetter, Roscoe 431, 432
Hilliard, Wally 460
Hill, Lee 345
Hill-Norton, Peter 451
Hilton, Paris 372

History Will Not Absolve Us 147
Hoffman, Abbie 279
Hoffman, Albert 319
Holloway, Natalee 354
Holographic Universe, The 265, 277, 400
Holroyd, Stuart 223
Holy Terror, Batman! 406
Honegger, Barbara 24, 25
Hoover Institution 38
Hoover, J Edgar 41
Hopkins, Budd 198, 203, 472
Hopsicker, Daniel 75, 79, 81, 426
Houck, Jack 301, 302
Hougan, Jim 207
Houston, Whitney 366, 367
Howe, Linda Moulton 165, 437, 472
Howland, Francine 277
Hubbard, L Ron 213-215, 233, 307, 332
Hudson Institute 38
Huguet, Daniel 448
Humanoids, The 462
Hunter, Alex 345, 347
Hunt for the Skinwalker 477-481
Hunt for Zero Point, The 92, 451-453
Hurtak, James 226
Hurtubise, Troy 248
Hutchison, John 248
Hynek, J. Allen 201, 295-297
Hyperspace and Parallel Worlds 196

I

Iannuzzi, Alberto 356
IG Farben 373
Illustrated Goetia of Aleister Crowley. The 443
Independent 328

In God's Name 23
Insight (magazine) 6
Intelligencer: Journal of US Intelligence Studies, The 153, 217
Invisibles, The 352, 357
Inter-Service Intelligence (ISI) 50, 84, 459
Into the Buzzsaw 44
Intruders 198, 204
Irwin, Gerry 12, 13, 14
Isikoff, Michael 74
Ivins, Bruce 463

J

Jackson, Jermaine 368, 369
Jackson, LaToya 369
Jackson, Michael 368, 369
Jacobs, Jane 267
Jane's Aviation Weekly 451
Jayhan, Phil 148
Jenny, Hans 261
Jerusalem Post 53, 55, 177
Jesus 29, 242, 480
JFK (movie) 381
Jillette, Penn 142
Joannides, George 45
Johnson, Bob 270
Johnson, Lyndon 41, 385
Johnson, Tim 425
Johnson, Vince 171
Jones, Alex 83, 144
Jones, Candy 303
Joo, Ilona 407
Journeys Out of the Body 316, 318, 320
Judge, John 84, 104, 370
Jung, Carl 265

K

Kaku, Michio 196
Karr, John 344

Kean, Thomas 67, 464
Keel, John 199, 200, 241, 243, 264, 305-311
Keith, Don Lee 21
Kekule, Friedrich 319
Kelleher, Colm 440, 477, 479, 481
Keller, Amanda 79, 366
Kelly, David 50, 52, 270
Kelly, Edward 181, 313, 408, 416
Kennedy, John F. (JFK) 21, 25, 34, 40, 41, 45, 51, 55, 85, 87, 114, 144, 146, 149, 156, 160, 161, 370, 381, 383, 385, 397, 398, 404, 455
Kennedy, Robert F. 28, 30, 45, 50, 80, 93, 374, 384
Kennedy, Ted 25
Kennedy, William H. 475
Kennett, Richard 219, 220
Keyhoe, Donald 431-434
Keys of Enoch, The 226
Khashoggi, Adnan 370
Kilburn, John 15
King, Lawrence 150, 194
King, Martin Luther 26, 35, 93, 144, 384, 455
Kirby, Jack 379, 380
Kissinger, Henry 24, 79
Klass, Philip 403
Kleinknecht, C. Fred 286
Knapp, George 477, 479, 481
Knowles, Herbert B. 431
Kohl, Helmut 79
Kostikov, Valery 40
Kouri, Jim 43
Krebs, Nancy 347
Kristofferson, Kris 26
Kroll Inc. 70-72
Kunz, Alfred 472, 475

L

LaFoon, Earl 28
Lam 237, 242, 292, 293, 307, 332
Lam Statement, The 293
Lammer, Helmut 250
Lamonica, Louis 411
Lankford, Mrs. 158
Larre, George 470
Larson, Bob 341
Last Investigation, The 46, 93, 152
Las Vegas Weekly 475, 476
LaVey, Anton 347
Ledeen, Michael 24, 99, 102
Leeb, Stephen 436
Lee, Henry 325, 337
Lee, William 71
Le Figaro 462
Legacy of the Beast, The 335
Leman, Patrick 36
Lemegton, The 243
Le Monde 420
Leno, Jay 373, 383
Levenda, Peter 159, 207, 227
Levine, Michael 43, 44
LeWinter, Oswald 371, 372
Lewis, Peter 395
Libby, Scooter 80, 81, 288
Liber Stellae Rubeae 189
Life Between Life 400
Life Eaters, The 405
Lilly, Doris 199
Lincoln, Abraham 398
Lindemann, Michael 7, 8
Litvinenko, Alexander 46, 48, 49, 51, 52, 425
Livneh, Tuvia 56
Lloyd, David 364
Lockheed Martin 308, 452
Lone Gunmen, The 273, 397
Long Trip, The 281
Loose Change 85, 362

Lorax, The 437
Los Alamos 308, 478
Los Angeles Times 143, 144, 330
Lost Highway 201, 202
Lourenco, Joaquim 209
Lovecraft, H.P. 192-194, 222,
    251, 307, 319, 469
Low, Robert 362
Lucas, Henry Lee 337
Luciani, Albino (John Paul I) 23, 26
*Lucifer's Lodge: Satanic Ritual
    Abuse in the Catholic
    Church* 475
Lynch, David 201, 362

M

Maariv 55
MacColl, Kirsty 360, 361, 363
MacGyver 370
Mack, John 141
Macy, William H. 50
Maddox, Alvis 264
Madison, Fred (fictional) 201, 202
Magic and Mystery in Tibet 390
Malcolm X 144
Malkin, Peter 177
Mamboozo 376
Mandelbaum, W. Adam 152, 153
Man Who Knew Too Much, The 93
Marchal, Paul 329
Marcinkus, Paul 25, 27
Marks, John 250, 469
Marley, Bob 256, 279
Marrs, Jim 20
Marshall, J. Howard 373
Marsh & McLennan 72
Martinez, Jorge 422
Martin, Malachi 211, 475, 476
Marto, Manuel 251
Marvin, Daniel 160, 161
Mary, Ferrie & the Monkey Virus 20
Mass Psychology of Fascism, The
    410

May, Edwin 152
Maynard, Curt 85
McClelland, Scott 147
McConnell, Leola 366
McCor, Dorris 158
McGowan, David 330
McGreevey, Jim 394
McKenna, Terence 184, 185, 416
McMoneagle, Joseph 153, 154,
    217, 218, 481
McTaggart, Lynne 249, 258,
    259, 392
McTell, Ralph 364
McVeigh, Timothy 79
McWilliam, Carey 147
Mercernaries2: World in Flames
    362, 363
Melanson, Phil 30
Melianovich, Walter 92
Memoirs of a Dutiful Daughter
    39
Mengele, Josef 93, 97, 177
Men Who Stare at Goats, The
    278
Menzel, Donald 164
*Merging Dimensions: The Open-
    ing Portals of Sedona*
    237, 480
Messengers of Deception 152,
    178, 474
MI5 433
MI6 81, 370, 371
Miami Vice 366
*MILABS: Mind Control and Alien
    Abduction* 469
Miller, Frank 287, 406
Miner, John 374
Mineta, Norman 434, 464
Minton, Bob 214
Mirror 328
Mitre Corp 308
Moen, Bruce 232-234, 400
Mohammed, Ali 86

Montini, Giovanni Battista Enrico Antonio Maria (Paul VI) 25
Monroe Institute 232, 316, 400
Monroe, James 316
Monroe, Marilyn 374
Monroe, Robert 320, 400
Moon, Sun Myung 44, 380
Moore, Alan 364
Moore, Bill 165, 446
Moore, Shaine 395
Morales, David Sanchez 45
Morales, Evo 42-46, 121
Moro, Aldo 24
Morrison, Earl 487
Morrison, Grant 352, 357
Morrison, Van 431
Mossadegh 405
Mothman Prophecies, The 200, 242, 305, 308
Moussaoui, Zacarias 75, 458
MSNBC 8, 353, 439
Mulder, Fox William (fictional) 35, 165
Mullis, Kary 195-197
Mundis Imaginalis 321
Murphy, Kim 144
Mussolini 356
Mysteries 226

N

Nadasdy, Ferencz 407
Naegeli-Osjord, Hans 276
Narby, Jeremy 245-247
Narco News 43
Nasrallah, Hassan 53
Nation, The 147, 455
National Aeronautics and Space Administration (NASA) 308, 314, 452, 453
National Institute for Discovery Science (NIDS) 439, 480-482
National Investigations Committee on Aerial Phenomena (NICAP) 431, 432
National Review 434
NATO's Secret Army: Operation Gladio and Terrorism in Western Europe 357
Nazarenko, Nicholas 78, 92
Necronomicon 192, 251, 303
Netanyahu 54
Neuburg, Victor 233
Nevzlin, Leonid 48
Newman, John 93
Newton-John, Olivia 358
New Orleans States Item 20
Newsweek 61, 65, 460
New York Daily News 368
New York Observer 76
New York Post 92
New York Sun 329, 384
New York Times 95, 98, 122, 172, 271, 382, 412, 426, 438
New York Times Magazine, The 432
New York World-Telegram 384
Nickel, Joe 14
Nicolson, Garth 458
Nightline 172
No Direction Home 270
Noguchi, Thomas 374
Norquist, Grover 463
Norris, Chuck 359
Notes on the Visual Stages of a DMT Trip 254
Nova, Guillermo Gonzalez 360
Nugan Hand Bank 456

O

O'Blivion, Brian 61, 359
O'Brien, Cathy 366
Observer, The 328
Occasional Letter No. 1 267
Ochsner, Alton 21
Octopus, The 372
Odio, Silvia 30

Index

Oldest History of the World Discovered by Occult Science in Detroit, Michigan, The 338
Old Nazis, the New Right, and the Republican Party 78
Omar, Abu 19
Omega Project, The 321, 399, 417
O'Neill, John 61, 72
On the Trail of the Assassins 150, 384
On the Trail of the Saucer Spies 432
Operation Gladio 37, 357
Operation Greenquest 65
Operation Mockingbird 147
Operation Ore 328, 396
Opus Dei 19
Orbison, Roy 283
Ordo Templi Orientis (OTO) 237, 241, 293, 306, 307, 334
O Seculo 209
O'Sullivan, Shane 45
Oswald and the CIA 93
Oswald, Lee Harvey 30, 31, 40, 41, 61, 146, 168, 381, 382, 398
Outer Gateways 237
Ovason, David 285, 286
Owen, Alex 233

P

Pahlavi, Reza 356
Pahl, Margaret Ann 325, 337, 340
Pak, Bo Hi 44
Palme, Olof 24, 371
Pandemic Studios 358
Parry, Robert 44
Parsons, Jack 215, 293, 294, 307, 332, 334, 478
Party's Over, The 436
Pasolini, Pier Paolo 410
Passport to Magonia 253
Patton, George 406

Paul, Henri 370
Pease, Lisa 455
Pemberton, Doug 232
Perkins, John 477, 478, 483-485
Perry, Arlis 340
Peterson, Otto 355
Peyote Dance, The 231
Phelan, Jim 383
Picknett, Lynn 218, 223-225
Pickover, Cliff 184
Pinchbeck, Daniel 231, 280, 281, 319
Pinkerton National Detective Agency 308
Pittsburgh Post-Gazette 5
Pitzer, William 160, 161
Plan Nine from Outer Space 159
Playboy 21
Podhoretz, Norman 91
Pogues (The) 360
Poincaré, Jules-Henri 319
Poletti, Ugo 25
Popp, Fritz-Albert 248, 249
Portman, Natalie 365
Posner, Gerald 20, 22, 381
Powell, Colin 195
Pratt, Bob 420, 421
Prelude to the Landing on Planet Earth 223
Presidential Commission on Radiation Experiments 104, 140
Pribram, Karl 259
Price, Pat 153, 215, 233
Prince, Clive 223, 225
Probe 30, 71, 361
Project ARTICHOKE 30, 109
Project Beta: The Story of Paul Bennewitz, National Security and the Creation of the Modern UFO Myth 446
Project Blue Book 424
Project MK-ULTRA 29, 97, 100, 109, 113, 149, 222, 305

Project Paperclip 92, 96, 108, 113, 120, 335

Project Stargate 152, 153, 481

Propaganda Due (P2) 24, 25, 356

Proyas, Alex 404

Psychic Battlefield (A History of the Military-Occult Complex), The 152

Ptech 64-68, 82, 84

Puharich, Andrija 222-225, 243, 244, 262

Puthoff, Hal 214, 220, 233, 257, 258, 301, 452, 453

Putin, Vladimir 37, 38, 46-48, 52, 95, 144

Q

Quispe, Felipe 43

R

Rabin, Yitzhak 54, 55, 56, 57, 133

Ramsey, Jon Benet 346-349, 357, 454

Rathke, William Thomas 29, 30

Ratzinger, Joseph Alois (Benedict XVI) 212

Raviv, Avishai 55, 57

Ray, James Earl 31, 455

Raynes, Brent 420-422

Reagan, Ronald 78, 279, 434

Redfern, Nick 432, 433, 460-463

Reich, William 249, 410

Remote Viewers 216, 232, 302

Remote Viewing Secrets 154

Re/Search 376

Return to Point Pleasant 254

Revelations: Alien Contact and Human Deception 447, 449

Reynolds, Morgan 386, 433, 465

Richardson, Greg 358

Ridge, Tom 66, 170

Riget ("The Kingdom") 413

Riguidel, Ray 470

Ring, Kenneth 321, 399, 417, 418

Robert F. Kennedy Assassination, The 30

Roberts, Paul Craig 434

Roberts, Ralph 374

Robinson, Gerald 325, 337, 340, 341

Rockefeller family 92

Rockefeller Foundation 96, 97

Rockefeller, David 79

Rockefeller, John D. Jr. 267

Rockefeller, Laurence 262

Roddenberry, Gene 224

Rodrigues, Claudiomira 421

Roemer, Bill 374

Romand, Raymond 423

Ronson, Jon 278

Rosselli, John 46, 374, 375

Rothstein, James 149

Rove, Karl 80

Roveraro, Gianmario 19

Rowe, Korey 85

Ruby, Jack 41, 61, 361

Rumsfeld, Donald 5, 6, 40, 127, 180, 406, 465

Ruppelt, Edward 424, 425

Ruppert, Michael 65, 68, 168, 437

Russell, Dick 93

Russo, Gus 381

Russo, Mike 218-220

S

Sacks, Bryan 16

Saeed Sheikh, Omar 50, 465

Sahl, Mort 93, 384, 385

Sakharov, Andrei 257

Salandria, Vince 147

Salo 410

Sampaio, Jorge 330, 331

Sane Occultism 399

San Francisco Chronicle 340
Sarfatti, Jack 219, 223, 227, 243
Satter, David 38
Scher, Arie 393-395
Schippers, David 76, 458
Schlemmer, Phyllis 224
Schmit, Loran 150
Schnabel, Jim 216-218, 220, 232, 302, 318
Schoenbrun, David 385
Schotz, Martin 147
Schrum, Donald 295, 296, 298, 300, 420
Schwartz, Jack 276
Scorsese, Martin 270
Scotsman, The 451
Scott, Peter Dale 38, 86, 383
Search for the Manchurian Candidate, The 250, 469
Secret Architecture of Our Nation's Capitol, The 285
Secret Cipher of the UFOnauts 241, 242
Secret Doctrine, The 410
Seed, Richard 250
Sense of Being Stared, The 272, 273
Sex and Rockets: the Occult World of Jack Parsons 334
Shaikh, Abdussattar 74
Shai, Yisrael 56
Shapeshifting: Shamanic Techniques for Global and Personal Transformation 477
Shatner, William 169
Shaw, Clay 21, 149
Shawn, Wallace 425
Shayler, David 433, 465
Sheehy, Gail 76
Sheen, Charlie 256
Sheldrake, Rupert 272, 274
Sherman, Mary 20-22, 287, 479
Sherwood, Ed 262

Shreve, Larry 379, 380
Shultz, Belinda 347
Siemer, Sidney 482
Sight Unseen 203
Silver, Joel 364
Simpsons, The 151
Sinatra, Frank 374, 375
Sin City 287, 288, 337, 406
Sindona, Michele 25, 26, 27
Singh, Indira 65, 67, 84, 457
Sinister Forces 159, 207
Sirag, Jean-Paul 243, 244
Sirhan, Sirhan B. 28-31, 303
Skeptic's Dictionary 140
Skeptics Society 139
Skolnick, Sherman 287
Skuratov, Yuri 47
Slavoff, Radi 92
Smith, Anna Nicole 373
Smith, Gaddis 382
Smith, George 371
Smith, Wayne 45
Solomon, Grant & Jane 312, 313, 416
Soros, George 49
Specter 327
Spencer, Diana Frances 370-372
Spiesel, Charles 149
Spitzer, Elliot 72
Sprague, Richard 361
Springmann, Michael 84, 457
SRI International (Stanford Research Institute) 214-216, 218-220, 243, 257, 301, 312, 452
Standard Oil 373
Stanford, Ray 244
Stanton, William 411
Stargate Conspiracy, The 218, 223
Starship Trooper 446
Star Trek 224, 225
Stevens, John 372
Stevenson, Ian 401, 402

Stillwell, Cinnamon 145
Stone, Harry 224
Stone, Oliver 385
Storm-Troopers of Satan: an Occult History of the Second World War 335
Strassman, Rick 185, 320, 399
Strassmeir, Andreas 79
Strieber, Whitley 404
Strong, Maurice 482
Stubblebine, Albert 215, 302, 433
Sullivan & Cromwell 93
Sullivan, Kathleen 277, 335
Sunday Herald (UK) 328, 329
Sunday Telegraph (UK) 329
Sunday Times (UK) 222, 328, 433
Supernatural 414
Suster, Gerald 335
Sutton family 15, 156-159
Swann, Ingo 214-218, 233
Swiatecki, Jerome 341

T

Talbot, Michael 265, 277, 400, 402
Talon News 147
Targ, Russell 301, 312
Tasco, John 263, 264
Taylor, Billy Ray 156, 159
Taylor, Busty 261
TechGnosis 201
Teeter, Lawrence 30
Teller, Edward 166
Temple of Set 113, 115, 153, 217, 377
Tesla, Nikola 249
Thatcher, Margaret 364
There Is No More Firmament 235
Thomas, Kenn 372
Thompson, Hunter S. 279
Thompson, Larry 65
Thompson, Richard L. 403
Toledo Blade 325

Tomlinson, Richard 370
Tonight Show 383, 384
Transformation 404
Trasco, Joe 187
Trepashkin, Mikhail 51
Trimble, George 452
Trine Day 161
Turner, William 28, 29

U

U2 359, 361
UFOs and the National Security State 179, 188, 402, 431
Ullman, Montague 266
Ultimate Con, The 83, 84
Underhill, Garrett 10, 11
United 93 62
Uri (book) 243, 244, 369

V

Vallee, Jacques 141, 151, 152, 162, 165, 178, 181-184, 186, 189, 201, 211, 253, 263, 264, 289, 290, 296-298, 308-310, 334, 336, 419, 420, 423, 424, 448-450, 474
Van Halen 366
Vanity Fair 62
Van Tassel, George 243
V for Vendetta 364
Videodrome 59, 61, 358
Vieira, Alves 15
Viera, Alfonso Lopes 210
Villot, Jean-Marie 25, 26
Vinod, D.G. 224, 227
Virtual Government 215
Visitors from Hidden Realms 421
Von Braun, Werner 13, 93
Von Daniken, Erich 208
Vonkleist, Dave 83

Von Trier, Lars 413
Voyages into the Unknown 232, 233, 400
Vreeland, Delmart 168

W

Wagner, Richard 70
Wall Street Journal 434
Ward, Thomas 44
Warnke, Mike 341, 342
Warren report 147, 381
Washington Post 62, 71, 271
Washington Times 44
Watson, Paul Joseph 397
Watts-Hughes, Margaret 261
WBZ-TV 64, 65
Weakland, Rembert 475, 476
Webb, Gary 143
Weekend 18
Weekly World News 201
Weil, Simone 37, 39
Welcome to Terrorland 75
Wells, Georgina 291, 292
Wellstone, Paul 426
Wheaton, Glenn 278
White, Thomas 6
Whitlam, Gough 396
Whitmore, John 222, 223
Whitton, Joel 400
Who Killed John O'Neill? 61
Why Johnny Can't Come Home 326
Wilson, Colin 225, 269
Wilson, Robert Anton 235, 240, 244, 356
Winnacker, Otto 84
Without Smoking Gun 160, 161
Wizard of Oz, The 438
Wojtyla, Karol Józef (John Paul II) 23, 27, 212
Wolfe, Donald 374
Wolf, Valerie 104, 106, 140

Wonder Years, The 366
Woodfield, Billy 374
Woodland, Robert 395
Woods, James 164
Woodward, Bob 304-306
Woolsey, John 91
World Is As You Dream It, The 484
Worley, Don 487, 488

X

X-Files, The 35

Y

Yale Daily News 382
Yallop, David 23, 25
Young, Neil 279
Youngquist, Walter 436

Z

Zaid, Mark 371
Zamora, Lonnie 290, 291, 294
Zardoz 438, 439, 443
Zevon, Warren 398, 467
Zvarych, Roman 143

Since 1954, the world's most powerful people have met in secret once a year ... until now!

The True Story of

Bilderberg Group

Daniel Estulin

3RD U.S. PRINTING – OVER 1,500,000 COPIES SOLD WORLDWIDE

The True Story of the Bilderberg Group
BY DANIEL ESTULIN

More than a center of influence, the Bilderberg Group is a shadow world government, hatching plans of domination at annual meetings ... and under a cone of media silence.

THE TRUE STORY OF THE BILDERBERG GROUP goes inside the secret meetings and sheds light on why a group of politicians, businessmen, bankers and other mighty individuals formed the world's most powerful society. As Benjamin Disraeli, one of England's greatest Prime Ministers, noted, "The world is governed by very different personages from what is imagined by those who are not behind the scenes."

Included are unpublished and never-before-seen photographs and other documentation of meetings, as this riveting account exposes the past, present and future plans of the Bilderberg elite.

Softcover: **$24.95** (ISBN: 9780977795345) • 366 pages • Size: 6 x 9

Dr. Mary's Monkey
How the Unsolved Murder of a Doctor, a Secret Laboratory in New Orleans and Cancer-Causing Monkey Viruses are Linked to Lee Harvey Oswald, the JFK Assassination and Emerging Global Epidemics
BY EDWARD T. HASLAM, FOREWORD BY JIM MARRS

Evidence of top-secret medical experiments and cover-ups of clinical blunders

The 1964 murder of a nationally known cancer researcher sets the stage for this gripping exposé of medical professionals enmeshed in covert government operations over the course of three decades. Following a trail of police records, FBI files, cancer statistics, and medical journals, this revealing book presents evidence of a web of medical secret-keeping that began with the handling of evidence in the JFK assassination and continued apace, sweeping doctors into cover-ups of cancer outbreaks, contaminated polio vaccine, the genesis of the AIDS virus, and biological weapon research using infected monkeys.

Softcover: **$19.95** (ISBN: 0977795306) • 320 pages • Size: 5 1/2 x 8 1/2

The Oil Card
Global Economic Warfare in the 21st Century
BY JAMES NORMAN

Challenging the conventional wisdom surrounding high oil prices, this compelling argument sheds an entirely new light on free-market industry fundamentals.

By deciphering past, present, and future geopolitical events, it makes the case that oil pricing and availability have a long history of being employed as economic weapons by the United States. Despite ample world supplies and reserves, high prices are now being used to try to rein in China—a reverse of the low-price strategy used in the 1980s to deprive the Soviets of hard currency. Far from conspiracy theory, the debate notes how the U.S. has previously used the oil majors, the Saudis, and market intervention to move markets—and shows how this is happening again.

Softcover **$14.95** (ISBN 0977795390) • 288 PAGES • Size: 5.5 x 8.5

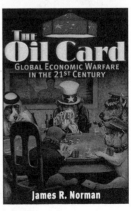

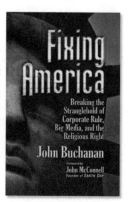

PERFECTIBILISTS
THE 18TH CENTURY BAVARIAN ORDER OF THE ILLUMINATI
BY TERRY MELANSON

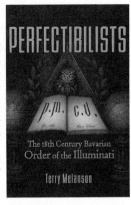

Presenting an advanced and authoritative perspective, this definitive study chronicles the rise and fall of the Order of the Illuminati, a mysterious Enlightenment-era guild surrounded by myth. Describing this enigmatic community in meticulous detail, more than 1,000 endnotes are included, citing scholars, professors, and academics. Contemporary accounts and the original documents of the Illuminati themselves are covered as well. Copiously illustrated and featuring biographies of more than 400 confirmed members, this survey brings to light a 200-year-old mystery.   *—Available Fall 2008—*

TERRY MELANSON is the owner and developer of the popular online Illuminati Conspiracy Archive and has been writing about the Illuminati since 2000. He lives in Moncton, New Brunswick.

Softcover: $19.95 (ISBN 9780-979988608) • 480 pages •200+ Illustration

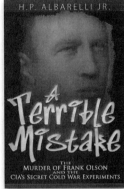

A TERRIBLE MISTAKE
THE MURDER OF FRANK OLSON AND THE CIA'S SECRET COLD WAR
EXPERIMENTS   *—Available Fall 2008—*
BY H.P. ALBARELLI JR.

In his nearly 10 years of research into the death of Dr. Frank Olson, writer and investigative journalist H.P. Albarelli Jr. gained unique and unprecedented access to many former CIA, FBI, and Federal Narcotics Bureau officials, including several who actually oversaw the CIA's mind- control programs from the 1950s to the early 1970s.

A Terrible Mistake takes readers into a frequently bizarre and always frightening world, colored and dominated by Cold War concerns and fears. For the past 30 years the death of biochemist Frank Olson has ranked high on the nation's list of unsolved and perplexing mysteries. A Terrible Mistake solves the mystery and reveals in shocking detail the identities of Olson's murderers. The book also takes readers into the strange world of government mind-control programs and close collaboration with the Mafia.

Fighting For G.O.D.
(Gold, Oil, Drugs)
BY JEREMY BEGIN, ART BY LAUREEN SALK

This racehorse tour of American history and current affairs scrutinizes key events transcending the commonly accepted liberal/conservative political ideologies — in a large-size comic-book format.

This book discusses key issues confronting America's citizenry and steps the populace can take to not only halt but reverse the march towards totalitarianism.

Softcover: **$9.95**, (ISBN 0977795330) 64 Pages, 8.5 x 11

America's Secret Establishment
An Introduction to the Order of Skull & Bones
BY ANTONY C. SUTTON

The book that first exposed the story behind America's most powerful secret society

For 170 years they have met in secret. From out of their initiates come presidents, senators, judges, cabinet secretaries, and plenty of spooks. They are the titans of finance and industry and have now installed a third member as United States President George W. Bush. This intriguing behind-the-scenes look documents Yale's secretive society, the Order of the Skull and Bones, and its prominent members, numbering among them Tafts, Rockefellers, Pillsburys, and Bushes. Far from being a campus fraternity, the society is more concerned with the success of its members in the post-collegiate world. Included are a verified membership list, rare reprints of original Order materials revealing the interlocking power centers dominated by Bonesmen, and a peek inside the Tomb, their 140-year-old private clubhouse.

Softcover: **$19.95** (ISBN 0972020748) 335 pages • Size: 5 x 8

OVERTHROW A FASCIST REGIME ON $15 A DAY
BY WAYNE MADSEN

The highs and lows of the Bush administration from the vantage point of a political dissenter are revealed in this undaunted analysis of American government.

Formerly an executive at a Fortune 500 company, Wayne Madsen quit his job and moved to Washington DC in 2000 to launch a journalistic, grassroots campaign seeking to cut through media hype and unveil the truth behind the politics. Writings included cover issues ranging from 9/11 and the Iraq war to the ousting of Bill Frist and Rick Santorum. As Madsen's whistle-blowing increased, his money from inside the Beltline dwindled, forcing him to prove some battles can be fought even on a shoestring budget.

Softcover: **$19.95** (ISBN 0977795365) • 312 pages

Sinister Forces
A Grimoire of American Political Witchcraft
Book One: The Nine
BY PETER LEVENDA, FOREWORD BY JIM HOUGAN

A shocking alternative to the conventional views of American history.

The roots of coincidence and conspiracy in American politics, crime, and culture are examined in this book, exposing new connections between religion, political conspiracy, and occultism. Readers are taken from ancient American civilization and the mysterious mound builder culture to the Salem witch trials, the birth of Mormonism during a ritual of ceremonial magic by Joseph Smith, Jr., and Operations Paperclip and Bluebird. Not a work of speculative history, this exposé is founded on primary source material and historical documents. Fascinating details are revealed, including the bizarre world of "wandering bishops" who appear throughout the Kennedy assassinations; a CIA mind control program run amok in the United States and Canada; a famous American spiritual leader who had ties to Lee Harvey Oswald in the weeks and months leading up to the assassination of President Kennedy; and the "Manson secret.

Hardcover: **$29.95** (ISBN 0975290622) • 396 pages • Size: 6 x 9

Book Two: A Warm Gun
The roots of coincidence and conspiracy in American politics, crime, and culture are investigated in this analysis that exposes new connections between religion, political conspiracy, terrorism, and occultism. Readers are provided with strange parallels between supernatural forces such as shaminism, ritual magic, and cult practices, and contemporary interrogation techniques such as those used by the CIA under the general rubric of MK-ULTRA. Not a work of speculative history, this exposé is founded on primary source material and historical documents. Fascinating details on Nixon and the "Dark Tower," the Assassin cult and more recent Islamic terrorism, and the bizarre themes that run through American history from its discovery by Columbus to the political assassinations of the 1960s are revealed.

Hardcover: **$29.95** (ISBN 0975290630) • 392 pages • Size: 6 x 9

Book Three: The Manson Secret
The Stanislavski Method as mind control and initiation. Filmmaker Kenneth Anger and Aleister Crowley, Marianne Faithfull, Anita Pallenberg, and the Rolling Stones. Filmmaker Donald Cammell (Performance) and his father, CJ Cammell (the first biographer of Aleister Crowley), and his suicide. Jane Fonda and Bluebird. The assassination of Marilyn Monroe. Fidel Castro's Hollywood career. Jim Morrison and witchcraft. David Lynch and spiritual transformation. The technology of sociopaths. How to create an assassin. The CIA, MK-ULTRA and programmed killers.

Hardcover: **$29.95** (ISBN 0975290649) • 422 pages • Size: 6 x 9